Tourism in China

MIX
Paper from
responsible sources

FSC
www.fsc.org FSC® C014540

ASPECTS OF TOURISM

Series Editors: Chris Cooper, *Oxford Brookes University, UK*, C. Michael Hall, *University of Canterbury, New Zealand* and Dallen J. Timothy, *Arizona State University, USA*

Aspects of Tourism is an innovative, multifaceted series, which comprises authoritative reference handbooks on global tourism regions, research volumes, texts and monographs. It is designed to provide readers with the latest thinking on tourism worldwide and push back the frontiers of tourism knowledge. The volumes are authoritative, readable and user friendly, providing accessible sources for further research. Books in the series are commissioned to probe the relationship between tourism and cognate subject areas such as strategy, development, retailing, sport and environmental studies.

Full details of all the books in this series and of all our other publications can be found on http://www.channelviewpublications.com, or by writing to Channel View Publications, St Nicholas House, 31–34 High Street, Bristol BS1 2AW, UK.

Tourism in China

Destinations, Planning and Experiences

Edited by
Chris Ryan and Songshan (Sam) Huang

CHANNEL VIEW PUBLICATIONS
Bristol • Buffalo • Toronto

Library of Congress Cataloging in Publication Data
A catalog record for this book is available from the Library of Congress.
Tourism in China: Destinations, Planning and Experiences/Edited by Chris Ryan and Songshan (Sam) Huang.
Aspects of Tourism: 59.
Includes bibliographical references and index.
1. Tourism—China—Planning. 2. Tourism—China—Management. I. Ryan, Chris, 1945-
G155.C55T683 2013
338.4'79151–dc23 2013011779

British Library Cataloguing in Publication Data
A catalogue entry for this book is available from the British Library.

ISBN-13: 978-1-84541-401-6 (hbk)
ISBN-13: 978-1-84541-400-9 (pbk)

Channel View Publications
UK: St Nicholas House, 31–34 High Street, Bristol BS1 2AW, UK.
USA: UTP, 2250 Military Road, Tonawanda, NY 14150, USA.
Canada: UTP, 5201 Dufferin Street, North York, Ontario M3H 5T8, Canada.

The policy of Multilingual Matters/Channel View Publications is to use papers that are natural, renewable and recyclable products, made from wood grown in sustainable forests. In the manufacturing process of our books, and to further support our policy, preference is given to printers that have FSC and PEFC Chain of Custody certification. The FSC and/or PEFC logos will appear on those books where full certification has been granted to the printer concerned.

Typeset by Techset Composition Ltd., Salisbury, UK.
Printed and bound in Great Britain by Short Run Press Ltd.

Contents

List of Tables

Contributors

Le Ai undertook research into Beijing's hutong as part of his Master's degree and currently works in Beijing as a Product Manager for a gift product company. Email: ailei-lelia@hotmail.com

Dr John Ap is an Associate Professor in the School of Hotel and Tourism Management (SHTM), The Hong Kong Polytechnic University, Hong Kong SAR, China. Email: hmjohnap@inet.polyu.edu.hk

Dr Jigang Bao is Professor and Dean of the School of Tourism Management, and Assistant President of Sun Yat-sen University, Guangzhou, China. He is a fellow of the International Academy for the Study of Tourism (IAST) Email: eesbjg@mail.sysu.edu.cn

Dr Humin Gu is Professor and Director of the China Hospitality Industry Research Center in the School of Tourism Management, Beijing International Studies University, Beijing, China. Email: guhuimin@bisu.edu.cn

Dr Weixia Hu is an Associate Professor in the School of History and Tourism Culture, Shanxi Normal University, China. Email: huweixia2002@163.com

Dr Songshan (Sam) Huang is Senior Lecturer in Tourism Management in the School of Management at the University of South Australia, Adelaide, Australia. He is also a full member of the Centre for Asian Business at the University of South Australia. Email: sam.huang@unisa.edu.au

Yifan Jiang is a postgraduate researcher in tourism planning in the Department of Tourism Management, School of Management at Zhejiang University, China.

Ping Li is completing her doctoral studies at the University of Waikato. She is a native of Beijing. Email: pl81@waikato.ac.nz

Professor Zhang Lingyun is Head of the Institute of Tourism at Beijing Union University and also editor of *Tourism Tribune*, China's leading tourism journal. Email: zhanglingyun1960@163.com

Preface

This book represents a collaboration between the editors and contributors in order to present issues in current Chinese tourism and tourism research to Western colleagues. The influences informing the book range from pragmatic concerns about destination planning in China, via senses of injustice about how that planning generates unequal distributions of revenue, concerns about needs for new conceptual approaches and observations about the changing nature of Chinese society and its political system, to commentary on the changing role of the Chinese state in tourism planning. Important and implicit throughout the text are the traditional classical patterns of Chinese thought based upon Taoist, Buddhist and Confucian principles, as these traditions grapple with the forces of secularism and commercialism in a new China. Traditional patterns of thought and growing senses of wealth are also both important to the maintenance of the Chinese Communist Party (CCP) as the party of government and the conservation of a one-party government. These tensions are thus played out within the CCP, and not between parties, and tourism is bound up with this process.

The occurrence and growth of tourism represents a symbol of economic success for the Party but, as has been commonly noted, tourism itself is not only an outcome of change, but a catalyst for further change. As a part of a consumerist society, tourism reflects a notion of choice – choices of where to go and how long to stay, and choices of with whom to communicate and how to behave. It has become a cliché to say that China is a nation and a state in transformation, but while it is known what it is transforming from, there seems little clarity as to what China is transforming into. This process of transformation and lack of clarity provide a backdrop to the chapters in this book.

The continued unfolding of this process also means that the contributions to this book are not complete and final. Each chapter simply represents a stage in a journey. But stages in such journeys represent points of comparison, and hence at some future stage other writers can use these chapters as a basis for comparison. At the same time, as interest in China grows, it is hoped that the chapters in this book will meet a need for information and concepts about the current state of tourism and its research in China.

Finally, we would also wish to acknowledge the support of the following. First, the support of Elinor Robertson of Channel View Publications is very much appreciated for overseeing this project from its initiation to its completion. We would also wish to acknowledge grant support from the Australian Centre for Asian Business (ACAB) at the University of South Australia provided to Songhsan (Sam) Huang. The editors are also grateful to Sun (Michael) Xuhua for putting together the index for this book. In addition, we would wish to thank Elsevier and the Birla Institute of Technology for being able to amend slightly previous material published in *Tourism Management* and the *Journal of Hospitality Application and Research*. These latter acknowledgements are duly made at the end of the respective chapters.

Songshan (Sam) Huang and Chris Ryan
October 2012

1 The Role of Tourism in China's Transition: An Introduction

Chris Ryan and Songshan (Sam) Huang

The Annual Development Report of China's Tourism 2011–2012, published by the China Tourism Academy (effectively the research arm of the China National Tourism Administration), continues a series of statistics that record growth in the numbers of tourists arriving in and leaving China. While domestic tourism growth slowed in 2008, the year of the Beijing Olympics, since that year it has continued to grow by in excess of 10% per annum and today domestic tourism accounts for over two billion tourist movements (CTA, 2012). Domestic tourism itself accounts for 65% of all tourism associated with China and dwarfs the two other components of inbound foreign tourists and outbound Chinese tourists. Outbound tourists now account for about 65 million passenger movements, and the number of inbound tourists is approximately the same number.

Impressive though these numbers are, of necessity they do not tell the complete story of tourism development within China. However, it is clear that Chinese tourism is coming of age, and increasingly China is not only a recipient of foreign investment but is now seeking to invest in tourism overseas. Gu et al. (2012), for example, note the mergers and acquisitions that the Chinese hotel industry is beginning to undertake in the USA. Niche tourism is also emerging and one such example is cruise tourism. Such is the importance of Chinese cruise tourism that the first China Cruise Industry Development Report was published in 2008 and this continues to be published annually by the Municipal Government of Shanghai Hongkou District, the Shanghai International Shipping Institute and the China Cruise and Yacht Industry Association (CCYIA). Spa tourism is another niche that is rapidly growing, while rural tourism continues apace, marked not only by growing numbers of tourists, but also by increasing investment, improved facilities and its own emergent niches such as tea tourism, as identified in Chapter 3 of this book.

Such is the rapidity of change that past research that is descriptive of places and their characteristics becomes part of a historical record and less of a description of the current situation. Does this therefore mean that any book on tourism in China is fated to become redundant almost as soon as it leaves the printing press or in these days becomes accessible on the internet? Different responses can be made to this question. First, the historian would probably argue that one cannot understand the present without being aware of the past – that the past serves as a benchmark from which change can be dated and traced. Second, the process of change itself is not neutral, but serves as a continuing lesson to inform the present and the future, and this is particularly so when researchers move from description into analysis and explanation. Conceptual thinking is thus important, as such thinking seeks to make sense of why and how circumstances have changed, what the causes were and how those factors might inform future policies.

Within China itself there exist several questions as to future directions at social, economic and political levels. Fulin (2010) identifies a meta-narrative of such changes when he states that China faces three 'termina-tions' in its current transitional phase. There will be the end of an export-led model of economic development, and this will be accompanied by the demise of the investment-led and GDP-centred models. The emergent theme will be one of equality and sustainable development. He argues that past policies cannot solve the problems caused by those same policies. They were introduced 30-years earlier to cope with a very different set of problems from those that face China today. In the 1980s the problem was one of find-ing a means for developing 'productive forces to a great extent (and) improv-ing the people's living standards' (Fulin, 2010: 42). Currently, he argues, reforms are being distorted for reasons of fatigue with economic models and a lack of consensus. Reform today is not a matter of 'the mere amelioration of systems' (Fulin, 2010: 44), but rather a comprehensive reform of 'eco-nomic, social and even political systems' (Fulin, 2010: 45). But his language is a language of transition, not revolution as occurred during Maoist times, and it is a viewpoint shared by many in the upper echelons of the Chinese Communist Party as it advocates the growth of a harmonious society, albeit in scientific ways and with Chinese characteristics, to cite the rhetoric of various Party Congresses. The issue is not one of resisting or promoting change, but of selecting a means that sustains the gains of the last three decades and generates further economic well-being for those millions that remain below the poverty line (some 130 million according to Zeng & Ryan, 2012), while creating a transition that meets the demands of a more affluent population seeking a less polluted environment in which to live, at the same time as recognising individual rights in the context of the mixed private–public economic sector that is emerging. All of this is to be achieved without putting at risk the social 'glue' that holds China together, a clue that includes the Chinese culture and heritage that forms such a large part of Chinese tourism. For Fulin (2010) the vision of the second 30-year development can be summarised as one of 'Consumption, Innovation, Green and Equality'. This requires the emergence of a consumer-led pattern of consumption based on a low carbon economy contextualised in a new theory of public service. Some writers have identified the role of corporate social responsibility as a key concept in this transition in China (e.g. Gu *et al.*, 2013; Zhou *et al.*, 2007).

These changes have a great bearing on the role of tourism within China, and that role has been recognised by tourism being given the status of one of the 'pillars' of the Chinese economy in November 2009 by the State Council (Sofield & Li, 2011). On Monday 27 August 2012, with the draft of the Tourism Law having first been audited and discussed by the Standing Committee of the National People's Congress, that status began to be legally implemented with the commencement of reforms relating to operational standards for travel agencies and scenic areas. With reference to the former, the draft law includes clauses stating that tour guide services fees must be clearly listed in travel contracts, and that travel agencies may not charge tourists for any expenses not included in the contracts. It also explicitly includes a clause that prohibits travel agencies from forcing tourists to purchase goods, thereby tackling the increasingly loathed practice of taking tourists to retail outlets selected on the basis of commission paid to tour guides rather than service to tourists (Xinhua, 2012). Such legislation illustrates a move towards greater consumer rights, an easing of inhibitions to future economic development and a social harmonisation with Chinese characteristics, by sustaining the intrusion of the state and its mechanisms into regulation adherence.

The different chapters in this book represent the thoughts of Chinese scholars seeking to understand these issues and are primarily based upon empirical or grounded research. They are for the most part based upon research undertaken by younger Chinese scholars in their doctoral theses, chosen to represent emergent ideas that hitherto have not been available to Western scholars in that they are derived from theses written in Mandarin, although some chapters have emanated from Chinese scholars working in Australia and New Zealand. However, for the most part these chapters are derived from ethnographic-style research which has required that their authors have lived in China for substantial periods of time, and again have been written by scholars with a past history of working in China, primarily in its tourism industry.

The voice articulated in these chapters is therefore different from that of many articles pertinent to Chinese tourism that appear in journals readily available to readers outside China. These were mainly written by Chinese scholars working or studying in universities, primarily in the USA or UK, and whose research may be predicated upon responses to questionnaires. While recognising that such research has the reliability normally measured by statistical tests there remains an issue of cultural understanding; this is particularly evident when dealing with tourism developments in the rural areas of China, as was evidenced by Yang *et al.* (2012) in their paper on

Chinese attitudes towards the completion of questionnaires. One might point out that the attitudes they uncovered, such as the wish to give the response 'wanted' by the researcher or that of the 'official response', is not unknown in countries other than China. However, given the transitional state of China as it emerges from a top-down policy-directed nation to an as yet ill-defined 'new China' as discussed by commentators like Fulin (2010), the potential responses described by Yang *et al.* (2012) are not uncommon, and the complexities of the situation often only become apparent through a process of immersion in given places and processes. It is this realisation that lends importance to the following chapters. Indeed, Chinese scholars have been critical of some of the research undertaken by those outside their own country who wish to understand China but who depend solely upon questionnaire-based data, while at the same time there is a need and a role for those who seek to bridge the differences (Chen & Bao, 2011). Over time, however, these differences appear – at least to these writers – to be diminishing, for many reasons. First, China is beginning to emulate Western patterns of being a consumer society. Second, the patterns of globalisation bring business practices and a realisation of a global village into an understanding of common interests, whether environmental or social. Hence China's Green Hotels reforms lean heavily in practice on a need for hotels to benchmark themselves against the best practice of their Western counterparts. For those inclined toward a conspiracy theory of history, the interweaving of governmental and corporate interests also prompts decision makers within their different respective societies towards seeking to sustain the status quo of power relationships, while equally resistance becomes more common when aided by the internet.

Tourism is partly a result and cause of these processes, and these issues are touched upon in various ways by the different contributors to the book. The book is divided into three parts, each with its own introduction. The three parts are 'Development Experiences', 'Policy Implementation and Destination Evolution' and 'Planning'. Within each part, chapters illustrate the theme, although by their nature overlaps occur. Indeed the fourth chapter in the book by Bao and Zuo could have found its way into the second, but eventually the editors thought that it possessed greater similarities to the other chapters within this part.

The first part of the book commences with a chapter by Zhou and Jiang and illustrates themes relating to the development of villages as tourist destinations in Chinese mountains. They note that mountain regions represent 69% of the land area of China and that the villages within them have experienced slower economic development than most other parts of China, and thereby represented a target for development under the Eleventh Five-year Plan in 2005, under the slogan of 'Constructing New Socialist Rural Communities'. The Happy Farmer's Home (HFH; *Nongjiale* in Chinese) has been one outcome of these policies, and Zhou and Jiang describe how these came into being, their dependence on external sources of capital and the lack of social capital within the villages. This theme is also apparent in the work of Bao and Zuo, in their chapter entitled 'Institutional Opportunism in Tourism Investment'. They describe processes only too familiar to many tourism researchers in China. It is not uncommon to find the wish to promote employment and income for a region becoming tied into the wish for corporate profit by private sector organisations still entwined in different ways with the State, especially at provincial and municipal levels, with both seemingly oblivious to the, at least short-term, losses incurred by local residents. Such processes are not always rational, being dominated by narrowly based considerations and vulnerable to corrupt practices.

In the following chapter Li, Wang and Ryan describe a case study that illustrates the themes of the two previous chapters, namely the case of Qiyunshan, a small mountain community not far from Huangshan City in Anhui Province. Based on its Taoist tradition and scenic beauty and subsistence agriculture including the growing of tea, the village has been rapidly developed between 2010 and 2012, with a new road being blasted through the mountain, and external capitalised resort complexes being built at the foot of the mountain on land compulsorily purchased from the local peasantry. Those of working age have lost their means of livelihood and need to seek new sources of income, often through migration, while profits go to the out-of-region developers, although the mountain villagers are now more wealthy than before. Apart from representing the unique Chinese tourism development experience at the village level, the Qiyunshan case as illustrated in this chapter taps into a social issue, more or less common as observers can see from China's general development realities and typically in the recent Wukan incident, which casts a gloomy future for those villagers who have lost their land as an essential means of living, out of all the optimism and short-sighted zeal from both the government and communities.

The last two chapters in Part 1 differ. Chapter 6 by Yong (Joe) Zhou describes the use of festival and special event tourism in China and illustrates frailties in the planning process because major events are often dictated by a wish to make 'the grand statement' and compete with other centres, but often are associated with a lack of post-event resource planning. The final chapter in this part is also based on ethnographic research by Jingjing Yang. However, instead of adopting conventional detailed descriptions of grounded research, the authors have recourse to the theories of Simmel and Coser in order to examine the nature of tension as not only a destabilising process but one that can be creative in formulating new alliances, group definitions and new modes of action.

Part 2 contains a chapter by Yang and Sun entitled 'Evolution of Tourism Destination Complex System: Theoretical Foundations' (Chapter 10) and a second by Yang, 'Evolution of Tourism Destination Complex System: Cases in China' (Chapter 11), offering amendments to the Butler (1980) Tourism

Area Life Cycle concept by drawing on systems and chaos theories to suggest that tourism planning in China is a complex, organic process wherein different tensions whirl around each other seeking a homeostasis that is at best only temporary. These theoretical processes are preceded by a chapter by Wang and Ap that sets the scene by describing policies put in place to handle tourism flows and numbers in the ancient town of Lijiang in Yunnan Province. They note the disparate authorities responsible for planning and promotion, and how these conflicting processes emasculate the authority of the Lijiang Tourism Bureau, the Lijiang Tourism Industry Association and the Ancient Town District Tourism Bureau, and the Ancient Town Preservation and Management Bureau. Indeed, the number of bodies specifically identified with tourism creates issues of a boundary and regulatory nature. Little wonder, therefore, that tourism administration is identified as a 'complex system' by Yang. The remaining two chapters by Huang, Ryan and Yang further analyse the nature of local administration (Chapter 12) and finally the discrepancies in perceptions based on differences between personal and altruistic notions of tourism impacts are examined with reference to the event policies of Hangzhou in a chapter by Zhou and Ryan (Chapter 13).

The final part comprises four chapters. The first by Hu examines the spatial relationships between the core area of a tourist destination and the peripheral regions around it, and the corridors that link the peripheries to the core. Drawing on the *Peripheral Environments of Tourist Attraction* (PETA) initiated in the Xi'an Manifesto, written by the International Council on Monument and Sites (ICOMOS) in 2005, Hu argues that the concepts have implications beyond those of heritage sites, and can be applied to the administration of tourist destinations and regions. She argues for an integrated form of destination management that requires recognition of the differing functions of these areas and a form of management that is cooperative, coordinating and responsive to the needs of stakeholders.

In Chapter 16 Wong and Ryan look at the impacts of religious tourism at Putuoshan on members of the monastic orders that reside there. One of the major Buddhist sites in the world, Putuoshan is chosen here as a representative site of religious, heritage and cultural tourism that is being promoted by the Chinese state. The chapter makes clear that those who are defined as 'true believers' are a minority among the visitors, and the majority are motivated to visit by a wish to see a site representative of China's classical past or by general sightseeing motives. Increasing numbers have, however, required the introduction of controls requesting the adherence to approved patterns of behaviour. The context of the text is, however, the unspoken notion that such tourism is promoted as a means of securing a sense of being Chinese that draws upon respect for authority by a controlling party that is increasingly moving away from the founding ideals of Maoism.

In Chapter 17 Wen examines the role of iconic sites more generally, but with reference to the Danxiashan Scenic Zone, which was declared a World

Heritage Site in 2010 for its natural features. The key attributes that are required for a site to obtain recognition as an 'iconic' site are listed, and the relationships between these features and their implications for management are analysed through a series of diagrams. The final chapter by Ai, Song, Ryan and Gu represents a stage in a longitudinal study of Beijing's Shi Cha Hai hutong that updates past research by the third and fourth authors.

Interspersed between the three parts of the book are introductory chapters by the editors that seek to highlight the similarities and differences between the chapters that make up each part, and do so with reference to research literature relating to China. As mentioned at the outset of this chapter, tourism in China has gone through significant changes. From the start in the Maoist period, when tourism was solely the reserve of higher political officials, it has grown tremendously in the last three decades. In the initial period of tourism development the government sought to encourage inbound tourism and inward capital investment while at the same time seeking to privatise assets such as hotels in a wish to upgrade existing hotels and build new hotels to international standards. In doing so, it used both the monies of the Chinese diaspora and hospitality companies based in locations like Singapore and Hong Kong, and the resources of the international Western-based hotel chains. Simultaneously though, economic growth produced a new well-educated middle class that, by comparison with the past, is affluent and who wish to travel. Today the emphasis is on domestic tourism, both as a means of generating economic impetus in the remaining underdeveloped regions, and to provide rewards for past sacrifice and hard work. For many Chinese, to be able to afford to be a tourist, to travel and to see the sights of their country while enjoying comfortable serviced accommodation is a symbol of being part of the modern world, or being a global citizen. It has been noted that, where once the Chinese may have travelled outside China to see the future and the new cities of the 21st century, now they achieve that by travelling within China, such have been the changes.

References

Butler, R. (1900) The concept of the tourist area lifecycle of evolution: Implications for the management of resources. *Canadian Geographer* 24, 5–12.

Chen, G. and Bao, J. (2011) Progress on overseas studies on China tourism: A review from the perspective of academic contributions. *Tourism Tribune* 26 (2), 28–35.

CTA (China Tourism Academy) (2012) *Annual Report on China Regional Tourism Development 2011/2012*. Beijing: China Tourism Press.

Fulin, C. (2010) *Change of China's Development Models at the Crossroads*. Beijing: China International Press.

Gu, H., Ryan C. and Yu, L. (2012) The changing structure of the Chinese hotel industry: 1980–2012. *Tourism Management Perspectives* 4, 56–63.

Gu, H., Ryan, C., Li, B. and Gao, W. (2013) Political connections, *guanxi*, and adoption of CSR policies in the Chinese hotel industry: Is there a link? *Tourism Management* 34 (1), 231–235.

2 Experiences in Developing Places

Chris Ryan and Songshan (Sam) Huang

Introduction

This chapter has primarily three sections. The first picks up a theme that is implicit in many chapters in this book, that is, the changing nature of the tourist destination. The role of the tourist destination is, by the very nature of tourism, a key component in the tourism research literature. In early models of tourism, such as Leiper's (1990) concept of the 'tourism system', the spatial relationships of travel between tourist-generating and tourist-receiving areas received significant attention. Researchers have adopted different perspectives – whether logistical as in studies of air routes, scheduling and transport systems (e.g. Duval, 2008; Page, 2005) or from positions of image, perception and usage of space (e.g. Beerli & Martin, 2004; Walmsley & Jenkins, 1992). It is also recognised that one of the most cited pieces in the tourism academic literature is that of Butler's (1980, 2006a, 2006b) tourism area life cycle. Consequently, the first theme in this chapter represents a review of the tourist area life cycle primarily drawing on Western literature.

The second part of the chapter then takes this theme of destination development and change and relates it to China and current emerging patterns. These themes are generalised from the case studies that follow in Chapters 3–7, and the content of these chapters is briefly stated at the conclusion of this chapter. Consequently, it can be stated that the purpose of the introduction is to provide the reader with first a generic review of current issues, and then to identify applications of those themes in current Chinese tourist destination developments.

The Tourist Area Life Cycle

The tourism destination life cycle is deceptively simple. At one level it replicates many life cycles of growth and demise as it traces the initial exploration of a destination by a few tourists who seek new and 'authentic' places through various stages that include involvement, development, consolidation and stagnation through to decline. However Butler (1980) also pointed out, as in marketing and branding exercises, that a destination may also be rejuvenated. The original concept used the variables of numbers of tourists and time with which to measure this process. Initially, writers sought to identify case studies that illustrated these different stages, while some, such as Hayward (1986), asked whether the cycle could be made operational by identifying measures that in turn could be used to identify turning points for the various stages. Intuitively the concept made sense, and in hindsight a number of cases were examined (for example, Cooper & Jackson's (1989) study of the Isle of Man). The concept also had important implications for destination planning – but the issue for Hayward as for other commentators was: how can we forecast the key turning points so that the concept could be made operational rather than simply being a description of past events? Consequently, a number of measures were advanced, one being the ratio of returning visitors to total visitors (Hayward, 1986) while others pointed to parallel theories of tourist typologies such as Cohen's (1972, 1979) groupings of drifters to mass packaged tourists, or Plog's (1973) allocentric, mid-centric and psychocentric types to identify the nature of the tourist market as a key determinant of destination stage. These issues are taken up further in Chapters 10 and 11 of this book.

However, just as some researchers were finding examples of the S-shaped curve, so others pointed out that the life cycle was a consequence of a process, and not all destinations shared the same process. For example, many destinations such as purpose-built resort complexes like Cancun (Papatheodorou, 2006) or Playa de las Americas (Padilla & McElroy, 2005) did not have exploration or early involvement stages, but were purpose built by property developers to emerge as fully fledged resorts with immediately high occupancy rates for the hotels within them. Indeed, as Hoosie (1990) indicates, some resorts of this nature involved the corruption of local officials, as the original landowners were induced to sell at prices that failed to reflect the market value associated with such resorts. In short, the search for quantifiable measures was misguided unless one was more conversant with the variables that formed a process, and the nature of the interaction between those factors. As noted below, these issues are not unknown in China and perhaps, some might argue, altogether far too prevalent. Bao and Zuo in Chapter 4 of this book provide such an illustration.

Additionally, the destination life cycle does not, however, solely relate to numbers and types of tourists. Young (1983) was an early commentator who, in his example of a Maltese fishing-farming village, traced the changing land usage patterns as development occurred. He illustrated how, over a comparatively short period of time, a simple land use pattern by a small community could grow into an international resort complete with marinas, hotels, apartments and villas that evoked a response by planning and local government authorities to impose zones that prohibited further development. His example highlighted the relationship between local entrepreneurs and external capital. As local residents respond to the economic opportunities presented by tourism by building bed and breakfast accommodation, and new rooms or holiday homes for let, their very activity initiates further growth that, in the European situation at least, leads to tour operators entering the market place. At one stage in his career the first editor worked for a niche Association of Independent Tour Operators (AITO) company located in the UK, who would, on identifying such an embryonic holiday destination, approach a local small hotelier or restaurant owner with funds to further develop their own facilities while guaranteeing a given volume of guests. In time, however, the success of the destination would attract larger operators and hotel companies and capital and ownership external to the host community would enter into the market place. Requiring larger volumes of business to generate the required rates of return meant that the destination proceeded on the path described by Butler. One consequence of this, as noted by Kermath and Thomas (1992), was the increased business and spatial marginalisation of the original community businesses, as external companies purchased prime sites or created new foci of activity in their developments within the location. In short, local communities and local capital owners slowly lost control of their own place according to these scenarios in the absence of constraints that might be imposed by governmental organisations. Again examples abound in China, where local communities are found to have little say in the planning of destinations; one of these examples is provided by Li, Wang and Ryan in Chapter 5.

Another side effect of this process is that local businesses and politicians even begin to lose control over the marketing of their own destination. The marketing increasingly shifts to the tour operators, who operate in their home markets of the tourist-generating rather than the tourist-receiving zone. The destination becomes a product in brochures that fit a house style and brand that belongs to the tour operator rather than the destination. Local businesses in the tourist-receiving zone increasingly have to feed off a derived demand for the destination in order to sell their own activities – that is, their marketing is directed to visitors once they have arrived at the destination. Previously, prior to the wide-scale adoption of the internet, they lacked the ability to directly market to potential visitors in the tourist-generating zone. Indeed, as Bastakis *et al.* (2004) argued with reference to Greece, such was the lack of control in local hands that external tour operators were able, through the threat of withdrawing business by the promotion of a competitor's destination, to hold local businesses to prices lower than they might otherwise have been able to charge.

Given the frequent reference to the tourist destination life cycle, it is perhaps worth noting that the concept has its significant detractors. Dhalla and Yuspeh, as early as 1976 (and before Butler's paper), argued that products are not organisms, are not living things, and thus the metaphor is misplaced. More significantly, the curve itself is not an independent variable, but simply an outcome; in short, as noted above, it results from a process that it does not prescribe. Thomas (1991) also argued that over-dependence on the model may lead to destination planners and marketers abandoning activities too early, misinterpreting the factors that led to a change in visitor numbers (consumers) and trying to pioneer new activities when the core product retains significant potential. Coles (2006) for his part argues that instead of an S-curve, one could equally borrow from the concept of the retail wheel (Brown, 1988) wherein change is perpetuated within a destination through the presence of innovative entrepreneurs who continually renew the destination from within. Under these circumstances, numbers of visitors may well be less important than another measure such as total expenditure. Under this scenario a destination may remain static in many of its spatial considerations, but be successful in eliciting higher levels of expenditure from visitors.

The Chinese Situation

How relevant is this to the Chinese situation? It is true that, as shown in Chapter 12, much of Chinese tourism policy is top down. General policies are determined by Beijing and the state comprehensive ministries enact and shape policies approved by the Party Congresses; through these approaches tourism has come to be recognised as one of the pillars of the emerging new China. However, Huang, Ryan and Yang in Chapter 12, as do others in this book, paint a more complex picture whereby the private and public sectors at the local level are becoming increasingly entwined in relationships that may owe as much to *guanxi* and political careers as to commercial objectives. Yet, arguably, in the socialist market economy that Chinese economic policy seeks, the realities of the market place will begin increasingly to determine the feasibilities of any tourism policy. Certainly by the end of October 2012 reports were emerging in the Chinese financial press of growing pressures on local government budgets, and there is evidence that many of the past prestigious developments such as the building of sports stadia have come at a high financial cost, as evidenced at Guangzhou and Shenzhen. Thus Huang, Ryan and Yang note the RMB (Renminbi) 210 billion deficit incurred by Guangzhou after the Asian Games – and early in 2012 the Chinese state commenced an investigation into these matters, an investigation that included senior elected officials of the city. As a consequence *Sina Weibo* in August 2012 was full of speculation about the future of former Guangzhou Communist Party Boss, Zhang Guangning, and his alleged involvement in corruption surrounding the Asian Games. It has been estimated that the debt left by those Games is equivalent to four years of Guangzhou's budget.

Another disturbing feature of the Chinese financial landscape is the growing problem of bad debt that has been becoming more apparent in 2012, as reported by *Caixin* in September 2012. The percentage of non-performing bank loans (NPLs), especially in the Delta region, has been growing, but currently is still sustainable at only a maximum of 4% of total debt for some banks. However, much of this is thought to be associated with real estate and, as noted by Gu *et al.* (2012) with their reference to developments in Xi'an, much of this is associated with mixed public and private sector property development, and its growth is a concern against a backdrop of growing local government sector debt. In March 2012 Yang Kaisheng, President of the Industrial and Commercial Bank of China, was reported as saying that China's debt to GDP ratio was about 43%, with a total government debt of RMB 17.5 trillion. Of this, local government debt was RMB 10.7 trillion. There was sufficient concern in early 2012 for Premier Wen Jiabao to need to address the issue on 14 March. Generally speaking there are two concerns: firstly that local government debt has risen quickly in the period since 2010, and secondly the proportion of total debt that may prove to be bad. Standard and Poor's (S&P) has stated that perhaps as much as 30% may prove to be irredeemable. Associated with this are two other concerns, the first of which is related in part to tourism, that is, the role of lending associated with the combined retail, leisure, cultural and tourism park and resort developments that have become part of the Chinese urban landscape. The question is: to what extent are these developments vulnerable to bad debt or a failure in financing? The second is the question as to what degree this debt is associated with corruption.

Alongside these developments has been the arrival of the internet, which has created an active Chinese 'netizen' base. Any quick perusal of the Chinese press indicates just how active it is in publicising alleged issues of corruption. Nonetheless, the playing field remains far from equal when it comes to the development of the capital-intensive resort complexes that are much favoured in China for various reasons. As demonstrated in the chapters by Bao and Zuo, and again by Li, Wang and Ryan, many possibilities exist for local residents to lose the sources of their livelihoods, and while promises are made that tourism development will generate economic improvement for local communities, all too often migrant labour is used and the higher managerial tasks are filled by outsiders, many of whom wish to work in larger centres. The consequence is that there is little reversal of migration from the rural to the urban areas, and the stated objectives of the policies are defeated. An additional problem for the organisation is that the resorts may be far away from the urban areas that are more attractive to career-minded younger managers, and consequently there can be problems in the retention of a cadre of professional, well-educated managers recruited from other than the local region.

These problems, however, are not always present, and for every example of disappointed hopes there are many cases of success. In this sense the

tourism was to be the theme for that year, thereby recognising the importance of the countryside in tourism development, especially for the domestic market. Certainly areas near to major conurbations have gained from tourism; for example, it has been estimated that in the wider Beijing Municipality income from tourism accounted for over 30% of rural income, while Zhang *et al.* (2006) provide evidence of a growing mix of more specialist rural tourist products in that region, hence the importance of, and challenge to tourism that is represented by the mountainous regions discussed by Zhou and Jiang in Chapter 3.

Chapter 4 by Jigang Bao and Bing Zuo provides a detailed case study of the machinations of large-scale capital in developing resort complexes in western China. They provide a record of changing patterns of ownership that effectively reinforce control over development within the hands of the east China-based companies, where broken promises are not properly held to account by local government who, in turn, are held at arms' length by a lack of transparency in financial details and, it is implied, by the establishment of relationships in the region studied that are for the financial benefit of both immediately involved parties, but not for the wider benefit of the local communities. The same theme, albeit in a different context, also emerges in the following chapter by Li, Wang and Ryan as they describe the changes that have taken place over a three-year period in an Anhui village. In this chapter they develop one part of their longitudinal study to concentrate on the views of local villagers. These local people complain of how the higher level jobs are not open to them, while continuing research at the site has also found evidence similar to that voiced by Bao and Zuo, namely that the major gains are made by external capital being permitted to build on land previously owned by local people, but which is compulsorily purchased by the local authority to permit the development of larger scale resort complexes.

In Chapter 6 Yong Zhou traces the development of special events and festivals in China. As in other parts of the world he indicates how such events have been motivated by many reasons, and that for China an important motive has been to establish Chinese cities as part of the modern world. Events become a statement of China's place in the modern world. But he also notes that several such events have been strategic errors, possibly due to an excess of enthusiasm, a misplaced statement of local pride or for political career enhancement. There is little doubt that such motives have played their role in China's history of events and indeed, as Zhou notes, such events had their precedents several hundreds of years previously when emperors sought to reinforce their power. Equally it needs to be stated that the faults noted by Zhou are not unique to China. As Pacione (2012) comments in his review of events in urban regeneration, the rhetoric of events does not always match the reality, while even successful events may well be disruptive because, when used as part of urban renewal, they often entail the movement and break-up of communities already residing in an area.

The final chapter in Part 1 is by Yang *et al.* and represents a slightly different approach as indicated above. In this case the study was based on the ways in which Kazakh and other entrepreneurs took advantage of the state's promotion of tourism, based on the culture of a minority people, namely the Tuva who inhabit the Kanas Scenic Area of Xinjiang Province in northwest China. In many ways this represents concerns that have long been expressed in the literature, namely an exploitation of culture by people other than those to whom the heritage belongs, and a commodification and watering-down of the culture as it is delivered to tourists on scheduled trips by non-native peoples. Yet the truth is not so simple, as it is the Tuva who condone those performances as a means of deriving an income from tourism through the illegal renting of their homes; by doing so they are able to retain many aspects of their traditional summer practices of herding on the grasslands. The authors present an analysis of conflict and tension between competing stakeholders – the entrepreneurs who offer product to the tourists, the tourists who wish to be entertained by seeing something new, the tour guides who want income, the Tuva who wish not to be disturbed but who also want supplementary income, and local government at various levels, who wish to generate tourism development, to ensure that the local situation remains 'harmonious' while wishing to avoid undue interference from either Urumqi or Beijing. Out of the new social interactions and networks that occur, new hybrid economic and social positions are formed.

Thus it can be seen that the interaction between destination evolution, management and the experiences they deliver to tourists and residents is far from uniform. It is complex, reflecting not only internal structures but also the vulnerabilities and the reactive processes that those structures possess when faced with external shocks. Equally those structures are open to endogenous shocks. Destinations are rarely static, and it is this theme of change that will be explored in Part 2 of this book.

References

Bastakis, C., Buhalis, D. and Butler, R.W. (2004) The perception of small and medium sized tourism accommodation providers on the impacts of the tour operators' power in Eastern Mediterranean. *Tourism Management* 25 (2), 151–170.

Beerli, A. and Martín, J.D. (2004) Factors influencing destination image. *Annals of Tourism Research* 31 (3), 657–681.

Brown, S. (1988) The wheel of the Wheel of Retailing. *International Journal of Retailing* 3 (1), 16–37.

Butler, R.W. (1980) The concept of a tourist area cycle of evolution: Implications for management of resources. *Canadian Geographer* 24, 5–12.

Butler, R.W. (2006a) *The Tourism Area Life Cycle: Applications and Modification.* Clevedon: Channel View Publications.

Butler, R.W. (2006b) *The Tourism Area Life Cycle: Conceptual and Theoretical Issues.* Clevedon: Channel View Publications.

Cohen, E. (1972) Toward a sociology of international tourism. *Social Research* 39 (1), 164–182.

Cohen, E. (1979) Rethinking the sociology of tourism. *Annals of Tourism Research* 6 (1), 18–35.

Coles, T. (2006) Enigma variations? The TALC, marketing models and the descendants of the Product Life Cycle. In R.W. Butler (ed.) *The Tourism Area Life Cycle Vol. 2: Conceptual and Theoretical Issues* (pp. 49–66). Clevedon: Channel View Publications.

Cooper, C. and Jackson, S. (1989) Destination Life Cycle: The Isle of Man case study. *Annals of Tourism Research* 16 (3), 377–398.

Dhalla, N.K. and Yuspeh, S. (1976) Forget the product life cycle concept. *Harvard Business Review* 54 (January/February), 102–112.

Dumreicher, H. (2008) Chinese villages and their sustainable future. *Journal of Environmental Management* 87 (2), 201–203.

Duval, D.T. (2008) *Tourism and Transport: Modes, Networks and Flows.* Clevedon: Channel View Publications.

Gu, H. and Ryan, C. (2010) Hungcon, China – residents' perceptions of the impacts of tourism on a rural community: A mixed methods approach. *Journal of China Tourism Research* 6 (3), 216–244.

Gu, H., Ryan, C. and Yu, L. (2012) The changing structure of the Chinese hotel industry: 1980–2012. *Tourism Management Perspectives* 4, 56–63.

Hayward, K.M. (1986) Can the tourist area life-cycle be made operational? *Tourism Management* 7 (3), 154–167.

Hoosie, L. (1990) Gringos in paradise. *Business Magazine, Toronto Globe and Mail* February, 65–70.

Kermath, B.M. and Thomas, R.N. (1992) Spatial dynamics of resorts: Sosúa, Dominican Republic. *Annals of Tourism Research* 19 (2), 173–190.

Leiper, N. (1990) Tourism systems. Department of Management Systems Occasional Paper No. 2, Massey University, Auckland.

Li, Y. (2010) Remedies for breach of contract in international sales of goods. PhD thesis, Faculty of Law, Arts and Social Sciences, University of Southampton.

Lu, Y. and Tao, Z. (2009) Contract enforcement and family control of business: Evidence from China. *Journal of Comparative Economics* 37 (4), 597–609.

Ma, A., Si, L. and Zhang, H. (2009) The evolution of cultural tourism: The example of Qufu, the birthplace of Confucius. In C. Ryan and H. Gu (eds) *Tourism in China: Destination, Cultures and Communities* (pp. 182–196). New York: Routledge.

Pacione, M. (2012) The role of events in urban regeneration. In S.J. Page and J. Connell (eds) *The Routledge Handbook of Events* (pp. 385–400). London: Routledge.

Padilla, A. and McElroy, J.L. (2005) The tourism penetration index in large islands: The case of Dominican Republic. *Journal of Sustainable Tourism* 13 (4), 353–372.

Page, S.J. (2005) *Transport and Tourism: Global Perspectives* (2nd edn). Harlow: Pearson Books.

Papatheodorou, A. (2006) TALC and the spatial implications of competition. In R.W. Butler (ed.) *The Tourism Area Life Cycle, Vol. 2. Conceptual and Theoretical Issues* (pp. 49–66). Clevedon: Channel View Publications.

Plog, S.C. (1973) Why destinations rise and fall in popularity. *Cornell Hotel and Restaurant Association Quarterly* 13, 6–13.

Thomas, M.J. (1991) Product development and management. In M. Baker (ed.) *The Marketing Book, Vol. 2* (pp. 284–296). Oxford: Butterworth Heinemann.

Walmsley, D.J. and Jenkins, J. (1992) Tourism cognitive mapping of unfamiliar environments. *Annals of Tourism Research* 19 (3), 268–286.

Young, B. (1983) Touristization of traditional Maltese fishing-farming villages. *Tourism Management* 4 (1), 35–41.

Yang, J., Ryan, C. and Zhang, L. (2013) Social conflict in communities impacted by tourism. *Tourism Management* 35 (1), 82–93.

Zhang, W., An, Y.Y. and Sun, H.L. (2006) The impacts of rural tourism on the social and economic development in rural areas – a case study of the suburbs of Beijing. *China Tourism Research* 2 (4), 546–562.

Zhou, Y-G. and Ma, E. (2009) Maintaining the authenticity of rural tourism experiences through community participation: The case of two Baiyang Lake island villages. In C. Ryan and H. Gu (eds) *Tourism in China: Destination, Cultures and Communities* (pp. 293–307). New York: Routledge.

3 A Model of Mountain Region Rural Tourism Development: The Case of Suichang

Yongguang Zhou and Yifan Jiang

Introduction

Definition of 'mountain villages'

There has been no specific and agreed definition of 'mountain villages' in both Chinese and foreign extant literatures with reference to their being tourist destinations. According to the Mountains and Mountain Forests Global Statistical Summary published by the United Nations Environment Programme (UNEP) in 2000, mountain regions can be summarised as including: (1) regions with an altitude of above 2500 m; (2) regions with an altitude between 1500 and 2500 m as well as a slope of not less than 2 degrees; (3) regions with an altitude between 1000 and 1500 m as well as a slope of not less than 5 degrees; and (4) regions with an altitude between 300 and 1500 m as well as a relative altitude difference of more than 300 m Blyth *et al.* (2002). Accordingly, the generalised usage of mountain villages in this chapter refers to the countryside in the above-mentioned mountain areas and a comparison is made between mountain villages and villages located on plains or lowlands.

Consequently, prior to any tourism development and the infrastructure that it attracts, a series of hypothesised differences may be said to potentially exist wherein each of these two types of village may differ. These differences are summarised in Table 3.1 and include differences in ease of accessibility, degrees of contact with the outside world, the extent of human impact on the surrounding landscape and the retention of long-established traditions. The purpose of this chapter is to describe some of the implications of this classification for the development of village-based tourism in China, taking as a case study mountain villages in Suichang County, Zhejiang Province.

Table 3.1 A conceptual comparison between 'mountain villages' and 'plain villages'

	Mountain villages	Plain villages
Traffic condition	Low accessibility, remote location	Good accessibility, around better developed cities and towns
Living condition	Less contact with the outside world; mostly keep the original lifestyle	Nearly assimilated by the outside world; no great difference from cities in lifestyle
Natural environment	Unique natural scenery	Notwithstanding the beautiful scenery, heavy imprint of industrialisation and urbanisation
Human landscape	Relatively well preserved folk customs	Fading or changed traditional customs

The development of mountain village tourism in China

Mountain regions occupy 69% of the territory in China and the people living in these regions account for one-third of China's total population. They also account for a large proportion of China's poverty-stricken communities (Zeng & Ryan, 2012). When compared to lowland villages, many mountain villages have experienced slower economic development and remain stricken by problems such as poverty and ecological degradation. At present, on the global scale, economic backwardness, poor infrastructure including road access and an increasing deterioration of the mountains' ecology have led to many problems which include a loss of population and labour, an ageing of the remaining local residents and a stultification of local patterns of life. The maintenance and the development of mountain regions and their populations had become such a compelling international concern that the year 2002 was announced as 'The UN International Year of Mountains'.

Many scholars have tried to analyse the consequences of economic recession and environmental degradation on mountain regions from differing perspectives of policy making and economics. As far as policies are concerned, the Chinese government has neglected the development of mountain regions for many years; consequently, little public investment has been available to support mountain region development. Zeng (2008) attributed poverty in the vast areas of rural China to poor infrastructure and a lack of capacity building and social capital due to a long period of past neglect of rural development. Additionally, past governmental mistakes in agricultural and land reform created subsequent dilemmas for mountain villages, which included issues of land and property ownership, as noted by Li, Wang and

Ryan in Chapter 5. Deficiencies such as these at the grassroots of mountain communities have rendered endogenous development difficult.

Since the beginning of the Eleventh Five-Year Plan in 2005, under the slogan of 'Constructing New Socialist Rural Communities', the Chinese government has lent much more support to the development of rural areas in terms of funding and policies. Exploratory rural development patterns and approaches have been trialled to develop the lowland villages. One of these trials is to generate linkages between rural residents and urban areas as the countryside becomes a place for short-stay breaks for the populations of towns and cities. This approach also promotes the industrialisation of agriculture to lead rural development. However, mountain villages are different from those lowland villages in resources and socioeconomic environments. While in the eastern developed provinces, mountain region development issues can be addressed by patterns of migration and repatriated earnings combined with developing mountain-based agriculture and farm-oriented tourism, there are generally not many effective measures to develop mountain villages other than in agriculture, forestry and animal husbandry.

Based on this background, this chapter focuses specifically on mountain village tourism development rather than rural tourism development in general. Mountain regions do possess advantages including being far away from urban pollution, possessing a cleaner ecological environment, fresh air and scenic views. Additionally, mountain villages are not uncommonly geographically close to river heads that prove to be key reserves of biodiversity, and at the same time often possess tangible and intangible cultural heritage from old routes that long ago fell into disuse. A further factor is that in many such villages, tourism development is considered an effective means of preventing the decline of agriculture, increasing household income and readjusting the economic structure, while serving as a proxy for membership of the modern world (Cui & Ryan, 2011).

The 'Happy Farmer's Home' (*Nongjiale*): Development and Predicament

Originating in China in the 1980s, the Happy Farmer's Home (HFH; *Nongjiale* in Chinese) is a form of tourism product designed to attract urban residents to live in peasants' homes, enjoy fresh air and experience traditional rural life. Household-based accommodations sited around scenic spots are the embryonic forms of HFH. Gao *et al.* (2009) treat HFH as a cluster of rural tourism products in China. They described HFH as having the following salient characteristics: (1) it serves the mass tourism market in China from a market perspective; (2) it should be classified as a leisure and holiday product; and (3) it is a tourism product complementing core tourism attractions and large-scale tourism provisions. Generally acknowledged as the origin of HFH,

Sansheng Township in Chengdu is an example of a place where urban office workers can escape from the hustle and bustle of their city life. According to the statistics from the Ministry of Agriculture (MoA) in 2010, more than 1,500,000 households nationwide had used their own houses to provide HFH services to city dwellers.

Unlike the farming situation in Europe and America, Chinese peasants only possess an average of about 1000 m^2 of arable land per capita. On the other hand, rural residents in China usually live together with people from the same clan. A village is normally composed of several hundred, or perhaps even 3000–4000 residents with a common ancestry. In these rural communities, traditional Chinese customs are still extremely influential in people's lives.

Because of the past slow economic growth of the rural areas over many years, Chinese peasants, especially those in mountain regions, have a relatively poorer standard of living when compared with their urban counterparts. As a matter of fact, most of the HFH products provided by farmers are comparatively inferior and poor in quality (not only by Western standards, but also by those of the new urban affluent groups). They are operated by farmers who remain primarily engaged in agriculture, and have limited capability for service quality improvement. Some of the barriers inhibiting improvement of the HFH products are due to 'Chinese characteristics'. For example, HFH are mainly operated on the basis of farmers' homes built on land granted by the government, and generally these lands should not legally be used for business purposes other than agriculture; consequently HFH businesses are often unlicensed and illegal. Additionally, because most farmers' houses are small and generally occupy no more than 140 m^2, they can only provide two to four guestrooms at most. Thus they cannot achieve high levels of profits and often simply supplement farm revenues, although as noted by Zeng and Ryan (2012) such supplements are significant to those who earn them. In the meantime, there are very few large-scale farms that can be operated as modern enterprises and achieve notable branding, because Chinese peasants lack both social capital and investment funds.

Two patterns can be discerned from the recent developments of rural tourism destinations in China. The first is represented by household-based guesthouses operated by individual farmers. Such accommodation offers genuine peasant household facilities and the rural landscape as attractions. However, the rural landscape is not intentionally maintained as a tourist resource and can be subject to change or degradation. The second pattern is represented by tourism enterprises based on historic or heritage villages or large-scale farms that provide a less authentic form of peasant accommodation but maintain a specific tourism rural landscape attraction. Such an example may be found in the recent tea tourism initiatives of Ping Lee County in Shaanxi Province (see Figure 3.1). While the first pattern fails to retain an unspoilt 'rurality' in rural tourism destinations, the second faces

Figure 3.1 'Modern' Tea Tourism Village, Ping Lee, Shaanxi

the challenge of meeting the tourists' quest for an 'authentic' experience. We believe both patterns are far from offering an idyllic rural life experience to tourists. It is therefore possible to identify a series of predicaments inherent in the situation, as described below.

Predicament 1: Low efficiency and short-term orientation of individual HFH operations

Our previous studies show that self-employed HFH businesses like those in Xianhuashan Village in Pujiang County (Zhang *et al.*, 2008) and the island villages in Baiyang Lake, Hebei Province (Zhou & Ma, 2009) would face 'bottlenecks' after 3–5 years' development, and display the following two characteristics.

- Firstly, as catering/dining service provisions are the core business of HFH operations, farmers face increasing competition with a low level of differentiation of their products, thus leading to a vicious circle of competing on lower and lower price, which will seriously and adversely affect the villages' sustainable development. During the cycle of evolution, natural and authentic agrarian operations often give way to extremely commercialised and manipulated product, previous community resources are gradually encroached on by a few dominant families, new residential houses are built primarily for tourism on tourists routes

Figure 3.2 Transferred vernacular architecture

(see Figure 3.1) and, more importantly, conflicts and attritions may arise between neighbourhoods.

- Secondly and alternatively, mountain villages involved in rural tourism are gradually urbanised. Guesthouses in mountain villages tend to copy modern building styles, often poorly, thereby losing their 'rurality' in appearance. An alternative example found in Shaanxi is the importation of a desired rural style from another part of China. For example, tea tourism villages in that province have imitated a rural Anhui style as seen in Figure 3.2. One potential consequence is that tourists find themselves eating in 'restaurants' and living in 'villas', which have lost the local cultural colours and are easily duplicated in other locations. It is suggested that mountain village tourist destinations of this type are destined to have a short life cycle.

Predicament 2: 'Imported' tourism development isolating rural communities

The second predicament is where tourism development is funded by investment capital sourced by entrepreneurs and businesses external to the village. This seems to be the main development model in mountain regions. Such an approach was evident in the case of Shangougou Scenic Zone (Chi & Cui, 2006), and in that of Hongcun in Huangshan Mountain (World Heritage Site), characterised by Ying and Zhou (2007) as 'travel agencies plus peasant households'. Although this 'import' tourism development model permits the introduction of external finance and professional management, its profit generation mainly relies on admission fees that may not trickle down to the local village community (Gu & Ryan, 2010). In such cases, while tourism has been developed on a local scale, there are also factors that inhibit the healthy development of local communities. External investors are interested in high-value tourism resources in mountain villages, especially those rooted in ancient villages with traditional culture and customs, but they lack interest in local community welfare. At the same time such developments make it difficult for other villages to develop their product, while additionally external business interests are not drawn to less historic mountain villages because the potential rate of return on investment (ROI) can rarely meet the capital requirements of the investor.

In practice, local governments often grant external companies so-called 'tourism management rights', yet the term has a dubious legality. It confuses the collective ownership of rural land with farmers' rights to lease land, and reinforces the likelihood of conflict between the tourism development company and the local community due to a lack of legal clarity. If the village is integrated into an attraction (as often happens in the case of an ancient village), direct and long-term conflicts will occur between the developer and the villagers, as exemplified by the case of Hungcon in Anhui Province (Gu & Ryan, 2010).

There is also the issue of the degree to which peasant communities feel able to be proactive. Even if tourism development is successful, the economic benefits that local farmers obtain are often very limited. In a survey in Huangshan Mountain conducted in 2002, it was found that villagers gained less than 10% of the ticket earnings on average (Zhou & Zhou, 2002). Even in cases where external investors valued the ecological environment surrounding the mountain villages and developed tourism-related real estate, the majority of the revenues generated through land sales went to the local government, leaving little positive impact on the development of the village community. Yet there are signs of a changing political environment as rural China finds its voice. As indicated in this book by Li, Wang and Ryan (Chapter 5), the rural mountainous village of Qiyunshan sees itself as the protector of the mountain, while in the period of September–November 2011 the village of Wukan attracted worldwide attention as it sought proper compensation for the illegal seizure of land from the Shanwei jurisdiction of the Guangdong government.

Predicament 3: Shortage of capital and talents

Generally speaking, the strong traditional community ties based on extended family relationships still found in mountain villages predispose local villagers to be actively involved in rural tourism development.

Additionally, the relatively low cost of developing tourism in mountain villages promises economic benefits for relatively little initial outlay. Therefore, tourism development is often seen by provincial and municipal governments as a significant means to help peasants improve their standards of living and enter the mainstream of economic activity. However, due to poor infrastructure in road, water and electricity supplies, and the relatively small scale of local populations, such governments prefer to choose more populated plain villages as the focus of 'building new socialist rural communities' in distributing financial resources; thus mountain villages are left behind. Furthermore, due to the outflow of young and middle-aged peasants to seek temporary jobs in the industrialised coastal regions, it becomes even difficult to set up effective organisations in mountain villages that can compete with outside enterprises in rural tourism development.

Based on the above discussions, we think it is worthwhile exploring more effective patterns and approaches to better cope with these predicaments in mountain village tourism development.

Target Model: Endogenous Development

In dealing with the problems of development in rural areas, the 'exogenous development' approach was employed in early development models. Exogenous development means developing the region through external enterprises or government subsidies, and pursuing economic growth through continuous modernisation and industrialisation. This approach, following past patterns of European and American modernisation, once played a leading role in many developing countries. However, with the passing of time the drawbacks of this development approach also emerged. For example, it tended to lead to a loss of economic and cultural independence at the local level and also oversimplified the diversity and complexity of rural community structures in villages. Moreover, it tended to neglect the importance of non-economic issues such as social justice, quality of life and ecological conservation.

Based on a review of the 'exogenous development' approach, in 1975 the Dag Hammarskjold Foundation in Sweden introduced the concept of 'endogenous development' for the first time in a report to the United Nations Assembly (Tsurumi, 1996). The following five key points were mentioned in the report:

- if development is understood from the viewpoint of liberating individuals and a holistic development of mankind, development can only be propelled from within a society;
- development should be need oriented;
- development should be self-reliant;

- development should be ecologically sound;
- development should be based on structural transformation.

The endogenous development approach is thus a self-oriented process. The development process will be controlled by the local community; development choices are made by an informed local community and benefits retained for that community. In summary, the following three aspects are essential in realising endogenous development.

- First, the ultimate goal of regional development is to cultivate the internal growth of the local community, to make full use of rural resources, and to retain and maintain the local ecological environment, cultural tradition and cultural diversity.
- Second, to achieve the goal stated above, the best strategies are to make local people the principal party in the development, construct local identity, and eventually enable local people to become active participants in local development as well as the main beneficiaries.
- Third, to ensure the implementation of the above strategies, villages must be involved and internally motivated. An effective grass-roots organisation should be established to represent the will of local people. The grass-roots organisation should have the authority to intervene with regional development decision making, and promote implementation of all measures from the bottom up.

The endogenous development approach has become one of the criteria for the UN and other international organisations to support subsidised projects. Among the organisations that have adopted the endogenous development approach as one of their project funding criteria, the most influential include the Ford Foundation of the US, and the COMPAS and LEADER programmes of the European Union. In China, influential organisations include non-governmental environmental conservation organisations such as the See Ecological Association (http://see.sina.com.cn/), and Friends of Nature (http://www.fon.org.cn).

The implementation of the endogenous development approach is of special importance to China. China had followed the simple 'exogenous development' approach for more than 30 years after 1979, leading to a series of serious social problems. Hence, in mountain villages, exogenous development proved to bring no sustained economic growth momentum, due to insufficient infrastructure and to labour migration and local recessions. In this chapter, therefore, by focusing on the endogenous development approach, we intend to explore a model for the sustainable development of the mountain regions which, as noted initially, account for 69% of total Chinese territory. To construct the new socialist rural communities as promoted by the government agenda, more than support funds are required; more important are innovative means and mechanisms to turn 'poverty alleviation with tourism' from the traditional 'blood-transfusion' pattern into a new blood generation pattern. The new pattern should be led by grass-roots rural organisations, with the active participation of community members and the capacity of cultivating community operation and self-development.

The Study Case of Suichang County

The 'Communal Model'

Suichang is a county located in the mountainous region of Zhejiang Province. It covers 2539 km² of land area and has a population of 226,000. As a typical mountain county, Suichang is known for its spectacular forest landscape, its gold mine and quality tea products, and as the origin of both the Qiantang and Ou rivers. It is also known as a place producing bamboo charcoal and the wild chrysanthemum flower bud. From December 2005 to May 2008 the first author of this chapter was involved in the county's tourism development as an appointed assistant governor in charge of tourism. The research described here is based on his direct experience of working in the county.

Suichang is about 220 km away from its nearest large city, Hangzhou. Thus it does not possess the location advantage possessed by suburban HFH operations. To develop rural tourism in Suichang, it was imperative to avoid low-price cutthroat competition among tourism operators, while at the same time it was important to guard against the visual destruction caused by the 'cement plus steel' rural building style. The primary purpose was to maintain the 'rurality' of the village landscapes and local customs and culture, which are the key components of the core competency of rural tourism in Suichang. It is worth mentioning that attracting external investment to develop HFH is unrealistic in such a context as Suichang as the low rates of return would not attract commercial external investment.

It was hence proposed that, during the initial stages of the county's rural tourism development, the county government would work on unified branding and marketing strategies, while village-level tourism organisations took the path of developing product based on shareholding cooperatives. Villagers were encouraged to establish shareholding cooperative organisations (e.g. a village-based HFH association) in which the villagers held shares; they cooperated by identifying tasks and deciding who would complete them, while operating as an autonomous enterprise (Zhou, 2006). Such a proposed model is further elaborated as follows.

First, unified planning and management is carried out at the village level. Hence, households would not bother to obtain individual business licenses. The whole village works as a unified HFH corporation, with one sales telephone

create an experience-centred product that combined a tour with a number of activities.

Projecting an image of 'Special Landscape, Indulgent Suichang'

In China it is thought many urban residents tire of city pollution, noise and congestion, and long for peace and serenity in the countryside, while at the same time seeking cleanliness, freshness and wilderness close to nature. Based on such urban residents' needs, Suichang's destination image has been designed along the theme of 'Special Landscape, Indulgent Suichang'. The word 'Indulgent' embodies the authentic nature of Suichang, implying that Suichang is a place where tourists can travel in a carefree way and without restraints. The self-drive tour is a focus for Suichang's rural tourism. 'Indulgence' rightly meets self-drive travellers' interests and preferences for independent travel and conforms to the marketing messages of the self-drive tours.

Internet marketing in the information age

The self-drive tourists, for the most part, are urban middle-class residents who earn a relatively high income. Consequently, the internet is the most cost-effective way to disseminate information while enabling communication between the parties. Apart from that, as tourism development in mountain villages is restricted by a lack of capital, the internet permits the villages to overcome a number of problems involved in other forms of marketing and so, for Suichang, the internet has come to play a leading role in its rural tourism marketing activities.

The brand of 'Suichang Commune' and the image of 'Special Landscape, Indulgent Suichang' convey a particular set of authentic tourism resources and products that can be displayed to tourists in a detailed and vivid way. These messages are communicated to the target audience through the establishment of a tourism channel on the local TV station (http://www.suichang.gov.cn/lypd/) and a dedicated marketing website – Suichang Tourism Web (http://www.sclyj.com/), supplemented by electronic magazines and news bulletins. In addition, trial experiential tours were offered to media journalists, travel agents and automobile club managers as complimentary marketing communication measures.

Effects of the Suichang Communal Model

As a result of these efforts, Suichang's rural tourism has developed rapidly since 2006. After just one year, the number of beds in HFH operations reached 900 (in 2007). During the week-long National Day holiday in 2007, tourist arrivals to the county reached 11,000, up 675% over the same period compared to the previous year. At the beginning of 2008, the management pattern of the Communal Model was officially extended to the whole county and 135 households operating HFH businesses in 25 villages were incorporated into the unified management of the Commune. A non-profit HFH service centre was set up in each village, following the 'centre plus house-hold' business operation pattern. 'Suichang Commune' was employed as a unified brand in all sales and marketing campaigns and activities; a HFH service standard was issued and thus market entry has been regulated with quality assurance. A visitor information and consultation office was set up in each village to effectively deal with tourist queries and complaints.

After two years of following the Communal Model, the number of vil-lages (spots) running HFH-style leisure tourism businesses had increased from 14 in 2007 to 34 by 2008; the number of employees in the sector increased to 475, and tourist arrivals amounted to 276,000, with the revenue climbing to more than RMB 12 million. By the end of 2008, the enhanced tourist capacity included 2200 beds and 10,000 dining seats, and tourist arrivals climbed yet further to 460,000. Due to its outstanding achievements, Suichang was awarded the first prize in the Provincial HFH Work Assessment for three consecutive years, namely from 2008 to 2010.

With these outcomes and the growing confidence of the communities, product development of the 'Suichang Commune' was further strengthened by initiating new product to present village culture and traditions. Some folk festivals like the July Fair, Coloured Lantern Fair, Tea Culture Festival and folk art performances like the Kunqu Opera, Tea Lantern Drama, Horse Lantern and Eight Treasures Lantern have been rediscovered and revived. Tourists can now enjoy various forms of colourful HFH activities associated with revived folk cultures while appreciating the rural landscapes.

Success has bred further success. For the whole year of 2009, the county hosted 2.5 million tourists from home and abroad with a total tourism income of RMB 1 billion. In comparison, these figures were only 125,000 in tourist arrivals and RMB 32 million in tourism income, respectively, in 2004 (Ye, 2011). Suichang has created for itself a national reputation in a short time and has been called 'a dark horse in the market' in the tourism industry of Zhejiang Province (Xue, 2005). Its development model has thus caught industry-wide attention.

Discussion

'Community-driven' vs. 'community participation'

We found from our study that, in order to ensure a fair distribution of the benefits derived from rural tourism, to minimise economic leakage, and ultimately to alleviate local poverty, a 'community-driven' development model under grassroots government leadership is necessary in the Chinese context. Simply calling for community participation is not adequate. This model is now being recognised by Chinese scholars (e.g. Zou et al., 2007) and it does seem that community-driven rural tourism development can lead to an extension of the industry supply chain and a maximisation of farmers' benefits.

Through a fair system of benefit sharing, avoiding over-commercialisation and preserving indigenous culture in the process of rural tourism development, rural destinations can enhance local residents' sense of pride in their communities and consolidate the basis for sustainable tourism development. While the more glamorous or ambitious rural resort features are not sustained in the individual household-based HFH model, the model does permit long-term sustainable development in the Chinese context.

The Communal Model: A refined version of HFH in China

For the most part, current mainstream HFH operations in China are usually based on individual households or family units, but their scale of operation does not guarantee independent branding and effective marketing. On the other hand, the Communal Model, under the unified planning and guidance of county-level authorities in agriculture and tourism, and taking villages as tourism operation units, can foster an orderly and unified network of tourism operations that permit the development of outstanding brands in the market.

HFH operations can meet tourists' basic needs of 'dining and lodging at peasants' homes'. On this basis the Communal Model can also generate enjoyable leisure tourism experiences, thus contributing to the creation of an atmosphere of 'joy at peasants' homes'. Furthermore, a healthy development in rural tourism can lead to the development of multiple related industries and generate a sustainable industry cluster based in the first instance on culinary arts, folk culture and the other arts. In turn these create new commercial opportunities for other businesses.

In terms of management, current HFH operations mainly follow localised accommodation service standards that closely follow the national hotel star rating system. As a result, HFH operations are required to provide the 'modernised' facilities found in urban hotels, missing the essential market distinctiveness of 'rurality' in rural tourism. In contrast, the Communal Model helps form a mutually beneficial unit consisting of different villages to form a holistic hub of tourism activities. Such a model represents a strategic exploration into constructing new rural communities that efficiently adapt to industrial restructuring while sustaining, preserving and developing the traditional cultures of rural China.

References

Blyth, S., Groombridge, B., Lysenko, I., Miles, L. and Newton, A. (2002) *Mountain Watch: environmental change & sustainable development in mountains.* Washington DC: World Conservation Monitoring Center United Nations Environment Programme.

Chi, J. and Cui, F. (2006) A study on the tragedy of the commons in the process of the development of on-limits rural tourism destinations – a case of Meijiawu, Longwu and Shangougou in Hangzhou. *Tourism Tribune* 7, 17–23.

Cui, X. and Ryan, C. (2011) Perceptions of place, modernity and the impacts of tourism – differences among rural and urban residents of Ankang, China: A likelihood ratio analysis. *Tourism Management* 32 (3), 604–615.

Gao, S., Huang, S. and Huang, Y. (2009) Rural tourism development in China. *International Journal of Tourism Research* 11 (5), 439–450.

Gu, H. and Ryan, C. (2010) Hungcon, China – residents' perceptions of the impacts of tourism on a rural community: A mixed methods approach. *Journal of China Tourism Research* 6 (3), 216–244.

Tsurumi, K. (1996) *Evolvement of Endogenous Development Theory.* Tokyo: Chikuma Shobo.

Xue, Y. (2005) Suichang tourism: A dark horse in the market. *Lisui.gov.cn*, accessed 27 February 2012. http://www.lishui.gov.cn/lypd/lydt/t20051104_115689.htm.

Ye, X. (2011) A study on the measurement of tourism economic contribution based on the added value: The case of Suichang, Zhejiang. *Enterprise Economy* 6, 163–165.

Ying, T. and Zhou, Y. (2007) Community, governments and external capitals in China's rural cultural tourism: A comparative study of two adjacent villages. *Tourism Management* 28 (4), 96 107.

Zeng, B. (2008) *Tourism Development and Local Poverty: A Case Study of Qinling Mountain Region, Shaanxi Province, China.* Saarbrucken: VDM Verlag Dr. Müller.

Zeng, B. and Ryan, C. (2012) Assisting the poor in China through tourism development: A review of the research. *Tourism Management* 33 (2), 239–248.

Zhang, H., Zhou, Y., Wei, H. and Huang, C. (2008) An empirical study of rural tourism endogenous development based on actor-network theory – a case of Xianhuashan village, Pujiang County, Zhejiang Province. *Tourism Tribune* 85 (2), 65 71.

Zhou, M. and Zhou, Y. (2002) Survey report of rural tourism development in Huangshan City. *Huizhou Social Science* 3, 25–29.

Zou, T., Wang, Y. and Cong, R. (2007) On the community-based development model of rural tourism – a case study of Daying Village, Tongzhou District, Beijing. *Journal of Beijing International Studies University* 1, 53–60.

Zhou, Y. (2006) *Rural Tourism Plan in Suichang (2006–2010).* Zhejiang: Tourism Institute of Zhejiang University.

Zhou, Y. and Ma, E. (2009) Maintaining authenticity of rural tourism experiences through community participation: The case of two Baiyang Lake Island villages. In C. Ryan and H. Gu (eds) *Tourism in China: Destination, Cultures and Communities* (pp. 293–307). New York: Routledge.

4 Institutional Opportunism in Tourism Investment

Jigang Bao and Bing Zuo

Introduction

Every developmental process requires the generation and capitalisation of resources. Early academic reviews of past policies relating to economic development within the context of developing economies, as exemplified by the *Great Push-forward, Low Level Development Trap* and the *Vicious Loops of Poverty*, all emphasised the role capital plays in development. Even in the current period, which may be classified as the Knowledge Economy, investment is still believed to be the principal driver of future development. Consequently, capital and capital accumulation will still be influential in regional development. In the three decades since the reform and opening-up of China to the global economy, a clear spatial economic structure has emerged with an advanced eastern coastal region and a less-developed centre and western region becoming evident. Indeed, the accumulation of capital and the ease of credit in the east had led to examples of excess liquidity chasing resources to the point of generating inflationary pressures in the period 2006–2009 when the government began to exercise more direct controls on bank lending policies – for example, on mortgages and, in Beijing, on the purchase of new cars.

Simultaneously, capital accumulation still remained in what may be described as a 'primary state' in the west, with provincial government in particular driving infrastructure development. For such governments tourism has become important for a number of reasons. One has been to create a demand that will utilise the new investments, while in addition tourism ventures help to attract the private sector and capital from the richer eastern seaboard regions. As a result, local governments have joined the 'race' for attracting external investment, but in doing so they have become increasingly submissive to investors external to their region, who garner excessive returns from the current institutional arrangements.

This chapter presents a case study of a tourism investment project involving external capital in western China. The case study discloses how investors were able to obtain an opportunistic rent from the then current institutional arrangements that were characterised by unequal bilateral power relations and the policy 'black holes' of a transition economy (Gu *et al.*, 2013), during which capital flowed from a developed region to a developing region. It is hoped such a case can provide insights into understanding local governments' behaviours in attracting and introducing external investments and their possible economic consequences.

Literature Review

There has been a haphazard path in understanding the role of tourism in the economic development of developing countries. An early consensus was that a high level of tourism consumption is of great significance for tourism destinations, as it can improve the destination country's international trade balance, thus alleviating a country's economic dependency on others, which is especially important to those developing countries whose economies rely on primary products (Sinclair & Stabler, 2004). Such an understanding tends to lead to 'blindly trusting' in tourism among developing countries, which state of mind overemphasises the potential advantages of developing tourism. However, after the 1970s many studies on tourism's economic impacts in developing countries suggested that tourism was a double-edge sword; tourism in less-developed regions does not play the role of a 'development agency' (Oppermann & Chon, 1997). Due to past long-term historical processes and a consequent lack of capital, in order to escape the *Vicious Loops of Poverty*, developing countries have had to resort to overseas capital and often companies from developed countries to fund tourism development. Consequently, the question of how to attract foreign investment into the tourism industry of a developing country becomes one of the central concerns on the tourism development agenda. This leads to a reliance on cross-border capital flows in these countries' tourism development; accordingly, contradictions and conflicts arise due to the development patterns and models rooted in developed countries and the different expectations and practices of overseas stakeholders.

In the initial stages of tourism development, most developing countries tend to prioritise mass inbound tourism to earn foreign exchange. Because of poor infrastructure and low educational attainment among citizens, a high level of investment is needed to implement such a non-spontaneous development strategy. As the implementation requires managerial and operational standards akin to those of developed countries, there is also a high level of dependence on foreign capital, talent and staff for developing countries to initiate their tourism industry (Bryden, 1973). This will, as Diamond (1977)

noted, force less-developed countries and regions to increase importing services and goods, leading to reduced tourism multiplier effects and generating
large amounts of leakage in tourism monetary flows. The existence of 'leakages' not only reduces the economic benefits generated from tourism development, it also seriously impairs a developing country's national tourism
development potential in the long term. In fact, the small sum that remains
after economic leakages is often earned by selling quality natural resource
materials at a lower price (Mathews & Richer, 1991). However, mass tourism
is often price competitive and sensitive and the flood of new mass tourists
into a new tourist region may well create an overdependence on tourism as
the dominant industry and inhibit the flexibility of the local economy to
diversify into other sectors. This will in turn exacerbate the fragility and
vulnerability of a country's national economy towards international market
changes, and increase the likelihood of the local economy being controlled
by multinational companies (DeKadt, 1992).

Technological, economic and business characteristics associated with
mass tourism tend to support large-scale and enclosed tourism attraction
development. Such a development mode imposes an 'enclave tourism' nature
on the development of tourism in developing countries (Jenkins, 1982).
Enclave tourism exhibits a high degree of spatial concentration, restricting
tourism development effects to zones only within the vicinities of an attraction or holiday resort (Page, 2004). Tourists would usually reach a hotel in
a metropolitan city from an international tourist transportation terminus,
shuttle flying among enclave tourism spots or resorts, and then returning
home from a metropolitan centre. Weaver (1991) depicts such types of tourist movement as a spatial dichotomy which is characterised by elite-
controlled modern resort enclaves and poverty-stricken local labour supplies.
Tourism therefore maintains structural and spatial inequality previously
existing in the traditional economy or, even worse, reinforces a structural
tendency toward tourism spatial polarisation. There is little contact between
elite-controlled tourism/enclave tourism and local enterprises. Job opportunities created by tourism are limited to a few direct employment positions.
Except for low-paid and trivial menial jobs, a large number of local people
benefit little or nothing from tourism (Pavaskar, 1982). The result of enclave
tourism cannot ameliorate the original regional development difference; on
the contrary, it leads to intensified inequality and spatial imbalance in the
society and economy, even serving as the source of social differentiation and
alienation (Britton, 1982).

In addition to examining the economic impacts of multinational corporations (MNCs) on host countries, researchers have also studied the consequences of tourism development from a political perspective. Research
suggests that tourism can not only adapt to or reinforce existing social and
spatial inequality; it can also transform economic inequality into political
inequality. Tourism development will not necessarily bring benefits to

developing countries; on the contrary, it can cause an overreliance by these countries on external forces, or cause some developing economies to be manipulated by a few multinational groups, thus reinstating the subjugation of developing countries to developed countries in the tourism industries. This represents a form of economic imperialism in the postcolonial era (Nash, 1989), and a new form of colonialism (neo-colonialism) spreading to less-developed countries in economic activities (Brohman, 1996). Under the influence of neo-colonialism, foreign capital is utilised to exploit those less-developed regions in the world, rather than helping them to develop; investment can therefore only enlarge, rather than narrow the gap in development between rich and poor counties, thereby replicating the structural inequality in the development history of both types of economies (Britton, 1980). Nevertheless, although reliance on developed countries or MNCs by developed countries can raise economic risks in destination countries, it can also improve the redistribution of wealth among different regions. Without foreign capital involvement, it is very hard for developing economies to maintain their market shares in the face of intense competition; they may even lose the capability for long-term investment and the safeguarding of existing assets. Moreover, with the further development of tourism, an increasing number of companies seek multinational operations, and host countries accommodating foreign capital can increase their bargaining power by requiring multinationals to compete for operational rights (Bull, 2004).

Researchers have positioned tourism within globalised trade relations to examine the role of foreign-derived tourism capital in the socio-economic development of developing countries. Such research explores broad political relationships among nations, and generates insights into the nature and consequence of economic relations in tourism development between developed and less-developed regions. Similar to problems facing other Third World countries, tourism development in western China bears the characteristics of both mass and enclave tourism, with a high degree of reliance on capital from outside the region. In the process of introducing external capital and investment, there also exist the imbalances noted above between the advanced and host Chinese regions and their authorities. Although within a sovereign country there is no issue of international dependency, within a country such as China complex intranational relationships emerge. The complexity of the issue is rooted in the different causes which include the nature of relationships between market-oriented private sector companies and regional, inter-regional and central governmental agendas and institutions – all of which give rise to mutually supporting and contradictory relationships between the parties. Many existing Western studies have a common flaw: most focus on analysing the impacts and consequences of tourism development and overlook the role of power bases in developed and developing zones and, over time, the changing pattern of inequality relationships between those zones. For example, the Butler Tourist Area Life Cycle fails to specifically consider the role of forces external to the destination, and how destination-externalities inter-relationships change over time. Consequently, studies on the inequality between developed and less developed regions appear to be general, static and lacking detail. In this chapter, we argue that relationships between tourism investors from the developed regions and the host region have characteristics different from those disclosed by prior studies when considering an economy in transition such as China.

Methods

For this study a qualitative approach was employed to explore the consequences of introducing external capital to a region in western China. The researchers started to pay attention to the region (designated as A) in western China and it tourism development in 1988. Systematic studies commenced in 2002. Over the years we have kept close observation on the tourism development of the region; many site visits were made over the years to better understand the development process. In July 2007 a trip was undertaken to investigate and revalidate the process that X Company in the A Region had adopted with reference to its investment strategies, their financing and their operations; interviews were used as the main method of collecting data. At the same time, secondary textual and statistical data were also collected. During our trip, we interviewed over 30 stakeholders in relation to tourism development in the A Region. Interviewees included: (a) key figures in the region's government and their civil servants; (b) senior management and staff in the X Company; (c) tourism managers and staff in other companies; (d) ex-staff who had resigned from the X Company; (e) staff from companies that the X Company had acquired; and, finally, (f) a journalist. Interview data were recorded. In the following sections, names of the place and companies are replaced with symbols. Data about the A Region were from the region's tourism bureau; those pertinent to the X Company were sourced from the Company's finance office.

The Case Study

In 1995 a private group company (hereafter the Group) from an eastern coastal province of China started investing in tourism development in the A Region of the B Province in western China. At that time the region's tourism development was in a trough. On 16 April 1995 the company signed a contract with the Forestry Bureau of the A Region to lease unworked forest land of 1675 hectares for 70 years. The company paid a lump sum of RMB 350,000[1] as rent for the first 10 years (annual rent per ha: RMB 20.89) and invested RMB 86 million in developing the S1 Scenic Zone (originally as a holiday resort, later renamed S1 Scenic Zone), which is located along a national driveway 8 km away from the city centre of the A Region. With such an investment, the company enjoyed a favourable local policy of 'Three Year Exemption and Two Year Half' in the A Region, which means that company was exempted from revenue taxes in the first 3 years of operation while only half the required tax needs to be paid in the following fourth and fifth years. Such a policy is more favourable than that adopted for local investors, which is categorised as being for 'Two Year Exemption and Three Year Half', but reflects the larger sums involved. The investment of RMB 86 million was used to renovate and build a 4–5 km long county level road connecting the Scenic Zone to the national driveway, and the construction of two small buildings in the Scenic Zone (a visitor centre and a dormitory). There were 201 ha of development land in the Scenic Zone, which were part of a primitive forest. In 2001 the S1 Scenic Zone was rated a 4A attraction by the China National Tourism Administration (CNTA). In 2002 it acquired ISO9001 and ISO14001 Environmental Quality Certification. When the S1 Scenic Zone started its operation in 1999, it received approximately 60,000 visitors in the first 7 months. Visitor numbers increased to 120,000 in 2000 and 320,000 in 2001. In 2002, to reinforce market order and avoid unhealthy competition, the A Region Tourism Authority stopped approving the establishment of similar types of tourist attractions, with the effect of issuing the *Notification on Reinforcing Tourism Market Management and Reorganization*. The Notification requested that all tourist groups to the A Region organised by travel agencies must have 4A attractions in the A Region included in their itineraries, while other attractions were optional. This policy placed the S1 Scenic Zone under government protection in terms of market entry barrier and profit earning. Under this dual protection, the S1 Scenic Zone grew and expanded quickly. In the first half of 2007 its accumulated visitor arrivals reached 380,000, becoming the second largest tourist attraction after the S3 Scenic Zone in the A Region.

In 2002 the Group invested RMB 100,453,500 in the A Region to establish the X Company, taking charge of all assets and investment projects of the Group in the region, thereby initiating capital expansion in the zone by X Company. On 26 September 2002 the X Company signed a contract with the D City[2] Forestry Administration of the B Province, investing RMB 150 million for the use of forest land of 2800 ha in the suburb of D City to build the S2 Scenic Zone in a cooperative way. The lease of the forest land was for 60 years. The S2 Scenic Zone started operations on 4 July 2004. According to our investigation, the RMB 150 million investment used for the construction of the S2 was not from the self-accumulated capital of the X Company, but through a loan mortgaged on the ticketing rights of the S1 Scenic Zone.

On 27 October 2003 the X Company signed a preliminary agreement with the A Region National Reserve Bureau, acquiring the F Company in the A Region and its debts. This led to the X Company's successful acquisition of the S3 Scenic Zone and its bundled S4 Scenic Zone under the F Company. The S3 Scenic Zone is located in the south of a national reserve in the A Region, only 47 km from the A City, enabling very convenient transportation. S3 occupied 340 ha of land, containing rare species and various protected wild animals listed in the *White Paper of Global Endangered Wildlife*. It is the only place in the A Region for tourists to observe rare species and animals. Starting in 1994, the A Region Natural Reserve Bureau continuously invested over RMB 40 million to develop tourism attractions based on threatened species and unspoilt forest sightseeing. On 8 September 1996 these attractions began to receive both domestic and international tourists. In 2003, according to the government audit, the S3 Scenic Zone owed a debt of RMB 43.34 million with total assets of RMB 18 million. There were over 200 staff working in the S3. The total operating revenue was RMB 6.7 million. As its assets could not cover the debts, S3 had to be sold by the government in open bidding. Two companies participated in the bidding: the F Company and the X Company. Finally, the X Company won the bid, buying the S3 at a price of RMB 26 million. An even more generous taxation policy was granted to the S3 Scenic Zone after the bidding. Within five years of offsetting the debt, S3 would enjoy complete tax exemption. Furthermore, the resource protection charge on the Scenic Zone was applied using the lowest standard, which is 8% of the total ticket revenue. In 2004 S3 won the title of national 4A attraction. In the first half of 2007 visitor arrivals to S3 reached 400,000, with ticket revenue of RMB 30 million, making S3 one of the more important tourism brands in the A Region, occupying 85% of the local market.

In 2004 the X Company successfully became the major shareholder of the S5 International Travel Agency in the A Region through investing RMB 2.636 million to buy 51% of S5's shares, and taking over all S5's businesses. Before the acquisition, the government-audited asset value of S5 was RMB 4.383 million, with a profit of RMB 1 million. The staff of S5 volunteered to collectively buy out the enterprise before the acquisition, but the initiative was not approved by the government. After the acquisition, all the former staff in S5 were laid off. The X Company used the national minimum standard (RMB 1,000 per work year per capita) to compensate the laid-off workers. It actually paid the compensation and other related fees of about RMB 780,000. However, at the date of our field investigation (July 2007), other payments remained overdue.

In addition to S5, on 17 September 2003 the X Company acquired the G Tourism Transportation Company with a price of over RMB 1 million, and founded the S6 Tourism Transportation Company. At the end of 2003 the X Company invested RMB 33.16 million when developing a small-scale tourism attraction, S7, next to the national driveway in the A Region, while at the same time, compared to S3's bundled attractions, S4 maintained its previous status due to its weaker ability to attract visitors. Up to this point, the

Table 4.1 Three-year financial profiles of S1 and S2 (RMB)

Items	S1			S3			
	2004	2005	2006	2004	2005	2006	3-year total
Ticket revenue (in 1000)	14,600	18,400	20,800	10,400	19,900	27,600	111,700
Profit (in 1000)	5,860	7,860	9,720	−760	8,360	12,960	44,000
Tax (in 1000)	730	920	1,040+ 1,480*	300	580	750	5,800
Rental and resources protection charges (in 1000s)	35	35	35	330	640	900	1,975

Source: X Company financial office.
*As income tax.

X Company had almost completed its capital expansion in the A Region, becoming the strongest tourism enterprise in the Region. In 2006 the X Company reviewed the assets for S1, S2 and S3 and came to the conclusion that over the past 10 years the total operational revenue net present value for the three attractions was RMB 400 million. As far as we know, the A Region government attempted to negotiate with the X Company to buy S1 and S3 back. However, as the X Company asked for RMB 400 million, a deal was not achieved. Table 4.1 shows the increasing revenues of companies S1 and S3 for the period 2004–2006.

Case Analysis and Discussion

Although currently there are no commonly agreed evaluation methods to assess the impact of external investment on host economic development, we can still run some simple calculations. Taking S1 and S3 as examples, the two attractions had a total of RMB 112 million in accumulated ticket revenue and a total of RMB 44 million in accumulated profits in the three years 2004–2006, averaging a profit rate of nearly 40%. However, in those three years, the accumulated tax, land rental and resource protection charges, and staff salary were RMB 5.8 million, RMB 1.975 million and RMB 21.7 million, respectively, which in total only accounts for 26.4% of the ticket revenue, or the equivalent of one year's ticket revenue of S3 in 2006 (see Table 4.1).

It should be acknowledged that, although some profit earned by the X Company was reinvested locally, more was returned to the parent company (the Group). Large sum local investments were mostly bank loans with the government as a guarantor, mortgaged through the Company's ticketing rights earned by a previous round of investment. In this way the Company paid little to move a huge rock ('四两拨千斤', as the Chinese proverb says). Although both the local government and other tourism enterprises admitted that the participation of the X Company in the local tourism market had been a catalyst for development, generating competitive awareness among local enterprises and applying advanced management methods from which others could learn, negative impacts of the X Company on the destination were emerging.

Firstly, the development of a local free market was impaired. Mortgage loans with the government as guarantor mean that, when the company cannot pay its debt, the government will assume the liability for losses. Thus, the government had to issue the regulation that 'all tour groups must visit local 4A attractions'. This not only infringes on the rights of tourists to visit where they wish, but also creates unfair competition for other tourism companies, causing a serious violation of free market principles.[3]

Secondly, it intensifies a dual labour market structure. It was noted that in the X Company, all those above middle-level managers or supervisors were staff assigned by the Group headquarters. Locally recruited employees were mostly frontline staff or actors in folk culture performances and had limited if any opportunities for promotion to senior posts. Such a human resource management practice meets the local government's expectation of importing management expertise and skills, but it also blocks local staff from 'learning from their work' and thus is not beneficial to the accumulation of local human capital.

Thirdly, serious social problems arose. The acquisition of the S3 Scenic Zone by the X Company and the X Company's breaking of the contract afterwards was resented by the local government and former employees in the acquired enterprise. The X Company took over operations of the S3 Scenic Zone on the same evening as the preliminary agreement was signed; however, a formal contract was only put in place after 18 months of S3's operation under the name of the X Company. The payment to the government was not completed until July 2007. According to the contract, the X Company should increase investment to upgrade the S3 Scenic Zone into a national 5A attraction; yet the Company did not fulfil its promise until 1.5 years later. It only implemented some small-scale renovations after the local tourism authority had issued multiple reminders and warnings. While the acquisition agreement requested that the X Company retain all the former staff in S3 after the takeover, the X Company used various excuses to lay off many of these staff, and by 2007 less than 50% of the former staff were working in S3. Similarly, many former employees were laid off after the S5 shares came predominately under the control of the X Company. Due to only low levels of compensation being paid to the laid-off workers, high levels of resentment prevailed among the former staff of S5. So many workers complained that the local government felt significant pressure to maintain local social stability. In 2007, when newly appointed government officials took office,[4] they were immediately overwhelmed by stacks of complaint papers.

After reviewing the X Company's patterns of investment in the A Region, we contend that the company's opportunistic behaviour is typical of the process of introducing or attracting external investment in a majority of western and some eastern less-developed regions. Prominent investor behaviours include fake promises, contract infringement, fraud and other revenue-seeking behaviours to gain benefits. When probing further into underlying reasons, such opportunistic behaviours can be explained by inequitable power relationships between the A Region government and the X Company, which are essentially determined by the dependence of less-developed regions on the capital from developed regions, and an inability by governments to properly implement legal processes, in part due to corrupt practices by both government officials and senior management. If this unequal relationship is permitted to continue and investors' opportunistic behaviours are not curbed, local governments' attempts at 'capitalising resources' will be hard to realise. Indeed, high social costs will be incurred and local control of tourism development might be lost. This in turn will reinforce the return and concentration of resources and wealth from less-developed to developed regions, and intensify the income distribution gap between rich and poor, perpetuating an imbalanced spatial structure of economic development in China. The consequences could be similar to the 'dependence' of some developing countries on the capital from developed countries (Brohman, 1996; Drakakis & Williams, 1983). Some Western scholars defined such a phenomenon as 'internal colonialism' (Dicken, 2007). The authors of this chapter would rather interpret such a phenomenon as a type of institutional opportunistic behaviour in the specific context of a transition economy. We trace the origins of such institutional opportunistic behaviours to the unequal power relations between investors from the developed regions and the host governments and the institutional black holes in the transition period.

Unequal power relations structure between external investors and the host government

Governments in less-developed regions hope to develop local economy and maximize social wealth through capitalising resources; investors from developed areas seek to maximize the added value of capital by finding investment opportunities. The combination of resources from less-developed regions with capital from developed regions serves as a link between investors and the host region. The relations between these two parties evolve on the basis of their respective negotiation power, while the gaming results are determined by various variables. As shown in Figure 4.1, both investors and the host government own certain 'power resources', determining their major power in the negotiation. The two parties tend to negotiate for their own benefit under some constraints, which in turn help define that level of power structure where decisions are made. Burns (1996) argues that one important

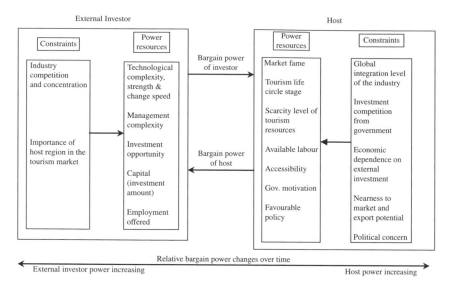

Figure 4.1 Uneven power relationship structure between external investors and host regions (adapted from Dicken, 2007)

source of power is the ownership of resources. Generally speaking, the scarcer the resource sought by both parties (e.g. capital needed by the A Region), the more powerful the party with such resource in the negotiation process would be. When many host regions run a 'rat race' to attract external investment, apparently host governments are increasingly disadvantaged in the negotiation. For the time being, local governments in China apply cut-throat strategies in competing for the limited amount of capital flows; such competitions for capital enable investors to gain better returns from regional conflicts and confrontations. These returns are embodied by virtually free land use (the annual land lease of the S1 Scenic Zone is only RMB 20.89 per ha), favourable taxation treatments, or other 'special treatments'. Of course, timing is also very important for investors. We see from the case that those important investments of the X Company in the A Region happened in the early and recession stages of the Region's tourism development (Figure 4.2). If the host region has a high reputation in the market and in a booming stage of tourism development, its government would have more control power (for example, in Lijiang, Yunnan Province). Nevertheless, the host region is generally more constrained than the investor and faces a bigger predicament. Economic distortions caused by overly favoured investment policies will also generate social costs larger than expected benefits. However, if host governments do not compete, they will not be selected by investors. Consequently, although economic harm could be circumvented, the benefits generated by external investors are also forgone. Therefore, local governments would rather sacrifice returns by accepting inequitable terms and conditions than

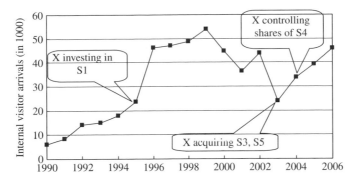

Figure 4.2 Tourism development in the A Region and the X Company's involvement

run the risk of failing to attract any externally funded capital to their region. An additional risk is that the failure to achieve economic development will attract unwelcome attention from the Beijing central government.

Investors' opportunistic behaviours induced by information asymmetry and lack of monitoring

Opportunistic behaviours refer to fraudulent revenue-seeking practices conducted for self-interest, and include lying, laziness and fraud (Williamson, 1975). People with an opportunistic tendency are likely to promote self-interest by means of fraud, false information and breaking promises. One precondition for opportunistic behaviours is information asymmetry. During the process of introducing external investment, information asymmetry favours the investor's financial situation. As local governments cannot obtain real financial information from the investor, the investor, as a party that can gain advantage through information manipulation, is more likely to release information selectively or in a distorted way, so as to formulate and implement a contract benefiting itself. It can promise larger amounts of investment to seek more favourable policy treatment, or make false financial statements to reduce tax payments, or cheat for bank loans. For instance, an officer in charge of tourism statistics in the A Region commented on the investments made by the X Company in the A Region: 'in fact it (the X Company) has little investment in the A Region. It is said its investment in the S1 Scenic Zone is over 80 million. But in reality it is not that much (judging by completed constructions). But you have to calculate according to what they said. Our indicators can only go up if they report more. And accordingly they can pay less tax.'

The frequency of opportunistic behaviours correlates with moral sensitivities on the subject of personal gain. If individuals wish to adhere to best practice, there is less opportunism in private personal contracts. However, in public contracts seeking to attract external investment, although local government officials may in practice control actual local benefits gained, they often do not accept any liability even if they have the control of resources. They are not held responsible for their behaviour, and do not accept the social costs, risks or loss caused by their behaviour. This is the real reason that led to the X Company's breaking of the contract, delaying their overdue payments to government, and other post-contractual opportunistic behaviours.

An improper officialdom evaluation system as an institutional basis for investors' opportunistic behaviours

After the mid-1990s, with its institutional change of separate taxation in distributing fiscal resources between central government and local governments, local governments in China increasingly adopt 'corporatized' views and practices, thus intensifying competition among the economies of administrative regions (Oi, 1992). Accordingly, economic performance indices, especially the growth of local GDP, rather than political and social criteria, become the norms on which local government officials get selected and promoted. Local government officials in different regions not only compete with each other for GDP and tax revenues in economic development, but also run political tournaments for promotion in their officialdom (Zhou, 2004). Investment can promote local economic development, increase tax income and enhance employment, and thus improve government officials' performance. Therefore, local government officials tend to resort to their control over local public resources, and introduce external investments to reach their political goals. Under such circumstances, attracting/introducing tourism investment in less-developed regions becomes in essence a political tool for local officials to seek promotion opportunities, making them overlook negative impacts caused by external investments.

The selfish motivation of local officials in order to maximize their personal economic benefit is a reason for the abuse of investor opportunistic behaviours. As approval of investments and control of local resources are all in the hands of the government, only the government can negotiate the introduction of external investment. In reality, a given departmental official with access to resources or approval procedures 'owns' the rights to 'legitimate' negotiation processes. This gives investors opportunities to 'seek rent' or 'using something small to get something big', and nourishes official corruption. Abnormal government behaviours emerge, including, for example, providing land use rights at low cost or free of charge, breaking state norms for 'favourable policies', investor protectionism, government interventionism. The losses and damage to local communities, enterprises and the market economic system are overlooked.

However, we should not indiscriminately blame investors' opportunistic behaviour or government officials' corrupt behaviour, without reference to the realities of the institutional environment that permit such behaviour. Thus, rectifying anti-social behaviour should start with building and improving the institutions. Hence it is of importance to improve the following systems: namely, the evaluation processes of staff and investments.

Firstly, the GDP-oriented government official performance evaluation system should be reformed, and a scientific local official performance evaluation and accountability system should be established. Good guidelines should be provided to regulate government officials' behavioural orientation and patterns, and to prevent officials from linking personal benefits to the introduction of external investment.

Secondly, an investment monitoring system should be established to prevent investors from over promising policy benefits and breaking contracts. Relevant international systems can be borrowed. For instance, in the USA, all foreign companies with an investment above a certain level, although enjoying favourable policy treatments, pay property taxes to the local government on the basis of the value of completed investment, and pay annual property tax according to the market value of the company's assets after the completion of the investment. Property tax is applied to farms, housing land, business-use land, forest, factories, houses and enterprise, and to physical properties such as furniture, vehicles and goods, as well as to non-physical properties like stocks, bonds, mortgaged contracts and bank deposits. Such taxation arrangements can prevent investors from reporting fake investment amounts designed to enjoy excessive benefit, while at the same time can compensate for financial deficits experienced by local governments in the provision of tax breaks and grants to investors.

Thirdly, a new form of tourism investment arrangement – land shareholding – can be explored. Shareholding arrangements can replace the leasing of land in the existing models of tourism development. All the land under tourism development, despite its 'state' or 'collective' ownership, should first be assessed as a usable land asset. Assessments should be conducted by a certified third party, a land evaluation agency, after the land user (developer) and the land holder (the collective village) submit an application to the land management authority. Land shares should be calculated on the basis of such assessments. The developer can also hold management or technological shares as the management party, apart from shares gained through capital investment. If the land is owned by the 'state', the land shareholder should be the local government; if it is owned by the 'village as a collective body', the land shares can be divided and allocated to each household in the village. Under such an arrangement, part of the profits can be retained by the local community to hire professional lawyers and accountants as legal and financial consultants to review and monitor the company's financial management and profit distribution. It should be made clear that farmers can join the shareholding voluntarily; they can also refrain from holding land shares and freely transfer their shares. Making host governments or local farmers shareholders can provide an effective monitoring system on the developer's investment behaviour. In addition, local government/residents can form a commonwealth body sharing both benefit and risks with the investor, enabling local communities to gain more of the benefit brought by external investors to the local economy.

Conclusion

Introducing investment by foreign and external capital is one of the common economic development strategies and means adopted by developing countries to finance economic growth. Although transnational companies can bring more tourism flows to a destination and improve the marginal returns of the productive elements in the destinations, they may also bring negative impacts to the local communities and environment in the absence of strict controls or moral imperatives to combat corrupt practices. It is likely that outside companies can monopolise the better local resources while staying distant from the destination both geographically and culturally. Favourable local government policies designed to attract external investments can lead to a long-term loss in market efficiency. This chapter comes to the following conclusion through a case study on the investment process of the X Company in the A Region of western China: during the process of introducing tourism investment by local governments, external investors can use the inequitable power relationship structure and system leakages present in transition economies to implement business opportunism though negotiating, cheating, rent-seeking and contract-breaking; they try to obtain economic policies benefiting themselves to the maximum, enabling a transfer of resources and wealth in the host region to their hands in non-transparent or opaque means. This will disadvantage local residents and enterprises, and ultimately means that less-developed regions lose control over tourism development. If investment opportunism is not curbed, the trend of wealth flowing from underdeveloped regions to developed regions will be intensified, further consolidating and intensifying the already alarming income gap between rich and poor and unbalancing further the spatial economic development of China. The current practice of local governments attracting external investments will not play a constructive role in the tourism development of western China. It could be contrastingly a damaging force. Therefore, it is imperative to improve the current system to curb opportunistic behaviours in tourism investment. It is recommended a proper local government official performance evaluation and an investment monitoring system with a reorganised land shareholding system be promoted; in doing so, a fair and just institutional environment can be fostered to allow tourism investments to run in an orderly and effective manner, enabling local residents to benefit from tourism development in a real sense.

Acknowledgements

An earlier Chinese version of this chapter was published in the Chinese journal *Human Geography*, Volume 3 in 2008. The chapter was translated by Dr Songshan (Sam) Huang and edited by Chris Ryan.

Notes

(1) In 1995 the US$/RMB exchange rate was approximately 1:8.7.
(2) Capital city of the B Province.
(3) In China officials were appointed, rather than elected. When the election system is combined with the discourse dominance of developmentalism, the growth of local GDP naturally becomes the key norm on which local government officials get selected and promoted. Thus, Chinese officials only need to pay attention to investment which is an important part of GDP, while not having to take responsibility for the possible negative effects. If a local government provides loan guarantees, it can attract more investors. Thus it was very popular that local governments provided credit guarantees for the enterprises before the year 2009 (but such practices have been forbidden by the central government since 2010 after the global financial crisis). To control and reduce the governmental credit risks, local governments had to issue regulations to favour the enterprise. The policy 'All tour groups must visit local 4A attractions' was issued in 2002. At that time, there were three 4A attractions. S1 was one of them. The X Company consequently became an oligopoly in the local market.
(4) In China local governments were reshuffled every three or five years; officials were appointed, rather than elected.

References

Britton, S.G. (1980) The spatial organisation of tourism in a neo-colonial economy: A Fiji case study. *Pacific Viewpoint* 21 (2), 144–165.
Britton, S.G. (1982) The political economy of tourism in the Third World. *Annals of Tourism Research* 9 (3), 332–358.
Brohman, J. (1996) New directions in tourism for Third World development. *Annals of Tourism Research* 23 (1), 48–70.
Bryden, J.M. (1973) *Tourism and Development: A Case Study of the Commonwealth Caribbean.* Cambridge: Cambridge University Press.
Bull, A. (2004) *The Economics of Travel and Tourism* (in Chinese; Long Jiangzhi, trans.). Dailian: Northeast University of Finance Press.
Burns, J.M. (1996) *Leadership* (in Chinese; Chang Jian, trans.). Beijing: China Renmin University Press.
DeKadt, E. (1992) Making the alternative sustainable: Lessons from development for tourism. In V. Smith and W. Eadington (eds) *Tourism Alternatives: Potentials and Problems in the Development of Tourism.* Philadelphia: University of Pennsylvania Press.
Diamond, J. (1977) Tourism's role in economic development: The case reexamined. *Economic Development and Cultural Change* 25 (13), 538–553.
Dicken. P. (2007) *Global Shift: Reshaping the Global Economic Map in the 21st Century* (in Chinese; Liu Weidong, trans.). Beijing: Commercial Press.
Drakakis, S.D. and Williams, S. (1983) *Internal Colonialism: Essays Around a Theme.* Edinburgh: Developing Areas Research Group, Institute of British Geographers.
Gu, H., Ryan, C., Bin, L. and Wei, G. (2013) Political connections, *guanxi* and adoption of CSR policies in the Chinese hotel industry: Is there a link? *Tourism Management* 34 (1), 231–235.

Jenkins, C. (1982) The effects of scale in tourism projects in developing countries. *Annals of Tourism Research* 9 (2), 229–249.

Mathews, H.G. and Richer, L.K. (1991) Political science and tourism. *Annals of Tourism Research* 18 (1), 120–135.

Nash, D.L. (1989) Tourism as a form of imperialism. In V. Smith (ed.) *Hosts and Guests: The Anthropology of Tourism*. Philadelphia: University of Pennsylvania Press.

Oi, C.J. (1992) Fiscal reform and the economic foundation of local state corporatism in China. *World Politics* 45 (1), 99–126.

Oppermann, M. and Chon, K.S. (1997) *Tourism in Developing Countries*. London: International Thomson Business Press.

Page, S.J. (2004) *Tourism Management: Managing for Change* (in Chinese; Liu Jili, trans.). Beijing: Electronic Industry Press.

Pavaskar, M. (1982) Employment effects of tourism and the Indian experience. *Journal of Tourism Research* 21 (2), 32–38.

Sinclair, M.T. and Stabler, M.J. (2004) *The Tourism Industry: An International Analysis* (in Chinese; Song Haiyan and Shen Shujie, trans.). Beijing: Higher Education Press.

Weaver, D. (1991) Alternatives to mass tourism in Dominica. *Annals of Tourism Research* 18 (3), 414–432.

Williamson, O.E. (1975) *Markets and Hierarchies, Analysis and Antitrust Implications*. Beijing: Commercial Press.

Zhou, L. (2004) The incentive and cooperation of government officials in the political tournaments: An interpretation of the prolonged local protectionism and duplicative investments in China [in Chinese]. *Journal of Economic Research* 6, 33–40.

5 The Impacts of Tourism on an Anhui Village: The Second Stage of a Longitudinal Study of Mount Qiyun

Ping Li, Qian (Nicola) Wang and Chris Ryan

Introduction

This chapter examines tourism impacts in a Taoist village (Mount Qiyun) in Anhui Province, China, based on the researchers' experience of living in the village and surveying residents and visitors. The researchers lived in the village in September and October of 2010, selecting those dates because the suitability of the weather encourages travel, while the National Day's Holiday in October lasts for seven days nationwide. It was thus possible to observe a peak holiday period, and to assess villagers' thoughts and behaviour prior to, during and after the holiday week. Additionally, the long holiday not only brought more visitors but also enabled family members of residents to return to the village. The study represents an intermediate stage of a four-year project. Thus the first author has spent a further seven months in the village over a period in 2011 and 2012.

Certainly the pace of change in rural China for those villages able to capitalise on tourism has been, by Western standards, amazingly rapid. The findings reported in this study are primarily based on research from an initial visit by the third author and further research subsequently by the first two authors. The first author lived in the village for about seven months in total over two visits and the second stayed there for about five weeks in total. These subsequent visits occurred two and three years after the first visit, and hence over time the authors have had access to data derived from a growing longitudinal study. As noted below, in those years significant changes occurred and continue to occur. A road to the village has been constructed, investment in infrastructure has taken place, the village now has internet connection, television satellite dishes have proliferated and social attitudes have changed. These changing attitudes cannot wholly be explained by tourism, as social media and television have their role to play, but it is possible to argue that the advent of tourism and the income it generated made possible residents' expenditure on internet connections, cell phones and television sets. In addition, the municipal and provincial government has acquired land from farmers at the foot of the mountain and permitted external entrepreneurs to develop a hotel and resort complex, although problems have been identified in terms of the adequacy of compensation for these compulsory purchases. Additionally, controversy has surrounded the changing ownership of the mountain, as described below.

Literature Review

Tourism is always considered as consisting of tourists, a business, an environment and a community in which this industry operates (Williams & Lawson, 2001). Therefore, tourism development plays a significant role in shaping local communities, and can have major visible impacts in those areas where tourists interact with the local environment, economy, culture and society (Mason, 2008). Cohen (1984), in an early study, argued that tourism could help improve the standard of living, increase the availability of resources for recreation and entertainment, and may also contribute to local traditional culture. Furthermore, tourism also brings significant economic benefits, such as increasing employment opportunities, income generation, tax revenue, stimulating the supply sectors of tourism, improving the level of economic activity, and raising the standard of living in the local community. For these reasons governments often support the development of tourism, especially for areas outside the mainstream of economic life (Ap, 1992; Ivanov & Webster, 2007; Liu et al., 1987). However, there remains a negative aspect and scholars such as Mason (2008) have pointed out that the negative consequences of tourism can include inflation, opportunity costs and a potential over-dependence on tourism. Furthermore, while tourism was often perceived as a clean industry this is not always the case. It can create significant environmental damage at the local destination (Andereck et al., 2005). Ryan and Gu (2009) wrote that tourism has been responsible for overcrowding that degrades the natural environment, threatens wildlife habitats and poses potential negative impacts on local community life in terms of intrusion effects such as noise, congestion, increased litter, additional demands on water supplies, sewage and waste disposal, and challenges to customs, traditions and cultures. These potential impacts may be significantly increased when communities exposed to tourism for the first time may lack physical, financial and social capital that enables them to anticipate and plan for such impacts (Y. Li, 2002a; X. Li, 2002b).

Early in the 1980s, Butler developed the framework of the Tourism Area Life Cycle (TALC), which described the relationship between tourism development (exploration, involvement, development, consolidation, stagnation, decline and rejuvenation) and its impacts. In other words, it was found that the environmental, social and economic situation of a tourism area will change over time as an area moves through the different stages. Butler (1980) indicated that in one scenario of the final stage of tourism development, that of decline, negative impacts will surpass the positive, because the carrying capacity will be exceeded (Butler, 1980). At that stage Ryan and Gu (2007) argued that costs pass from the private to the public sector, that 'glocalisation' based on local culture and traditions sold through a global distribution system replaces the 'globalised' product and, while this may represent a way forward, economic realities mean that the original nature, culture and community of place will not be replicated. Consequently, when tourism expands rapidly, the impacts need to be anticipated, comprehended, planned for and managed (Wall & Mathieson, 2006). Tourism impact research can therefore provide planners with a database to develop an effective tourism plan to address local concerns and issues, and increase the awareness for public participation (Lankford, 2001).

Generally, research into tourism impacts on local destinations in China dates from the 1990s, when scholars began to notice that tourism development created impacts on residents and communities (Zhou & Wu, 2005). However, the majority of those studies focused on employing theoretical frameworks derived from empirical studies in developed countries (Zhang et al., 2008). Some, such as Ying and Zhou (2007), argued that in China it may not be possible to completely copy or apply Western-style community participation principles because of the special socio-economic, political and cultural setting of China. Li (2002b) found that many studies of tourism impacts placed an emphasis on ethnic minority communities in China or some Chinese remote rural regions. For example X. Li (2002b) and Li and Yan (2003) argued that in the less economically developed areas of China young residents would be particularly vulnerable to demonstration effects arising from the behaviour of higher income tourists. It was only in recent years that researchers started to explore the impacts of tourism on more famous and typical destinations. For instance, based on the investigation of Zhangjiajie National Forest Park in China, Zhong et al. (2008) found that the park's environment, air quality and groundwater quality had deteriorated over four different tourism development stages (e.g. the exploration, involvement, development and consolidation stages). Wang et al. (2005) undertook a study of residents' perception of tourism impact in Harbin, and noted that tourism made Harbin a more exciting place and had enriched its traditional local culture; however, the study also found that the residents ignored the negative impacts. Gu and Ryan (2008) examined the relationship between local community and tourism impacts in a Beijing hutong, and indicated that traffic congestion and visitors were considered as being intrusive into everyday life, but generally residents still considered tourism to have more rather than fewer advantages. Certainly there exist in China factors that are unique to that country which impinge on tourism and its impacts. For example, Zhang and Bao (2010) describe the impact of the *Hukou* on the spatial dynamics of Xidi, Anhui Province, as its growing tourism retains a resident population that might otherwise migrate, and also helps to reinforce an elite that adds 'nepotism to such an interests-pattern as they recommend relatives to work in tourism, which results in high dependence on the economic benefit tourism brings' (Zhang & Bao, 2010: 247). Given, however, the size of China and its variation in administrative practices, Ryan *et al.* (2011), basing their research on a study of the Kaiping Diaolou, questioned if metanarratives in the area of tourism impacts on residents are indeed possible, concluding perhaps that each situation is a case study with its own specific spatial, temporal and socio-economic conditions.

More specifically, therefore, this chapter reports findings from research into residents' perceptions of the impacts of tourism on the village, their evaluations of those impacts and their expectations, hopes and fears of future tourism development in the light of the rapid change experienced in the two years prior to data collection. While Ryan *et al.* (2012) had reported on prior research, noting the changes that had occurred since their study, it was decided to adopt an exploratory approach at this stage with a view to commence a third stage for the research in 2012.

The Study Area: Mt Qiyun

Mt Qiyun is located in Xiuning County, Huangshan City, Anhui province (Figure 5.1). Xiuning County is 33 km from Huangshan City (Mt Qiyun Scenic Area Management Committee, 2010), which is 'located at the most Southern end of Anhui Province and bordering on Zhejiang and Jiangxi provinces' (Xiuning County Tourism Administration, 2010: 1). Early Taoists chose Mt Qiyun as a place to live to practise austere meditation. Mt Qiyun occupies 110 km² (Qiyun Shan Tourism, 2011) and there are about 150 villagers living on the mountain. They are not only residents but also service providers at this unique scenic spot. Mt Qiyun is known as the 'First Taoist Country in China' because its records date from early in the Tang Dynasty (AD 758–760). Taoism was introduced to Mt Qiyun by a Taoist priest, Gong Xiayun (Mt Qiyun Scenic Area Management Committee, 2010). The ultimate goal (ideally) of Taoist priests is to train and cultivate themselves to attain immortality so that they can help people achieve their desires and be

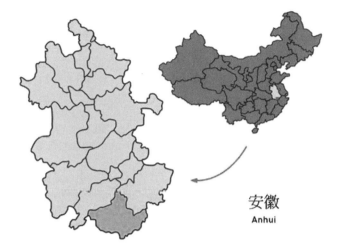

Figure 5.1 Geographical location of Mt Qiyun
Source: http://en.wikipedia.org/wiki/Huangshan_Shi.

blessed. In China, the four main Taoist mountains are Mt Wudang in Wuhan Province, Mt Longhu in Jiangxi Province, Mt Qiyun in Anhui Province and Mt Qingcheng in Sichuan Province (Zhang *et al.*, 2007). Mt Qiyun is seen as the 'second Mt Wudang' (Xiuning County Tourism Administration, 2010: 4), which demonstrates its high reputation since ancient times, although it is small when compared to other mountains in China, being only 584 m in height.

The most prosperous time of Mt Qiyun was during the Ming (1368–1644) and Qing (1644–1911) dynasties, when it attracted many pilgrims from different places (Mt Qiyun Scenic Area Management Committee, 2010). However, Mt Qiyun experienced a difficult time during the period of the 'Cultural Revolution' (1966–1976). Taoism was criticised 'as a fatalistic and passive religion during the Cultural Revolution' (Wang & Stringer, 2000: 34), and Mt Qiyun did not escape such criticisms. A large number of temples, statues and Taoist scriptures were destroyed by the Red Guard in 1966 (Cheng, personal communication, 29 September 2010) as part of a mission to smash the 'Four Olds' that were associated with 'traditional culture, ideas, customs and habits' (Ryan, 2011: 112). Fortunately, in 1982 the vice-governor of Anhui Province recognised that Qiyun had huge potential for tourism development and provided some funding for restoring temples and statues (Cheng, personal communication, 29 September 2010). Since 1994 Mt Qiyun has been accredited as a National AAAA Scenic Area, a National Forest Park, a National Geological Park, a Chinese Sacred Land of Daoism and a National Cultural Relic Protection Unit (Cheng, personal communication, 29 September 2010). In addition, Mt Qiyun has a rich cultural heritage value in addition to its significant geological values, due to its

Danxia red rock landscape and these are expressed in social and built forms that integrate Taoism cultural heritage, the typical architecture of residents' houses (i.e. Hui-style architecture; Figure 5.2), the Danxia landforms, and inscriptions on precipices and stone inscriptions. It has therefore been identified as a location for religious tourism, which is growing in China (Cao, 2007) and there has been local initiatives to prepare the site for UNESCO World Heritage status.

Today many tourists use a gondola that was built as a means of access to the mountain in about 1996. Prior to that development, access was by a path used for walking up and down the mountain, which still provides an alternative option for tourists (mainly pilgrims); it also remained as a major access path for residents due to the costs of the gondola ride at the time of research. In addition, a new road (Figure 5.3) was under construction at the back of mountain when the researchers were in the village, and this is now complete and was being used in 2012. There were also a number of lookouts under construction in 2010 and every lookout provides a good angle to see the mountain and the scenery at the bottom of the mountain. Excavating a tunnel through the mountain was under consideration when the researcher stayed in the village; on 29 April 2011 excavation of the tunnel started and it was then thought that construction would take about four months (Qiyun Shan Tourism, 2011). Certainly the opening of the tunnel has provided an alternative transportation route for both visitors and residents. During the first author's residency in 2012 a not uncommon topic of conversation among villagers was about what car they would buy. In addition, significant

Figure 5.2 The Hui-style architecture of Qiyuanshan

Figure 5.3 A new road under construction in 2010

small scale infrastructure improvements were noted; these included new paving of streets and the installation of themed rubbish bins, as well as new signposting and means of interpretation. In 2011 and 2012 new promotional videos of the village were made and released and it is significant that they also carry subtitles in English.

Methodology

The study employed mixed methods with an emphasis on qualitative methods and ethnography to provide data that might provide a basis for future empirical data collection and problem identification. It required researchers to became an 'insider', using participant observation techniques to experience local residents' daily life, with the aim of exploring their behaviours, activities, expectations and attitudes toward tourism development. Every day, the two lead researchers completed field notes to record that day's observations, feelings, and informal conversation arising during the daily events. Other specific methods in this research mainly involved the following:

(1) *In-depth semi-structured interview*. The target interviewee respondents were the local village residents, who lived and worked in Mt Qiyun. Twenty-four semi-structured interviews were conducted in Mt Qiyun village during four weeks of October 2010. The information was recorded by note taking and tape recording and were analysed by thematic

analysis and the use of the software package CATPAC™. In the process of interviewing, the researcher avoided the participants' busy business hours and chose times when they relaxed. Each interviewee was formally interviewed at least twice (about half an hour each time) to gain an understanding of the participants' previous experience, story, current life status and further expectations. Based on the reviewing of related literature on tourism impacts and residents' attitudes, four themes were designed to guide residents in this interview:

(i)   the overall attitude to Mt Qiyun tourism;
(ii) the impacts created by tourism (economic, social-cultural, environment);
(iii) views about the tourism authorities;
(iv) suggestions for further developments in Mt Qiyun.

(2) *Informal conversation.* These were conversations that arose in daily interaction with local people. For example, prior to the National Holiday period, village residents would talk about their relatives and friends returning to the village.

(3) *Photography and video taking.* The third author had taken a significant number of photographs on a prior visit and thus comparisons were possible. In addition, villagers started to show the researchers their old photographs and in some cases pictures.

The analysis of the qualitative data was subject to a number of checks to ensure as far as possible the credibility of the theme classification. The first two authors independently analysed the data using traditional thematic analysis prior to comparing results, and then worked together to achieve a congruency of classifications. The third author took the notes and comments and checked them through using textual analysis software to confirm the themes. The themes identified below were the result of such processes.

(4) *The self-completion of a quantitative questionnaire.* The survey used a seven-point scale (where seven was the highest score) to assess residents' perceptions of tourism impacts in their village. The survey was divided into four sections: (a) local residency; (b) opinion about the opening of a cable car to the village and its impacts; (c) general attitudes to tourism; and (d) socio-demographic data. Of the sample of 66, the majority comprised local residents living in Qiyun, and there were also a small number who did not live in the village but worked there. There was also access to students who were children of residents, who studied outside the village but returned to it, and other relatives of local residents who often visited Mt Qiyun and who were present during the National Holiday. They helped in this process of data collection. The Statistical Package for Social Sciences (SPSS) 17.0 was employed to analyse the data using descriptive, frequency, independent t-test, ANOVA and regression statistics as described later.

(5) *Secondary documentary evidence.* Finally, there was a document analysis based on official documents, printed tourism promotional materials and past research results on Mt Qiyun. These comprised five copies of local village documents, three sets of Mt Qiyun marketing materials, one newspaper article and the local governmental website.

Sample

The sample for semi-structured interviews consisted of 24 participants: seven females (29%) and 17 males (71%). The oldest participant was 88-years-old, while only seven of the total were below 40-years-old. The youngest was 19-years-old. The majority of participants were local villagers, except four respondents from villages below the mountain and three from Xiuning County. Nearly all of these participants work in Mt Qiyun, including an incense seller, tour guide, Taoist, restaurant owner, fortune-teller, etc. On the other hand, there were 66 residents who completed the questionnaire, and male and female participants accounted for 37.8% and 62.1% of the total sample. As might be expected, the majority of respondents were between the ages of 26–50 years (accounting for nearly 60% of the total sample), while respondents above 60-years-old and under 25-years-old took a similar proportion of the total sample (16.7% and 18.0% of total respondents). The number of respondents involved in the questionnaire is small; however, it is a high percentage of the actual number of total villagers (about 33%), and hence it could be considered as representative on that basis. One issue is the degree to which faith can be placed in such questionnaires given the varying degrees of literacy that exist in such villages. In this case, however, where respondents required help, such help was provided. Also, by the time the questionnaire was completed, the researchers had become familiar figures around the village and good relationships had been established with many of the residents. Indeed some retain contact via the internet and have hosted a third research project in 2012.

Findings

Many residents agreed that tourism development could help to improve living conditions by increasing their family's income. In particular, participants were willing to compare their current quality of life with that of a previous period, especially with the time when Mt Qiyun was not open to general tourists. Additionally, they identified a sub-theme; that is, the quality of life on the mountain was now better than that in the surrounding villages at the foot of the mountain because of the incremental income derived from tourism. This finding confirms the view expressed by many

However, a land sale in 2011 once again for the fifth time in recent history passed ownership of the mountain to an external business organisation, thereby nullifying hopes of a greater say in development that had occurred only two years earlier when the municipal government bought back ownership from a prior private sector company.

More than half of the respondents pointed out that tourism development had played a somewhat positive impact on local traditional culture and promoted Taoism. Residents felt pride in their Taoist history, the temple, the gods and the traditional festival. Each liked to tell visitors about the story and history of this Taoist Mountain.

For example, two incense sellers said:

> ... my father was a Taoist in mountain Qiyun when he was alive; hence, I know lots of stories about Taoism, I like Taoism ... hope tourism could stimulate the protection of Taoism ...

> ... because of tourism development, many temples had been repaired, old historic places also begin to be re-established; and some of our traditional things had been introduced to visitors ...

Indeed, many researchers have found that tourism has strengthened local folk customs (e.g. in Bali, see McKean, 1972). Collier (2003) also provided evidence to suggest that 'tourism can provide the impetus for a revival in local customs and traditions in many areas' (Collier, 2003: 331). Nonetheless, in China Xie (2011) has questioned whether such have been the impacts on the traditions of the Li people in Hainan that even the Li are today confused about their cultural traditions, a situation that has come into being due to private businesses creating their own legends simply to better entertain visitors.

The results also indicated that respondents showed high levels of agreement with the concept that 'tourism development could improve basic facilities for locals'. For example, transportation was more convenient than previously, street lighting provided, new forms of broadcasting TV and internet were installed, and a new tourist pathway was built. Moreover, the current study found four female respondents who specifically mentioned that tourism had definitely changed their life for the better after Mt Qiyun opened to visitors, because they now not only took care of their families but had also begun to go out of the house, faced a new environment and worked in a regular tourism job to earn money.

Respondents were also asked, 'How do you feel tourism affects Mt Qiyun environmentally (both positive and negative)?' The findings revealed that tourism development was not perceived as having brought significant environmental damage to the mountain, perhaps because of the, as yet, small number of visitors being attracted to Mt Qiyun. Compared with other attractions near Mt Qiyun such as Hongcun, Xidi and Huangshan, Qiyun

Mountain was receiving by far the smallest number of visitors per year. Indeed, despite the small number of visitors coming to the mountain, the government and authority is seeking to implement many policies to protect the mountain environment. This theme was illustrated by quotes such as:

... The government and authority were forbidding the illegal buildings, and stop local residents raising pigs and chickens to protect the environment ...

... The government also creates a family responsibility system to ensure the clean environment, green covering, and good social order outside each unit building ...

... The rubbish bins were designed as recycled and no recycled boxes ...

However, it is necessary to note that some small environmental problems still existed in the village. For instance, in the peak season, rubbish is becoming a more significant problem; many visitors tend to drop their rubbish anywhere if they cannot find conveniently sited rubbish bins. Many pilgrims wish to burn incense and joss paper in the Taoist temple, which creates much smoke and rubbish. This finding corresponds with that of Gurung (1995), who found that tourism in mountain communities was more likely to increase litter, as paper, and plastic or glass bottles were frequently found on routes. This echoes the work of Wong (2011) on the dangers presented to Buddhist temples in Putuoshan from the burning of incense sticks.

Yet, when asked to provide an overall judgment of the impacts of tourism, all the respondents supported tourism development in Mt Qiyun, and hoped the mountain could be further promoted to attract many more potential visitors. It was interesting to note that, despite some negative effects of tourism, all the respondents stated that they wanted tourists, because tourism could bring economic benefits to them. This finding was similar to Western studies that found that, while residents held mixed attitudes about tourism development, they still generally supported tourism despite perceived negative impacts (Besculides et al., 2002). However, this is not to say that residents were satisfied with every aspect of tourism. By reading original transcripts for this question, the researchers found 20 out of 24 respondents in the present study reported some disquiet with the Mt Qiyun authority and government. Indeed, to better understand these types of concerns, the first author found a former Xiuning government secretary who had made significant contributions in developing Qiyun Mountain. When asked why Qiyun Mountain's tourism had developed so slowly, he provided three essential reasons, as follows:

(1) Before 2010, the management right was sold to a private company. Those private companies only focus on ticket selling without planning and development.

(2)   Lack of local residents' support, because residents cannot receive any compensation ... (the company) ignored local residents' suggestions ... the residents never knew what was going on about Mt Qiyun.
(3)   Lack of government support, the Xiuning government cannot provide enough financial support, so the tourism facilities were quite old and limited.

Based on a statistical analysis, the majority of respondents held to an opinion that 'The tourism planning authority should encourage further tourism development in the area', with a mean of 6.66, on a seven-point scale where seven represented the highest score, and a standard deviation (S.D.) of 0.59, followed by the statement 'The money spent locally to attract more tourists is a good investment' (mean = 6.59; S.D. = 0.70). However, at the lower end of the scale was the variable relating to 'I feel the village's tourism planning authorities do an excellent job in making the right decision about the area' (mean = 3.64; S.D. = 1.38).

Discussion

From both the results of the qualitative and quantitative data, it might be said that the residents in Mt Qiyun were more likely to focus on the positive tourism impacts; indeed only a small number of respondents initiated any mention of the negative impacts during the research. With regard to the positive economic benefits, the majority stated that it was certainly true that their quality of life had improved a lot because of tourism (with a mean of 5.65), which is consistent with findings by researchers such as Jurowski and Gursoy (2004). Another finding was to confirm that tourism development in Mt Qiyun had created many basic job opportunities for local residents. On the other hand, it was also argued by several interviewees that the jobs created by tourism were considered as having low skill requirements, relatively low pay and status and were often seasonal in nature. It was suggested that the local authority should place an emphasis on training residents to become more skilled. On the other hand, tourism did supplement existing income earned from agriculture, and its seasonal nature meant it did not overly interfere with agricultural practices primarily relating to the growing of tea. It also provided employment for those not otherwise able to labour in the fields. So, while generating comparatively modest incomes, its supplementary effect was important as demonstrated in the higher incidence of ownership of consumer durables. On the social-cultural impacts, it was felt that tourism development could help to protect Taoism heritage culture (mean = 6.05), reinforcing local pride about Taoism, helping to sustain a traditional festival and to inform tourists about Chinese cultural traditions.

More importantly, the current research found nearly all respondents welcome tourists and want Mt Qiyun to develop even more quickly and attract more visitors. One main reason was the feeling that residents could earn even more if the number of tourists increased. This same wish also meant that residents expressed some dissatisfaction with the role played by the local government; however, a complex set of reasons lay behind this which are beyond the remit of this text, essentially concerned with the ownership of the land and the passing of that ownership to a private sector corporation. Although the present findings require future substantiation, they provide normative grounds for several recommendations relating to the development of Mt Qiyun, including:

- Cognisance must be taken of a growing feeling on the part of residents that they are best placed to protect the heritage and culture of the mountain, and government should eventually recognise them as an owner of the mountain.
- The local village should receive adequate compensation and dividends from tourism ventures in Qiyun Mountain.
- The local authority should work with communities rather than with individuals to avoid narrowly focused self-interests dominating and to ensure more harmonious community–governmental relationships.
- Thought needs to be given to the creation of more stable job opportunities and training programmes for middle-aged and elderly residents.
- Tourism should be more environmentally sustainable.
- There should be respect for traditional heritage Taoism culture.

Yuehua Street is the main residential area for villagers, so it was thought inappropriate to overdevelop this area in order to avoid undue intrusion into local life. As one of the Anhui provincial government's focal points for developing future tourism attractions, the strategic tourism planning for Mt Qiyun recommends an emphasis on Qiyun Daoism cuisine, Qiyun Taoist health practices, Daoism Qiyun Country, Qiyun tea, and encouraging collaboration with the other three famous Taoist mountains: Mt Wudang, Mt Qingcheng and Mt Longhu (Sai, personal communication, 27 September 2010). Due to the limited usage of Taoist culture as a tourist attraction prior to 2010, more ideas to develop Taoist cultural tourism products have been identified by local stakeholders, such as establishing China's Taoism museum and using Qiyun as a base for film production (Sai, personal communication, 27 September 2010). There was also a feeling that advertising could be further improved, for example by promoting the existence of restaurants and accommodation in the village both in print and on the web, and by enhancing relationships with tour operators and tour guides. What is omitted from much of this discussion is the actual nature of Taoism, for as Kirkland (1986) noted, the religion, while altruistic and tolerant, has its own traditions, including a stream of mysticism, and certainly its adherents may have their own views on the commodification of its rituals for the purposes of tourism.

A similar issue with reference to Buddhism is also discussed by Wong and Ryan in Chapter 16 of this book.

These findings would indicate that Mt Qiyun is at the early stage of tourism development, referring to Butler's (1980) evolution of a tourism area, and most residents want more visitors as indicated from the interviews. However, while the residents tend to be enthusiastic about tourism, and wish for more control and ownership, there are some ambiguities in their attitudes. On the one hand, they are motivated by economic considerations for more income and better employment opportunities. The degree to which this may potentially clash with the longer term sustainability of the village as a pilgrimage site and as a place of Taoist ritual and festivals seems to feature very little in the residents' thinking. Indeed, one might ask, 'why should it?', given the limited experience and education of many of the residents. This seeming inability to foresee any potential long-term consequences of unbridled growth in visitor numbers and the proliferation of tourism product based on the above ideas requires intervention by the planning authorities and/or the imposition of responsibilities on the part of researchers. The issue is whether the former are solely committed to a growth scenario, or whether there is a growing willingness to consider wider remits. Past history in the development of tourist sites in Anhui that extend the tourism product beyond Huangshang, such as Xidi, Hongcun and other sites including the Tangyue Arches of Bao Village and other promotions based on traditional architectural styles, suggest that the former scenario will dominate, but recent documentation from the Provincial government is suggesting a growing sensitivity to carrying capacities (Huang, 2003). However, this implies future difficult political decisions as constraints on growth may disappoint local residents. If researchers are to begin to inform residents as to possible future outcomes, that too poses problems in terms of the research paradigms being adopted. Current research has been post-positivistic in nature. Can future research by the lead author based on a longer stay in the village maintain that stance? Only time will tell. There remains, therefore, a requirement for monitoring of the situation – and this too poses a challenge for future research in China. Like their Western counterparts there is a relative lack of longitudinal research in China. In a country of such rapid change, benchmarks need to be established to trace progress or regress, and that can only be achieved by long-term relationships between researchers and the places being researched.

Finally, it should be noted that tourism development at Mt Qiyun is ongoing and dynamic; equally, the focus of the authors' research is also changing. Initially it concentrated on the village and also the visiting tourists, and a new dataset from the later work has yet to be analysed. But the current research has gone further to address some of the deficiencies in the research reported above. First, there has been a more detailed study of how the Mt Qiyun tourism has impacted on other surrounding villages and, secondly, more detailed interviews have been conducted with local government officials to provide a voice to officialdom in later reports. Taken as a whole, it can be seen that tourism in China at site-specific levels is dynamic, and so too must be the research methods adopted if this complexity is to be captured.

Acknowledgements

This paper is based upon an earlier article published in *Tourism Tribune* in Mandarin (Li *et al.*, 2012).

References

Andereck, K.L., Valentine, K.M., Knopf, R.C. and Vogt, C.A. (2005) Residents' perceptions of community tourism impacts. *Annuals of Tourism Research* 32 (4), 1056–1076.

Ap, J. (1992) Residents' perceptions on tourism impacts. *Annals of Tourism Research* 19 (4), 665–690.

Besculides, A., Lee, M.E. and McCormick, P.J. (2002) Residents' perceptions of the cultural benefits of tourism. *Annals of Tourism Research* 29 (2), 303–319.

Butler, R.W. (1980) The concept of a tourist area cycle of evolution: Implications for management of resources. *Canadian Geographer* 24, 5–12.

Cao, H. (2007) *Analysis of Religious Tourism Development and Operation Issues in Contemporary China.* Guang Dong Tourism Institute. Online at http://ly.gdcc.edu.cn/n12470c84.aspx.

Cohen, E. (1984) The sociology of tourism: Approaches, issues, and findings. *Annual Review of Sociology* 10, 373–392.

Collier, A. (2003) *Principles of Tourism: A New Zealand Perspective.* Auckland: Pearson.

Coser, L.A. (1957) Social conflict and the theory of social change. *British Journal of Sociology* 8 (3), 197–207.

Dogan, H. (1989) Forms of adjustment: Sociocultural impacts of tourism. *Annals of Tourism Research* 16, 216–236.

Gu, H. and Ryan, C. (2008) Place attachment, identity and community impacts of tourism – the case of a Beijing hutong. *Tourism Management* 29 (4), 637–647.

Gurung, C.P. (1995) People and their participation: New approaches to resolving conflicts and promoting cooperation. In A.J. McNeely (ed.) *Expanding Partnership in Conservation* (pp. 232–233). Washington, DC: Island Press.

Huang, C. (2003) Preliminary study of rural tourism of Huangshan City [黄山市乡村旅游初步研究]. *Geography* 18 (1), 24–28.

Ivanov, S. and Webster, C. (2007) Measuring the impact of tourism on economic growth. *Tourism Economics* 13 (3), 379–388.

Jurowski, C. and Gursoy, D. (2004) Distance effects on residents' attitudes toward tourism. *Annals of Tourism Research* 31 (2), 296–312.

Kirkland, J.R. (1986) The roots of altruism in the Taoist tradition. *Journal of the American Academy of Religion* 54 (1), 59–77.

Lankford, S.V. (2001) A comment concerning developing and testing a tourism impact scale. *Journal of Travel Research* 39, 315–316.

Li, P., Wang, Q. and Ryan, C. (2012) The impacts of tourism on traditional villages: A case study of Mt Qiyun, Anhui Province. *Tourism Tribune* 27 (4) , 57–63.

Li, Y.P. (2002a) The impacts of tourism in China on local communities. *Asian Studies Review* 26 (4), 471–486.

Li, X. (2002b) The impacts of tourists on the social-culture in developing countries. *Journal of Central China Normal University (Natural Sciences)* 2, 254–256.

Li, Z. and Yan, J. (2003) The vicissitude of social culture and the modernisation of social psychology in under-developed tourism destinations. *Journal of Beijing International Studies University* 5, 89–93.

Liu, J.C., Sheldon, P.J. and Var, T. (1987) Resident perception of the environmental impacts of tourism. *Annals of Tourism Research* 14, 17–37.

Mason, P. (2008) *Tourism Impacts, Planning and Management* (2nd edn). Oxford: Butterworth-Heinemann.

McKean, P. (1972) Tourism, culture change, and culture conservation in Bali. Paper presented at the 71st Annual Meeting of the American Anthropological Association, Toronto, Canada.

Mt Qiyun Scenic Area Management Committee (2010) *Qiyun Mountain*. Xiuning: Mt Qiyun Scenic Area Management Committee.

Page, S.J. and Connell, J. (2006) *Tourism: A Modern Synthesis*. London: Thomson.

Qiyun Shan Tourism (2011) *Coming to Qiyun Shan, Looking for Xu Xiake's Footprints*. Qiyun Shan Tourism website. www.chinahotel.com.cn/Attractions_2148.html.

Ryan, C. (2011) China: Tourism and religious sites. In F. Xu (ed.) *Religious Tourism in Asia and the Pacific* (pp. 110–124). Madrid: United Nations World Tourism Organisation.

Ryan, C. and Gu, H. (2007) The social impacts of tourism in a Beijing hutong – a case of environmental change. *China Tourism Research* 3 (2), 235–271.

Ryan, C. and Gu, H. (2009) *Tourism in China: Destination, Cultures and Communities*. New York: Routledge.

Ryan, C., Zhang, C. and Deng, Z. (2011) The impacts of tourism at a UNESCO heritage site in China – a need for a meta-narrative? The case of the Kaiping Diaolou. *Journal of Sustainable Tourism* 19 (6), 747–765.

Ryan, C., Jing, S., He, Y. and Gu, H. (2012) Touristic perceptions in a Taoist Chinese village. *Journal of China Tourism Research* 8 (1), 19–36.

Wall, G. and Mathieson, A. (2006) *Tourism: Change, Impacts and Opportunities*. Sydney: Pearson Education.

Wang, J. and Stringer, L.A. (2000) The impact of Taoism on Chinese leisure. *World Leisure Journal* 42 (3), 33–41.

Wang, Y., Li, G. and Bai, X.M. (2005) A residential survey on urban tourism impacts in Harbin. *China Tourism Research* 1 (1), 116–128.

Williams, J. and Lawson, R. (2001) Community issues and resident opinion of tourism. *Annual of Tourism Research* 28 (2), 269–290.

Wong, U.I.C. (2011) Religious tourists – belief and sightseeing – the behaviours of visitors to the Temples of Putuoshan, China. Unpublished doctoral thesis, Department of Tourism and Hospitality Management, University of Waikato Management School.

Xie, P.F. (2011) *Authenticating Ethnic Tourism*. Bristol: Channel View Publications.

Xiuning County Tourism Administration (2010) *Guidebook of Tourism*. Xiuning County: Xiuning County Tourism Administration.

Yang, J. and Ryan, C. (2011) A framework to research tourism impacts: The functions of social conflict. Paper presented at the Islands and Small States Conference, University of the South Pacific, Suva, Fiji, September.

Ying, T.Y. and Zhou, Y.G. (2007) Community, governments and external capitals in China's rural cultural tourism: A comparative study of two adjacent villages. *Tourism Management* 28 (1), 96–107.

Zhang, M., Huang, L., Wang, J., Liu, J., Jie, Y. and Lai, X. (2007) Religious tourism and cultural pilgrimage: A Chinese perspective. In R. Raj and N.D. Morpeth (eds) *Religious Tourism and Pilgrimage Festivals Management: An International Perspective* (pp. 98–112). Wallingford: CABI.

Zhang, X. and Bao, J. (2010) Tourism development and the rural change: The hypothesis of origin-dynamics. In P. Zhao (ed.) *Tourism Tribune (2008–2009) English Edition* (pp. 241–250). Beijing: Social Science Literature Press.

Zhang, X.M., Ding, P.Y. and Bao, J.G. (2008) Income distribution, tourism commercialisation, and Hukou status: A socioeconomic analysis of tourism in Xidi, China. *Current Issues in Tourism* 11 (6), 549–566.

Zhong, L.S., Deng, J.Y. and Xiang, B.H. (2008) Tourism development and the tourism area life-cycle model: A case study of Zhangjiajie National Forest Park, China. *Tourism Management* 29 (5), 841–856.

Zhou, H. and Wu, J. (2005) A summary of the research on the impacts of tourism on a destination's social culture in China. In P. Zhao (ed.) *Tourism Tribune (2003–2004) English Edition* (pp. 138–151). Beijing: Social Science Literature Press.

6 Festival and Special Event Development in Modern China: A 30-Year Practice

(Joe) Yong Zhou

Background

In China large-scale events (e.g. events related to national celebrations or royal family activities) regularly took place even before the foundation of the People's Republic in 1949. The Emperors' enthronements and weddings always meant that there would be nationwide celebrations and large-scale ceremonies. Religious sacrifices to the gods were also celebrated in the feudal age, some of which involved large numbers of people and had an importance beyond the personal. Evidence for this exists in many well-known historic buildings in China that were specifically built as venues for special events. For example, the Temple of Heaven, a World Heritage site in Beijing with an area of 270 ha, was exclusively constructed to worship Heaven in AD 1420 during the Ming Dynasty, and to mark the movement of the capital from Nanjing to Beijing. It was then used annually for this purpose by dynastic rulers until the beginning of the 20th century. After 1949, special events, especially those with large-scale attendance, were often related to political activities and arranged by the government, the Communist Party of China (CPC) and related bodies such as the Red Guards' gatherings in Tiananmen Square during the Cultural Revolution. Only after the country started its economic reform and open door policy in 1978, when tourism was recognised as an industry, did more general tourism events emerge in China.

Getz (2006) suggested that increased productivity and wealth would result in a large, diversified demand for consumer goods, leisure activities and travel. As world travel patterns have shifted towards the fast-growing East Asian economies since the 1990s, China and other Asian countries began to adopt themed years and organise events as new tourist attractions and generators of image. Increasingly, local governments realised that their traditional events might be popular with tourists anxious to discover the local culture, and that special events could be a cost-effective way to further tourism development. Meanwhile, with more leisure time and the rapid growth of disposable incomes, events and festivals have become an increasingly important part of China's domestic leisure scene.

Contemporary China's tourism development started at the end of the 1970s. Tourism infrastructure, especially hotel rooms and transport, were in significantly short supply in the early 1980s (Wen & Tisdell, 2001). As a consequence, initial tourism investment provided infrastructure and basic tourist facilities. For example, hotels, air routes and airports were included in the earliest investment projects, financed by external capital after inbound capital was permitted in China (Pomfret, 1991, Richter, 1983). During the years 1986–1991, the growth of inbound tourism to China experienced a period of slowdown not helped by the events of 1989, but domestic tourism began to flourish when the nation's economic reforms made domestic business and leisure trips more affordable for a growing number of Chinese. As Wen and Tisdell (2001) noted, China's focus was initially on the expansion of international tourism as a vehicle to acquire foreign exchange, but subsequently attention was also given to domestic tourism, and the government's attitude towards the role of domestic tourism became more positive. The overall demand for tourism in China exploded, while supply could not keep pace with the rapid growth in demand, although more hotels and aircraft were provided during this period (Mak, 2003). An excess of attractions of the same type such as nature-based sightseeing and historical heritage dominated itineraries, and the lack of new, alternative attractions hindered the development of the industry and tarnished its reputation. At the same time, festivals, public celebrations and special events were increasingly regarded as tourist attractions and attracted destination image-makers as in other parts of the world (Getz, 1991). Under these circumstances, albeit initially slowly in China, events tourism, together with other relatively 'new' types of attractions including theme parks and MICE (Meeting, Incentive, Convention and Exhibition) activities, began to emerge.

A number of special events and festival celebrations started to emerge during the second half of the 1980s and early 1990s. Table 6.1 lists some of the well-known special events and festivals that emerged and grew during the 1980s. Among them, probably the most widely renowned event was the 1990 Asian Games held in Beijing. It was the first international sports mega-event held in China. It was believed that the motivating factor for China's bid for the 1990 Asian Games in 1985 was the desire to abandon the previous 'friendship through sport' policy and to achieve recognition and prestige through sporting victories and a high-profile event (Riordan, 1991). As a consequence, the government used the 1990 Beijing Asian Games more for political ends than for economic or tourism purposes. In particular, it 'was used by the Chinese to help improve their image after the Tiananmen Square

Table 6.1 Special events in China (before 2000)

Event/festival	Current organiser	Features
National Games (since 1979)[a]	National Administration of Sports; hosts: provincial governments	Sports event, every 4 years
Beijing Marathon (since 1981)	Chinese Athletic Association	Annual event
Luoyang Peony Festival, Henan (since 1983)	Luoyang City Government	Annual flower show
Weifang Kite-flying Festival, Shandong (since 1984)	Weifang City Government; China Central Television	Annual event
Harbin Ice & Snow Festival, Heilongjiang (since 1985)[b]	Harbin City Government	Annual event
Wuqiao Circus Festival, Hebei (since 1987)	Ministry of Culture; Hebei Provincial Government	Biennial event
Dalian Garment Festival, Liaoning (since 1988)	Dalian City Government	Annual event with fair shows
National Book Fair (since 1989)[c]	Host city governments	Annual fair/exhibition
11th Asian Games, Beijing, 1990	Beijing Municipal Government; Chinese Olympic Committee	One-off mega sports event
Qingdao Beer Festival, Shandong (since 1991)	Qiandao City Government	Annual arts event
Shaolin Martial Arts Festival, Henan (since 1991)	Chinese Wushu Association; Zhengzhou City Government	Annual event
Shanghai Film Festival (since 1993)	State Administration of Radio, TV & Film; Shanghai Municipal Government	Annual event
Flower Expo '99, Kunming, 1999	Chinese Central Government	One-off World Expo

Sources: Dewar *et al.* (2001), COC (2003a), and various media resources
Notes
[a]There were three National Games of China held in Beijing in 1959, 1965 and 1975. Since the 4th games in 1979, the National Games have been held regularly every 4 years in different provinces and cities.
[b]Harbin Ice & Snow Festival originated in 1963 but was stopped temporarily after the 1966 festival due to the Cultural Revolution. The festival was revived in 1985 and has been held annually since then.
[c]The first national book fair was held in 1980 in Beijing, but only since the 2nd fair in 1989 has the event become an annual one.

massacre (incident)' (Hall, 1992: 90). He Zhenliang, the former International Olympic Committee (IOC) vice president and honorary chairman of the Chinese Olympic Committee (COC), also acknowledged the Asian Games' role in unifying the Chinese and presenting China to the world, an image-building exercise thought necessary one year after the Tiananmen Square incident (Sanlian, 2003). During the 16-day Games, the gathering of 6000 athletes and officials from 36 Asian countries attracted extensive media coverage and attention on China.

The most obvious outcome of the 1990 Asian Games was that it fostered the country's confidence in its ability to host large-scale international events. At the closing ceremony, a huge banner appeared in the stands which read: 'With the success of the Asian Games, we look forward to hosting the Olympic Games' (COC, 2003b). Across a street in the Dongcheng District of Beijing, another banner was hoisted with these words: 'We have successfully hosted the Asian Games and we can successfully host the Olympic Games' (COC, 2003b; Zhou et al., 2012). Moreover, the Beijing local government and its citizens also benefited from the urban development associated with the 1990 Asian Games. Beijing's infrastructure, such as roads, airport, sewage and communications systems, was improved and the city's layout altered. The Asian Games extended Beijing's expansion to the north (Sanlian, 2003). The newly built Olympic Centre and athletes' village, now known as the Asian Games Village, became a well-developed residential community in the northern part of the city. On the other hand, the impact of the Asian Games also caused new problems, such as the unbalanced development between the northern and southern areas of the metropolis, and an inefficient use of venues after the Games. In 2001 the Beijing Organising Committee for the Olympic Games (BOCOG) commented that the municipal government had noted these problems and taken them into account when Beijing bid and prepared for the 2004 and then 2008 Olympics Games (BOCOG, 2001).

One of the early research articles about China's festivals and special events in the English literature was that of Dewar et al. (2001). They examined the motivations of those visiting the 1998 Harbin Ice & Snow Festival with an existing cross-cultural instrument. According to Dewar et al. (2001: 524), the festival 'had grown substantially and is now among the largest of its kind and certainly one of the most spectacular'. In 1998 the festival included five major programmes in the arts, sports, culture, tourism and trade, and it was viewed not only as a festival for raising residents' spirits and providing cultural, recreational opportunities, but also as a way to 'bring much needed currency and employment to the city' (Dewar et al., 2001: 524). With an estimated 16,000 international and 2.8 million domestic visitors during the month-long festival, the city raised US$ 4.8 million in foreign exchange and RMB 360 million (approximately US$ 44 million) in domestic tourist receipts (Dewar et al., 2001).

Evolution and Development of Special Events in China

In the early years of event development in China, despite the large number of special events organised in many towns and cities, the development of special events took place more in a 'spontaneous manner' rather than being well planned and managed. The following summarises the evolution and developmental process of China's festivals and special events for the period 1980–2012.

From celebration purpose to economy/trade orientation

At the early stage of event development in the 1980s, festivals and special events were regarded mainly as opportunities for local celebration and recreation. The above-mentioned Harbin Ice & Snow Festival emphasised its function as a festival for raising residents' spirits and morale and providing cultural and recreational opportunities (Dewar et al., 2001). The Luoyang Peony Festival, first held in 1983 in central Henan Province, is another example. According to the Organising Office for the Peony Festival (OOPF), the then mayor of the city said in his welcoming speech at the first Festival that the main purpose was: '... to re-strengthen the reputation of Peony City, to enrich residents' everyday life, as well as to improve "Double Civilisation"[1] progress, (and) the City has avowed that a Peony Festival will be held from 15th to 25th every April in the future' (OOPF, 2003). Actually, most festivals and events initiated before 1987, such as the Kite Festival in Weifang which was first held in 1984 and the Circus Festival in Wuqiao, Shijiazhuang City first held in 1987, all evidenced similar purposes of celebration and local recreational aims. This phenomenon can be understood in an even broader sociopolitical background. China's economic reform first started in the countryside during 1978–1982 with the system of 'contracting land to individual households', i.e. in moving away from collectives towards a system of peasant-owned land. It spread to urban areas in the second half of the 1980s (Nolan, 2004). As a result, China's agriculture dramatically lifted productivity in most parts of the Chinese countryside. The output of the major crops increased at annual rates of 8% between 1978 and 1984, compared with the annual average rate of increase of 1.1% from 1952 to 1978 (National Bureau of Statistics, 1985). The rural residents benefited most from the reforms and the quality of their lives improved to an unprecedented level. The fundamental problem of feeding China's population, which had been a problem for centuries, was basically solved (Chen & Davis, 1998). Farmers and local governments sought festivals and special events to celebrate rich harvests and to share in a celebration of good fortune. When considering the geographical location of the above-mentioned festivals, it is found that almost all these festivals took place in small- or medium-sized inland cities. These cities relied on agriculture or were closely linked with a rural society. They were also rich in culture and tradition. Unsurprisingly, the themes of these festivals had close connections with agricultural activities and traditional local features, such as peonies, kite-flying and the circus.

After the success of these pioneering festivals, more cities, particularly large cities in coastal areas, started to realise the potential roles of festivals and special events in image-making and business generation. They began to plan and launch their own festivals and special events. Most of these destinations were industrially based and thus events covered themes such as fashion and garments in Dalian, beer in Qingdao and film in Shanghai (see Table 6.1). Additionally, these host cities were often located in the eastern coastal areas which had an increasing economic importance. They viewed festivals and special events as a means to complement and further business and trade. Therefore the events were always accompanied by government-backed industrial exhibitions and/or business conferences (*People's Daily*, 2002). As a result, other festivals, including the pioneers mentioned above, were progressively influenced by the new event–exhibition model. When China embarked on its market-oriented economic policy in 1992, boosting local business and attracting external investment became a dominant theme within most festival and event activities. Consequently, as *People's Daily* (2002) summarised, a typical festival in this period consisted of a splendid but analogous opening ceremony, an exhibition aimed at attracting external investment, and street parades. Even today this is still found in China. For example, Ryan and Gu (2010) report a case study reflecting these typical features of a festival programme.

A study conducted by Zhang (2004) examined event tourism development in eight Chinese cities. Two types of event activities, namely: (a) festivals and (b) cultural and sports events, were included in this study. Relevant data of the study are summarised in Table 6.2. The figures indicated that:

- The number of events varied between the coastal cities and inland cities. Four coastal cities held 1288 festivals and cultural and sports events, while the figure for the four inland cities was 518.
- Compared with the coastal cities, inland cities relied more on festivals than cultural and sports events. The possible reasons for these differences reflects the difference in resources – cultural and sports events require more resources (i.e. specialised facilities such as stadiums and theatres, professional and skilled expertise) which were not readily available in the inland cities.
- Festivals and events in inland cities are themed more on local culture and traditions such as food, fishing, martial arts and native operas, the influence of which would be limited more at a regional and only rarely at national level. On the other hand, the coastal cities hosted more national and international events (e.g. Beijing Marathon, Tennis Masters Cup Shanghai or the World Expo in Shanghai).

Table 6.2 Numbers of festivals and events in selected cities in 2002

		Festivals	Cultural and sports events	Total
Eastern coastal cities	Beijing	166	183	349
	Shanghai	228	233	461
	Guangzhou	135	163	298
	Hangzhou	105	75	180
	Sub-total	634	654	1288
Inland cities	Xi'an	48	24	72
	Chengdu	101	38	139
	Guilin	121	33	154
	Kunming	117	36	153
	Sub-total	387	131	518

Source: Zhang (2004)

After the turn of the century, especially after Beijing won the right to host the 2008 Olympic Games, several mega-events took place in China. Indeed, it seemed that festival and event tourism had become a fashion as noted by Zhou and Ryan in Chapter 13 of this book. This was particularly the case in leading cities such as Beijing and Shanghai, while important secondary cities such as Huangzhou, Shenzhen and Guangzhou also hosted significant events as listed below. This was in part fuelled by rapid economic growth which facilitated the development of a growing middle class (Wu & Cai, 2006) who demanded more leisure and entertainment events that had an international prestige (also see Chapter 13). The two-day weekend system introduced in 1995 in China also stimulated the need for more local leisure activities. Increased international business, commercial and recreational global communication after China's accession to the World Trade Organisation in 2001 additionally brought more opportunities for international special events. A number of mega-events took place in China in this period, among which the better known included the 2001 World University Games (Universiade), the 2001 Three Tenors Concert, the China Tennis Open (since 2004) in Beijing, the 2001 APEC Summit, the F1 Grand Prix (since 2004) in Shanghai and the International Floriade in Xi'an in 2011. Almost all these mega-events were located in major centres of population or in cities with special features (e.g. a cold climate for winter sports competitions). The mega-event strategy seems to have been influential in that an increasing number of cities have sought to replicate the formula. Besides the Beijing 2008 Olympic Games, there have been mega-events in cities such as Shenyang (2006 Horticultural Expo), Changchun (2007 Asian Winter Games), Harbin (2009 World University Winter Games), Shanghai

(2010 World Expo), Guangzhou (2010 Asian Games) and Shenzhen (2011 Universiade) – although not all have been financially viable, as can be seen in Chapter 12 of this book by Huang, Ryan and Yang. It is believed that Beijing's successful bid for and hosting of the 2008 Olympic Games and its perceived benefits for the host stimulated other cities to bid for and host international events, particularly mega sports events. Meanwhile, a large number of smaller scaled world sports championships started to shift to the second-tier cities (mostly provincial capital cities) or even third-tier coastal cities in China. A recent report showed that more than 350 international sports competitions were held in China in 2010, of which about a quarter happened in Beijing, Shanghai and Guangdong Province (*Nanfang Daily*, 2011).

From largely government involved to government oriented

As displayed in Table 6.1, the majority of these events in China were or still are directly run by government bodies. In practice, government bodies had often acted as organisers or were involved directly in other roles through the provision of venues and finance. For instance, for the Harbin Ice & Snow Festival, 'thousands of ice lanterns were produced both by individuals and as displays organised by the government' (Dewar *et al.*, 2001: 524). Local governments also often tend to seek co-organisers from a higher level of official bodies (such as national associations or the national media) to enhance the reputation and influence of the event. If the theme of an event is related to certain administrative organisations, that is, government ministries or national associations, these organisations are commonly invited as co-organisers. Nonetheless, in such situations most of the preparation and operational work would be conducted at a local level. A temporary or permanent event-organising office or committee headed by the local mayor with members including officials from related government departments such as culture, public security, finance, transport or tourism is generally established to coordinate and be responsible for the whole event. In some cases, local government has been engaged in running events through direct funding and enforcing local business or individual donations (*People's Daily*, 2002). In more recent years, because of the demands upon civic administration and the poor financial returns, some cities have started to change from a 'government-involved' strategy to a 'government-sponsored' one. This means more major festival events have introduced professional business operations and event management through a bidding and sponsoring process (*People's Daily*, 2002). For example, the Weifang City Government ceased their direct financial support for its Kite Festival in 1998. This process has been replicated in other events such as the Nanning International Folk Song Art Festival (Xinhua, 2002), where commercial operation by a specialist professional event-organising company (Nanning Dadifeige Culture Communication Co. Ltd) was introduced in 2002. Now the company has extended its business to other festivals and events nationwide and become a major player in the cultural event-organising market.

Challenges Facing Festivals and Special Events in China

There are no detailed statistics available about the numbers and scale of festivals and special events held in China. Some estimates indicate that more than 10,000 festivals were held in China in 2010 (ChinaNews, 2011). Today festivals and special events are common in many cities. For example, in 2002 it was reported that there were a total of 32 festivals held in the city of Qingdao in Shandong Province, which meant that, on average, a new festival would be staged every 12 days (*Workers' Daily*, 2003). Although a large number of festivals and special events are held, few can be regarded as successful in terms of 'hard' tangible outcomes and economic impact, although 'soft' gains in terms of personal and professional links may well result. So far, few events have attracted international attention or have developed an international reputation (ChinaNews, 2011). In addition to their short histories, other reasons for this may include the following aspects.

Poor organisation with misplaced aims and objectives

As mentioned above, the majority of festivals and special events in China are directly organised by various levels of government or with government support or involvement. Often the ideas for introducing new festivals or events come from senior officials and not from market research into potential demand (*Workers' Daily*, 2003). Before implementation of the festival or event, little or no market research is conducted about who the event should be held for and what kinds of events audiences and tourists are expecting. The primary aim of hosting festivals or special events is often to solicit and negotiate investment from external sources. An event with celebrities, who are often invited and paid by government bodies, may attract regional or national media coverage. As a result, hosting festivals and events has become a means to gain media attention for destinations and to obtain political prestige for senior and junior administrative staff. Moreover, external investment deals signed during the event often fail to materialise (*Workers' Daily*, 2003). Also, when events take place, local businesses are often forced to participate or to pay sponsorship fees to the organising government bodies in order to make the event appear successful. This, in turn, leads to dissatisfaction and less local support (Lamberti *et al.*, 2011; Wu, 2003). At the same time, under such mistaken purposes and practices, the interests of local residents and tourists are ignored. Faced with overly high admission fees and programmes that simply duplicate other events, visitors are becoming more discerning and thereby less enthusiastic for 'me too' event programming. Fortunately, in some cities, organisers have realised this, and visitor-centred festivals with more participatory celebration and leisure programmes have appeared. For example, since 2003 the Beer Festival in Qiandao has cancelled admission fees at some venues in order to attract visitors (Xinhua, 2004). In other cities, market-oriented events have emerged. For example, in 2002 the International Folk Song Festival held in Nanning, Guangxi started to adopt a private sector model and succeeded in meeting its objectives (*People's Daily*, 2002).

Lack of unique themes and features

Because of their experiential nature, Getz (2006) emphasised that festivals and events, especially periodic ones, must adopt a long-term perspective as to their themes and programmes, including a consideration of the life cycle of events and programme elements. However, inefficient organisation and duplicated themes have brought several festivals and events in China to a premature end (*People's Daily*, 2002; Wu, 2003). Wu (2003) noted there were many identical and indistinguishable events when he identified more than a dozen tea festivals throughout China and noted that none had achieved a good market reputation or a successful commercial outcome.

Conclusion

To sum up, modern China's festival and event industry has been developing during the past three decades. Festivals and special events have become a common form of attraction in many destinations. Despite the rapid growth of festivals and events in term of numbers, the industry is still at its infancy stage. Festivals and special events have been primarily organised for image-making purposes or local political advantage rather than as a tourism attraction. Often, the roles of different stakeholders are somewhat ambiguous and misplaced in many festivals and event activities. When compared with the hotel and tour operation sectors, there is more direct government involvement in the festival and events sector. The planning of festivals and special events is also often of a spontaneous nature with little regard for follow-up processes or the longer term usage of facilities built to host events. Systematic planning and guidelines for the event industry are notably absent. In addition, local residents' and tourists' needs and reactions are often ignored, and the interests of organisers and government are more focused on issues such as a city's image and attracting external investment. The adoption of market-oriented event strategies will provide one option towards developing sustainability for the event sector in China. Research on festival and event development in China is also far from adequate and more is needed. It is suggested that research on festivals and events be undertaken in the areas of: (a) the role of government and other stakeholders; (b) event market research; (c) event outcome and impact evaluation; and (d) resident and tourist attitudes and reactions. Such research would certainly benefit the development of systematic strategies for event tourism planning, marketing and management in China.

Note

(1)   Double civilisation is official Chinese jargon, meaning progress from both an ethical and physical aspect.

References

BOCOG (2001) *Beijing Olympic Action Plan,* accessed 15 February 2003, http://www.bei jing-2008.org/new_olympic/eolympic/plan.htm

Chen, F. and Davis, J. (1998) Land reform in rural China since the mid-1980s. *Land Reform* 2, 122–137.

ChinaNews (2011) *Scholars Estimated over 10,000 Festivals Held in China,* accessed 13 December 2011, http://www.chinanews.com/cul/2011/10-31/342522 3.shtml

COC (Chinese Olympic Committee) (2003a) *National Games,* accessed 4 December 2004, http://en.olympic.cn/games/national/list.html

COC (Chinese Olympic Committee) (2003b) *Bid for the 2000 Olympics,* accessed 6 December 2004, http://en.olympic.cn/china_oly/olympic_bids/2004-03-27/121850.html

Dewar, K., Meyer, D. and Li, W.M. (2001) Harbin: lanterns of ice, sculptures of snow. *Tourism Management* 22 (5), 523–532.

Getz, D. (1991) *Festivals, Special Events and Tourism.* New York: Van Nostrand Reinhold.

Getz, D. (2006) *Event Management and Event Tourism* (2nd edn). New York: Cognizant Communication Corporation.

Hall, C.M. (1992) *Hallmark Tourist Events: Impacts, Management and Planning.* London: Belhaven Press.

Lamberti, L., Noci, G., Guo, R. and Zhu, S. (2011) Mega-events as drivers of community participation in developing countries: The case of Shanghai World Expo. *Tourism Management* 32 (6), 1474–1483.

Mak, B. (2003) China's tourist transportation: Air, land, and water. In A. Lew, L. Yu, J. Ap and G. Zhang (eds) *Tourism in China* (pp. 165–194). New York: Haworth Hospitality Press.

Nanfang Daily (2011) Thousand sports competition matches in one year. *Nanfang Daily,* 1 November [in Chinese].

National Bureau of Statistics (of China) (1985) *China Statistical Yearbook, 1984.* Beijing: China Statistical Press.

Nolan, P. (2004) *Transforming China, Globalisation, Transition and Development.* London: Anthem Press.

OOPF (2003) *The First Luoyang Peony Festival,* accessed 9 December 2004, http://www.0379.info/show_news.asp?id=9

People's Daily (2002) Urban festivals need to seek actual outcome. *People's Daily,* 27 December, p. 5 [in Chinese].

Pomfret, R. (1991) *Investing in China: Ten Years of the Open Door Policy.* Ames: Iowa State University Press.

Richter, L.K. (1983) The political implications of Chinese tourism policy. *Annals of Tourism Research* 10, 395–414.

Riordan, J. (1991) *Sport, Politics and Communism*. Manchester: Manchester University Press.

Ryan, C. and Gu, H.M. (2010) Constructionism and culture in research: Understandings of the fourth Buddhist Festival, Wutaishan, China. *Tourism Management* 31 (2), 167–178.

Sanlian (2003) Over the gap between Asian Games and Olympics. *Sanlian Lifeweek* 255.

Wen, J. and Tisdell, C. (2001) *Tourism and China's Development: Politics, Regional Economic Growth and Ecotourism*. Singapore: World Scientific.

Workers' Daily (2003) Why (they are) high on festival-invention? *Workers' Daily*, 1 March, p. 6 [in Chinese].

Wu, B.H. (2003) *Research of Chinese Urban Events' Development and Management*, accessed 10 December 2004, http://www.china.org.cn/chinese/OP-c/458045.htm

Wu, B.H. and Cai, L.P. (2006) Spatial modeling: Suburban leisure in Shanghai. *Annals of Tourism Research* 33 (1), 179–198.

Xinhua (2002) *From Governmental Duty to Market Operation. Xinhuanet*, 24 November, accessed 8 December 2010, http://news3.xinhuanet.com/newscenter/2002-11/24/content_639113.htm

Xinhua (2004) *Most Visitors Attended the Festival this Year*, accessed 10 December 2010, http://www.sd.xinhuanet.com/news/2004-08/30/content_2770330.htm

Zhang, B.B. (2004) Studies on event tourism in hot tourism cities between the east and the west in China. *Forecasting* 23 (3), 16–19 [in Chinese].

Zhou, Y., Ap, J. and Bauer, T. (2012) Government motivations for hosting the Beijing 2008 Olympic Games. *Journal of Tourism and Cultural Change* 10 (2), 185–201.

7 The Impact of Tourism in Kanas Scenic Area: The Role of Conflict and Tension in Tourism Development

Jingjing Yang, Chris Ryan and Lingyun Zhang

Introduction

This chapter is derived from an ethnographic study undertaken by the first author who lived for 12 consecutive months among the Tuva and Kazakh communities of Kanas Scenic Area of Xinjiang Province, and became an 'adopted daughter' of a Tuva family. She participated in daily life, attended various festivals, including those held away from public areas and which were accessible only on horseback, and spoke the local languages. Data were derived from observation, informal conversations, daily note-taking, and informal and more formal interviews among residents, outside entrepreneurs, visitors and government officials (both local and provincial). Additional reports, papers and texts were also collected. The first author is Han from Inner Mongolia, but was living primarily in Beijing. She is thus of the same ethnicity as the majority of tourists and government officials, and many of the external entrepreneurs who come during the summer season, but unlike them she lived through the harshness of the winter when the villages are cut off from the outside world, even to the point of losing power supply. Figures 7.1–7.3 show aspects of life in one of the small Tuva villages.

What can be noted from the photographs is that the area is remote, but new infrastructure is being developed by both provincial and central governments, and a combination of a sense of being remote, possessing scenic values, unpolluted air and the patterns of life of minority peoples creates a

Figure 7.1 Winter time in Kanas

Figure 7.2 Summer season

tourism product for visitors from the central and eastern seafront cities of China. The photographs also indicate a lack of major hotel development, meaning that the villages are primarily destinations for day trip activity, away from the resorts built to house the tourists. It also means that the villages experience a seasonal and daily pattern of tourist intrusion – namely that tourists are generally present only in summer months, and even then primarily during the main daytime hours. While this lessens direct impacts,

Figure 7.3 Tuva Homestay site

it also means that the villages are effectively recipients of secondary expenditure by the tourists and are primarily dependent upon tour guides bringing tourists to the villages from the resort complexes. Nonetheless, the additional incomes generated are significant for these people and there lies one of the sources of tension described below, as the community tussles with issues of achieving a balance between the values of past nomadic lifestyles and an entry into the modern world of commodified cultures and monetary systems of commercial life.

This chapter is therefore structured around a discussion of concepts of social structure, identifying the key texts that informed an analysis of the data with respect to the role of social tensions within and between the community and outside groups. It subsequently describes some of the events that were observed and at times participated in that informed the analysis. A synthesis is finally generated in which the two prior parts come together to formulate new propositions and means of assessing the nature of tourism's impacts upon marginalised peoples, whose very marginality forms the focus of them and their culture becoming the subject of tourist gaze and tourism development.

The impacts of tourism upon minority peoples and their communities have attracted many studies (Butler & Hinch, 2007; Ryan & Aicken, 2005), but while reference has been made to the subsequent social and political tensions (Ryan *et al.*, 2007), relatively few such studies have had recourse to structured sociological theory. The purpose of this study is thus to analyse tensions found in the Kanas Scenic area of Northwest China by reference to Coser's (1956) social conflict theory. Ryan *et al.* (2011) have argued that many studies of tourism impacts are heavily contextualised within the specific characteristics of the case areas, and lack a comparison with other case areas and related studies. Indeed, although making comparisons between different rural areas in China, they go so far as to argue that a meta-narrative is not possible. This chapter seeks to address this claim by referring to a factor implicit in their study and others, namely that impacts generate tensions, and while the tensions may involve different actors and stakeholders, there does exist a meta-narrative that permits generalisation through the characteristics of social tension. Consequently in this chapter a tension-directed tourism development system is proposed that provides a tool for comparing and contrasting tourism impacts in different areas. It is further suggested that it is complementary to the Butler (1980, 2006) tourism area life cycle.

Consequently, a number of gaps in studies about tourism and social conflict are being addressed. First, there exists a relative lack of empirical evidence as to the functions of social conflict and its relationship with tourism development, especially with reference to locations inhabited by minority groups. Second, when such a concern does exist, it is directed primarily toward the reduction of conflict. However, following Coser (1956), social tensions and political conflict can be a necessary and positive part of all social relationships, and a requisite for social change (Coser, 1956). Third, conflict is often accompanied by cooperation, unity and the formation of alliances, but in tourism studies the relation between conflict and the emergence of cooperation/unity/alliance has rarely been discussed. Fourth, a theoretical base for social conflict is needed to support the empirical studies regarding tourism development and conflict. Fifth, although this last aspect is not the primary focus of this paper, it is suggested that this form of analysis is especially important in the context of common conflicts in China that arise over compensation for land seized for economic development such as that evidenced in Wukan Village, Guangdong Province in November and December 2011.

Social Conflict Theory

Social conflict as a subject has a long history in sociological theory, and obviously forms a central theme in not only general sociological theory but also within Chinese sociological theory due to the Marxian-Maoist tradition. Thus, for example, Oberschall (1978: 291) provided an early review of social conflict theory, defining social conflict as '... result(ing) from purposeful interaction among two or more parties in a competitive setting. It refers to overt behaviour rather than to potential for action and to subjective states', and he continues to review the work of various theorists including Paige, Dahrendorff and Coser.

From a Western perspective, a study of Leninist-Marxist-Maoist approaches was provided by Meisner (1971), who critiqued Maoist concepts of social conflict within the wider Marxian-Leninist paradigms by noting 'The whole question of the relationship between Leninism and Maoism is filled with ambiguities and the historic tie between the two has become exceedingly tenuous' (Meisner, 1971: 2). Contemporary Chinese writing is now imbued with reference to older Confucian traditions as the Chinese Communist Party seeks 'social harmony' and writers such as Hwang (1998) refer to symbolic interaction and social exchange as the means of solving disputes between in- and out-groups while, in the hospitality literature, Gu et al. (2013) argue that *guanxi* provides a social glue for settling disputes in the absence of a Western tradition of social and commercial contractual law while China currently exists as a transitional state as discussed in Chapter 1.

For its part this study rejects these multiple approaches and solely applies propositions from Coser's (1956) *Functions of Social Conflict* which are derived from the classical work of Georg Simmel's (1922/1955), *Conflict*. Three reasons exist for this approach. The first is an entirely pragmatic one: 'It seemed more convenient, for purposes of exposition, to follow an author with a consistent general orientation rather than to shift between writers whose orientations may be divergent' (Coser, 1956: 30). Second, the theories noted above tend to perceive social conflict either from a perspective whereby it should be mitigated (the social harmony approach) or radicalised to purposely generate change. Simmel and Coser's perspective of social tensions and conflicts as a process inherent in social relationships and one conducive to non-violent transformative change seemed more consistent with what was observed during the fieldwork that informed this chapter. In short, a theoretical structure providing a means of analysis and explanation for the conflicts arising in a community experiencing a developmental process better met the purpose of this study – namely the social transformation and cultural change of a society.

As just noted, studies about social conflict theory have a long history and are deeply rooted in human thought: 'Conflict provides many sociologists the central explanatory category for the analysis of social change and of "progress"' (Coser, 1956: 16). The social process is defined as 'incessant reaction of persons prompted by interests that in part conflict with the interests of their fellows, and in part comport with the interests of others' (Small, 1905: 205). Over the years, the study of social conflict has received attention from economists, historians, anthropologists, novelists, philosophers, political scientists, sociologists, psychologists and theologians.

Many of the contributions to social conflict theory come from philosophy and sociology, and some are derived from other disciplines, such as the biological sciences. The sociology of conflict is partially concerned with how social order is challenged and maintained (Easterbrook et al., 1993). Georg Simmel, Talcott Parsons, and Lewis A. Coser, among other classical sociologists, have made a significant contribution to the study of social conflict theory. Particular theories or hypotheses about conflict in general have been applied to various types of conflict. It is generally agreed that social conflict has both functional and dysfunctional consequences. If a social system is to benefit from conflict, the negative effects of conflict must be reduced and positive effects must be enhanced.

Lewis A. Coser's (1956) *The Functions of Social Conflict* was one work that critiqued the then dominant sociological paradigm – structural functionalism – and contributed to its subsequently diminishing influence in the discipline. Coser (1956: 31) depicts conflict as 'a form of socialization' and analyses conflict in terms of interactive processes. Some certain degree of conflict is an essential element in group formation, resulting in both association and dissociation which serve a social function. Coser (1956) reveals functionalism's conservative biases and its inability to capture the conflict, competition and tension that characterise group life, but he does not impetuously dismiss this paradigm's insights. Based on Durkheimian premises, Coser suggests that conflict is a persistent phenomenon and serves some latent social functions. However, by departing from functionalism's assumptions of stability and harmony, Coser also facilitates the shift towards the conflict paradigm by suggesting that conflict is ubiquitous and an inherent part of social relations. In order to devise a theory of social conflict, Coser reformulated and analysed 16 of Simmel's (1922/1955) dimensions regarding conflict, which may be classified as follows:

- conflict and group boundaries;
- hostility and tensions in conflict relationships;
- in-group conflict and group structure;
- conflict with out-group and group structure;
- conflict – the unifier;
- conflict calls for allies.

These hypotheses apply to a wide range of conflicts, from racial tensions to religious differences. They have valuable explanatory power for analysts of contemporary social relations, including the arena of tourism impacts on minority peoples. For example, Coser states that social conflict often acts as a 'safety valve', releasing tension while preserving social relations, and that conflict with an out-group enhances identity and consciousness for the in-group. Coser's (1956) work meets the purpose of studies of tourism impacts: to discuss the social transformation and cultural change of a society. To test these propositions' validity in contemporary society, the first author spent 12 months among the Tuva and Kazakh people of Kanas Scenic Region in Xinjiang to generate data to assess the extent to which Coser's (1956) 16 suppositions can be applied to tourism impact studies. In undertaking the study, Coser's (1956) 16 propositions are extended by making comparisons between Western and Chinese societies, by applying those concepts to an ethnic community, and by looking at the administrative realities of the Kanas Scenic Area.

Tourism impacts on ethnic communities

The impact of tourism on ethnic peoples has attracted attention among scholars in sociology (e.g. Cohen, 1996), anthropology (e.g. Chambers, 2000; Greenwood, 1977, 1989; Nash, 1977, 1989; Smith, 1977a, 1977b, 1996; Swain, 1977) and tourism (e.g. Fisher, 2000; McIntosh, 2004; McIntosh & Johnson, 2005; Ryan & Aicken, 2005; Ryan et al., 2007; Sofield, 1996; Tucker, 2003). Most of the reviewed studies focus on a specific group at a specific location, such as the hunter-gatherers in Thailand (Cohen, 1996) or the Maori in New Zealand (Carr, 2007; McIntosh & Johnson, 2005; McIntosh & Ryan, 2007).

The majority of these early studies follow the 'cautionary platform' established by Jafari (1989). Researchers were largely concerned about the negative impacts of tourism, such as those of social conflict, crime, commercialisation and degradation of indigenous culture, the decrease of value and sacrilege of religious belief and symbols (e.g. Greenwood, 1977; Pi-Sunyer, 1977). Kent (1975) defines tourism in Hawaii as a 'new kind of sugar', representing a parody on their premier agricultural export. On the other hand, some studies reflect the characteristics of the 'advocacy platform' (Jafari, 1989). Mckean's (1977) study about Bali in Indonesia and Deitch's (1977) study about Indians in the southwestern United States, among others, emphasise tourism's positive impacts, such as the preservation and production of traditional arts and crafts, and the enhancement of pride in heritage and ethnic identity. After, that research flows into the 'knowledge-based platform' (Jafari, 1989). The re-study of some communities and re-thinking about some earlier research sought to make the research more objective and holistic in the broader context that generated it, such as the studies of Smith (1989) and Greenwood (1989, 2004). Over time the studies have become both more critical as researchers have sought to address past wrongs and give voice to minorities (Swain, 1977; Swanson & De Vereaux, 2012), and more polyvocal as the complexities and differing value systems become more apparent (Greenwood, 2004).

The determinants of tourism impacts are complex. According to Prasad (1987), the magnitude of the impact is dependent upon a number of factors such as the nature of the society, its flexibility or resilience to change, the size of the host population relative to the number of visitors, the degree of dependence of the society upon tourism, and the economic state of the society. Ryan (2003: 152–158) suggests several variables that should be considered in discussing tourism economic impacts: tourism development of the destination area, the level of economic development of the destination area, the nature of the tourist facilities and their attractiveness, the degree of foreign or out-of-region ownership of hotels and tourism infrastructure, the employment of non-indigenous labour, the infrastructure provided by government, and tourist types and their association with other parts of the economy.

The impacts of tourism on ethnic peoples have been well researched but there is a lack of a holistic view and systematic research for a better understanding of tourism's impacts. More studies considering the multiple factors including tourists, government, tourism enterprises, local people and tourism development of the destinations are needed.

Social conflict and destination development

As discussed above, the study of social conflict has received attention from a variety of disciplines. In contrast, the social conflict issues in tourism destinations have not been systematically investigated by tourism scholars or, if analysing issues of power, they have chosen not to use the concepts of conflict resolution, being drawn more to the concepts of network theory (Dredge, 2006, 2010). However, in many tourism-directed communities, tourism development largely influences social conflict; tourism brings more groups and subgroups, varies and complicates conflict nature and forms, and therein influences social structure and cultural change of the communities.

Social conflict was mentioned in the early tourism studies that characterised the 'cautionary platform' (Jafari, 1989). Conflict of interest, values and goals happens between stakeholders. Examples are the conflict between the indigenous owners of the land and the foreign investor over tourism development (Sofield, 1996), the conflict between ethnic community and outsider entrepreneurs over economic benefits from tourism (Crystal, 1989; Goering, 1990), and the conflict between tourists and locals towards limited resources (Urbanowicz, 1977).

Cultural conflict, as one of the themes of tourism impact studies, has been addressed by researchers, such as the studies in the book *Tourism and Cultural Conflicts* (Robinson & Boniface, 1999). According to Robinson (1999: 7), cultural conflicts occur on a regular basis at different levels and between different interest groups in tourism. Robinson (1999) provides four dimensions in which cultural conflict happens: tourism industry–host conflicts, tourist–host conflicts, tourism–tourist conflicts and host–host conflict. The determinants which influence the conflict between tourism industry and host community are: (1) the nature and the extent of the commodification of the host culture; (2) the utilisation of natural resources and its cultural resources; and (3) the degree of economic dependency of the host community on tourism.

Economic benefit has been a major subject of conflict. It has been commonly believed that tourism brings economic benefit to tourism destinations; however, the economic benefits may not be distributed evenly across different groups. In Toops's (1992) discussion about the relationship between Han tour guides and ethnic groups in Xinjiang, China, the direct tourism income accrued disproportionately to Han as middlemen. Current research in China points to many instances where structural capital is developed as a consequence of compulsory purchases of land by governmental bodies who on-sell to private corporations that effectively deny the original farmers access to land, yet who have inadequate compensation (Feng, 2008; Shepherd, 2011). Who the main beneficiaries from tourism development should be is always the subject of conflict and tensions in developing countries. Conflict and tensions over economic benefits derived from tourism commonly happen between ethnic community and outsider entrepreneurs (Crystal, 1989; Feng, 2008; Goering, 1990), between local people and local tourism administration (Feng, 2008), and between other different groups and subgroups. From a political and social perspective some evidence suggests that conflict between a predominant and minority ethnic group may reduce the citizenship rights of particular groups and further reduce the multicultural character of a particular society (Medrano, 1996). On the other hand, community bonds have been enhanced because local groups become united against outside enterprises and against the local government, such as in Fenghuang County of China (Feng, 2008).

The Study

As noted in the opening paragraph, the data were derived from a 12-month residency among the Kanas Tuva and Kazakh settlements, Xinjiang, China. Before tourism development, the main stakeholders in the Kanas Scenic Area were only two groups – governments and local people. Tourism introduced the other two groups – tourism entrepreneurs and tourists. The former social structure was replaced by a new structure designed to meet the economic and social development of the local society as perceived by China's central government. The four groups together contribute to the social system of the community in the tourism season. The common interests and positions in the society of each group and the reciprocal antagonisms conserve social divisions and systems of stratification. Governments, entrepreneurs, tourists and local ethnic people each play their own roles in the system with their own goals and interests.

Tourism in Kanas is highly seasonal, but growing in numbers as the provincial government promotes the area for its scenic values and cultural differences, while additionally it is away from the Islamic areas of the north. Tourism is centred upon three small villages, each of which has its own characteristics and a differing duration of involvement in the industry. The main areas of accommodation are located some distance away from the villages, primarily to reduce potential negative social demonstration effects (Sofield, personal communication). The tourist activity is primarily based upon day trip activity (albeit not wholly as some will stay in the village under some legal pretence) and a main feature is the Tuva home stay visit. These visits primarily comprise a visit to a Tuva home, a welcome in a traditional manner, a performance of local music, singing, dance (which will often involve the visitors), and a meal based on local traditional foodstuffs. In addition, tourists may hire horses and go on accompanied horse rides across the grasslands, and can occasionally observe local festivities.

The culture that is featured in the brochures and the discourse of the tour guides is that of the Tuva people, but in practice many of the Tuva people retain a traditional summer nomadic lifestyle to graze their cattle. This is beginning to change, due not only to tourism, but also to other factors such as the need for children to attend schools and for them to be represented in consultations with government officials. Nonetheless, traditional practices remain strong. The outcome of this is that Tuva people illegally lease their homes to mainly Kazakh entrepreneurs (but also some Han) who replicate the Tuva culture and generally will act like Tuva hosts. Tuva people gain from rental income from tourism and retain for the most part a preferred traditional lifestyle, entrepreneurs and tour guides earn an income, tourists are satisfied and local officials condone illegal practices to write reports to superiors of economic development. On some occasions the first author participated in these home-stay visits in different guises, including being a performer handing out food.

The social setting is thus one of shifting liaisons and arrangements as each stakeholder seeks to sustain an income while working within and around local tourism regulations. For the most part these arrangements are functional, generally friendly as both Tuva and Kazakh live in the same villages, but on rare occasions violence was observed. It is not possible within this paper to describe all the events and incidents recorded, but the following provide some examples.

Exploration stage: Belief centred

As in many ethnic communities around the world, the intrusion of tourists and outsider entrepreneurs generated a cultural shock for this formerly isolated community. The opposition in the exploration stage of the Kanas Scenic Area can be characterised with reference to belief and value systems. According to an outsider who married a local lady and lived in Kanas Village for over 20 years, 'At the beginning of the tourism development, locals did not know how to adjust to the new environment, since so many outsiders suddenly came (to this isolated area)'. Locals could not understand the outsiders' behaviours and lifestyles that were too far removed from their own. Strictly speaking, this stage is characterised by cultural difference and curiosity, and few tensions and struggles were involved.

With reference to direct interaction between visitors and locals, visitors were impressed by the simplicity, kindness and primitive lifestyle of locals. According to some who visited Kanas in this period, the locals even tried to 'feed' grass to the vehicles, because in their minds the vehicles would be very hungry after a whole day running on the road. On the other hand, tourists' dress, behaviour, lifestyle, the 'advanced' cameras, cars etc., were a surprise to the locals.

The private outsider entrepreneurs were another source of culture shock. At this stage, locals had little sense of direct participation in tourism. Some Kazakhs even regarded operating a business as a source of shame. According to a local Kazakh:

> In the early stage of the tourism development, the restaurant operators asked tourists RMB 1000 for a rooster which was worth at most RMB 50. The boss told the tourists that the wild rooster was caught from forest and was very good for health. They talked nonsense.

The business tricks used by outsiders surprised the local ethnic people. On the other hand, locals also saw that these operators obtained significant profits from tourism. This represented another shock, but one which gradually led the locals to participate in tourism in the following stages, although initially the Tuva in particular were lacking in social capital including past business experience in a market-oriented economy. These deficiencies included no knowledge of commercial business methods and specifically little in the way of contacts with the travel agencies, tour guides and other industry intermediaries, and certainly no direct access to the tourist-generating regions.

It may also be noted that differences of values and beliefs existed between tourists and the local government. Local governmental staff failed to anticipate the rapid increase of tourist numbers, and many failed to understand why so many tourists should come to this 'small place'. It was the politicians and high-ranking officials from the Central and Xinjiang governments who provided details of the significance of tourism when they officially visited the area, and it was this visit that prompted the formation of the local tourism administrative institutions and measures. In 1987 the Buerjin Tourism Bureau was founded, enforcing the initial development and subsequent construction of facilities in the region and duly commencing the administration of Kanas tourism.

Involvement stage: Resource centred

In this stage, many groups including national and regional bureaux, public sector organisations, private enterprises and entrepreneurs from nearby counties and cities established facilities and commenced operating tourism businesses in Kanas. The process was probably at its peak between 1996 and 2000 when the local government called for 'the whole of society to develop tourism'. Consequently, resources became the subject of tensions between different parties.

Inter-group and intra-group tension coexisted during this period. Tension existed between outside entrepreneurs and locals, between administrative institutions, and even between tourists. Entrepreneurs (primarily small and medium in size), in open competition with each other, 'grabbed' places at which to establish tourist facilities. The shortage of tourism facilities forced the tour guides to 'grab' accommodation and food for their own group members, often at very short notice, thereby stressing what organisational arrangements had been made, and creating at least short-term annoyances and grievances. One of the consequences of this resource-centred tension was a degradation of tourism products and service quality, while at the same time there was some unconstrained building of tourist assets, especially those of small retail and catering outlets.

Development stage: Power centred

As the area moved into a more sustainable and increasingly ordered development stage under government remit, the profit motive as a determinant of policies became more apparent. Tension, therefore, is now characterised by whoever holds the power of influencing decision making in the area. This power represents both economic and administrative advantage, and is closely related in the Chinese context. The administration of the area experienced frequent changes in this stage. The administration and licensing of a horsemen team in each village and the home visit cultural performance businesses also experienced changes that represent changes in the balance of power between different levels of administrative initiatives and the local villagers' committees, and between village headmen, committee members and Han government officials.

Proposing a New Tension-driven Social Conflict Tourism Development Model

As noted previously, theories and hypotheses of social conflict have been applied in the discussion of various disciplines and subjects, such as religion, race and ethnicity (Dodson, 1958; Hager, 1956; Hines, 1966), inter-tribal relations (Murphy, 1957) and international relations (North et al., 1960; Timasheff, 1965). According to Arzensek (1972), a model for studying social conflict must contain at least three factors: (1) institutional identification of the society; (2) identification of social conflict; and (3) identification of institutional change.

Based on social conflict theory and in line with tourism development (especially in ethnic communities), a tension-directed tourism development model for studying tourism impacts can now be suggested.

A tension-directed tourism development system

This system consists of four parts.

- a tension-directed evolution of some ethnic tourism areas (Figure 7.4);
- the emergence of key power clusters (Figure 7.5);
- a community tension-directed mechanism of tourism impact (community development perspective) (Figure 7.6);
- an inter-personal tension-directed mechanism of tourism impact (Figure 7.7).

The four parts are detailed as follows.

A tension-directed evolution of some ethnic tourism areas

An evolutionary model generally demonstrates the development of some ethnic tourism areas directed by different types of tensions at different stages in destination development. Coser (1968: 232) defines conflict as 'a struggle over claims to resources, power and status, beliefs, and other preferences and desires'. It is suggested that, using the typologies of the Butler (1980) Tourist Area Life Cycle model, the exploration, involvement and development stages are sequentially centred upon beliefs, resource and power respectively, as shown in Figure 7.4, although a degree of co-existence of each conflict source are present in each of the destination stages.

In many ethnic communities around the world, the intrusion of tourists and outside entrepreneurs brings cultural shock to those formerly isolated communities. The opposition in the exploration stage can be characterised by processes of negotiation between the parties based upon their respective belief and value systems. In the subsequent involvement stage, various segments of both public and private public sectors come to participate in

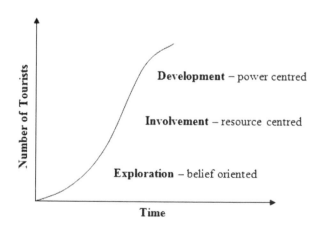

Figure 7.4 The tension-directed evolution of ethnic tourism areas

tourism. Consequently, resources became the object of tensions between different parties. The indigenous community commands the cultural resource but the other stakeholders generally control access to the other resources of tourist supply and external capital. The public sector retains the resource of granting licences and permissions through planning processes that may be entirely formal or subject to degrees of corrupt practices. This also means that the private sector also has the resource of policy enforcement. Both inter-group and intra-group tension may coexist during this period.

As areas enter into the development stage, the profit motive as a determinant of policies becomes more apparent. Tension, therefore, is characterised by who holds the power of influencing decision making in the area. Each party has by this stage engaged in processes of change. The indigenous community (or some part of it) may have acquired political and social connections in past dealings, but equally may have become more fractured unless held together by very strong belief systems. They may also have acquired some small financial capital. Such gains, however, increasingly bind them to the value systems of the dominant groups. As in Kanas the process may at times be accompanied by latent and actual violence through a riot, but the very act of increasing compensation actually reinforces and furthers the legitimisation of the government as the body able to make such concessions. Such concessions cannot be legally gained from other parties. For their part, private entrepreneurs gain economic returns, further the legitimacy of the government as providing the success the regional government requires in reporting to more senior levels of government in Beijing, but equally are dependent upon the forms of policy implementation required by the government, or alternatively seek their ends by trying to subvert government regulations by entering into informal arrangements with local peoples.

Conflicts' functions of establishing and maintaining power are mainly presented in the involvement and development stages. Individuals and groups may assert their claims when they feel discrepancies between the amount of power, status and wealth that they command and the amount that they feel to be due to them (Coser, 1956: 134). Failure to assert such claims may mean they fail to advance, and others may fail to consider claims on their behalf (Coser, 1956).

The emergence of key power clusters

Governments, tourism entrepreneurs, tourists and locals are identified as the four main stakeholders in tourism destinations, as shown in Figure 7.5. The unique elements and general positions of each group serve to establish the identity lines of societal groups; the conflict with other groups contributes to the reaffirmation of the identity of the group and the maintaining of its boundaries against the surrounding social world. They are the core features of the tension-directed tourism development system and determine the nature, extents, and forms of tension in tourism development.

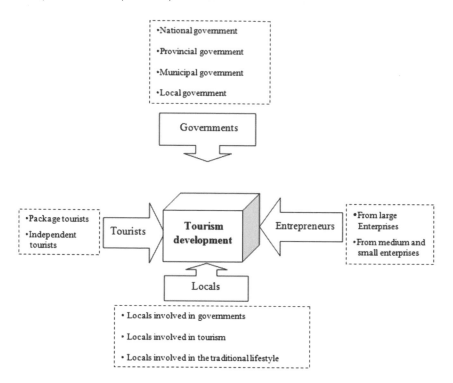

Figure 7.5 Four forces (groups) in tourism development

These main groups play different roles in tourism development. For the government, tourism development has sought to package and standardise ethnic culture into an exploitable resource for modernisation, thus necessitating the production, preservation and representation of an 'authentic' cultural heritage that contributes to nation building (Oakes, 1998). For tourism entrepreneurs, they are more interested in economic benefits. Economic motives often outweigh other goals in a tourism business. As Oakes (1998: 158) suggests, whether propagandised as poverty alleviation or legitimised as cultural development, tourism for those most actively involved in its development is simply about 'making money'. For tourists, they visit ethnic destinations for multiple purposes, and their real motivations are often inconsistent with those they express verbally or in response to a survey (Yang *et al.*, 2012). Their gazing and travel behaviours influence locals. For local ethnic people, they are often marginalised or disadvantaged economically and politically and they have a low level of control over their resources and tourism activities. Noticeably, tourism permits the occurrence of more subgroups with different demands and broadens the differences and demands between subgroups.

It should be acknowledged that there is some overlap among the groups defined. Members of one group may have multiple interests which draw them into a second or even third group, as in the example of a local who is involved in governments and is also involved with a small enterprise. Conflict may arise from this notion of multiple memberships. From the perspective of network theory such persons can hold central positions and thus also acquire a communicative power as a resource in addition to those other powers noted above. Equally outliers in the network may also possess social and network capital by being links with networks outside the local or regional network within Kanas, as may be the case of tour guides accompanying groups from Beijing.

A complicating factor is the relationship between resident groups of Kazakh and Tuva who live within the same village all year round. A symbiotic relationship of pecuniary interests and close proximity is woven into a system of ethnic, linguistic and cultural differences. Boundary maintenance becomes fuzzy, and the fuzziness is itself a source of both tension and strength in the fluidity of inter- and intra-group negotiations. It is, however, the tensions that act as creative forces, but the need for the changes in the status quo is due to the catalyst of tourism development. It is these social groups that together contribute to the social system of the community and the reciprocal tensions create a balance between various groups, therein maintaining the total social system (Simmel, 1922/1955).

A community tension-directed mechanism of tourism impact (community development perspective)

The intra- and inter-group conflicts and cooperations contribute to the changes of societal structure which therein, reiteratively, permits the changes of group positions in impacted society. These promote a subsequent community development stage. Meanwhile, stakeholders' positions in society and demands resulting from and on them may also change in the subsequent development stage. This perspective is consistent with the schema suggested by Yang and Sun in Chapter 10 in their application of complexity theory to tourist destination evolution in China. Adopting the principle of small changes causing significant outcomes, they envisage a process of continuing feedback mechanisms in the development of a destination where each part of the subsystem (tourists, capital, government, local and external actors) all initiate and respond to small and increasingly larger changes in the initial status quo. The system thus comprises continuing responses, but from the perspective of this chapter, such response patterns emerge from the inequalities of the social, political and economic capital of the varying parties (see Figure 7.6).

An inter-personal tension-directed mechanism of tourism impact

Mach and Snyder (1957) list the characteristics of and empirical conditions for the identification and characterisation of conflict phenomena and situations, namely: (1) at least two parties or analytically distinct units

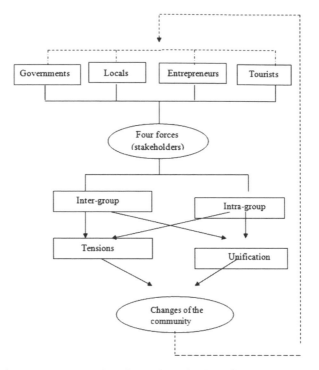

Figure 7.6 The community tension-directed mechanism of tourism's impacts

(actors, groups, collectivities, etc.) are necessary for social conflict; and (2) social conflict derives from two types of scarcity, 'position scarcity' and 'resource scarcity'. Position scarcity prevails when a certain object cannot be in two places at the same time or cannot perform two different functions simultaneously. Scarcity of resources prevails when the desired object is limited in such a way that the actors cannot obtain as much as they would like. A third condition is conflict behaviour that is oriented toward destroying, thwarting or otherwise controlling the opposing side. Fourth, social conflict requires interaction between the sides so that actions and counter-actions are mutually opposed and, last, conflict relations always include the striving for control of scarce resources or the striving to influence behaviours in a desired direction.

Among the communal changes, the inter-personal relationships of the stakeholders may also change. Under the conditions of behavioural, demographic and structural differences, tension/conflict occurs between individuals and leads to behavioural and attitudinal changes. The tension/conflict aftermath will further influence the antecedent conditions and create new interpersonal relationships in the subsequent development stage of the community (see Figure 7.7).

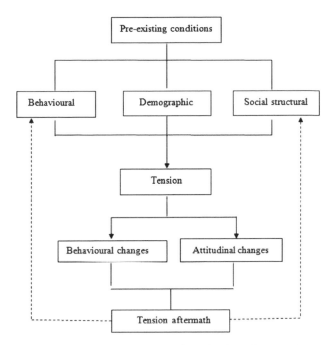

Figure 7.7 The interporsonal tension-directed mechanism of tourism's impacts

Theoretical Implications of the System

It is suggested that the proposed model possesses six implications, each of which is described below.

The functions of conflict/tension in relation to social change in the community

Conflict is important in terms of 'interactive processes' and is a 'form of socialization' (Coser, 1956: 31). It is a necessary and positive part of all social relationships, and a necessity for social change. Group formation is a result of both association and dissociation, so that both conflict and cooperation serve a social function and contribute to changes in a society.

Stakeholders in tourism development

A society consists of groups with different demands. While tensions serve to establish the identity and boundary lines of the four groups (governments, tourism entrepreneurs, tourists and locals), more generally it is the unique elements and general positions of such groups that individually and together serve to establish the identity lines of societal groups. In this instance, the four groups of locals, governments, tourists and entrepreneurs together contribute to the social system of the community and the reciprocal tensions create a balance between the various groups, thereby maintaining the total social system (Simmel, 1922/1955). This requires a commonality of purpose, and in this case that commonality was served by a need for income on the part of locals and tourism intermediaries, and for government, approval from Beijing and Urumqi. A symbiotic relationship was generated whereby tourism permitted additional incomes to be gained, a peaceful set of relationships secured that process, the threat of disquiet won concessions, and concessions further confirmed legitimacy on the part of the government.

The heterogeneity of a community/group

The extents, approaches, and results of tourism impacts on different populations of any one community are different within a heterogeneous social structure. It is argued that over time the interpersonal relationships would change and the structure of the community would be influenced by the area's tourism development. Tourism development of an area may contribute to the changing relationships between subgroups and the structure of the community. The result is that tourism generates an increasing amount of congruence between parties in the absence of an intrusion by external forces with which the local system cannot cope. The process reinforces the identification of joint interests, which in turn begin to link with external factors such as tourism companies located in large cities. A tension thereby exists between maintaining a homogeneity of linked local interests to deal with externally imposed change, and the need for permitting some external change to continue dynamism within the system.

The distinction between behaviour (conflict) and attitude (hostility)

Behavioural changes may differ from attitudinal changes in that the former may, at least initially, be latent while the latter may become overt. There is thus a temporal component to the changes. Hostile feelings may arise in the interplay of 'impulses of hostility' and opposing groups, and interaction greatly contributes to the potential occurrence of conflict (Simmel, 1922/1955). Tourism has increased the levels of interaction between groups, and has also increased competition, hostility and jealousy, which can be confined within acceptable levels by shifting alliances designed to achieve group benefits so long as those benefits continue to be generated and are valued by the recipients.

Pre-existing conditions for conflict/tension

Pre-existing conditions, such as social positions, cultural norms, demographics and social structure, should be considered in the analysis of conflict

(Coser, 1956). These factors influence the occurrence, modes, extents and also the resolution of conflict. Social structure is a key factor in determining whether the conflict will threaten the legitimacy of the social system (Coser, 1956).

The correlation between conflict and unification

Conflict is often accompanied by cooperation/unity/alliance. Conflict may create alliance between individuals/groups when they are faced with a common threat. The conflict with out-groups may increase the cohesion of the in-groups; it may even permit alliance between individuals of different groups if they are faced with a common threat. It is suggested that conflict fulfils a functional role by establishing and maintaining a balance of power between the stakeholders.

Practical Implications of the System

In line with the theoretical implications of the system above, a series of issues emerge for the management of tourism development in areas where such tourism is based upon the culture of local ethnic and cultural minorities.

An objective attitude towards conflict

It is suggested that the social conflict inherent in tourism development needs to be viewed objectively, especially by governments. The governments need to have an objective understanding about the nature of potential conflicts and to distinguish realistic from unrealistic conflict in order to resolve tensions. Although the distinctions between realistic and unrealistic conflict theoretically show that the social phenomena of conflict can be potentially explained in terms of tension release, its reality is commonplace in the real world and not simply an abstract theoretical concept. There is a danger that, if the local government overlooks the possibility of realistic conflict as a factor inherent in any social system, the local administration will only look for 'therapeutic measures' of a short-term nature (Coser, 1956: 52) instead of investigating the causes of conflict. They see all conflict as a 'social disease' and the lack of conflict as 'social health' (Coser, 1956: 53). The functions of conflict in contributing to social development should be considered and emphasised. This requires local administrations to become knowledgeable about the cultures they wish to promote as tourism product, to be patient with cultural difference, and to be prepared to negotiate and to value difference. Equally it may be claimed that ethnic minorities have the right to reject tourism; in practice, most societies will welcome it instead for the opportunities that it generates for their children and the improvements it can bring to their daily lives. In the case of poor marginalised communities such as those of Kanas these can be quite basic, such as the provision of power supplies in the winter and better access to basic provisions. What is required is a vision of what is required, and what is not.

In the Chinese situation, however, the political reality is that such visions are centrally determined, but there remains evidence that the powerless do possess power, as evidenced by the albeit patchy success of rural riots such as those at Wukan in 2011.

A balance of stakeholders' interest

The 'merit' in conflict largely depends on the ability to assert a perspective considered by others to be legitimate. Conflict can be regarded as a balance of the comparative strengths of two or more parties. If conflict is to be avoided, some other means for measuring relative power must be available as a counterpoint to the basis of the original claim (Coser, 1956). Posner (1979, 1983, 2000) suggests that the Kaldor–Hicks model of efficiency (Hicks, 1939; Kaldor, 1939) whereby participants seek to maximise monetary returns has a proven ability to quantify power relationships between stakeholders. The 'optimal outcome' is reached when the administration, entrepreneurs and tourists arrange sufficient compensation to those who are made worse off so that all end up no worse off than before the introduction of change. This quantification of change offers a measure by which the success of management may be gauged, and even indeed budgeted for.

An attention to subgroups' interests

In practice, groups, such as governments, are often regarded as homogeneous. Locals may view tourists as 'good' or 'bad', rather than considering what kinds of tourists are 'good' and what kinds of tourists are 'bad'. The government may consider the community as a whole, and thereby ignores the different interests and demands of different segments. Many residents of Kanas do not hope to be involved in regional tourism decision making and management (Wang et al., 2010). On the other hand, there is a minority willing to participate in tourism decision making. Furthermore, the locals who are engaged in local government aspire to gain more decision-making power; one reason is that such power is closely related to personal benefit. This issue is especially important for planning. Different subgroups and their needs and desires should not be ignored or overly advantaged.

Poverty as the major concern of the people

In underdeveloped and/or developing countries and regions, especially among indigenous communities with a very low level of economic development, poverty is still the major concern of the people. The gain or loss of income largely determines the reactions of locals towards the conflict with outer-groups. Within China, an issue exists with reference to relative political and economic power centres in the wider nexus of groups, and in some situations where the government makes concessions in relation to economic profits, the very concession may (as noted above) paradoxically reinforce the role of government as the source of economic benefaction. Certainly observation during the fieldwork found several examples where changes in regulations gained acceptance because of pecuniary advantage accruing to affected parties. However, the long-term sustainability of this policy may be open to question, but at this stage of development increasing tourist numbers more or less guarantees increasing government, corporate and private revenues.

Ethnic people's psychological problems during social change

The social transformational process of ethnic communities, such as from nomadic to an agricultural lifestyle and from subsistence farming to business operations and management, requires a change of attitudes, norms and other psychological adjustments for some ethnic peoples. Such issues require to be addressed by governments, researchers and related non-governmental organisations. These issues may influence long-term national and regional stability and have significance for social development. The practical management implications again point to the need for an emic approach to the management of change, and that the etic will not be wholly satisfactory in the outcomes it will achieve.

Consideration of antecedent conditions for tension

Factors such as social positions, cultural norms, demographics and social structure require consideration when dealing with conflict. The consideration of such factors permits thorough analysis of conflict and right conflict resolution measures.

Conflict and cooperation/unity/alliance

Cooperation/unity/alliance between individuals/groups is important for conflict resolution. In addition, when launching policies and measures thought undesirable by other stakeholders, government may be required to consider the potential cooperation/unity/alliance of those stakeholders who seek to oppose these policies and measures. Such opposition may cause the policies and measures not to be implemented and thereby undermine governmental credibility. One practical implication for the Chinese situation is that the need for 'social harmony' may create potential tortuous negotiations in the search for a solution – and the more practical process of sustaining *mianzi* (face) represents a mid-point between a more Western perspective where it is simply recognised that not all can be equally satisfied and, on the other hand, an ideal of harmonious relationships being realised. *Realpolitik* has a role to play, even in China, because political realities cannot be ignored.

One problem in Chinese administration is that the more able administrators in marginal areas quickly seek promotion to the more powerful centres of decision making, and thus this can impede policies based on the emic unless a civil service can achieve recruitment of local ethnic people. However, unfortunately at this stage, the ethnic minorities may not have the necessary educational qualifications or understanding, as their traditional pre-modern world of nomadic cattle grazing in this example does not prepare them for a career in governmental circles. However, again observation reveals change occurring as both old and young, for example, adopt cell phone technologies in those centres where cell phone towers exist.

Conclusion

This study employs Coser's (1956) social conflict theory for a discussion of tourism impacts on the ethnic communities, and proposes a tension-directed tourism development system with which to analyse tourism impacts. This system involves both macro and micro perspectives of tourism impacts. It embodies the evolutionary mechanism of tourism destinations, an emphasis on, in this case, four primary groups (tourists, governments, tourism entrepreneurs and local community) and subgroups, and the changes of interpersonal relationships during tourism development. Not only are the consequences of tourism on the locals assessed, but also the determinants and the mechanism of tourism impacts are involved. It demonstrates the conflict and negotiations between the groups and subgroups, thereby contributing to an understanding of the functions of social conflict on tourism destination development.

Many tourism impact studies are empirical studies that emphasise the specific characteristics of the case areas, and lack a comparison with other case areas and related studies. The framework of analysis and the tension-directed tourism development system provide a tool for comparing and contrasting tourism impacts on different areas. It permits a discussion of the determinants of different tourism impacts on different destinations. It permits cross-case study analysis from which generalisation becomes possible.

The evidence is restricted to the Kanas Scenic Area. To research tourism development in multi-ethnic destinations and to compare and contrast such issues in Eastern and Western counties is one direction for future study. In contrast to the minority peoples in the Kanas Scenic Area having little power in politics, the native Fijians have political power and to some extent take advantage of the Indians by denying them a full range of political rights (Sofield, personal communication), even while wishing to retain their entrepreneurial business capabilities. The application of this system in other countries will permit the extension and improvement of the proposed system of analysis.

As an exploratory analysis of the functions of social conflict in tourism, this study discusses groups in tourism, the hostility and tensions in conflict relationships, and also intra- and inter-group conflict. However, there remains a lack of a more comprehensive analysis of conflict management and conflict resolution in tourism. This is both a limitation of this study, and a future research direction. There is a need to establish a systematic theory about social conflict in tourism that comprises such elements as the nature of conflict, conflict management, conflict resolution, etc. Hopefully this research will attract interest from researchers and scholars on conflict in tourism and contribute to this domain.

Acknowledgement

This paper is based upon Yang, J., Ryan, C. and Zhang, L. (2013) Social conflict in communities impacted by tourism. *Tourism Management* 35 (1), 82–93 with the permission of the publishers.

References

Arzensek, V. (1972) A 'conflict model' and the structure of Yugoslav society. *International Journal of Sociology* 2 (4), 364–383.

Butler, R.W. (1980) The concept of a tourist area cycle of evolution: Implications for management of resources. *Canadian Geographer* 24, 5–12.

Butler, R.W. (2006) The origins of the Tourism Area Life Cycle. In R.W. Butler (ed.) *The Tourism Area Life Cycle, Volume 1: Applications and Modifications* (pp. 13–26). Clevedon: Channel View Publications.

Butler, R. and Hinch, T. (2007) *Tourism and Indigenous Peoples: Issues and Implications.* Oxford: Butterworth Heinemann.

Carr, A. (2007) Maori nature tourism businesses: Connecting with the land. In R. Butler and T. Hinch (eds) *Tourism and Indigenous Peoples: Issues and Implications* (pp. 113–127). Oxford: Butterworth-Heinemann.

Chambers, E. (2000) *Native Tours: The Anthropology of Travel and Tourism.* Long Grove, IL: Waveland Press.

Cohen, E. (1996) Hunter-gatherer tourism in Thailand. In R. Butler and T Hinch (eds) *Tourism and Indigenous Peoples* (pp. 227–254). London: International Thomson Business Press.

Coser, L.A. (1956) *The Functions of Social Conflict.* London: Routledge & Kegan Paul.

Coser, L.A. (1968) Conflict: III. Social aspects. In D.L. Sills (ed.) *International Encyclopedia of the Social Sciences* (Vol. 3, pp. 232–236). New York: Crowell Collier & Macmillan.

Crystal, E. (1989) Tourism in Toraja (Sulawesi Indonesia). In V.L. Smith (ed.) *Hosts and Guests: The Anthropology of Tourism* (2nd edn) (pp. 139–168). Philadelphia, PA: University of Pennsylvania Press.

Deitch, L.I. (1977) The impact of tourism upon the arts and crafts of the Indians of the southwestern United States. In V.L. Smith (ed.) *Hosts and Guests: The Anthropology of Tourism.* Philadelphia, PA: University of Pennsylvania Press.

Dodson, D.W. (1958) The creative role of conflict in intergroup relations. *Merrill-Palmer Quarterly* 4, 189–195.

Dredge, D. (2006) Policy networks and the local organisation of tourism. *Tourism Management* 27 (2), 269–280.

Dredge, D. (2010) Place change and tourism development conflict: Evaluating public interest. *Tourism Management* 31 (1), 104–112.

Easterbrook, S., Beck, E., Goodlet, L., Plowman, L., Sharples, M. and Wood, C. (1993) A survey of empirical studies of conflict. In S.M. Easterbrook (ed.) *CSCW: Cooperation or Conflict?* (pp. 1–68). London: Springer-Verlag.

Feng, X.-H. (2008) Who benefits? Tourism development in Fenghuang County, China. *Human Organization* 67 (2), 207–220.

Fisher, D. (2000) The Social-economic Consequences of Tourism in Levuka, Fiji. Unpublished doctoral thesis, Lincoln University, Canterbury, New Zealand.

Goering, P.G. (1990) The response to tourism in Ladakh. *Cultural Survival Quarterly* 14 (1), 20–25.

Greenwood, D.J. (1977) Culture by the pound: An anthropological perspective on tourism as cultural commoditization. In V.L. Smith (ed.) *Hosts and Guests: The Anthropology of Tourism* (pp. 129–138). Philadelphia, PA: University of Pennsylvania Press.

Greenwood, D.J. (1989) Culture by the pound: An anthropological perspective on tourism as cultural commoditization. In V.L. Smith (ed.) *Hosts and Guests: The Anthropology of Tourism* (2nd edn) (pp. 171–185). Philadelphia, PA: University of Pennsylvania Press.

Greenwood, D.J. (2004) Culture by the pound: An anthropological perspective on tourism as cultural commoditization. In S.B. Gmelch. *Tourists and Tourism: A Reader* (pp. 157–170). Long Grove, IL: Waveland Press.

Gu, H., Ryan, C., Bin, L. and Wei, G. (2013) Political connections, guanxi and adoption of CSR policies in the Chinese hotel industry: Is there a link? *Tourism Management* 34, 231–235. doi:10.1016/j.tourman.2012.01.017.

Hager, D.H. (1956) Religious conflict in the US. *Journal of Social Issues* 12 (3), 3–11.

Hicks, J.R. (1939) The foundations of welfare economics. *Economic Journal* 49 (196), 696–712.

Hines, J.S. (1966) The functions of racial conflict. *Social Forces* 45 (1), 1–10.

Hwang, K.-K. (1998) Guanxi and mientze: Conflict resolution in Chinese society. *Intercultural Communications* 7 (1), 17–38.

Jafari, J. (1989) Sociocultural dimensions of tourism: An English language literature review. In J. Bystrzanowski (ed.) *Tourism as a Factor of Change: A Social Cultural Study* (pp. 17–60). Vienna: International Social Science Council, European Coordination Centre for Research and Documentation in Social Sciences.

Kaldor, N. (1939) Welfare propositions in economics and interpersonal comparisons of utility. *Economic Journal* 49 (145), 549–552.

Kent, N. (1975) A new kind of sugar. In B.R. Finney and K.A. Watson (eds) *A New Kind of Sugar: Tourism in the Pacific* (pp. 169–198). Honolulu, HI: East-West Center.

Mach, R. and Snyder, R. (1957) The analysis of social conflict – toward an overview and synthesis. *Journal of Conflict Resolution* 1 (2), 212–248.

McIntosh, A.J. (2004) Tourists' appreciation of Maori culture in New Zealand. *Tourism Management* 25 (1), 1–15.

McIntosh, A.J. and Johnson, H. (2005) Understanding the nature of the Marae experience: Views from hosts and visitors at the Nga Hau E Wha National Marae, Christchurch, New Zealand. In C. Ryan and M. Aicken (eds) *Indigenous Tourism: The Commodification and Management of Culture* (pp. 36–50). Amsterdam: Elsevier.

McIntosh, A.J. and Ryan, C. (2007) The market perspective of indigenous tourism. In R. Butler and T. Hinch (eds) *Tourism and Indigenous Peoples: Issues and Implications* (pp. 73–83). Oxford: Butterworth-Heinemann.

Mckean, P.F. (1977) Towards a theoretical analysis of tourism: Economic dualism and cultural involution in Bali. In V.L. Smith (ed.) *Hosts and Guests: The Anthropology of Tourism* (pp. 93–107). Philadelphia, PA: University of Pennsylvania Press.

Medrano, J.D. (1996) Some thematic and strategic priorities for developing research on multi-ethnic and multi-cultural societies. *Management of Social Transformations* (Discussion Paper Series No. 13). Paris: UNESCO.

Meisner, M. (1971) Leninism and Maoism: Some populist perspectives in Marxism-Leninism in China. *China Quarterly* 45, 2–36.

Murphy, R.F. (1957) Intergroup hostility and social cohesion. *American Anthropologist* 59 (6), 1018–1035.

Nash, D. (1977) Tourism as a form of imperialism. In V.L. Smith (ed.) *Hosts and Guests: The Anthropology of Tourism* (pp. 33–47). Philadelphia, PA: University of Pennsylvania Press.

Nash, D. (1909) Tourism as a form of imperialism. In V.L. Smith (ed.) *Hosts and Guests: The Anthropology of Tourism* (2nd edn) (pp. 37–52). Philadelphia, PA: University of Pennsylvania Press.

North, R., Koch, H.E., Jr. and Zinnes, D. (1960) The integrative functions of conflict. *Journal of Conflict Resolution* 4 (3), 355–374.

Oakes, T. (1998) *Tourism and Modernity in China*. London: Routledge.

Oberschall, A. (1978) Theories of social conflict. *Annual Review of Sociology* 4, 291–315.

Pi-Sunyer, O. (1977) Through native eyes: Tourists and tourism in a Catalan maritime community. In V.L. Smith (ed.) *Hosts and Guests: The Anthropology of Tourism* (pp. 149–155). Philadelphia, PA: University of Pennsylvania Press.

Posner, R. (1979) Utilitarianism, economics, and legal theory. *Journal of Legal Studies* 8, 103–140.

Posner, R. (1983) *The Economics of Justice*. Cambridge, MA: Harvard University Press.

Posner, R. (2000) Cost-benefit analysis: Definition, justification, and comment on conference papers. *Journal of Legal Studies* 29, 1153–1177.

Prasad, P. (1987) The impact of tourism on small developing countries – an introductory view from Fiji and the Pacific. In S. Britton and W. Clarke (eds) *Ambiguous Alternative-tourism in Small Developing Countries* (pp. 9–15). Suva, Fiji: University Press of the South Pacific.

Robinson, M. (1999) Cultural conflicts in tourism: Inevitability and inequality. In M. Robinson and P. Boniface (eds) *Tourism and Cultural Conflicts*. Oxford: CABI Publishing.

Robinson, M. and Boniface, P. (eds) (1999) *Tourism and Cultural Conflicts*. Oxford: CABI Publishing.

Ryan, C. (2003) *Recreational Tourism: Demand and Impacts*. Clevedon: Channel View Publications.

Ryan, C. and Aicken, M. (eds) (2005) *Indigenous Tourism: The Commodification and Management of Culture*. Amsterdam: Elsevier.

Ryan, C., Chang, J. and Huan, T.C. (2007) The Aboriginal people of Taiwan. Discourse and silence. In R. Butler and T. Hinch (eds) *Tourism and Indigenous Peoples: Issues and Implications* (pp. 188–204). Oxford: Butterworth-Heinemann.

Ryan, C., Zhang, C. and Zeng, D. (2011) The impacts of tourism at a UNESCO heritage site in China – a need for meta-narrative? The case of the Kaiping Dialou. *Journal of Sustainable Tourism* 19 (6), 747–765.

Shepherd, R.J. (2011) Historicity, fieldwork, and the allure of the post-modern: A reply to Ryan and Gu. *Tourism Management* 32 (1), 187–190.

Simmel, G. (1922/1955) *Conflict and the Web of Group Affiliations* (K.H. Wolff, trans.). New York: Free Press.

Small, A.W. (1905) *General Sociology*. Chicago, IL: University of Chicago Press.

Smith, V.L. (ed.) (1977a) *Hosts and Guests: The Anthropology of Tourism*. Philadelphia, PA: University of Pennsylvania Press.

Smith, V.L. (1977b) Eskimo tourism: Micro-models and marginal men. In V.L. Smith (ed.) *Hosts and Guests: The Anthropology of Tourism*. Philadelphia, PA: University of Pennsylvania Press.

Smith, V.L. (ed.) (1989) *Hosts and Guests: The Anthropology of Tourism* (2nd edn). Philadelphia, PA: University of Pennsylvania Press.

Smith, V.L. (1996) Indigenous tourism: The four Hs. In R. Butler and T. Hinch (eds) *Tourism and Indigenous Peoples* (pp. 283–307). London: International Thomson Business Press.

Sofield, T.H.B. (1996) Anuha Island Resort, Solomon Islands: A case study of failure. In R. Butler and T. Hinch (eds) *Tourism and Indigenous Peoples* (pp. 176–202). London: International Thomson Business Press.

Swain, M.B. (1977) Cuna women and ethnic tourism: A way to persist and an avenue to change. In V.L. Smith (ed.) *Hosts and Guests: The Anthropology of Tourism* (pp. 71–81). Philadelphia, PA: University of Pennsylvania Press.

Swanson, K.K. and De Vereaux, C. (2012) Culturally sustainable entrepreneurship: A case study for Hopi tourism. In K.F. Hyde, C. Ryan and A.G. Woodside (eds) *Field Guide to Case Study Research in Tourism, Hospitality and Leisure* (pp. 479–496). Bingley: Emerald Publishing.

Timasheff, N.S. (1965) *War and Revolution*. New York: Sheed and Ward.

Toops, S. (1992) Tourism in Xinjiang, China. *Journal of Cultural Geography* 12 (2), 19–34.

Tucker, H. (2003) *Living with Tourism: Negotiating Identities in a Turkish Village*. London: Routledge.

Urbanowicz, C.F. (1977) Tourism in Tonga: Troubled times. In V.L. Smith (ed.) *Hosts and Guests: The Anthropology of Tourism*. Philadelphia, PA: University of Pennsylvania Press.

Wang, H., Yang, Z-P., Chen, L., Yang, J-J. and Li, R. (2010) Minority community participation in tourism: A case of Kanas Tuva villages in Xinjiang, China. *Tourism Management* 31 (6), 759–764.

Yang, J.-J., Ryan, C. and Zhang, L. (2012) The use of questionnaires in Chinese tourism research. *Annals of Tourism Research* 39 (3), 1690–1693. doi: 10.1016/j.annals.2012.02.002.

Yang, J., Ryan, C. and Zhang, L. (2013) Social conflict in communities impacted by tourism. *Tourism Management* 35, 82–93. doi: 10.1016/j.tourman.2012.06.002.

Part 2

Policy Implementation and Destination Evolution

8 Policy Implementation, Destination Evolution and Resident Perceptions of MICE Tourism

Songshan (Sam) Huang and Chris Ryan

Introduction

This chapter serves to introduce the following chapters in this part. Nevertheless, the discussion goes beyond simply providing brief reviews of the chapters included. It further offers critical comments on the various issues covered in the chapters and assists readers to develop their understanding by connecting the issues in different chapters. Broader contextual discussions on China's political, social and cultural systems and the linkages of research efforts as covered in the chapters to the international tourism academic circle are also provided.

Tourism Policy Implementation

As tourism becomes a more significant economic sector in a country or at the global level, it not only attracts more attention from the business sector but also more government intervention. This can be explained by the fact that tourism, when becoming a significant tertiary economic sector, can function as economic stimulator, foreign exchange generator and employment provider, and can thereby fulfil functions that are among the major concerns of most governments. Government in turn can exert its influence on tourism through different policy instruments, including advocacy, money, direct government action and legislation (Bridgman & Davis, 2004). The degree to which this happens depends on many factors. These include a country's political tradition and culture, its system of government as defined in its constitution, and the market importance of its tourism industry, all of which may work as discursive forces to shape government intervention in tourism development. As for the mode of such involvement, variations exist among governments, even those with similar political traditions. While tourism is strongly represented in some central government ministries and departments, in others, government direct involvement in tourism development is negligible, with little or no governmental functions dedicated to tourism.

In comparison with Western countries like the USA and Australia, China has a centralised government system where power is relatively concentrated toward the centre. However, as noted in Chapter 12 of this book by Huang, Ryan and Yang, the Chinese form of government has undergone several rounds of restructuring and there is an apparent trend for Beijing to decentralise some of its functions, especially those relating to policy implementation. While both economic and social system transitions are under way as China embraces the world, political reform in China is believed to have been more cautious and to be moving much more slowly than economic reform (Zheng, 2010). Recognising government restructuring and decentralisation in China, although representing one of the major moves in China's political transition, is not in itself sufficient in aiding understanding of China's complex political realities. However, some political realities in China can be understood through the case study of tourism policy implementation at the local government level as demonstrated by Wang and Ap's work which immediately follows this chapter.

Wang and Ap, in Chapter 9, employing a case study approach, provide a close look at tourism policy implementation at local government level. Using the Ancient Town Preservation Fee policy of the famous heritage tourism site, Lijiang, they interviewed key informants from relevant government agencies and representative industry organisations, and identified both constraints and facilitators of policy implementation in the study case. Three constraints identified by the study were: (a) conflicts of interests among key actors; (b) the combination of government and state-owned business; and (c) competing public administrative arrangements for tourism management. While these issues appear to replicate the literature (e.g. Airey & Chong, 2010; Zhang & Yan, 2009; Zhang et al., 2002) and are more or less echoed by other chapters in this book (e.g. Chapter 12), the emic perspective and real voice from the interviewees should by no means be overlooked. A couple of related issues need to be pondered and further discussed here. Both are associated with the third constraint issue as identified above. The authors differentiate 'comprehensive government agencies' from 'sector agencies' in the public administrative arrangement of tourism management. Comprehensive government agencies such as the State Development Planning Commission and the Ministry of Finance are generally perceived to be more powerful in the government system. However, sector agencies, in which category both national and local level tourism administrations would fit, are less powerful and have little say in the government system. Such an arrangement makes it difficult for tourism government agencies to implement a 'tourism' policy, which actually belongs to the jurisdictions of comprehensive government agencies. Interestingly, tourism as an industry in China has been long perceived as a 'comprehensive' industry and one that can promote the development of other industries due to its strong association with major economic sectors (Shao, 2012). It has been observed that when tourism administrative issues become more regulated, tourism government agencies may feel less awkward and more confident in coordinating various aspects of tourism development in the country (see also Chapter 12). And with the importance of tourism recognised as both an economic and social function in Chinese society, the power and status of tourism government agencies might be strengthened accordingly. We should keep an open mind to see how future developments change or adjust this discourse.

The above discussion naturally leads to the issue of the legislative system in China. As one interviewee in the Wang and Ap study noted, 'the inadequacy of the legislation system could be compensated for by administrative procedures …'. Nevertheless, we should take a developmental view with regard to the legislative system in China. Despite the inadequacy of legislation in arranging either policy making or policy implementation, there is a trend whereby China is moving toward to a more mature legal system. Symbolised by the political discourse of 'Yifa Zhiguo' (依法治国, running the country by law) or 'Yifa Xingzheng' (依法行政, administering by law), the country has been improving its legislative system. A milestone event was the promulgation of the Law of Administrative Permission in 2003 by the National People's Congress Standing Committee. Under the law, government agencies' responsibilities and obligations in various administrative procedures were more clearly defined, thus effectively preventing unlawful government interventions or interferences in policy implementations and making intergovernmental coordination in policy implementations relatively easy to undertake. However, in reality, policy implementation proves to be a more complicated issue, as demonstrated by Wang and Ap in the case study.

Wang and Ap go further to identify three facilitators in the case study for policy implementation, namely, (a) support of international community; (b) leadership of Lijiang Municipal Government; and (c) guanxi (personal relations). The first facilitator should be interpreted with care in the specific context of the study. As the policy itself was initiated by UNESCO in consideration of the world heritage status of Lijiang City, the external persuasive force exerted by UNESCO in legitimising the policy among different levels of Chinese authorities is unique in this case. In most local-level tourism policy implementation cases, such international community support would be non-existent. The complex system view as expressed in the two chapters authored by Chunyu Yang (Chapters 10 and 11) may help explain the situation. Applying complex system theory, the international community support may represent a significant input to the subsystem of tourism policy implementation, which itself is a coupling network that exchanges flows of material, energy and information with other subsystems in the local tourism destination system. (Please refer to Chapters 10 and 11 for a more detailed discussion of tourism destination complex systems.) Having said this, we do need to acknowledge that, as China opens up to globalisation, international factors and influences will play more decisive roles in directing China's internal issues and development. For instance, researchers have noted how the internet as a global force has driven changes in Chinese society and prompted the Chinese leadership to move towards liberalism (Kluver & Yang, 2005; Yang, 2003; Zheng, 2004).

It should be noted that even with concerted efforts from different social, business and political circles to advance China to be a country ruled by law, modern China had both its political philosophy and cultural tradition largely influenced by Confucianism. Confucius (551–479 bc) clearly favoured a society ruled by noble men (*Junzi,* 君子) rather than by laws, for as he said, 'Govern the people by regulations, keep order among them by chastisements, and they will flee from you, and lose all self-respect. Govern them by moral force, keep order among them by ritual and they will keep their self-respect and come to you of their own accord' (Confucius, 1998). With this inherited cultural norm and programming (Hofstede, 1991), one may argue that the men-ruling mentality and cultural tradition among the Chinese people may not be easily eradicated. This may help explain the third facilitator as identified by Wang and Ap, namely *guanxi* (personal relations). There is a significant literature about how *guanxi* dominates Chinese life in different aspects (e.g. Kipnis, 1997; Luo, 1997, 2007). Yet it is especially worth noting that even in the more liberalised government system in China that has emerged over the past two decades or so, officials still resort to *guanxi* or personal social networks to deal with governmental matters. With the involvement of *guanxi*, the boundary between official matters and personal affairs is not clearly defined. In terms of policy implementation, the possibility in China could be that an official in a less powerful government agency, but with strong *guanxi* with officials in other government agencies, could get a policy implemented better that that achieved through more formal, hierarchical channels.

Somewhat coincidentally, Huang, Ryan and Yang's chapter (Chapter 12) also talks about government functions in tourism. In their chapter, Huang, Ryan and Yang focus on local government roles in China's tourism development. They also review the evolution of central government's role in the development of tourism in China. By noting that the literature does not differentiate local from central government when examining the government's functions in tourism development and that past studies have mainly examined the roles of central government in China, the authors emphasise the role of local governments in China. They found that the roles taken by the central government in developing tourism are also more or less held by local governments; however, while the central government forsook its operator's role in tourism, local governments renewed or transformed this role from operating tourism enterprises to managing tourism resource properties. They suggested that the dyadic relationship between the central government and local governments should be further studied. The study hints that local governments are becoming more substantial and influential as stakeholders in China's tourism development.

Destination as a Complex System and Destination Evolution

The tourist destination has been widely researched as the key component forming or inducing tourism phenomena and associated activities. Multiple perspectives can be found in the literature in attempts to understand the tourist destination. Leiper was among the few scholars who conceptualised tourism as a system. In Leiper's (1979) model, the tourist destination is among the key geographic elements of tourism, connected to the tourist-generating region through transit routes. Jafari (1987), in his conceptualisation of tourism taking a sociocultural perspective, emphasised the tourist at the centre of defining tourism. He used 'the receiving system' or 'tourist site' to denote the non-ordinary environment a tourist normally experiences at a destination (Jafari, 1987: 157). Although these authors conceived tourism as composed of different systems and implied that the tourist destination is a system that could be disaggregated into subordinate systems, their contributions are mainly on providing conceptual understanding of tourism phenomena in an analytical framework, rather than providing a holistic view of the relationships of system components.

Butler's (1980) tourism area life-cycle model (TALC) may be among the few well-received theories in tourism research. The TALC model has been debated, tested, revalidated, revised and extended since its inception in 1980 (Baum, 1998; Butler, 2011; Cooper & Jackson, 1989; Getz, 1992). The TALC's origins are the belief that tourist destinations and resorts are essentially products that demonstrate similarities to other goods and services (Butler, 2006). This assumption postulates a rather linear view of the evolution of tourist destination. While the simplicity and overall utility of the model in understanding tourism development and planning issues should be recommended, the model as a tool in tourism planning is questioned for its practical value, as many empirical studies provided considerable variance from the model (e.g. Getz, 1992; Lundtorp & Wanhill, 2001). The real situations of destination evolution have proved to be far more complicated than that suggested by the TALC.

The state-of-the-art research on tourist destination and destination evolution seems to be at a crossroads, where more solid and applicable theoretical foundations are needed. The TALC model mainly takes into consideration the economic laws of market supply and demand in describing a destination's evolution. However, in reality, a destination is subject to many different forces including social, political factors at both regional and national scales, and unexpected events like natural and manmade disasters. Understanding a destination's evolution from the economic perspective oversimplifies the complexities as demonstrated in real-world situations. A more holistic view integrating both economic factors and other factors to understand destination evolution would be more helpful. In Chapters 10 and 11 of this book, Chunyu Yang and Xuhua Sun make valuable contributions towards providing this alternative view to destination evolution.

The first chapter authored by Yang and Sun (Chapter 10) offers theoretical and conceptual discussions, taking the assumption that a tourist destination is a complex system, rather than a simple mechanical system determined by physical forces. As complex systems, tourist destinations are composed of subsystems that constantly exchange flows of material, energy and information with each other as well as the outside world. The evolution of the complex systems is thus determined by the overall coupling force informed by numerous internal and external factors, their relations with each other and the outside world. By treating tourist destination as complex systems, we are open to alternative theories that can provide better explanations of real-world situations. The authors resort to different scientific theories to construct the tourism destination complex system (TDCS) theory, including general systems theory, dissipative structure theory, system control theory and chaos theory. However, we as the editors of this book would suggest that complexity theory (see Anderson, 1999; Lewin, 1992; Manson, 2001) may provide better theoretical underpinnings for such work. Nevertheless, both the chapter and its sister chapter (Chapter 11) provide Chinese case studies to illustrate the nature of the debate.

Another point as suggested in the Yang chapters is non-linear and holistic thinking to understand destination evolution. The authors mention Chinese Taoist philosophy to understand destination evolution. This indicates a paradigmatic transition in this stream of research. As noted by some scholars, tourism research so far has been predominately guided by Western research paradigms. However, as more researchers with Asian cultural backgrounds enter the field of tourism research (Ryan, 2009), a more pluralistic knowledge approach is foreseeable (Huang, 2011a). Research camps and tribes in the tourism academy (Tribe, 2010) may be revamped with new epistemological enquiry approaches from the Eastern civilisations. In 2012 the *Annals of Tourism Research* published an article exploring tourism representations of

Chinese cosmology (Buzinde *et al.*, 2012), hinting that such a knowledge creation transition is already happening. Chinese traditional wisdoms (knowledge) and philosophies, while currently still largely remaining in the Chinese language and among Chinese peoples, will further enrich our globalised knowledge creation platforms, especially providing alternative interpretations and understanding of the complexities of the world. Yang borrowed the Taoist world view and the universal change law of 'profit-deficiency-consumption-ceasing' to depict the circular evolution of tourist destinations. While Chinese epistemology has dominated indigenous Chinese scholars' research methodologies, it is only recently that the Chinese way of thinking could exert a substantial influence on the international tourism research community. For example, the concept of *Feng Shui* and its application in tourism planning was discussed by tourism scholars in China in the 1990s (Chen, 1996); however, it is not until 2011 that we see an article talking about *Feng Shui* in the *Annals of Tourism Research*. In terms of destination evolution, we also see the potential in the applicability of the Chinese Theory of Change (*Yijing*, 易经). Widely conceived as the 'classic of the Chinese classics', *Yijing* has been regarded as the origin of Chinese philosophies and culture (Smith, 1998). The paradoxical (some authors refer to it as 'bipolar change' even though the term 'bipolar' may not capture its meaning; see Schöter, 2008) change patterns and mechanism informed by the forces of *Yin* and *Yang* may also offer us more solid theoretical foundations to understand destination evolution. However, the highly abstract and metaphysical nature of *Yijing* theories and the long tradition of treating *Yijing* as mythology rather than science in Chinese history may prove to be a roadblock for Yijing theories to be widely adopted in tourism research.

Resident Perceptions of MICE Tourism

Resident perception of tourism impacts has remained a key focus of tourism academic inquiry and has evolved over the years with theoretical adaptations and paradigmatic shift as shown in Table 8.1, derived from Ryan *et al.* (2011). Starting from Doxey's (1975) work, marked by the Irritation Index (Irridex), this stream of research has progressed along a continuous flow path with various theoretical underpinnings in the English language literature (e.g. Ap, 1990, 1992; Ap & Crompton, 1998; Gu & Ryan, 2008, 2010; Liu & Var, 1986; Long *et al.*, 1990). By comparison, resident perception of tourism development has been less well studied among tourism scholars in China until very recently (Hsu *et al.*, 2010; Huang, 2011b; Huang & Hsu, 2008). The difference may be because tourism research in China has been guided to a larger extent by government policies and concerns (Xie, 2003). Unlike Western democracies, China still maintains its social hierarchy in which government takes the central and most powerful position (*Guan Benwei*,

Table 8.1 Stages in moving towards a multi-nuanced understanding of the impacts of tourism on communities: a meta-narrative?

Stage	Period	Nomenclature	Indicative literature	Characteristics
1	1960s, 1970s	The Linear Association – the period of observation	Doxey, 1975; Greenwood, 1972, 1974; V. Smith, 1977; G. Young, 1973; B. Young, 1983	Articles tend to be based on observation of trends – little empirical data.
2	1980s and 1990s	The period of empirical data gathering – the standardisation of items	Allen et al., 1988, 1993; Davis et al., 1988; Long et al., 1990; Liu and Var, 1986; Liu et al., 1987; Sheldon and Var, 1984	The emergence of survey-based articles with a commonality of items relating to researcher-identified negative and positive impacts.
3	1990s	The period of questioning homogeneity of residents	Getz and Jamal, 1997; Lawson et al., 1998; Ryan and Montgomery, 1994	The increased ability to undertake more sophisticated analysis due to better computing permits clustering techniques, while in a series of papers Getz and Jamal report on a multi-million dollar initiative in Alberta.
4	1990–2010	The emergence of concepts	Ap, 1992; Ap and Crompton, 1998; Gu and Ryan, 2008; Ko and Stewart, 2002; Lindberg and Johnson, 1997; McCool and Martin, 1994; Ryan et al., 1998	Researchers combine data capture with concepts drawn from social psychology derived from other than tourism studies. In addition, purely quantitative studies continue to be published.

| 5 | 2000– present | The role of local culture and the need for more ethnographic study – the role of the emic and the etic – begins to inform study, particularly with the growing importance of tourism impacts in a non-English speaking world | The role of Indigenous Peoples Studies in adopting different world views: Albers and James, 1983; Bennett. 1997; Butler and Hinch, 1996, 2007; Cohen, 1989; Johnston, 2006; McIntosh et al., 2004; Robinson and Boniface, 1999; Zeppel, 2006

The role of an emergent China-based study: Chio, 2009; Su and Wall, 2010; Sun and Bao, 2006; Wang and Xu, 2009; Wong et al., 2013; Wu et al., 2009; Yang et al., 2013; Zhang and Yan, 2009 | Early research tended to the etic – the researcher gazing at the researcher – but more ethnographic/emic perspectives have been emerging as native scholars write independently of non-indigenous scholars or in partnership with them, while researchers such as Yang et al. (2013), Wong (2011) adopt far more sustained ethnographic studies by living in the communities of the researched to observe tourism impacts. Links exist with the earlier ethnographic work of Grabarn, Nash, Cohen, etc. |

Source: Derived from Ryan et al. (2011)

官本位) and dominates the public domain (*Min*, 民). However, as noted by Ryan and Gu (2009), such statism in China is gradually decaying. The Chinese leadership headed by President Hu Jintao upheld a Scientific Development View (*Kexue Fazhan Guan*, 科学发展观), which stresses humanism as its core value (*Yi Ren Wei Ben*, 以人为本). With the ultimate goal being to construct a harmonious society (*Hexie Shehui*, 和谐社会), the political discourse in China may drive tourism research to become associated with more humanistic colour. Increasing collaborations between Chinese scholars and their overseas counterparts are also contributing to such a transition of research foci.

As evidenced in other parts of the world, rapid economic growth and further integration of China into the global economy have also induced a promising Meetings, Incentives, Conferences and Events (MICE) industry in China. In response to the booming MICE industry in China, research has been developed to address various aspects and issues in this specific field. Jin *et al.* (2012) examined the cluster effects on exhibition destination attractiveness in China. They found that while large cities like Beijing, Shanghai, and Guangzhou as leading Chinese cities have consolidated their leadership status in the MICE industry, encompassing more heterogeneous industry sectors, second- or third-tier Chinese cities tend to have more homogeneous industry concentration by attracting exhibitors from more locally specialised industry backgrounds. While, understandably, business or industry supply issues attracted research attention, residents' perceptions towards significant events in China did not exist in a research void. Zhou and Ap (2009) examined Beijing residents' perceptions of the 2008 Olympic Games. Residents were classified into two groups, labelled 'embracers' and 'tolerators', generally suggesting a positive attitude towards the event. Such an optimistic attitude held by local residents towards MICE events was somewhat echoed by the study of Zhou and Ryan as featured in Chapter 13.

The Zhou and Ryan study also revealed more contextual realities in China's MICE industry by exploring conversational data with Hangzhou residents over Hangzhou as a host city and the World Leisure Expo in 2006 as an event held in the city. Two aspects of the study findings warrant further discussion. First, the study reveals a perceptual map of residents from the qualitative data which shows little direct interaction between the host city and the event itself. This raises the question as to what extent a well-conceived and established tourist city like Hangzhou can be promoted and enhanced through hosting a new event. There seems to be a derived research need to further test the co-branding and image transfer issues in the MICE sectors (Jago *et al.*, 2003; Xing & Chalip, 2006). Second, the study found little community involvement in the event under examination. The World Leisure Expo, like most other large events held in China, was largely directed and organised by the 'government'. It should be acknowledged that the Chinese government in its political system has demonstrated exceptional mobilisation power and capacity in hosting mega-events like the Beijing 2008 Olympic Games or the Shanghai World Expo in 2010. However, a lack of local community involvement in MICE planning and development may lead to residents' resentment, as suggested in the study, although subject to the caveat that communities must feel they possess efficacy (as suggested in Gu & Ryan's (2008) study of place attachment in the hutong). As China's MICE sectors develop, the issues disclosed in the Zhou and Ryan study will yet further unfold.

Conclusion

In this chapter, we have sought to identify the major themes covered by the following chapters in this part. In the implementation of China's tourism policy both international/global forces and Chinese unique cultural features such as *guanxi* need to be considered as salient factors that forge the policy discourse. As an alternative paradigm by which to study tourist destination evolution, treating tourist destinations as complex systems opens up the research avenue in this area to a variety of theoretical approaches, including systems sciences, complexity theory, or even Chinese Theory of Change, namely *Yijing*. New developments such as those of China's MICE industry will also introduce new research topics such as event-host city co-branding and community involvement in MICE planning and development. While noting these contextual and topic-relevant issues, we believe readers will also reconstruct their own interpretations that will resonate in their own distinctive ways.

References

Airey D. and Chong, K. (2010) National policy-makers for tourism in China. *Annals of Tourism Research* 37 (2), 295–314.

Albers, P.C. and James, W.R. (1983) Tourism and the changing photographic image of the Great Lakes Indians. *Annals of Tourism Research* 10 (1), 123–148.

Allen, R.L., Hafer, H.R., Long, P.T. and Perdue, R.R. (1993) Rural Residents' Attitudes Toward Recreation and Tourism Development. *Journal of Travel Research* 31 (4), 27–33.

Allen, R.L., Long, P.T., Perdue, R.R. and Kieselbach, S. (1900) The impact of tourism development on residents' perceptions of community life. *Journal of Travel Research*, Summer, 27 (1), 16–21.

Anderson, P. (1999) Complexity theory and organization science. *Organization Science* 10 (3), 216–232.

Ap, J. (1990) Resident perception research of the social impacts of tourism. *Annals of Tourism Research* 17 (7), 481–494.

Ap, J. (1992) Residents' perceptions of tourism impacts. *Annals of Tourism Research* 19 (3), 665–690.

Ap, J. and Crompton, J.L. (1998) Developing and testing a tourism impact scale. *Journal of Travel Research* 37 (2), 120–130.

Baum, T. (1998) Taking the exit route: Extending the tourism area life cycle model. *Current Issues in Tourism* 1 (2), 167–175.

Bennett, S. (1997) Maori Tourism. *Tourism Management* 18 (7), 471–473.
Bridgman, P. and Davis, G. (2004) *The Australian Policy Handbook* (3rd edn). Sydney: Allen & Unwin.
Butler, R. (1980) The concept of the tourist area lifecycle of evolution: Implications for the management of resources. *Canadian Geographer* 24, 5–12.
Butler, R. and Hinch, T. (1996) *Tourism and Indigenous Peoples*. London: Thomson Business Press.
Butler, R. and Hinch, T. (2007) *Tourism and Indigenous Peoples* (2nd edn). London: Thomson Business Press.
Butler, R.W. (2006) The origins of the Tourism Area Life Cycle. In R.W. Butler (ed.) *The Tourism Area Life Cycle Volume 1: Applications and Modifications* (pp. 13–26). Clevedon: Channel View Publications.
Butler, R.W. (2011) *Tourism Area Life Cycle*. Contemporary Tourism Reviews series. Oxford: Goodfellow Publishers.
Buzinde, C., Choi, Y. and Wang, A.Y. (2012) Tourism representations of Chinese cosmology: The case of Feng Shui tourism. *Annals of Tourism Research* 39 (2), 975–996.
Chen, C. (1996) The modernization of geomantic omen (feng shui) and its tourist values. *Human Geography* 11 (1), 29–35.
Chio, J. (2009) The internal expansion of China. In T. Winter, P. Teo and T.C. Chang (eds) *Asia on Tour: Exploring the Rise of Asian Tourism* (pp. 210–222). London: Routledge.
Cohen, E. (1989) Primitive and remote: Hill tribe trekking in Thailand. *Annals of Tourism Research* 16 (1), 30–61.
Confucius (1998) *The Analects* (A. Waley, trans.). Beijing: Foreign Language Teaching and Research Press.
Cooper, C. and Jackson, S. (1989) Destination life cycle: The Isle of Man case study. *Annals of Tourism Research* 16 (3), 377–398.
Davis, D., Allen, J. and Cosenza, R.M. (1988) Segmenting Local Residents by their Attitudes, Interests, and Opinions toward Tourism. *Journal of Travel Research*, Fall, 2–21.
Doxey, G.V. (1975) A causation theory of visitor–resident irritants: Methodology and research inferences. In *Proceedings of the 6th Annual Conference of Travel Research Association* (pp. 195–198). San Diego, CA: Travel and Tourism Research Association.
Getz, D. (1992) Tourism planning and destination life cycle. *Annals of Tourism Research* 19 (4), 752–770.
Greenwood, D.J. (1972) Tourism as an agent of change. A Spanish Basque case. *Ethnology* 11, 80–91.
Greenwood, D.J. (1974) *Culture by the Pound,* paper read at the 1974 annual meetings of the American Anthropological Association, Mexico City, Mexico.
Gu, H. and Ryan, C. (2008) Place attachment, identity and community impacts of tourism – the case of a Beijing hutong. *Tourism Management* 29 (4), 637–647.
Gu, H. and Ryan, C. (2010) Hongcun, China – residents' perceptions of the impacts of tourism on a rural community: A mixed methods approach. *Journal of China Tourism Research* 6 (3), 216–243.
Hofstede, G. (1991) *Cultures and Organizations: Software of the Mind*. London: McGraw-Hill.
Hsu, C.H.C., Huang, J. and Huang, S. (2010) Tourism and hospitality research in Mainland China: Trends from 2000 to 2008. In D. Pearce and R. Butler (eds) *Tourism Research: A 20:20 Vision* (pp. 147–160). Oxford: Goodfellow Publishers.
Huang, S. (2011a) 'China, forever': Orientalism revisited. *Annals of Tourism Research* 38 (3), 1188–1192.
Huang, S. (2011b) Tourism as the subject of China's doctoral dissertations. *Annals of Tourism Research* 38 (1), 316–319.
Huang, S. and Hsu, C.H.C. (2008) Recent tourism and hospitality research in China. *International Journal of Hospitality and Tourism Administration* 9 (3), 267–287.

Jafari, J. (1987) Tourism models: The sociocultural aspects. *Tourism Management* 8 (2), 151–159.

Jago, L., Chalip, L., Brown, G., Mules, T. and Ali, S. (2003) Building events into destination branding: Insights from exports. *Event Management* 8 (1), 3–14.

Jin, X., Weber, K. and Bauer, T. (2012) Impact of clusters on exhibition destination attractiveness: Evidence from mainland China. *Tourism Management* 33 (6), 1429–1439.

Johnston, A.M. (2006) *Is the sacred for sale: Tourism and Indigenous Peoples.* London: Earthscan.

Kipnis, A.B. (1997) *Producing Guanxi: Sentiment, Self and Sub-culture in a North China Village.* Durham, AC: Duke University Press.

Kluver, R. and Yang, C. (2005) The internet in China: A meta-review of research. *Information Society: An International Journal* 21 (4), 301–308.

Ko, D-W. and Stewart, W.P. (2002) A structural equation model of residents' attitudes for tourism development. *Tourism Management* 23 (5), 521–530.

Leiper, N. (1979) The framework of tourism: Towards a definition of tourism, tourist, and the tourist industry. *Annals of Tourism Research* 6 (4), 390–407.

Lewin, R. (1992) *Complexity: Life at the Edge of Chaos.* New York: MacMillan.

Lindberg, K. and Johnson, R. (1997) Modeling resident attitudes toward tourism. *Annals of Tourism Research* 24 (2), 402–424.

Liu, J.C. and Var, T. (1986) Resident attitudes toward tourism impacts in Hawaii. *Annals of Tourism Research* 13 (2), 193–214.

Liu, J.C., Sheldon, P. and Var, T. (1987) Resident perception of the environmental impacts of tourism. *Annals of Tourism Research* 14 (1), 17–37.

Long, P.T., Perdue, R.R. and Allen, L. (1990) Rural resident tourist perceptions and attitudes by community level of tourism. *Journal of Travel Research* 28 (3), 3–9.

Lundtorp, S. and Wanhill, S. (2001) The resort lifecycle theory – generating processes and estimation. *Annals of Tourism Research* 28 (4), 947–964.

Luo, Y. (1997) *Guanxi:* Principles, philosophies and implications. *Human Systems Management* 16 (1), 43–51.

Luo, Y. (2007) *Guanxi and Business* (2nd edn). Singapore: World Scientific.

Manson, S.M. (2001) Simplifying complexity: A review of complexity theory. *Geoforum* 32 (3), 405–414.

McCool, S.F. and Martin, S.R. (1994) Community attachment and attitudes toward tourism development. *Journal of Travel Research* 32 (3), 29–34.

McIntosh, A.J., Zygadlo, F.K. and Matunga, H. (2004) Rethinking Maori tourism. *Asia Pacific Journal of Tourism Research* 9 (4), 331–352.

Robinson, M. and Boniface, P. (1999) *Tourism and Cultural Conflicts.* Wallingford: CAB International.

Ryan, C. (2009) Thirty years of tourism management. *Tourism Management* 30 (1), 1–2.

Ryan, C. and Gu, H. (eds) (2009) *Tourism in China: Destination, Cultures and Communities.* New York: Routledge.

Ryan, C., Scotland, A. and Montgomery, D. (1998) Resident attitudes to tourism development – a comparative study between the Rangitikei, New Zealand and Bakewell, United Kingdom. *Progress in Tourism and Hospitality Research* 4 (2), 115–130.

Ryan, C., Zhang, C. and Deng, Z. (2011) The impacts of tourism at a UNESCO heritage site for China – a need for a meta-narrative? The case of the Kaiping Diaolou. *Journal of Sustainable Tourism* 19 (6), 747–765.

Schöter, A. (2008) Bipolar change. *Journal of Chinese Philosophy* 35 (2), 297–317.

Shao, Q. (2012) *The Chairperson's Message.* CNTA official website, accessed 7 March 2012. http://www.cnta.gov.cn/html/common/AbountUs/LeaderAddress.aspx

Sheldon, P. and Var, T. (1984) Resident attitudes to tourism in North Wales. *Tourism Management* 5 (1), 40–47.

Smith, R.J. (1998) The place of *Yijing* in world culture: Some historical and contemporary perspectives. *Journal of Chinese Philosophy* 25 (4), 391–422.

Smith, V. (1977) *Hosts and Guests – The Anthropology of Tourism* (1st edn). Philadelphia: University of Pennsylvania Press.

Su, M.M. and Wall, G. (2010) Place attachment and heritage tourism at the Great Wall. *Journal of China Tourism Research* 6 (4), 396–409.

Sun, J.X. and Bao, J.G. (2006) The community participation model of tourism: an empirical study of Yunnan and Guangxi. *China Tourism Research* 2 (1/2), 137–145.

Tribe, J. (2010) Tribes, territories and networks in the tourism academy. *Annals of Tourism Research* 37 (1), 7–33.

Wang, C. and Xu, H. (2009) Is diversification a good strategy for Chinese tourism companies. *Journal of China Tourism Research* 5 (2), 188–209.

Wong, C.U.I., McIntosh, A. and Ryan, C. (2013) Buddhism and Tourism: Perceptions of the Monastic Communities in Putuoshan. *Annals of Tourism Research* 40, 213–234.

Wu, J., Xu, J. and Ekiz, E.H. (2009) Investigating the push and pull motivation of visiting domestic destinations in China: A means-end approach. *Journal of China Tourism Research* 5 (3), 287–315.

Xie, Y. (2003) Tourism and hospitality industry studies: A comparative research between China and the overseas countries. *Tourism Tribune* 18 (5), 20–25.

Xing, X. and Chalip, L. (2006) Effects of hosting a sport event on destination brand: A test of co-branding and match-up models. *Sport Management Review* 9 (1), 49–78.

Yang, G. (2003) The co-evolution of the internet and civil society in China. *Asian Survey* 43 (3), 405–422.

Yang, J., Ryan, C. and Zhang, L. (2013) Ethnic Minority Tourism in China: Han perspectives of Tuva figures in a landscape. *Tourism Management* 36, 45–56.

Young, B. (1983) Touristization of traditional Maltese fishing-farming villages: A general model. *Tourism Management* 4 (1), 35–41.

Young, G. (1973) *Tourism: Blessing or Blight.* Harmondsworth: Penguin.

Zeppel, H. (2006) *Indigenous Eco-tourism: Sustainable Development and Management.* Wallingford: CAB International.

Zhang, H.Q. and Yan, Q. (2009) The effects of power, ideology, interest groups, and the government on tourism policy making – a conceptual model. *Journal of China Tourism Research* 5 (2), 158–173.

Zhang, H.Q., Chong, K. and Jenkins, C.L. (2002) Tourism policy implementation in mainland China: An enterprise perspective. *International Journal of Contemporary Hospitality Management* 14 (1), 38–42.

Zheng, Y. (2004) *Globalization and State Transformation in China.* Cambridge: Cambridge University Press.

Zheng, Y. (2010) Where to go for China's political reform? Zaobao.com, accessed 7 March 2012. http://www.zaobao.com/special/forum/pages8/forum_zp101011.shtml

Zhou, Y. and Ap, J. (2009) Residents' perceptions towards the impacts of the Beijing 2008 Olympic Games. *Journal of Travel Research* 48 (1), 78–91.

9 Tourism Policy Implementation at the Local Level in China: A Case Study of Lijiang

Dan Wang and John Ap

Introduction

In most economically developing regions and countries, local government often plays a dominant role in tourism development for several reasons, one of which may be because of a small or non-existent private sector (Shivji, 1973). Additionally, in most socialist countries, local and national government will often initiate tourism development because the resources necessary for tourism are controlled by the government (Jenkins & Henry, 1982). China is one such country that has adopted a government-led tourism development strategy as evidenced in other contributions to this book. Consequently, the quality of those policies, and their implementation, is critical as the success of these policies helps determine relationships with an emergent private sector in contemporary China and the success of policies that seek to generate income and employment. However, the implementation of tourism policy has been found to be fraught with challenges (Cai, 2000; Ding & Liao, 2004; Kuang, 2001a, 2001b; Lai et al., 2006; Lo et al., 2000). Given the varying dynamics of different regions of China and the diversity of local tourism policies, it is important to explore tourism policy implementation at the local level to assess the effectiveness of those policies and provide empirical information on how the process works and for future theoretical generalisation.

The purpose of this chapter is to identify the factors influencing tourism policy implementation at the local level in China, using as a case study the 'Ancient Town Preservation Fee' (ATPF) policy adopted in Lijiang, China. Through this case study, the constraints and facilitators that influence tourism policy implementation are described and analysed. Data were obtained by interviewing government officials in charge of tourism policy making, through observation and the use of secondary sources. This study identified key players in the ATPF policy implementation and identified conflicts of interests, their relationships and interactions.

Literature Review

Tourism policy implementation in China

Although possessing a centralised governance system, the Central Government in China has left tourism public administration to the local level in China, which in this arena enjoys a high level of autonomy (Chong, 2000). One reason for this, at least in the past, has been ideological, because tourism has, until recently, been regarded as of secondary political and economic importance. Consequently, no significant problems were envisaged in leaving local government with discretionary authority in initiating tourism policies and implementing them. However, as tourism grows in importance the local autonomy of tourism public administration has led to modes of implementation that further fragment existing authority structures (Chen, 1999; He, 2001; Kuang, 2001b; Lin, 1996; Wang, 1998; Wei, 2000). Due to historical administrative arrangements, China has several separate government agencies which manage its natural and cultural tourism resources. These agencies include departments responsible for construction, forestry, gardens, culture and heritage, even at the lower county or town government levels. Additionally, given the multi-sectoral nature of the tourism industry, the implementation of tourism policies needs the assistance of other government organisations such as the commerce bureau, municipal construction departments, and the police and security departments. As such, effective implementation of tourism policy cannot be accomplished without high levels of cooperation being achieved across a range of related organisations (Lo et al., 2000). Therefore, tourism policy implementation in China can be conceptualised as an inter-organisational process. It is a process where a local tourism agency seeks to coordinate and establish cooperation with other actors to obtain the resources required to implement policy.

Factors influencing policy implementation

Tourism policy implementation is 'the process through which policy ideas and plans are translated into practice' (Dredge & Jenkins, 2007: 170). Three main approaches exist, namely: (1) 'top-down'; (2) 'bottom up'; and (3) hybrid (i.e. a synthesis of the first two). The top-down approach focuses on how implementation of policy is exercised by the policy maker. Here the nature, environment and modes of central policy implementation are critical factors for success (Gunn, 1978; Hogwood & Gunn, 1984; Mazmanian & Sabatier, 1983). The bottom-up approach focuses on how local communities or street-level bureaucrats negotiate with people at the 'top' level, such as those at the national, federal or regional levels (Lipsky, 1980) when devising and implementing policy. Limitations of both approaches have been revealed in practice (Goggin et al., 1990; Younis & Davidson, 1990), leading to attempts to integrate the best features of both (e.g. Goggin et al., 1990; Mazmainan & Sabatier, 1989; Ryan, 1996; Sabatier, 1986; Stoker, 1991). For example, Goggin et al. (1990: 32) developed 'the communications model of inter-governmental policy implementation' (Figure 9.1), which integrated the major concerns and variables of the top-down and bottom-up research studies into a single framework. They proposed that the outcomes of policy implementation depend on: (1) national-level inducements and constraints (i.e. policy messages, and reputation of the communicators); (2) local-level inducements and constraints (i.e. local officials, power of implementation agency, local politics and interest groups); (3) local decisional outcomes (i.e. decision makers' interpretation of national decisions based on the integrated consideration of the inducements and constraints at the local level); and (4) local capacity (i.e. the organisational capacity of implementation agency, the local socio-economic and political conditions). Krutwaysho and Bramwell (2010) proposed a 'society-centred' and 'relational' approach to the study of policy implementation. They argued that policy implementation is an

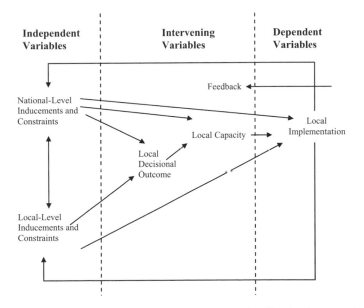

Figure 9.1 Communications model of inter-governmental policy implementation
Source: Adapted from Goggin *et al.* (1990: 32).

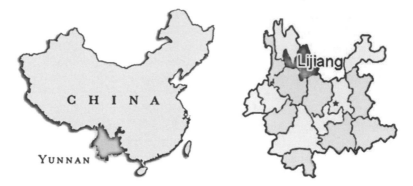

Figure 9.2 Location of Yunnan Province and Lijiang, China

interactive and negotiated process between implementers and those who will bear the outcomes of policy. This process reflects the social context such as the socio-economic, cultural and political relations in society (Bramwell & Meyer, 2007). Therefore, factors influencing policy implementation should be considered in a broad sense by assessing the local environment, examining the negotiation and bargaining between social groups and individuals around the policy, and recognising the power of government. This is shown in Figure 9.1, which highlights the importance of capacities and feedback processes.

Studies on tourism policy suggest that the implementation of tourism policy can be influenced by diverse factors depending on the local political system, such as the ideology and administrative arrangements, etc., as well as the role of the tourism industry in the social-economic environment and the attitudes of local people towards tourism (Dodds, 2007; Lai *et al.*, 2006; Puppim de Oliveira, 2008). As such, investigations of tourism policy implementation often conclude that policy makers should adopt a hybrid or synthesised approach that considers factors from both the top-down and bottom-up approaches. Considering the factors proposed by Goggin *et al.* (1990) and Krutwaysho and Bramwell (2010), this study explored the factors influencing tourism policy implementation at the local level in China by analysing the context of tourism policy implementation with the introduction of a preservation fee (i.e. entry fee) for the UNESCO cultural heritage listed ancient town of Lijiang in the northwest of Yunnan Province (see Figure 9.2). The major actors involved in tourism policy implementation and the dialectic relationships between the actors are analysed in this case study.

Methods

The selection of the case was purposeful and criteria based, which is a strategy 'in which particular settings, persons, or activities are selected deliberately in order to provide information that cannot be gotten as well from other choices' (Maxwell, 2005: 88). By its nature the study required a case that reflects the complexity of the involvement of multiple government organisations. This, as described below, was present in this instance. In addition, this policy had been implemented for nine years prior to the study being undertaken in 2010. Consequently, problems in policy implementation had emerged and measures taken to resolve them have been identified.

Both primary and secondary data were used in this study. The primary data were collected through interviews (Yin, 2003) and a 'snowball' sampling technique was used to select representatives of the stakeholders involved in collection of the ATPF. A total of six government officials working in the Lijiang Tourism Bureau, the Lijiang Tourism Industry Association, the Ancient Town District Tourism Bureau and the Ancient Town Preservation and Management Bureau were interviewed. One interview was also conducted with an employee working in the industry association and one with an employee from the hotel industry. This was because hotels were required to collect the preservation fee on behalf of the local government. The profiles of the interviewees are listed in Table 9.1. The interviews were audio recorded and focused on two questions: (1) How was the ATPF policy implemented? and (2) What are the factors that constrain or facilitate implementation of fee collection?

Secondary data were also collected and these served as supplementary material for the primary data. The secondary data came from a wide variety of sources, such as internal government documents, government publications, international tourism organisation publications and newspapers and magazine articles.

Content analysis was employed to systematically analyse the data and assess its inferences. The procedures suggested by Berg (2001) were followed. First, the raw data were read and re-read for the purpose of familiarity and preparation for coding. Second, the code frame was generated from open

Table 9.1 Profile of interviewees

Label	Gender	Organisation
(1) LJ1	Male	Lijiang Tourism Bureau
(2) LJ2	Male	Lijiang Tourism Bureau
(3) LJ3	Male	Lijiang Tourism Bureau
(4) LJ4	Male	Lijiang Tourism Industry Association
(5) LJ5	Male	Ancient Town District Tourism Bureau
(6) LJ6	Male	Ancient Town Protection Bureau
(7) LJ7	Female	Jinquan Hotel employee (Lijiang)

Notes: LJ, Lijiang interviewees. Details of the position or title of the interviewees are not provided to maintain their privacy and confidentiality.

coding (Strauss, 1987) at two levels, the manifest and latent content (Berg, 2001). Third, the data were coded combining inductive and deductive approaches that compared codes with the categories included in the conceptual framework. The two sets of codes (i.e. open coding and theoretical coding) were integrated to generate the final coding frames. Finally, the codes were categorised into themes, and the data sorted according to the themes that emerged from this analysis. In addition, the triangulation of the data and systematic documentation of the raw data and data analysis process were undertaken to ensure the 'trustworthiness' (Lincoln & Guba, 1985) of the findings.

Findings

Study setting

Lijiang is located in the northwest of Yunnan Province, China (Figure 9.2). It consists of one district (the ancient town district) and four counties (Yulong, Yongsheng, Huaping and Ninglang). Before 2002, it was called the Lijiang Prefecture, and the current Lijiang city was a county at that time. Lijiang is known for its abundant natural and cultural tourism resources, such as the spectacular Tiger Leaping Gorge, picturesque Lugu Lake, snow-capped Jade Dragon Snow Mountain and Lijiang Ancient Town. Among these attractions, the most famous is Lijiang Ancient Town, an old town with a history of 800 years. Lijiang Ancient Town, as it is commonly known, is more correctly called Dayan Ancient Town (大研古镇). It was registered on the UNESCO World Heritage List in December 1997 (World Heritage Center, 1997). In the late 1980s, the major industry in Lijiang was agriculture, and Lijiang was one of poorest counties in Yunnan because of the limitations of accessibility and cultivated area. Since the mid-1990s, the economic structure of Lijiang has been changed by the development of tourism. Currently, tourism is the most important industry in Lijiang. Its contribution to local GDP was more than 70% in 2007 (Lijiang Municipal Government, 2008).

The ATPF is part of the Lijiang Ancient Town Protection Plan initiated by UNESCO. The purpose of this policy is to provide funds to manage and maintain the ancient town. The Lijiang Municipal Government is responsible for the policy's implementation. The agencies which undertake the actual implementation of the policy are the Lijiang Tourism Bureau and the Ancient Town Preservation and Management Bureau. Four other government organisations were also involved in this project. They are the Lijiang Industrial and Commercial Bureau, Lijiang Merchandise Price Bureau, Lijiang Financial Bureau and Lijiang Construction Bureau. The ATPF was introduced as an administrative tax to be used for the preservation, management, revitalisation and restoration of Lijiang Ancient Town. Every tourist who visits Lijiang

Ancient Town was charged RMB 40 (with the fee being raised to RMB 80 per person in 2007) and it is, in effect, an entrance fee. As it was difficult to set up a specific entrance point to collect the fee, local travel agents and hotels were asked to collect the tax from visitors on behalf of the local government. The ATPF has been collected since January 2001. By the end of 2009 the Lijiang Tourism Bureau and Ancient Town Preservation and Management Bureau had collected around RMB 180 million (US$27 million) (China Daily, 2009). Although the fee serves a simple function, its implementation involved numerous parties which highlights the complexity of implementing a simple fee collection measure.

Factors influencing the implementation of the Ancient Town Preservation Fee Policy

Due to the involvement of multiple government and non-government organisations, the implementation of the ATPF policy has proven to be fraught with challenges. However, the special social, economic and political context of Lijiang created some facilitators for policy implementation. This section analyses three environmental facilitators and three constraints originating from the public administrative arrangements of tourism in Lijiang and illustrates the nature of the relationships between these factors (as shown in Figure 9.3).

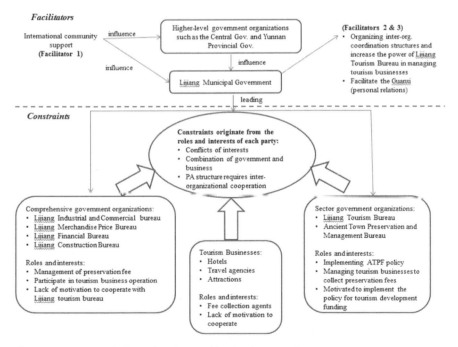

Figure 9.3 Factors influencing ATPF policy implementation

Constraint 1. Conflicts of interests among key actors

The vested interests of the main players have created conflicts between the varying organisations and the implementation agents. The primary organisations (the Lijiang Tourism Bureau and the Ancient Town Preservation and Management Bureau) have the motivation to pursue the success of policy implementation. However, at the same time they are subordinates of the Lijiang Municipal Government, which still expects successful implementation of the policy in spite of a scarcity of funding for ancient town preservation and in the face of pressure from the higher levels of government such as the Yunnan Provincial Government, State Council and the international community (UNESCO) to promote tourism for economic and political reasons. Also, both local agencies can benefit from the collection of the preservation fee because around 2% of the total preservation fee is allocated to them as part of their administration fee. However, the tax collecting agencies, including hotels, travel agents and attractions, lack the motivation to cooperate as they view it as an added administrative burden. These organisations were asked to collect the fee from tourists on behalf of the government because of their direct connection with tourists. In practice, fee collection is never easy. Tourists have usually been found to hold negative opinions about the preservation fee and resist paying for it as it increases the costs of a stay, and the current rates are already significant for many visitors, given Chinese wage levels. For their part, the collection agencies (i.e. hotels and travel agencies) need to take time and effort to explain the ATPF and its purposes to tourists. However, there were no benefits for these business organisations and there is a risk of incurring the tourists' displeasure. For example, one of interviewees (LJ7), who had to face unpleasant situations and handle tourist complaints about the fee, said:

> Some tourists misunderstood us. They thought that we just want to charge more. So they don't trust us and don't want to pay for the preservation fee. The communication sometimes proves to be very unpleasant. Particularly, in peak seasons, we feel that we don't have spare time and energy to explain the policy to visitors.

Constraint 2. Combination of government and state-owned business

In order to boost tourism industry development, the Central Government released the 'Five Together' policy in 1984 to encourage the state, together with local governments, individual government agencies, collectives and individuals, to get involved in tourism business operations through the establishment of enterprises. As such, government organisations at various levels became actively involved in running tourism businesses. Such a practice has distorted the natural order of the market mechanism and also affected the effective implementation of tourism policy because initiatives based on self-interests encourage the abuse of administrative authority, the violation of economic rules, and lead to situations involving a conflict of interest. In the implementation of the ATPF policy, conflicts between the two primary organisations and tourism business organisations were caught up in wider tensions between the different organisations, including those of government. The collection of the preservation fee was deemed to harm the interests of the state-owned and private sector tourism businesses, because they not only had to set aside the fee from their revenues, but also needed to allocate resources to collect the fee. Therefore, the government agencies supporting the businesses were also reluctant to cooperate because additional bureaucratic procedures were involved. Thus, inter-organisational coordination becomes a key point for the successful implementation of the ATPF policy. However, due to the nature of the institutional arrangements of tourism administration in China, inter-organisational coordination between the different organisations turned out to be complicated and difficult. This introduces the third constraint that arose in this situation.

Constraint 3. Public administrative arrangement of tourism management

As noted, the implementation of the ATPF policy requires the cooperation of multiple government organisations. As the agency in charge of ATPF fee collection, the Lijiang Tourism Bureau sought cooperation from relevant government organisations. However, in the hierarchy of public administrative arrangements in China such bodies as the Lijiang Tourism Bureau are ranked towards the lower end of the administrative scale. At the national level, government agencies in China can be divided into two categories, namely: (1) comprehensive government agencies such as the State Development Planning Commission (国家发展计划委员会) and Ministry of Finance (财政部); and (2) sector government agencies such as the Ministry of Construction (建设部) and the National Forestry Bureau (国家林业局) (Chong, 2000). Within a centralised public administration system, local governments at various levels are required to adopt the same administrative structures and arrangements. The administrative portfolios of the comprehensive government agencies are more holistic than those of sector government agencies. Consequently, in the reaches of public administration, the comprehensive government agencies are more influential than the government agencies. For example, the funding of policy implementation is allocated by the Finance Bureau and tourism businesses require an operating license from the Commercial and Industry Bureau. Sector government organisations are therefore dependent on the decisions of the comprehensive government organisations. As noted by Huang, Ryan and Yang in Chapter 12 of this book, this also applies at the national level to the China National Tourism Administration (CNTA). The Tourism Administrative Organisation (TAO) is thus a *sector agency* (Interviewee LJ5). With this type of administrative arrangement, constraints may be imposed by some comprehensive government agencies on the local TAO's ability to initiate and implement a policy or plan.

Within these institutional arrangements, the Lijiang City Tourism Bureau has a 'weak voice' in inter-organisational coordination, as Interviewee LJ2 summed up:

> Sometimes, we feel frustrated in the coordination with other government organisations; most of them are more powerful than us. They just show their support at a superficial level. A few of them will actively participate in the cooperation with us. Some of them are often absent in the meetings called by us for the purpose of cooperation discussion.

Also, due to the low status and administrative rank of the Lijiang Tourism Bureau, other government organisations barely consider or heed suggestions from the Lijiang Tourism Bureau and they view cooperation as *'doing a favour'* (Interviewee LJ3) for the bureau. It is important to change officials' understanding of the importance of tourism and the role of the TAO. Other interviewees supported this viewpoint, including respondents LJ1 and LJ4. One identified understanding and values as the foremost key to improving the effectiveness of tourism policy implementation. He said:

> The inadequacy of the legislation system could be made up by administrative procedures. However, if people's understanding of tourism administration and the role of tourism bureau is unclear and biased, the procedures cannot be established and management measures cannot be adopted. (Interviewee LJ1)

Facilitator 1. Support of the international community

International attention and support was the foremost factor in facilitating the collection of the preservation fee. As stated above, in 1997 Lijiang was approved and listed by UNESCO as a world cultural heritage site. At the time this was perceived as bringing significant benefits to China as well as to the region in terms of reputation and economic and cultural development. Therefore, the protection and development of the ancient town attracted the attention of the Central Government and Yunnan Provincial Government. Influential and important leaders such as former President Jiang Zemin, former Premier Zhu Rongji and the key officials of Yunan Provincial Government each paid separate official visits to the ancient town. The attention of the higher level government brought more pressure on the local government. As one of interviewees (LJ4) commented:

> In China, once higher-level leaders pay attention to an issue, the conflicts between government organisations at the local level can be easily resolved. For example, in Lijiang, the ancient town has been recognised

as a world culture heritage site. The status of ancient town can influence the image of China in international society. Therefore, the issues related with the preservation of the ancient town become the focus of local government. Thus, the support of the Lijiang Municipal Government can motivate cooperation between Lijiang Tourism Bureau and other government organisations. The heads of different government organisations would like to accept the suggestions and requests from Lijiang Tourism Bureau.

According to another of the interviewees, before UNESCO proposed the ancient town preservation fee in 2000, some officials in Lijiang Tourism Bureau and the previous Ancient Town County Government (currently the Ancient Town District Government) had made a similar proposal to the Lijiang Municipal Government as they realised that the increase in the number of tourists since 1998 threatened the town's carrying capacities and there was a need for an additional revenue stream to better finance their management strategies. However, considering that the implementation of this initiative would involve many government departments and that coordination work would be difficult, the municipal government chose not to support the proposal. Given the low status of a local tourism bureau in the public administration system, the support of a local government is critical for success. In this case the support and attention from the international community was decisive in subsequently gaining that support – both from officials at national and at local levels of government.

Facilitator 2. Leadership of Lijiang Municipal Government
The leadership of the Lijiang Municipal Government was also key for the implementation of the preservation fee. Together, the abilities of the Lijiang Tourism Bureau and the Ancient Town Management Bureau would, under normal circumstances, have been inadequate to secure the necessary coordination with other more senior and influential government organisations, but under pressure from the international community and higher level leaders, the Lijiang Municipal Government adopted a leadership role in securing the implementation of the fee and overcoming conflicts of interests

To secure an effective long-term collection of the preservation fee the Lijiang Municipal Government established complementary institutions to regulate the actors in the policy implementation network and encouraged voluntary cooperation. In 2000 the Lijiang Ancient Town Preservation and Management Committee was established by the Municipal Government. It was comprised of government officials from various government agencies involved in the collection of the fee. The goals of this committee were to 'create awareness of the preservation fee among government agencies, provide a channel for relevant parties to address concerns and discuss the division of tasks, and resolve problems' (Lijiang Municipal Government, 2000). In

2003 this committee was reorganised and upgraded to form the Lijiang Ancient Town Protection and Management Bureau as a formal government agency under the Lijiang Municipal Government. A division, named the Ancient Town Preservation Fee Collection Division, was established within the Bureau with responsibilities to assist and monitor the collection of the preservation fee. For example, if some hotel guests refused to pay the fee, employees in this division, who work in 24-hour shifts, had the authority to visit hotels to explain the policy to the guests and ensure the collection of the fee. This division also sends employees to each of the main attractions in Lijiang to facilitate the collection of fees at entry points to the ancient town.

A mechanism was also established to ensure the cooperation of travel agents and hotels in collecting fees on behalf of the government. In China, the hotel star grade assessment and evaluation is conducted by the local TAO and the CNTA. Therefore, in Lijiang the municipal government decided to establish a connection between performance in collecting preservation fees and the evaluation of the hotel's star grading. Although the government organisations involved in the operation of hotels were unwilling to accept such an evaluation method, they effectively had little choice but to accept it and cooperate with the Lijiang Tourism Bureau because they are subordinate to the Lijiang Municipal Government. As one interviewee commented (LJ6):

> The supportive position of Lijiang Municipal Government is very strong. Therefore, almost all government organisations take the collection of ancient town preservation fee seriously, because no one wants to annoy their boss (the Lijiang Municipal Government).

With the travel agents, a link was formed by the Lijiang Municipal Government between their quality guarantee fund and the collection of the preservation fees. The quality guarantee fund is an insurance scheme managed by the Lijiang Municipal Government to compensate tourists in the event of accidents due to inappropriate management on the part of the travel agent. The Lijiang Municipal Government permitted the Lijiang Tourism Bureau to make deductions from the quality guarantee fund if the travel agents failed to collect the ATPF from their clients or did not submit the required sums to the Ancient Town Preservation and Management Bureau. Thus, there was an enforced cooperation required of travel agents and hotels with the local TAO in collecting the fee.

Facilitator 3. Guanxi (personal relations)

In China, *guanxi* is identified as an important parameter that cannot be neglected in understanding both business activity and political phenomena (e.g. Buttery & Wong, 1999; Pye, 1995; Schramm & Taube, 2003; Xin & Pearce, 1996). It also plays a role in the establishment of hotels and, arguably, other aspects of tourism (Gu et al., 2013). It not only means the relations created by law, consanguinity or affection, but it is also a network of subtle interpersonal connections for the purpose of mutual interests and benefits. The term *guanxi* generally means 'special relationships' or 'personal connections' literally. In her extended research, Yang (1994) described *guanxi* like this:

> When it is used to refer to relationships between people, not only can it be applied to husband-wife, kinship, and friendship relations, it can also have the sense of 'social connections,' dyadic relationships that are based implicitly (rather than explicitly) on mutual interest and benefit. Once guanxi is established between two people, each can ask a favor of the other with the expectation that the debt incurred will be repaid sometime in the future. (Yang, 1994: 1)

Gu *et al.* (2013) contextualise *guanxi* as follows:

> From a classical Chinese philosophical perspective *guanxi* relates to social networks within which people perform specific roles and in achieving this they express *ren* (which may be translated as 'humanity'). Following Mozi (ca. 470 BC–ca. 391 BC), this *dao* (way) requires a *chang* (constant) that tends to the well-being of all – hence the Chinese State's pursuit of a 'harmonious society'. (Gu *et al.*, 2013: xx)

They also suggest that, in a transition economy such as that of China, *guanxi* possesses an added importance where legislative and administrative gaps exist as the economy moves from one of centralised control to a mixed public–private sector model where relationships and responsibilities remain, at least for the moment, unclear. Without an institutionalised mechanism, coordination and cooperation among organisations are generally manipulated by some key official/officials within the organisations. Their personal *guanxi* with the key officials of another organisation or their *guanxi* network may influence the relationships at the organisational level. At the beginning of the preservation fee collection, the communication channels between the primary implementation agencies and other government organisations had not been established. The coordination of the local TAO with other players in the policy implementation largely depended on *guanxi*. As described by one interviewee (LJ3):

> Due to multiple government organisations being relevant to the implementation of this policy, the progress of policy implementation depends on other government organisations. The *guanxi* of key officials in our bureau (Lijiang Tourism Bureau) with officials in those organisations helped a lot. If there is a good *guanxi* there, the coordination and cooperation would be much easier.

Guanxi is also identified as an efficient and transaction-cost-reduction coordinating mechanism in the implementation of tourism policy. This study confirmed the findings of the study conducted by Schramm and Taube (2003), who commented that the Chinese *guanxi* network could enable initiative, and conduct and control transactions more efficiently, especially in an environment featuring high degrees of institutional uncertainty. As stated by one interviewee (LJ4):

> Good *guanxi* can create trust between us and other people (in other government organisations). This means we don't need to worry about the complicated meeting procedures, and we will help each other to get things done efficiently.

In China, *guanxi* is symbolic, or social capital, or even political capital to correct any disadvantages in economic institutions, and administrative and legal systems (Buttery & Wong, 1999; Dasgupta & Serageldin, 1999 in Schramm & Taube, 2003; Pye, 1995). *Guanxi* is an alternative means for people to generate personal wealth and establish security under the centrally managed system. It is an alternative to contracts and legal rights in an institutionally disordered environment with great institutional uncertainty in terms of economic interaction. The functions of legal norms present and transparent in most political systems are currently replaced by the more opaque workings of *guanxi* in China, at least in this present stage of economic, social and political transition. As a consequence, the authority and order of Chinese governance is still partially shaped by the processes of *guanxi*. In this study one interviewee defined *guanxi* as the 'complementary resources of institutions', and thus it takes on a function of binding and connecting players in the policy network when they cannot be connected under institutional arrangements.

Conclusion

This study investigated the implementation of the ATPF policy in Lijiang, China. The case study identified the conflicts of interests among key actors, the combinations of government and state-owned business, and the public administrative arrangements of tourism management which have constrained policy implementation. Achievements in the eventual implementation of the preservation fee collection at the current stage can be attributed to the support of the international community, the leadership of local government and the role of *guanxi* (personal relationships).

Constraints in tourism policy implementation, as shown this study, are thought to originate from the system of public administration currently in place. As such, it is difficult to change these constraints because there is strong political resistance to any fundamental change in the public administrative structure in China (Zhang *et al.*, 1999). The facilitating factors identified in this case study are interconnected. The supportive attitude of the international community influenced the attitude of the Central Government which, in turn, exerted pressure on the Lijiang Municipal Government. The actions of the Lijiang Municipal Government in initiating inter-organisational cooperation and designing mechanisms to facilitate inter-organisational coordination helped and reinforced the processes of *guanxi* among the various parties included in implementing the policy to collect the preservation fee.

This case study demonstrates the challenges and difficulties the local tourism administrative organisations face. Also, this case study demonstrates the flexibility and autonomy of local public administration in taking advantage of the social and economic environment to identify remedies to overcome current deficiencies in public administration. This study implies that policy makers should be aware of the strong institutional constraints that exist in the administration of tourism policies in China and the low ranking that is attributed to tourism in the policy making process in spite of the obvious economic significance of the various industry sectors that comprise tourism. Consequently, to facilitate policy implementation, it is important to design mechanisms to address the interests of different parties created by the unequal hierarchies of power and the overlapping areas of responsibilities between government organisations and tourism businesses. Hence one lesson from this case study is that the leadership of the local TAO is critical in achieving inter-organisational coordination and cooperation, and this requires the appropriate exploitation of social, economic and political factors in the local environment.

References

Berg, B.L. (2001) *Qualitative Research Methods for the Social Sciences* (4th edn). Boston, MA: Allyn & Bacon.

Bramwell, B. and Meyer, D. (2007) Power and tourism policy relations in transition. *Annals of Tourism Research* 34 (3), 766–788.

Buttery, E.A. and Wong, Y.H. (1999) The development of a Guanxi framework. *Marketing Intelligence & Planning* 17 (3), 147–154.

Cai, J.C. (2000) On the reform of China's outbound travel management [in Chinese, 试论我国出境旅游管理体制改革问题]. *Tourism Tribune* 15 (3), 13–18.

Chen, W.M. (1999) Some views on the administrative behaviour of tourism industry and its characteristics in China [in Chinese, 风景区保护与发展统一论的若干商榷意见]. *Tourism Tribune* 14 (4), 14–17.

China Daily (2009) The collection of Lijiang Ancient Town Preservation Fee and the protection of World Culture Heritage. ChinaDaily, 31 August, Online at http://www.chinadaily.com.cn/zgzx/2009-08/31/content_8636825_2.htm

Chong, K. (2000) Development of an inter-relationship model of the policy-making process and its application in the Chinese mainland tourism context. Unpublished master's thesis, Hong Kong Polytechnic University, Hong Kong, China.

Ding, R.Z. and Liao, J. (2004) Study on the conflicts in tourism development in China [in Chinese, 中国旅游业发展中的矛盾及调整思路]. *Finance & Economics* 2, 4–7.

Dodds, R. (2007) Sustainable tourism and policy implementation: Lessons from the case of Calvia, Spain. *Current Issues in Tourism* 10 (1), 46–66.

Dredge, D. and Jenkins, J. (2007) *Tourism Planning and Policy*. Brisbane: John Wiley.

Goggin, M.L., Bowman, A.O'M., Lester, J.P. and O'Toole, L.J., Jr. (1990) *Implementation Theory and Practice: Toward a Third Generation*. Glenview, IL: Scott Foresman/ Little, Brown and Company.

Gu, H., Ryan, C., Li, B. and Gao, W. (2013) Political connections, *guanxi* and adoption of CSR policies in the Chinese hotel industry: Is there a link? *Tourism Management* 34, 231–235. doi:10.1016/j.tourman.2012.01.017.

Gunn, L. (1978) Why is implementation so difficult? *Management Services in Government* 33, 169–176.

He, L. (2001) Work report on 'Tourism Standard' implementation [in Chinese, 大力推进旅游标准化工作]. *Tourism Tribune* 16 (2), 5–6.

Hogwood, B.W. and Gunn, L. (1984) *Policy Analysis for the Real World*. Oxford: Oxford University Press.

Jenkins, C.L. and Henry, B.M. (1982) Government involvement in tourism in developing countries. *Annals of Tourism Research* 9 (4), 499–521.

Krutwaysho, O. and Bramwell, B. (2010) Tourism policy implementation and society. *Annals of Tourism Research* 37 (3), 670–691.

Kuang, L. (2001a) Centralization or decentralization: The governments are in a dilemma in developing tourism industry [in Chinese, 集权还是分权：政府发展旅游业的两难境地]. *Tourism Tribune* 2, 23–26.

Kuang, L. (2001b) *Study on Tourism Industry Government-led Development Strategy* [in Chinese, 旅游业政府主导型发展战略研究]. Beijing: China Tourism Publications.

Lai, K., Li, Y. and Feng, X. (2006) Gap between tourism planning and implementation: A case of China. *Tourism Management* 27 (6), 1171–1180.

Lijiang Municipal Government (2000) *Suggestions on Dayan Ancient Town Preservation Fee*. Lijiang: Internal Government Document.

Lijiang Municipal Government (2008) *Suggestions on Tourism Development in Lijiang*. Lijiang: Internal Government Document.

Lin, C.R. (1996) On the predicament of the development of the tourism industry in Fujian Province and its way out [in Chinese, 武汉市东湖风景区的旅游功能定位于开发问题探讨]. *Tourism Tribune* 11 (1), 41–44.

Lincoln, Y.S. and Guba, E.G. (1985) *Naturalistic Inquiry*. Beverly Hills, CA: Sage Publications.

Lipsky, M. (1980) *Street-level Bureaucracy: Dilemmas of the Individual in Public Services*. New York: Russell SAGE Foundation.

Lo, C.W.H., Yip, P.K.T. and Cheung, K.C. (2000) The regulatory style of environmental governance in China: The case of EIA regulation in Shanghai. *Public Administration and Development* 20 (4), 305–318.

Maxwell, J.A. (2005) *Qualitative Research Design: An Interactive Approach*. Thousand Oaks, CA: Sage Publications.

Mazmanian, D.A. and Sabatier, P.A. (1983) *Implementation and Public Policy with a New Postscript*. Lanham, MD: University Press of America.

Puppim de Oliveira, J.A. (2008) Property rights, land conflicts and deforestation in the eastern Amazon. *Forest Policy and Economics* 10 (5), 303–315.

Pye, L.W. (1995) Factions and the politics of Guanxi: Paradoxes in Chinese administrative and political behaviour. *China Journal* 34 (July), 35–53.

Ryan, N. (1996) Some advantages of an integrated approach to implementation analysis: A study of Australian industry policy. *Public Administration* 75, 737–753.

Sabatier, P.A. (1986) Top-down and bottom-up approaches to implementation research: A critical analysis and suggested synthesis. *Journal of Public Policy* 6, 21–48.

Schramm, M. and Taube, M. (2003) The institutional economics of legal institutions, guanxi, and corruption in the PR China. In J. Kidd and F. Richter (eds) *Fighting Corruption in Asia: Causes, Effects, and Remedies* (pp. 271–296). Singapore: World Scientific Publishing.

Shivji, I. (1973) *Tourism and Socialist Development*. Dar es Salaam: Tanzania Publishing House.

Stoker, R.P. (1991) *Reluctant Partners: Implementing Federal Policy*. Pittsburgh, PA: University of Pittsburgh Press.

Strauss, A.L. (1987) *Qualitative Analysis for Social Scientists*. New York: Cambridge University Press.

Wang, G.X. (1998) On the development and management of tourist holiday resorts in the country [in Chinese, 国内旅游度假区开发与管理分析]. *Tourism Tribune* 13 (4), 38–40.

Wei, X.A. (2000) Several problems in tourism development in China [in Chinese, 于旅游发展的几个阶段性问题]. *Tourism Tribune* 15 (5), 9–14.

World Heritage Center (1997) *Old Town of Lijiang. Inscription N26 52 0.012E100 13 59.988*. Washington DC: United Nations Educational, Scientific and Cultural Organization.

Xin, K.R. and Pearce, J.L. (1996) Guanxi. Connections as substitutes for formal institutional support. *Academy of Management Journal* 39 (6), 1641–1658.

Yang, M.M. (1994) *Gifts, Favours and Bouquets: The Art of Social Relations in China*. New York: Cornell University Press.

Yin, R.K. (2003) *Case Study Research: Design and Methods*. Thousand Oaks, CA: Sage Publications.

Younis, T. and Davidson, I. (1990) The study of implementation. In T. Younis (ed.) *Implementation in Public Policy* (pp. 3–14). Aldershot. Dartmouth.

Zhang, H.Q., Chong, K. and Ap, J. (1999) An analysis of tourism policy development in modern China. *Tourism Management* 20 (4), 471–485.

10 Evolution of a Tourism Destination Complex System: Theoretical Foundations

Chunyu Yang and Xuhua (Michael) Sun

Introduction

While there are a number of case studies relating to tourist destination evolution, many are descriptive and fail to properly analyse the determinants of change within the destination. Given this, a better understanding of the complexities of destination evolution has failed to emerge, and the literature lacks a theory of a tourism destination complex system (TDCS), even though generally research in tourism tends toward the empirical (Wang *et al.*, 2005). Current theoretical studies still lie in the phase of drawing on and assimilating the multi-disciplinary experiences of different schools of theory, rather than establishing their own research ideas, methods and theoretical systems based on cross-disciplinary perspectives, and they may be said to still be within a pre-paradigmatic stage.

There are several reasons accounting for this. On one hand, the evolution of TDCS develops with spatial and temporal changes from an initially simple to a more complex structure, and from disorder to order. This evolution highlights modes of action and the relationships among elements of TDCS, which in the space–time continuum is one of endless deconstruction and reconstruction. Inevitably, it results in the fact that TDCS evolves dynamically with spatial and temporal changes as it cycles through different means, directions, speeds and stages, which makes it nearly impossible to attempt to examine the nature and evolutionary mechanisms of TDCS through traditional mechanical or static research thinking and methods. On the other hand, scholars have adopted many different systematic scientific theories including general systems theory, dissipative structure theory, system control theory, system dynamics theory and chaos theory in studies of the tourism destination. Yet while the core concepts, theoretical systems and research methods of different schools of thought have left their distinctive marks, a lack of consensus still remains. There remains no assimilation of these different theories. In part this may reflect the nature of tourism space. Tourism space is composed of tourist source places, tourism destinations and tourism channels linking tourist source places and tourism destinations. For the purposes of this chapter, the concept of tourism space refers to the destination where certain geographical tourism resources, tourism-specific facilities, tourism infrastructure and other relevant conditions are integrated in a systematic way for tourists' stay and activity involvement. It is therefore a complex of urban planning, landscape aesthetics, spatial usage and transport systems within physical geographical features where tourist activities may or may not co-exist with other economic zones and/or activities.

Based on the aforementioned issues, this chapter proposes, under the guidance of system science, explorative methods of 'nonlinear thinking', 'holistic thinking', 'relationship thinking' and 'process thinking' (Peng, 2003), to examine different levels or parts of TDCS. In view of this, this chapter retrospectively examines the roots of basic relationships among key elements forming the tourism destination so as to determine objects, concepts and characteristics of a theory still under construction. Consequently, the chapter explores fundamental problems in the theory of TDCS evolution by tracing from the micro-level relations between the constituent elements to the macro-level relationship of the system. Theoretical issues examined in this chapter include the meaning and features of TDCS and the evolutionary mechanism of TDCS and associated concepts. The research aims to construct a theoretical framework of TDCS evolution in order to enrich and improve a specific research stream in tourism studies, and help achieve sustainable development of tourism destinations.

Conceptual Grounds of a TDCS

Meaning of TDCS

Definitions of 'system' vary with different schools of system studies. However, the concept of TDCS can be understood from the common ground already established in system theories. First, TDCSs are composed of interrelated material objects. As Bunge (1981) argues, any object of a substance is a system or an integral part of the system; not only physical and chemical systems are material, but so too are organisms and social systems. Second, TDCSs are built and arranged by human beings. The TDCS is the entity constructed by the people at the place to be recognized. It is 'a hypothesis or model' (Rosen, 1985: 47) where people use symbols and rules of syntax to construct selectively, based on the people's 'experience unit'. According to Gaines (1979), the system is what we want to identify as a system; we create and build a system instead of expecting to find a system; many different systems can be constructed in terms of the same experience.

Therefore, the meaning of TDCSs is required to contain at least the following three characteristics (Yan *et al.*, 2006):

- the existence of entities distinguishable from one another in the system, which are called elements;
- relationships or relation networks among all the elements;
- these relationships sufficiently produce a newly organized whole as well as new system-analysing levels that can be differentiated from the surrounding environment.

The above features should be included in defining TDCS either from the standpoint of general system theory, dissipative structure theory or from the standpoint of other system science theories.

TDCS as a system has various elements that are not accidentally stacked together without any relationship, but are closely interrelated and interacted. The interaction of the so-called system elements refers to mutual influence, reciprocal restraint or mutual control and even the state of being coupled together. Namely, they change each other's status or state space, and change other's behaviour routes or ways of acting. For example, a change in the political and economic situation would impact on tourism activities, because politics and economics act as social determinants of tourism development. Tourism development is restricted by political and economic conditions, yet at the same time, under certain conditions, tourism can also affect political and economic situations. The same interactive relationship applies between the tourism environment's carrying capacity and tourist arrivals. The tourism environment may undergo corresponding variations of carrying capacity as tourist arrivals change in volume and type. In the initial stages of tourism destination development, a pristine ecological environment (here we mean a broadly defined ecological environment covering natural, social, economic and cultural environment carrying capacity issues) attracts admiring visitors; when a TDCS develops to a certain extent, a deterioration in the ecological environment, in turn, would slow down the continuous increase of tourist numbers. The coupling relationship between elements of TDCSs can be illustrated in depth with Bertalanffy's system equations (Bertalanffy, 1987).

Supposing a TDCS has n elements, any element will be represented by X_i ($i = 1, 2, \ldots n$). It is also assumed that Q_i is a certain measure of X_i, and its changing amount will be $\Delta Q_i/\Delta t$ or dQ_i/dt. If the change is continuous, the interaction between elements of the TDCS can be represented by a set of differential equations, namely:

$$\frac{dQ_i}{dt} = f_i(Q_1, Q_2, \ldots, Q_n) \quad i = 1, 2, \ldots, n \qquad (10.1)$$

This equation shows that state changes (dQ_i/dt) of any element in a TDCS are the functions or results of all the elements, and that the character changes of any element (changes of Q_i on the right side of the equation) may cause the changes of all other elements' characters (dQ_i/dt). This equation expresses the interactions and the interaction networks of the elements of a TDCS, different from the general expression of individual causation.

The relationship expressed here includes not only the relationship of Q_i acting on Q_j (i.e. Q_i and Q_j respectively represent the reason and the result), but also the circular causality of Q_i acting on Q_j and Q_j reacting on Q_i. This circular causality is called *feedback*. We can take the relationship between supply and demand of tourists at a tourist destination as an example and conduct the feedback analysis on its process of evolution. First, at the initial stages of tourism destination development with the demand of a small number of tourists, some local residents begin to provide tourists with simple food service and accommodation. As the popularity of the tourist destination grows, tourism demand increases rapidly, resulting in a shortage of supply at the destination. In the phase of tourist rapid growth, local employment is initially generated and tourism supplies increase due to a large number of local and externally generated investments. At this stage, tourism demand and tourism supply synchronously leap in line with rapid development. This is the process of positive feedback in the system development. However, booms come to an end. Further growth of tourist numbers exceeds what the destination's carrying capacity allows, exerting in turn a negative impact on the destination. The marked issues are likely to be overcrowding, serious environmental pollution and tourism quality degradation, which trigger a decline in travel demand and force the destination into recession. At the signs of early decline in the tourism destinations, due to reduced travel demand, local and foreign investors speculating in tourism correspondingly begin to reduce or withdraw their investment. The economy of the destination may decline rapidly, consequently leading to diminishing tourism supplies and exacerbated unemployment. On the other hand, reduced tourism demand, excessive tourism supply and the reductions in the price of tourism products cause loss of profit in tourism enterprises, which also lead to reduced investments by firms. Following the trend, tourism revenues will continue to drop and eventually depress economic development. At this stage, there exists significant unemployment or an emigration of labour, excessive idle tourist facilities, and losses of tourism enterprises or even bankruptcies. At this critical moment, the destination faces either decline or revival, which represents the negative feedback process of the TDCS evolution (see Figure 10.1).

Evidently, both positive and negative feedbacks co-exist in the evolution process of TDCS. They do not differ in sequence and importance, but vary as to which type of feedback dominates at different times and exhibit quantity accumulation. In the early state of TDCS evolution, due to a low level of

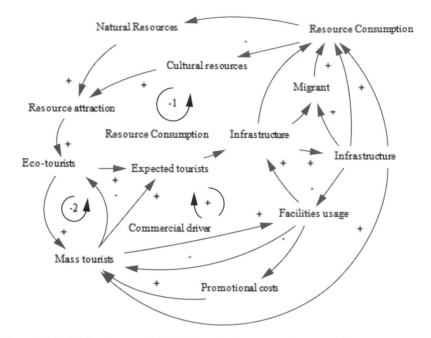

Figure 10.1 Feedback map of the TDCS evolution process (adapted from Xu, 2006)

quantity accumulation and insignificant negative feedback, the negative effects generated are not strong enough to adversely influence tourism destination evolution. During this period, positive feedback plays a leading role in the rapid development of tourism destinations. As tourism develops further, a variety of negative factors increase and thereby negative feedback is strengthened. When negative feedback dominates, tourism development will suffer from the recession until the collapse of the TDCS, or a new equilibrium under new conditions is achieved.

Figure 10.1 describes the process, not as a simplified causality by examining only a few specific factors, but as illustrating the universal interactions and diverse networks among the elements of a TDCS.

Modern natural science contends that any system contains three factors, i.e. material, energy and information; by exchanging these three factors, varying interactions and interrelationships among system elements can be achieved. There is no exception for TDCS. The interactions and interrelations among the constituent elements of a TDCS originate from the formation of tourist flows and consequent exchanges of both internal and external material flows, energy flows and information flows at the destination. In this process, the relationship of mutual restraint, mutual control and reciprocal influence formed among the constituent elements of a TDCS can be called coupling relationships. These coupling relationships are commonly found among the elements with associations and can be demonstrated both between elements in pairs which constitute TDCS and at the organizational level among different subsystems. Such coupling relationships cannot be built once and/or unchangingly. They have the characteristic that the first 'adaption' works as the reason for triggering the second 'adaption', which in turn results in the interchange of a causal loop network. The summed total of these relationships constitutes a stable structure within a certain period of time, space and state, thus forming the organizational structure of the destination and its way of integration, that is, the structure of the TDCS, which differentiates a TDCS from other systems and environments. The constraints and controls posed by the coupling relationships among elements of TDCS do not mean that elements are associated with each other in an entirely unchanged and static way; they nevertheless define modes of *law and order* to the activities and variations in the system.

Therefore, we conclude that a TDCS is a complex adaptive system evolving with time and space. On the basis of mutual adaptation, constituent elements of TDCS form a specific structure and functions by coupling themselves to affect each other. They gradually form a more complex function-coupling system at different levels by exchanging material flows, energy flows and information flows within and outside the system to improve and regulate their rules of conduct, thus continuously perfecting the system's structure and functions so as to adapt to a complex and ever-changing external environment.

Characteristics of TDCS

Through examining the meaning of TDCS, we found that a TDCS has the following features in addition to the features of nonlinearity, complexity and integrity that characterize any general complex system.

Subjectivity

The subject status and the subjectivity existence of the system's constituent elements are among the most basic features of TDCS. Without the subject status and subjectivity existence of the key elements, tourism destination complex adaptive systems would not come into being, because the involvement of human beings with prominent cognitive ability has equipped a TDCS with more proactive *sense of organization, learning* and *adaptability*. However, the initiative to adapt must be based on subject status and subjectivity existence as an essential precondition.

Because constituent elements of a TDCS with the nature of subjectivity have cognitive differences and distinct motivations, they *collaborate* through *competition*. On the basis of *collaboration*, they form *coupling forces* whose direction and size vary with time and space, and improve their behaviours to adapt to the complicated external environment through the feedback mechanism of systems. The entire evolution of TDCS, including the generation, differentiation of new levels and emergence of diversity, gradually derives from such a foundation. As a dynamic system, the performance of a TDCS is characterized by the fact that, rather than a passive recipient of environmental impact, the system exerts influences on the environment while keeping itself independent of the environment. Accordingly, the behaviours of a TDCS are self-motivated with the integration of environmental stimuli and their own purposes. Through acquiring and processing information from the environments and interacting with the environments, relevant *regularity* can be extracted as a reference for the behaviours to achieve their objectives (Tan, 2007).

Adaptability

Compared to other complex systems, the TDCS has a more proactive *sense of organization, learning* and *adaptability* in some unique forms and states, such as unexpected effects caused by accidental events like war, epidemics and earthquakes, change of competition-and-cooperation relationship among destinations, and dynamic adjustments of tourism policies. TDCS possesses the ability to self-adjust its structure and behaviours so as to adapt to the environment. In other words, the relationship among the constituent elements of a TDCS and the external environment is no longer the traditional simple, passive, one-way causal relationship, but embodies the process of active learning, adjustment and adaptation. They couple themselves to influence each other and are united on the basis of the mutual *adaptation*. The positive and the negative feedback loops formed in the coupling process play a stimulating and suppressing effect on the evolution of tourism destinations, impelling tourism destinations to learn from the environment and gain experiences. By improving and controlling their behavioural rules to adapt to the complicated external environment, tourism destinations as a whole can demonstrate coordination and sustain their behavioural patterns.

Dynamic balance

The tourism destination complex adaptive system itself, involving people-to-people and people-to-place subsystems, has the nature of self-stability. In other words, it always has a condition or mechanism to resist constant interference from the external environment (such as the impact of natural disasters on the physical environment, transportation, accommodation and other infrastructural subsystems in tourism destinations, as well as the system oscillation caused by the abnormal fluctuations of tourist numbers at certain periods due to changes in the political, economic, social and cultural factors). When the external environment breaks the balance of the destination's system by force, it can always return to equilibrium, or maintain itself to the extent permitted by its structure. It can be called a homeostatic mechanism (living structure) which is inherent in the adaptability of TDCS (Jin, 2005).

The functioning process of the homeostatic mechanism in TDCS predisposes the overall evolution of tourism destinations to equilibrium, but its internal balance is continually subject to change. The balance of its evolution is not static, but dynamic, which can be manifested in an evolution curve of a nonlinear developmental process with short-term *oscillation* and long-term *cycles*. However, the dynamic balance of TDCS functions within its limits. The dynamic balance will be broken if the system is stressed beyond a certain range of current capacity. However, at any one period of time, the state of dynamic equilibrium in TDCS ensures that we can understand its characteristics and evolutionary mechanisms.

Evolution Mechanism and Regularity of a TDCS

Evolution mechanism

Coupling forces

Constituent elements of TDCS, through their own force, affect the evolution of tourism destinations. Such forces include changes in environmental carrying capacity, exchange rate fluctuation, political relations between countries (harmonious or otherwise), quality and range of tourism resources, transportation, guidelines of government policy making, and tourism supply and demand. However, instead of directly influencing the evolution of TDCS, they exert an overall impact on the evolutionary process of tourism destinations by coupling with other system elements. Different in nature, size, directions, these forces vary constantly with different spatial and temporal dimensions. There are many factors triggering change of these individual forces, including change of spatial and temporal dimensions in which constituent elements of tourism destinations are located, the volatility of other forces, the disturbance of environmental factors and their own fluctuations, etc. A TDCS structure relies on the existence of the forces and their interactions, and the constituent factors of the system interact in a jointly comprised open environment. Through the interactions, a comprehensive impact forms, shaped by the collective power of the coupling forces.

Coupling forces are the power source of TDCS evolution

When we examine from different levels or parts of TDCS and probe apparent one-way causal relationships, closer examination reveals positive and negative feedback loops formed by coupling forces (Xu, 2001, 2005, 2006) that universally exist among the various constituent parts of tourism destinations. Under the three combined conditions of irreversibility, limitation and self-organization, one force can be generated from the system within a certain tempo-spatial scope; it then passes on and transforms several times, and eventually returns to form a loop. This process can be called *self-coupling*. Positive and negative feedbacks make self-coupling oscillating circuits to form circles, i.e. positive and negative feedback loops. The former *self-stimulates* and *self-encourages* the evolution of tourism destination, thus contributing to continuous generation of new things. This represents the normal pattern for tourism destinations' self-renewal, development and evolution. However, either a positive or negative feedback loop amplifies the tourism destination's departure from equilibrium. For example, in the initial development of a tourism destination, the arrival of tourists signals for increasing investment. Under the amplification of positive and negative feedbacks, a series of factors interact to increase the tourist numbers at the destination. At the same time, the cumulated adverse effects caused by the continuous development of tourism in the destination will take it beyond its initial carrying capacity at some future time, thus paving the way for the destination's decline. Negative feedback plays the role of *self-stability* and *suppression* of the destination's tourism evolution. It regulates tourism destinations to maintain its stability by comparing the difference between the inputs and outputs in a destination (see Figure 10.2). Once the destination is overloaded with large tourist numbers that go beyond the tourism environmental carrying capacity, the TDCS automatically detects the signal by comparative devices, and applies various restrictive measures through the adjustment mechanism to ensure an orderly and stable development.

Positive and negative feedback loops, like a pair of push and pull forces interacting and influencing each other in the evolution process of a TDCS, would propel the destination to *fluctuate* around the equilibrium point of its evolution, thus providing the endless developmental power for the evolution. These two feedback loops, along the process of the destination's development

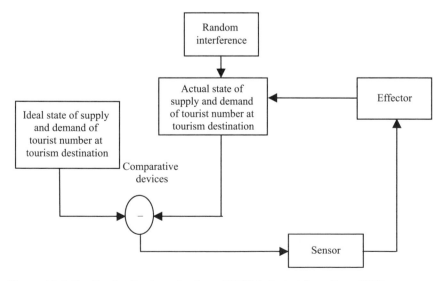

Figure 10.2 Feedback-adjust mechanism of TDCS (adapted from Bao, 1986)

and evolution, can also generate more complicated coupling networks functioning at different levels, which in turn promote the evolution of TDCS. It is in this sense that coupling forces can be regarded as the *engine* of the TDCS evolution.

Coupling forces explain the origin of the homeostatic mechanism of TDCS evolution

The concept of coupling forces emphasizes that TDCS is a whole unit of interrelated and interactive constituent elements. In other words, forces of the constituent elements, by *accommodating each other*, form an *ultimate system coupling force* to influence the evolution process of TDCS. *Accommodating each other* refers to the interaction among various elements; each element can not only effectively stretch/contract or fluctuate but also form the harmonious state of accommodating each other through its stretching/contracting or fluctuation, thereby serving as the basis of the homeostatic mechanism of TDCS (see Figure 10.2).

However, the adjustment mechanism of negative feedback in the TDCS evolution only explains the maintenance of the system's homeostatic mechanism; it does not reveal the origin of this adjustment mechanism. First, we need to determine the constants which must remain unchanged in the homeostasis of TDCS; afterwards we can identify and find the information agencies with targeted differences as well as the association between the information-transfer agency and the effector. From the perspective of coupling relationships among the constituent elements of TDCS, we can interpret how the target values are determined in the homeostatic system.

When we analyse the relationship between the environmental carrying capacity and the life cycle of TDCS, taking into account feedback mechanisms in examining the system homeostasis, we must determine the equilibrium values in order to analyse the entire system; however, we cannot ascertain what the system equilibrium is. From the perspective of the coupling relationship discussed above, we found that both carrying capacity and life cycle of TDCS influence and act on each other. For example, changes of tourist numbers in each stage on the evolutionary curve of the tourism destination life cycle will impact on the tourism environmental carrying capacity. There exists a corresponding threshold value for the tourism environmental carrying capacity and these threshold values at different stages will in turn affect the tourist numbers and types of tourists being attracted. It is this relationship that determines the existence of the TDCS equilibrium; it is also this relationship that maintains the feedback regulation in tourism destinations on the destinations' departure from equilibrium. In fact, the coupling relationship which lies among the constituent elements of TDCS has determined the possible existence of its equilibrium point. According to Ashby's Control Theory and methods, the number of equilibrium points can be deduced from the interaction patterns of coupling relationships in TDCS (Zhang, 1965); whether the feedback is positive or negative can be judged by the stability of equilibrium points. As a result, the origin of homeostatic mechanism can be adequately explained by coupling forces and relationships of TDCS.

Coupling networks

With mutual adaptation and competition among the large number of constituent elements, tourism destinations continually evolve into a self-organized, multi-dimensional, multi-level, multi-variable complex evolutionary system; the coupling relationships among the constituent elements of tourism destinations form even more complicated coupling networks functioning at different levels as time passes. The coupling networks are generally characterized by the system elements' coupling relationships possessing a clear hierarchy and significantly increased self-control as well as competitiveness as the system evolves. Coupling relationships not only blend together the constituent elements of TDCS but also, in a higher structural level, bridge different subsystems of a tourism destination. Thus, a fully functional coupling system can be formed whereby the output of a subsystem services the input of another (or its own) subsystem. Within a certain time, space and state, a stable structural model can be formed, as can the organizational forms and the integrative patterns of a destination, i.e. the TDCS structure. Therefore, the TDCS evolves as an integrative system.

In a market economy, the price is the fundamental factor in determining tourism supply and demand. According to the laws of demand and supply, the higher the price, the less demand will be, and the more supply will be; on the contrary, the lower the price the more tourism demand will be, and the less tourism supply will be. Therefore, tourism product prices balance supply and demand, while the reciprocal relationship is that tourism supply and demand generate a balanced price in the tourism market. This is further illustrated in Figure 10.3.

With the horizontal axis Q representing the number of tourism products and the vertical axis P representing the price of tourism products, the price curve D of tourism demand and the price curve S of tourism supply can be plotted in the same graph (Figure 10.3). The price curve D of tourism demand and the price curve S intersect at point E. Point E can be called the equilibrium of tourism supply and tourism demand as tourism supply equals tourism demand; then the corresponding price P_0 is called the equilibrium price, and the corresponding number of tourism products Q_0 is called the balanced output. If the price of tourism products rises from P_0 to P_1, the travel demand will be reduced to Q_1, while tourism supply will increase to Q_2; thus supply exceeds demand in the tourism market ($S > D$), by namely, $Q_2 - Q_1$. If the price of tourism products drops from P_0 to P_2, tourism demand will increase to Q_3, while tourism supply reduces to Q_4; thus demand exceeds supply in tourism market ($D > S$), by namely, $Q_4 - Q_3 = -(Q_3 - Q_4)$.

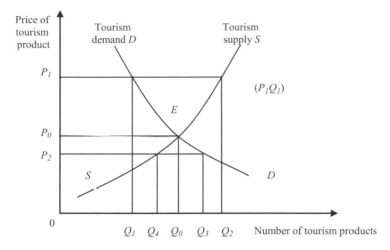

Figure 10.3 Relationship of tourism destination supply and demand

The equilibrium relationship between tourism demand and tourism supply has been analysed from a static perspective in the above-mentioned relationship. However, from the actual mechanism of economic operation, once tourism supply forms, it will be relatively stable; however, tourism supply varies with the price of tourism products within its capacity. The relationship between tourism supply and demand is informed by a dynamic equilibrium. Theorems in microeconomics prove that, holding other conditions unchanged, the market price of commodities and their production quantity are determined by the intersection point (P_0Q_0) of the curve $S - S$ and the curve $D - D$. When the market price is $P_1 \neq P_0$, and the production quantity is $Q_1 \neq Q_0$, the price will automatically converge toward P_0 and Q_0, as shown in Figure 10.4 by the trajectories of the cobweb, and maintain the stability of P_0 and Q_0 to some extent. The same law applies to the determination of tourism product price and tourism supply-and-demand relationship.

What Figure 10.4 discloses is part of the universally known law of economic value functioning in a market economy system. Why does such a law function in a market economy system? Jin (2005) elaborated this from a methodological perspective and posits that microeconomics regards the market system as a functional coupling system. We hereby borrow his theoretical lens to run a detailed analysis on the functional coupling network in TDCS.

Initially, each subsystem in a tourism destination's functional coupling system follows the general law of causality. The first causal relationship lies between the price of tourism products and tourism demand. Holding other conditions constant, the higher the price, the lower the demand, and consumers can buy alternative products (certain types of tourism products can be substituted and tourism products demonstrate high price elasticity on

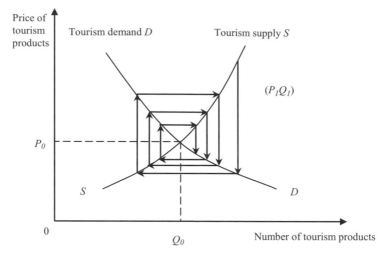

Figure 10.4 Convergence map of tourism destination supply and demand

demand). Thus, as illustrated in Figure 10.5, the first subsystem D is generated in which the input is the price P and the output is the purchasing quantity Q_1. With other conditions unchanged, when P increases, purchasing quantity Q_1 decreases. The curve $D - D$ in Figure 10.4 represents the relationship between the input P and the output Q_1. What can affect the structure of this subsystem is a variety of social psychological factors. The second subsystem S represents another well-known general causal relationship in microeconomics. With other conditions unchanged, the higher the price of tourism products, the more tourism suppliers are willing to produce. The structure of S is mostly determined by suppliers' motive of pursuing profits. The input of the subsystem S is also P, so the greater P is, the greater Q (actual production quantity), the output of S, will be. It can be illustrated by the curve $S - S$ in Figure 10.4. However, these two subsystems alone are not sufficient to form the tourism market economy system. In the tourism

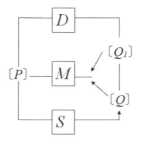

Figure 10.5 Tourism market functional coupling network

market system there is another key subsystem, M, i.e. the subsystem of tourism market mechanism. In a market economy, the functional role of the tourism market is achieved through the market mechanism. The market mechanism refers to the internal relationships of mutual influence and mutual restraint formed in the exchange activities and transactions by all the parties in the tourism market. Specifically, it is an approach of combining such factors as supply and demand, price, competition, risk and so on, employed by each tourism market player to conduct economic activities in the tourism market. It is the process of combined forces of the supply-and-demand mechanism, price mechanism, competition mechanism and risk mechanism. It can also be explained by the general causality law; however, in this subsystem, the input is Q_1 and Q and the output is P. The output of M is determined by Q_1 and Q. Obviously the tourism market mechanism can also regarded as an embodiment of causality.

When tourism product supply is greater than demand, the seller on the market will tend to reduce price P; when supply is less than demand, the seller will increase price P. If $Q_1 < Q$, M will not make the price change. The inputs Q_1 and Q affecting P cannot be written out by a simple function, but it is a generalized causality. With other conditions unchanged, the function of M can be simplified as follows: when the demand Q_d is unequal to the supply Q_s, M will respond respectively by lowering or increasing prices or maintaining the same price based on whether $Q_d > Q_s$ or $Q_d > Q_s$ or $Q_d = Q_s$. Obviously, the input and the output of these three subsystems couple each other to form a typical functional coupling system, which partly represents the tourism market system (see Figure 10.5). The law of value determines the function of this coupling network. As long as we make some simplifications, we can get the equilibrium shown in Figure 10.4.

In general, it is impossible for the tourism products to be extremely scarce and overstocked. Tourism product suppliers always want the products to be sold out. Thus, M always adjusts the price P to the state in which the demand controlled by price was equal to the supply at that time, i.e. $Q_d = Q_s$. Under the condition of no overstocking of tourism products, the tourism market mechanism will quickly adjust the price of tourism products at a time to the extent that the market demand equals the tourism product supply. Once Q_s is determined, so is Q_d, and P is subsequently determined. Therefore, the coupling of M and D can be simplified into a new subsystem D to handle: the input of D is $\{Q\}$, while the output is $\{P\}$; the function of Q and P is the same as the demand curve. Thus, we can get a more simplified illustration (Figure 10.6) coupled by these two subsystems: P and S.

Through the above analysis we can understand the implications reflected in Figure 10.4. The equilibrium price drawn by intersecting the curve $D - D$ and the curve $S - S$ not only possesses mathematical significance; more importantly, it also represents the function coupling of two subsystems. Thus, it clarifies why P_1Q_1 moves along the track of a cobweb.

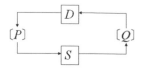

Figure 10.6 Simplified chart of system function coupling

The movement track mimics the change process of the input and the output in the function coupling system. For example, supposing $Q = Q_1$ at the beginning, the price will be determined by the result of inputting Q_1 into D, i.e. $P_1 = D (Q_1)$; when P_1 is determined, Q at the next time will be redefined, because tourism product providers will determine a new production scale based on the price. Q_2 at the next time will be determined by the result of inputting P_1 into S, i.e. $Q_2 = S (P_1)$; the function coupling makes the values of P and Q constantly change. Clearly, Q_1 determines P_1, *and then* P_1 determines Q_2... This process can be marked by the $P \times Q$ phase plane with the supply curve and the demand curve. It follows the rule of finding the corresponding P_1 in the $D - D$ line according to Q_1 and then locating P_1 into the $S - S$ line to find the corresponding Q_2, and so on. The whole trajectory of P and Q is shown in Figure 10.4, i.e. the convergence map. The system can return to the original equilibrium point through the tourism market mechanism in the case of external interference, making the tourism economic system stabilized. However, this only represents one case of the real-world tourism economic system evolution. There are two modes resulting from the interaction of the mutually conditioning and reciprocally causal coupling loops between tourism supply and demand: *self-affirmation* and *self-negation*. The former shows that the tourism economic system is in a steady state; the latter shows that the system is unstable. This mutually conditioning and reciprocally causal relationship is the basic mechanism in which each part of the tourism economic system adjusts one to another to maintain their vitality. Figures 10.7, 10.8, 10.9, and 10.10, respectively,

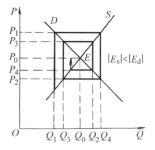

Figure 10.7 Convergent cobweb

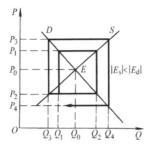

Figure 10.8 Divergent cobweb

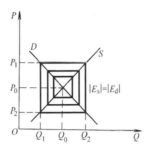

Figure 10.9 Proprietary cobweb

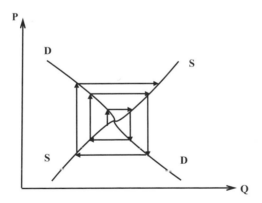

Figure 10.10 Nonlinearities fluctuation

represent the four types of mutually causal relationships between tourism product demand and supply as well as their manifestations.

The first form, as demonstrated in Figure 10.7, is the cobweb convergent at the intersection point (P_0, Q_0) of the supply curve and the demand curve. Relative to the price axis, the absolute value of the demand curve slope is greater than the absolute value of the supply curve slope. When the tourism market deviates from the original state of equilibrium due to any external interference, the actual price and the actual production will fluctuate around the equilibrium level; however, the fluctuation diminishes gradually towards the equilibrium point E. Thus, the state represented by the equilibrium point E is stable. In other words, due to external factors, when tourism product prices and production deviate from the equilibrium value (P_0, Q_0), the homeostatic mechanism in the tourism economy system can make tourism product prices and output automatically restore equilibrium.

The second form, as shown in Figure 10.8, represents a divergent cobweb. Relative to the price axis, the absolute value of the demand curve slope is less than the absolute value of the supply curve slope. When the tourism market deviates from the original state of equilibrium due to any external interference, the actual price and the actual yield will fluctuate divergently, moving away from the price and production quantity determined by the equilibrium point E. In this form, the equilibrium state represented by the equilibrium point E is unstable, and thus is called unstable equilibrium.

The third form is called proprietary cobweb. In such a system, the absolute value of the supply curve slope is equal to the absolute value of the supply demand slope. When the tourism market deviates from the original state of equilibrium due to external interference, the actual price and actual yield fluctuate around the equilibrium point at the same rate (Figure 10.9). The fluctuation does not further deviate from the equilibrium point, nor does it converge toward the equilibrium point.

The fourth form is called nonlinearities fluctuation. In such a system, demand and supply are both nonlinear. When the tourism market deviates from the original state of equilibrium due to external interference, the actual output of tourism products and the actual price show the nonlinear fluctuation shown in Figure 10.10.

The mutually causal relationships between tourism product demand and supply in a tourism market economy system also include an alternative mode of interaction, i.e. the imbalance between supply and demand. When travel demand and supply elasticities do not match each other, the price will be in an unstable state with endless fluctuations. No matter what the supply is at the beginning, there will always be squared spirals, enclosed circles or irregular fluctuations that catch the system in an endless oscillation as it seeks homeostasis. This is the negative mode of mutual causality between tourism product demand and supply. This mode of self-negation indicates the instability of tourism product price, uncertain production, and constant disturbance of the whole TDCS.

When such a conceptualization is extended from economic systems to TDCS, the overall conceptual framework of TDCS can be established. In our framework, the holistic entity of TDCS is symbolized as W, and it is coupled with lower-level functions like $W_A, W_B, W_C, W_D \ldots W_M \ldots$. Within the holistic entity, there exist different parts $A, B, C, D \ldots M \ldots$ with the functions of W_A,

W_B, W_C, W_D...W_M... So the overall TDCS W can be regarded as the organizational system through coupling different functions by the subsystems A, B, C, D...M.... Because each subsystem follows the general causal law, both the input and the output can be regulated and allocated. The input is the condition of a subsystem while the output serves as its function. Suppose the condition set of subsystem M is $X_m = \{X_1, X_2, \ldots X_i\}$, and the function set for M is $Y_m = \{Y_1, Y_2, \ldots Y_i\}$. As the function is determined by the condition, the follow formula is generated (Jin, 2005):

$$Y_m = M \ [X_m] \tag{2}$$

Here, M mirrors the relationships between X_m and Y_m and represents the structure of subsystem M. $Y_m = M \ [X_m]$ indicates that when the condition set X_m exists and the system structure has been determined, the function set Y_m is determined. This is also a demonstration of the general causal law. A subsystem can be illustrated as the following equation (3):

$$\{Y_m\} \leftarrow \boxed{M} \rightarrow \{X_m\} \tag{3}$$

In a TDCS, different tourism subsystems like A, B, C, D ... M... are coupled together, making the output of some subsystems act as the input of others or themselves. This is how a tourism destination, as a multi-organizational, multi-level structure involving both people-to-people and people-to-place relations, can be developed into a complex system through functional coupling networks. Obviously, functional coupling networks are not some unknown entities in the system. Jin (2005) argued that if we treat the input and output sets in an organizational system as the observable (physical) parts in the organization, the functional coupling networks are the relationships among them. That any organization has a corresponding living system structure does not mean that a new unknown entity in the structure is found; rather, it means that self-coupling does exist in the relationships among these parts and purports to maintain functional coupling.

TDCS evolution

Based on the above discussion, it should be noted that the TDCS evolution is one type of evolution with the characteristic of unified diversity. This marks a big difference from our previous understanding of the TDCS evolution. The TDCS evolution is not only an evolving process of destruction and disintegration from simplicity to complexity and from low level to high level, but also an evolution of unified diversity from one specification to another and from one complex state to another (Yan, 1993). The meaning of the evolution can be defined in broad and narrow senses. The TDCS evolution in a broad sense includes any possible change, such as its birth, growth, maturity, stagnation and demise. Judging internally, the evolution in a narrow sense refers to the fundamental change of its structure mode, from one structure to another structure with a different nature; judging externally, the evolution in a narrow sense refers to the fundamental change of its overall morphology and behaviour patterns, from one pattern to another pattern with a different nature.

Second, the TDCS evolution is not the restructuring of various original components, but a new unified diversity. Symmetry breaking (referring to the sub-stable state) reflects tempo-spatial evolution of destinations inevitably making new diversity to replace old diversity, new unity to replace old unity, and making the process irreversible.

Third, the TDCS evolution contains coupling functions of constituent elements. A tourism destination developing from one version of unified diversity to another reflects the outcome of coupling relationship development among its constituent elements. *Self-coupling* and self-winding and the resultant looping circles formed by them constitute the rise and fall of tourism destinations, thus proving a steady power to promote destination evolution and development.

To conclude, the TDCS evolution is a specific process of transferring one form of unified diversity to another form of unified diversity. This evolution process has been endlessly motivated by self-coupling and self-winding among constituent elements of a TDCS as well as the system fluctuation informed by its feedback loops. The homeostatic mechanism derived from coupling forces of system elements defines the essence of system development and evolution. Tourism destinations are self-organizing systems under the influence of complicated competition and coordination of internal and external factors. It is through such a holistic approach that tourism destinations form, evolve, develop and decline, and that the process can be observed and studied.

Bifurcation points

Leiper (1995) argues that tourism is an industry with great diversity with two major factors, i.e. tourism supply and travel demand. Tourism demand from source markets is unstable, seasonal and disorderly; tourism supply in destinations is vulnerable and inflexible in the short term, and thus both contribute to the fluctuating fortunes of tourism destinations. The TDCS evolutionary process is in the fluctuations caused by change in these two determining variables. Adaptability, due to human decision making, is a characteristic of TDCS, but outcomes are subject to the environment *and* the system's self-evolution. Therefore, the fluctuations in the evolution process differ from those that arise alone from the system's low-level passive responses to environmental changes.

Tourism destinations' ways of coping with environmental changes tend to be diverse. Passive responses include those toward climate change, short-term dramatic environmental changes like rain and snow, and those caused by various social and natural emergencies like strikes, demonstrations, terrorist attacks, violence, war, epidemics and plague. Active responses, on the other hand, include relevant policies that aim to enhance tourism destination system functions, increase efficiency, promote harmonious development of tourism, or to adjust the exchange rate, amend the national holiday system (e.g. China's 'Golden Week' holiday system was introduced to stimulate domestic demand in 1999), improve competition and/or cooperative relationships among tourist destinations, develop new resources, and utilize new technologies.

No matter what causes the fluctuations, whether it is due to passive responses caused by the environment or an active adjustment for the sake of system development, once the fluctuations of a variable meet or exceed the threshold value a system can support, there will be an essential change in the structure of the destination. Such a threshold value point can be called a *bifurcation point* in the TDCS evolution (Russell & Faulkner, 1999; Zahra & Ryan, 2007). Due to uncertainties, multiple possibilities lie at bifurcation points in the TDCS evolution. Ultimately, the actualization of any given possibility will be determined by the system coupling force informed through the combination of various elements and conditions in the vicinity of bifurcation points (the coupling force's nature, size and direction will affect the whole TDCS choice of next move at a bifurcation point). A destination is provided with multiple possible path choices at a bifurcation point, making its self-organizing process follow different possible ways, directions, speeds and phases, and consequently forming new system structures and functions. The existence of bifurcation points also highlights the nature of uncertainty and non-repeatability of TDCS. In other words, the existence of bifurcation points renders the destination self-organizing process complicated and irreversible. This explains why destination evolution life cycle curves described in the literature differ from each other. Figures 10.11–10.14

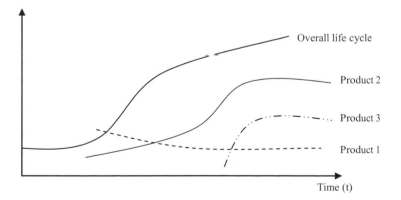

Figure 10.11 The components of tourism product life cycle (adapted from Haywood, 1986)

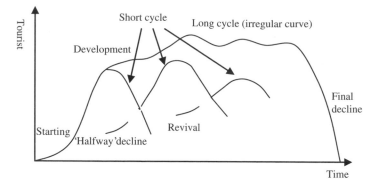

Figure 10.12 Model of dual life cycle (adapted from Yu, 1997)

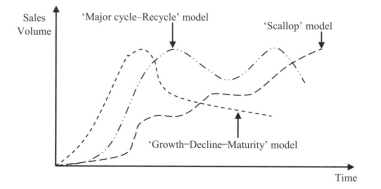

Figure 10.13 Three models of product life cycle (adapted from Lundtorp & Wanhill, 2001)

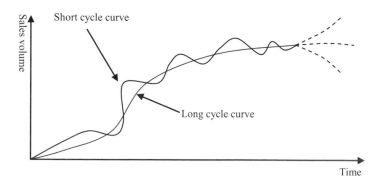

Figure 10.14 Model of two-cycle of tourism product structure (adapted from Yang & Lu, 2004)

show different shapes of destination evolution curve we found in the literature (Haywood, 1986; Lundtorp & Wanhill, 2001; Yang & Lu, 2004; Yu, 1997). These empirical studies evidenced that in reality very few tourism destinations follow the standard S-shaped curve described in Butler's (1980) model, but are characterized by various abnormal development trends.

Conclusion

Tourism destination evolution is influenced by numerous factors that are themselves intertwined and correlated. In essence, tourism destinations are directed by the same evolution mechanism and its associated meanings and rules; however, in reality, different destinations demonstrate contrastingly distinct evolution patterns. Therefore, discrepancies exist between the realities of TDCS evolution and those conceived by the initial Butler's tourism area lifecycle (TALC) model. Numerous studies on destination evolution and their findings unanimously confirm the discrepancies as indicated above. However, the key issue underlying theoretical disputes in this study field is that the essence and meaning of the TDCS evolution is yet to be fully disclosed and understood as Butler's also represents a highly abstract theoretical model. In fact, the TDCS evolution process can be characterized by a seemingly Daoist version of philosophical understanding that order is in disorder and disorder also contains order. The certainties of the TDCS evolution process can be disclosed by probing and tracing coupling relationships and functional coupling networks among constituent elements of a TDCS. On the other hand, holding these certainties, explanations of uncertainties of TDCS evolution demonstrations can be sought.

References

Bao, J. (1986) *Tourism System Research – Taking Beijing as an Example*. Beijing: University of Beijing.

Bertalanffy, V.L. (1987) *General System Theory* (T. Qiu and J. Yuan, trans.). Beijing: Social Sciences Academic Press.

Bunge, M. (1981) *Scientific Materialism*. Dordrecht: D. Reidel Publishing

Butler, R. (1980) The concept of the tourist area lifecycle of evolution: Implications for the management of resources. *Canadian Geographer* 24, 5–12.

Gaines, B.R. (1979) General systems research: Quo vadis. *General Systems Yearbook*, 24, 1–9. Louisville, KY: Society for General Systems Research.

Haywood, K.M. (1986) Can the tourist area life cycle be made operational? *Tourism Management* 7 (3), 154–167.

Jin, G. (2005) *System Philosophy*. Beijing: New Star Press.

Leiper, N. (1995) *Tourism Management*. Collingwood: TAFE Publications.

Lundtorp, S. and Wanhill, S. (2001) The resort lifecycle theory – generating processes and estimation. *Annals of Tourism Research* 28 (4), 947–964.

Peng, X. (2003) *Complex Thinking and Social Development*. Beijing: Renmin University of China Press.

Rosen, R. (1985) *Anticipatory Systems*. New York: Pergamon Press.

Russell, R. and Faulkner, B. (1999) Movers and shakers: Chaos makers in tourism development. *Tourism Management* 20 (4), 411–423.

Tan, C. (2007) Subjective existence and accomplishment in a complex adaptive system. *Academic Research* 4, 66–71.

Wang, Q., Chen, Y. and Hu, M. (2005) Analysis on territorial tourism systems of Henan Province. *Areal Research and Development* 24 (4), 92–95.

Xu, H. (2001) Study on the potential tourists and life cycle of tourism product: A system dynamics approach. *Systems Engineering* 19 (3), 69–75.

Xu, H. (2005) Dynamic system model of the life cycle at urban tourism destinations. *Human Geography* 20 (5), 66–69.

Xu, H. (2006) A model study in the development of ecotourism destination. *Tourism Tribune* 21 (8), 75–80.

Yan, Z. (1993) *Evolution of Complex Systems*. Beijing: People's Publishing House.

Yan, Z., Fan, D. and Zhang, H. (2006) *Introduction to System Science – Complexity Exploration*. Beijing: People's Publishing House.

Yang, X. and Lu, L. (2004) Retrospect and prospect or study on resort life cycle. *Human Geography* 19 (5), 5–10.

Yu, S. (1997) Discourse about tourism destination life cycle theory – to be discussed with Senlin Yang. *Tourism Tribune* 12 (1), 32–37.

Zahra, A. and Ryan, C. (2007) From chaos to cohesion – complexity theory in tourism structures: An analysis of New Zealand's regional tourism organizations. *Tourism Management* 28 (7), 854–862.

Zhang, L. (1965) *Introduction to Cybernetics* (originally written by W.R. Ashby). Beijing: Science Press.

11 Evolution of a Tourism Destination Complex System: Cases in China

Chunyu Yang

Following the conceptual and theoretical discussions on the evolution of the tourism destination complex systems (TDCS) in the previous chapter, the current chapter analyses cases of TDCS in China and assesses their characteristics.

The Certainty in the TDCS Evolution Process

Development and changes appear to follow inherent laws. Decline follows peaks; construction versus destruction, growth versus decline – things in the universe are destined to abide by such an objective law of development. Historical development shows a distinctive process of *'gaining-emptying-depleting-resting'*. Originally *gaining* and *emptying, depleting* and *resting* represent contradiction and opposition, respectively. However, *gaining* turns to *emptying* by the process of *depleting; depleting* evolves to *resting* by the process of *emptying*. Thus, a *S*-shaped development curve and cycle has been formed (Li, 2004). The TDCS process is no exception. Once visitors appear at an underdeveloped region with the potential to become a tourism destination, the region becomes the site of a relationship of tourism supply and demand. The causal relationship between tourism supply and demand and their inherent feedback loops couple with each other to form a system with the emergent new structure and functioning of the TDCS. Its development must go through the several above-mentioned stages.

Such a conclusion can also be drawn from the probabilities inherent in the *law of large numbers* (Feller, 2006). Although TDCS is surrounded by confounding factors, the choice of potential paths at bifurcation points will always be restrained by certain internal and external conditions, making conditional and limited the system's scope of divergence at a given space and time. A number of factors involved in the divergence functions of evolution are relatively certain in quality, quantity, functional degree and functional scope, etc., and so too is the result caused by mutual cooperation and competition. The possible paths of destination evolution and their speed of change are always finite, countable and show certain regularities. By investigating and studying in detail these regularities, scholars can predict tourist numbers and tourism economic cycles (Kuang, 2000; Li & Sun, 1998; Sun, 2000, 2001; Wei & Yu, 2005). However, due to the presence of intervening factors, the reliability of prediction of tourist flows at destinations can only be relative and not definitive.

The Uncertainty in the TDCS Evolution Process

The interaction of coupling forces in TDCS at evolutionary points of disagreement (structural instability points) will encourage TDCS to enter a new steady state, either actively or passively. This new steady state is usually not unique, for alternative stable states may exist for future periods after other periods of instability. As shown in Figure 11.1, starting from the points of disagreement (bifurcation), TDCS steadily tends not only to go toward a given point (*b*), but also toward another momentary state (*b′*). In the three-dimensional space-time as well as multi-dimensional space-time, there exist several possible paths of evolution, and evolution forms in the selection process of TDCS at the evolutionary points of bifurcation; thereby arise the complexity of evolution and the diversity of evolutionary paths. This situation agrees to some extent with Chinese Taoist thoughts on evolution. Lao Tzu, who is widely accepted as the founder of Taoism, argued that the law of development is determined by an Absolute Truth, the so-called Tao. For the development of a thing, its interior must be divided into two and there is a nonlinear interaction; a nonlinear system with internal contradictions always has certain states of tension with external factors. Hence, through internal nonlinear interference and appropriate external change, the system

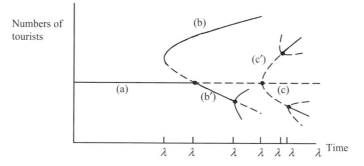

Figure 11.1 Evolutionary bifurcation map

will be bifurcated and produce new things. Such is true with the formation, development and evolution of things.

Certainty and uncertainty in the evolution of TDCS are intertwined. Certainty is characterised by such stages as 'gaining-emptying-depleting-resting' which the evolution of TDCS is bound to undergo, as well as the emergence of S-shaped development curves; uncertainty is characterised by the different times of emergence and duration in several stages through which the TDCS evolution must pass under the influence of confounding factors. S-shaped evolution curve analysis reveals the existence of vastly different evolutionary paths for destinations. This is why it is difficult to find two tourism destinations with an identical evolutionary process. This difficulty accounts for the disputes in tourism destination life cycle theory. Under these circumstances, research should focus on probing the evolutionary mechanism of TDCS to seek for its intrinsic universality and regularity in the evolutionary process.

The Oscillation of the TDCS Evolution Process

There are numerous complicating factors affecting numbers of tourists in TDCS. According to the factors' nature, origin, mechanism and other criteria for the classification, factors can be classified as internal and external, tourism supply and demand factors, natural and social factors, primary factors and complementary, secondary factors, random and periodic factors, etc. The division of these factors in the space-time evolution in tourism destinations is relative and dynamically changeable. For the unity of research and the convenience of analysis, we classify the factors affecting the fluctuating evolution of TDCS into periodic and random factors.

Periodic factors

The so-called periodic factors refer to the repeated cycle effect on the TDCS evolution process, meaning that tourist numbers oscillate on a regular basis. In terms of the mechanism of periodic factors and their frequency, it can be correspondingly divided into regular and non-regular periodic factors. Regular periodic factors include the Golden Week holiday system and seasonal fluctuations.

The Golden Week holiday policy

Since China began to implement the Golden Week holiday system in 1999, it has given rise to the phenomenon of the periodic holiday economy. Taking several major attractions of Nanjing, Jiangsu Province for example, Liu (2006) analysed the influence of the Golden Week holiday system on tourist demand. By calculating monthly tourist flow volumes at different times at Dr Sun Yat-sen's Mausoleum, Tomb of the Ming Emperors and Linggu Temple in Nanjing, Jiangsu Province, it can be seen that, in the period 2000–2002 when compared to 1993–1998, tourist arrivals in May and October to each of three scenic areas significantly increased (see Table 11.1). Tourist arrivals at Dr Sun Yat-sen's Mausoleum scenic area increased respectively by 4.3% and 3.6%; Tomb of Ming Emperor scenic area by 3.9% and 2.4%; and Linggu Temple scenic area by 3.2% and 7.4%. And in April, June, September and November, there was a large decline in tourist arrivals; tourist arrivals at Dr Sun Yat-sen's Mausoleum scenic area decreased respectively by 2.5%, 1.7%, 1.2% and 2.5%; Tomb of Ming Emperor scenic area by 2.6%, 0.8%, 1.0% and 1.2%; and Linggu Temple scenic area by 4.4%, 1.2%, 0.1% and 2.5%. Tourist arrivals in September showed little change, due to the Osmanthus Festival which led to more stable tourist volumes at the scenic areas.

The reason for the above phenomenon can be analysed as follows: in April and September, tourists look forward to the long holidays of 1 May (Labor Day) and 1 October (National Day), so their travel demand is postponed; in June and November, tourists have taken their holiday outings, also leading to a reduced travel demand. Figures 11.2 and 11.3 show the trend lines of tourist arrivals to Dr Sun Yat-sen's Mausoleum and the Linggu Temple before and after the Golden Week policy implementation. As indicated, the Golden Week holiday system has a significant effect on the yearly distribution of tourist flows at the scenic areas, with tourist arrivals concentrated towards May and October and decreased in the adjacent months.

The overcrowding experienced during the Golden Weeks, combined with other issues as to what type of holiday to take, or indeed whether to take a holiday, has become a focus of public concern. Today, as a consequence of the lack of capacity during the Golden Weeks, the phenomenon of *Golden Week holiday aversion* has emerged in terms of public attitudes toward holiday travel, travel time and travel destinations (Li, 2006). This will affect the evolutionary process of TDCS in China.

Climatic fluctuations

Generally, tourists are sensitive to the climate and potential climatic changes at destinations (Hamilton *et al.*, 2003; Lise & Tol, 2002) because climatic characteristics are usually highly valued (Hu & Ritchie, 1993). Climatic fluctuations will affect the landscapes of tourist destinations and their appeal to tourists. In recent years global climatic changes have affected ski seasons, produced heat waves and led tourists to consider destination switching for given times of the year.

As shown in Figure 11.4, monthly tourist arrivals data in 2000–2002 at Zhangjiajie City, which takes its name from a well-known Chinese National Forest Park in China, have clearly shown the importance of seasonal factors. Table 11.2 shows for the three years 2000–2003 significant seasonal fluctuations in tourist arrivals as measured by the percentage that arrive in any given month. May, July, August and October can be seen as peak seasons; April, June, September and November as the shoulder months; and November,

Table 11.1 Monthly proportional changes of tourist arrivals in three scenic areas, Jiangsu Province (unit: 10,000)

Year	Dr Sun Yat-sen's Mausoleum				Tomb of Ming Emperor				Linggu Temple			
Month	1993–1998	1999	2000–2002	D-value	1993–1998	1999	2000–2002	D-value	1993–1998	1999	2000–2002	D-value
1	3.7	4.8	4.4	+0.8	2.7	3.7	4.0	+1.3	4.0	5.5	4.7	+0.7
2	5.8	6.1	4.7	−1.1	28.3	35.4	25.9	−2.4	5.9	7.3	5.3	−0.6
3	8.0	6.8	9.3	+1.3					8.2	7.3	7.5	−0.6
4	12.6	9.8	10.0	−2.5	9.5	9.4	6.9	−2.6	14.4	10.0	10.0	−4.4
5	13.4	12.1	17.7	+4.3	9.1	10.1	13.1	+3.9	14.4	11.5	17.6	+3.2
6	7.4	6.4	5.7	−1.7	4.5	5.4	3.7	−0.8	6.3	7.6	5.2	−1.2
7	8.0	8.7	8.5	+0.5	7.0	5.4	5.5	−1.5	7.2	8.3	6.9	−0.3
8	8.3	9.2	8.7	+0.5	6.2	5.8	5.6	−0.6	8.1	8.0	7.7	−0.4
9	7.0	5.7	5.9	−1.2	4.4	3.7	3.4	−1.0	6.2	5.4	6.1	−0.1
10	12.6	18.5	16.3	+3.6	8.8	13.7	11.2	+2.4	12.8	19.0	20.2	+7.4
11	7.9	7.9	5.4	−2.5	5.3	5.3	4.1	−1.2	7.9	6.4	5.3	−2.5
12	5.4	4.1	3.3	−2.1	3.4	2.3	2.8	−0.6	4.7	3.6	3.5	−1.2

Note: D-value refers to the proportional difference in monthly accumulated tourist arrivals between 2000/2002 and 1993/1998.

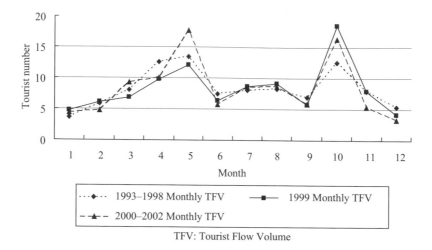

Figure 11.2 Tourist visitor numbers to Dr Sun Yat-sen's Mausoleum scenic area before and after the Golden Week policy implementation

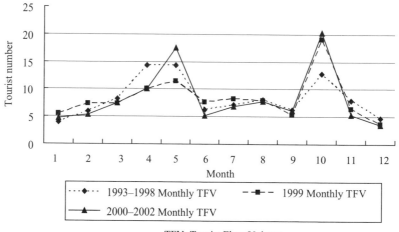

Figure 11.3 Tourist visitor numbers to Linggu Temple scenic area before and after the Golden Week policy implementation

January, February and March as the off-season. The maximum daily visitor numbers during the year reached 23,000, the lowest being less than 100.

Taking the *Happy Valley* of Shenzhen as a case study, Dong and Liu (2005) analysed the characteristics of tourist flow over time at the scenic area and discovered that Happy Valley also demonstrated seasonal cyclical fluctuations. The volatility was relatively large, with winter and summer vacations as peak seasons, May and October as shoulder seasons, and June

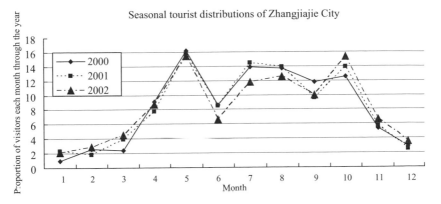

Figure 11.4 Seasonal tourist distributions of Zhangjiajie City (adapted from Yan, 2004)

Table 11.2 Yearly seasonal tourist distributions of Zhangjiajie City (%)

Year	Jan.	Feb.	Mar.	Apr.	May	Jun.	Jul.	Aug.	Sept.	Oct.	Nov.	Dec.	Yearly
2000	0.97	2.60	2.35	9.08	16.20	8.59	13.89	13.72	11.76	12.56	5.39	2.89	100
2001	2.29	1.79	3.94	7.72	15.72	8.54	14.48	13.91	9.57	13.85	5.66	2.53	100
2002	2.10	2.89	4.47	8.72	15.46	6.63	11.82	12.56	9.93	15.32	6.56	3.54	100

and September as the off-season. Sun (2007) used climatic data for the past 30 years to evaluate the climatic comfort levels for tourism in Xi'an and its surrounding mountains. Accordingly, he developed a rating scale of tourism suitability and time-line distribution. In combination with the changes of annual inbound tourist flow between 2000 and 2002, the peak and off seasons of travel activities and monthly indices were identified. Based on climatic comfort levels and special factors, the correlation between the monthly index of tourist flows and climatic comfort levels was established by the adoption of ordinary least square (OLS) estimation. Results indicated that changes of inbound tourist numbers over the year in Xi'an City followed an *M*-shaped distribution. The distribution saw April-May-June and August-September-October as the peak seasons, with an average monthly index of tourist flows ranging between 12.4% and 14.1%. In July, due to the hot weather, there is then a dip in inbound tourist arrivals and the average monthly index of tourist flow was 9.4%. January, February and December were the off-seasons of inbound tourism in Xi'an because of the cold weather, with a monthly index of tourist flow ranging between 2.7% and 3.8%. As temperatures rise from February to May each year, there is a significant growth in inbound tourist numbers; as temperatures drop from October to December, the number of inbound tourists declines rapidly. A significant correlation was evidenced between the changes of inbound tourist numbers during the year and the climatic comfort levels.

Irregular cyclical factors

Economic cyclical fluctuations

Economic cyclical fluctuation is again an important factor affecting the cyclical oscillations in tourism. Economic factors like exchange rate changes, inflation and trade disputes between countries can cause the TDCS evolution to undergo non-regular periodic expansion or dramatic contractions. Due to global economic integration, tourism appears to be more susceptible to cyclical fluctuations in the trans-regional or trans-national economy. Zhang (1999) explored the effect of currency exchange rates on the number of visitors to Hong Kong. The paper listed eight main tourist source markets including Mainland China, Taiwan, Japan, the USA, the UK, Canada, France and Germany, with the time frame from 1980 to 1993. It concluded that currency exchange rates had a high impact on visitor numbers from different source markets. Luo (2007) confirmed that the exchange rate was negatively correlated with travel demand through case studies of Japanese tourists to China, and that the appreciation of the Renminbi (Chinese Yuan) would reduce Japanese inbound travel demand to China. Figures 11.5 and 11.6 show negative correlations between the higher exchange rate of Renbinbi to Japanese Yen and Japanese visitor arrivals to China in 1990–2005. It was calculated that every 1% appreciation of Renminbi would reduce Japanese travel demand to China by 0.449%.

Kuang (2000) argued that tourism, as an economic activity, is characterised by its volatility in the developmental process. The tourism industry has a strong connection with other industries and the cyclical fluctuations of related industries will periodically influence the tourism market, creating regular cyclical fluctuations in tourism development. Tourism demand, especially demand for business travel, represents a form of conspicuous demand that closely follows fluctuations in the wider economy; for example, there is a high correlation between economic prosperity and business travel demand. International tourism engages cross-border economies and different national

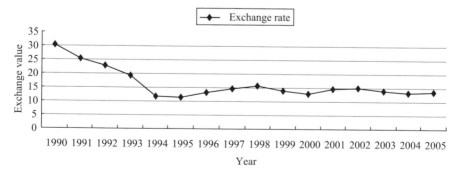

Figure 11.5 Chinese/Japanese money exchange rate fluctuation 1990–2005 (after Luo, 2007)

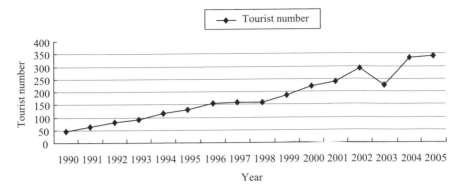

Figure 11.6 Japanese tourist arrivals to China 1990–2000 (unit, 10,000)

tourism markets are inter-correlated, again causing cyclical fluctuations in tourism transferable from one country to another.

By analysing the cyclical fluctuations of both global tourism and aspects of China's tourism, Kuang (2000) pointed out that the global tourism market had experienced a total of 10 cycles in 37 years between 1961 and 1998. After an analysis of China's tourism, he claimed that the level of fluctuation had declined from high to medium and classical fluctuations and growth-oriented fluctuations co-existed in China's tourism growth (Table 11.3).

Sun (2001) used two indicators, namely, inbound tourist arrivals for Xi'an and tourism revenue to construct a trend-line equation. He found three time-scale fluctuation cycles regarding the changes of both tourist arrivals

Table 11.3 Fluctuation in international tourist arrivals

Before the 1990s			After the 1990s		
Cycle no.	Year	Growth rate of tourist receipts (%)	Cycle no.	Year	Growth rate of tourist receipts (%)
1	1979	32.36	3	1990	12.1
	1980	35.65		1991	21.4
	1981	36.20		1992	14.3
	1982	2.02		1993	8.9
2	1983	19.60		1994	5.2
	1984	35.60	4	1995	6.2
	1985	38.71		1996	10.2
	1986	27.96		1997	12.6
	1987	17.89		1998	10.22
	1988	17.80			
	1989	−22.70			

Source: Kuang (2000)

and tourism revenue growth, particularly the *Juglar cycles* of 6–7 years being the most typical. Similarly, Wang *et al.* (2004) analysed cycles in China's tourism based on inbound tourist arrivals and tourism revenues within 20 years (1979–2002). They concluded that the growth of China's inbound tourism has experienced five small cycles from 1979 to 2002 (i.e. 1979–1982, 1983–1989, 1990–1994, 1995–1998 and 1999–2001).

Zhang and Lu (2004) conducted a time series analysis of cyclical fluctuations based on both annual (1978–2002) and monthly data (1989–2002) of inbound tourist arrivals. Their results suggested the existence of irregular cyclical fluctuations. The annual data were divided into three periods: the first two cycles are of great amplitude and with relatively short cyclical length; the latter cycle is of relatively small amplitude but with a longer cyclical length. The monthly data from 1989 to 2002 demonstrated one cycle, namely a 'pioneering' cycle with a relatively long period of contraction. The factors resulting in the large cyclical fluctuations are those events with a greater impact, which are characterised by peaks and troughs in the cyclical curve. Low-impact events often lead to mild fluctuations within a cycle.

Tourism consumption changes

What can be learned from these studies is that irregular fluctuations in the economic cycle (that is, economic fluctuations not following any simple rules or fixed cycles) and consequent irregular cyclical oscillations in tourism caused by those economic fluctuations are real, measurable and inevitable. Among various economic factors, price, inflation and exchange rates are closely associated with cyclical fluctuations in tourism.

Changes in tourists' preferences and purchase patterns are one of the major factors affecting tourism cycles at tourist destinations. Tourists' repeat visits to tourism destinations in China tend to be low, as they generally prefer to experience new destinations. On the global scale, coastal tourism was quite popular in the 1960s and 1970s; sightseeing tours and cultural tourism played a leading role in the 1980s; while in the 1990s ecotourism and industrial tourism gradually became fashionable. All these popular travel patterns are closely related to consumers' awareness and propensities at a certain time.

Random factors

Random factors refer to non-cyclical disturbances generated in the evolutionary process of TDCS that cause the tourist flow to show irregular oscillations in arrivals. Such factors include short-term weather occurrences (storms, blizzards, heat waves, tornadoes, tsunamis and drought, etc.) and major unexpected incidents. They have a strong impact on travel demand and can cause strong fluctuations in tourist numbers within a short time.

Unexpected events in recent years that have left a great impact on the global tourism industry and China's inbound tourism are shown in Table 11.4.

Table 11.4 Comparative analysis of major incidents' effects on Chinese inbound tourism

Incident name	Year of occurrence	Scope	Nature of incident	China's tourism development status at that time	Impact degree
'June 4' incident, Tiananmen Square	1989	China	Political event	Relatively simple structure of inbound tourist source; weak anti-risk capability	In 1989 inbound tourist numbers fell by 20.7%; foreign exchange earnings declined by 17.2%
The Gulf War	1991	Middle East	Armed conflict	Relatively simple structure of inbound tourist source; weak anti-risk capability	In 1991 inbound tourist numbers rose by 55.1%; foreign exchange earnings increased by 28.3%
Asian financial crisis	1997–1998	Southeast Asia, around the world	Economic event	Diverse structure of inbound tourist source; enhanced anti-risk capability	In 1998 inbound tourist numbers rose by 10.2%; foreign exchange earnings increased by 4.4%
Kosovo conflict	1999	Eastern Europe	Armed conflict	Diverse structure of inbound tourist source; strong economic growth; enhanced anti-risk capability	In 1999 inbound tourist numbers rose by 14.7%; foreign exchange earnings increased by 11.9%
'9-11' incident	2001	America, Afghanistan, around the world	Terrorist attacks	Diverse structure of inbound tourist source; still strong economic growth; strong anti-risk capability	In 2001 inbound tourist numbers rose by 6.7%; foreign exchange earnings increased by 9.7%
SARS	2003	China	Disease and epidemics	Diverse structure of inbound tourist source; still strong economic growth; strong anti-risk capability	In 2003 inbound tourist numbers rose by −6.37%, foreign exchange earnings increased by −14.6%

These events include the 4 June Tiananmen Square incident in 1989, the Gulf War in 1991, the Asian financial crisis between 1997 and 1998, the Kosovo conflict in 1999, and 11 September terrorist attacks in 2001. When these events occurred, China's tourism was at different periods of development; consequently the impacts of the events on China's inbound tourism were dissimilar. As the industry matures it might be expected that endogenous shocks may become less, although any system may still remain susceptible to exogenous shocks.

Combined effects of cyclical and random factors

Given the combined impacts of a variety of different intervening variables at differing times and places, tourism destinations will inevitably produce unique evolutionary processes. Nonetheless, from the perspective of economic analysis, regular cyclical fluctuations can be identified, thereby also permitting identification of random factors. In the following sections, China's inbound tourism and domestic tourism development processes are hereby analysed.

Evolution of China's Inbound Tourism

For a TDCS, especially a tourist destination like China with a huge territory, tourism arrivals, both holistically and regionally, represent the overall outcome of coupling effects of multiple factors in a period. The economic periodic fluctuation in China's international tourism is conspicuous by its growth and fluctuations. Table 11.5 shows the growth rate of China's international tourism foreign exchange earnings in the years from 1979 to 2004. There were five major fluctuations. The first lasted for six years from 1979 to 1984, the second lasted for eight years from 1985 to 1992, the third from 1993 to 1997, the fourth from 1998 to 2000, and the fifth from 2001 to 2004, after which the evolution enters its sixth fluctuation. As shown in Table 11.5, the highest annual growth in China's international tourism foreign exchange earnings was 70.70% in 1979, but three years later it dropped rapidly to 7.40%; the growth rate of the earnings was as high as 20.70% in 1988, but the next year it declined sharply by 17.20%; similarly, the growth rate of the earnings was as high as 14.57% in 2002, but it suddenly dropped by 14.60% in 2003.

The factors leading to the fluctuations are very complex and difficult to accurately predict and control. Overall, the main factors involve politics, economy, nature, psychology, and in many cases the factors intertwining together play a decisive role in the fluctuation of international tourism. Equally these fluctuations have had significant impacts on the development of destinations within China. For example, the growth rate of China's

Table 11.5 Fluctuation in Chinese international tourism revenues

Before 1992			After 1992		
Circle	Year	International tourism income growth rate (%)	Circle	Year	International tourism income growth rate (%)
1	1979	70.70	3	1993	18.70
	1980	37.30		1994	56.36
	1981	27.30		1995	19.25
	1982	7.40		1996	16.81
	1983	11.60		1997	18.37
	1984	20.20	4	1998	4.37
2	1985	10.50		1999	11.88
	1986	22.50		2000	15.08
	1987	21.60			
	1988	20.70	5	2001	9.67
	1989	−17.20		2002	14.57
	1990	19.20		2003	−14.60
	1991	28.30		2004	47.87
	1992	38.70			

Source: *China Tourism Statistics Yearbook* (2004) and http://www.cnta.com.

international tourism foreign exchange earnings was as high as 70.70% in 1979. This was because the decision at the Third Plenary Session of the 11th CPC Central Committee to implement reforms and open China up to the global economy produced significant impacts on China's international tourism. Hence, politics and resulting policies have exerted a major influence on China's international tourism.

Other factors include investment and consumption as well as fiscal and financial factors. Investment is not only an important means to enhance economic development, but also a lever for realising economic resource allocation. Investment in China's tourism was also an important factor causing fluctuations in China's international tourism sector. In the context of the initial development stage after the 1979 reforms, a lack of sufficient infrastructure proved to be a major problem in developing China's tourism. The investment made subsequently in hotels and other tourism infrastructure has met many of the initial problems, but more recently signs have emerged of overcapacity (Gu et al., 2012).

Tourism revenue relies on tourist expenditure, which in turn is determined by income and competing demands on consumers' budgets. Theoretically, consumer demand in tourism is restrained by three conditions, i.e. travel motivation, the ability to pay and available discretionary time. In this discussion only the effect of disposable income is taken into consideration. Generally, people's overall disposable income level is influenced by the overall economic situation. It is surmised that fluctuations in China's international tourism are related to the world economic situation. For example, the global economic recession in 1982 caused a sharp decline in China's international tourism, and the growth rate of China's international tourism receipts also showed a downward trend. Financial factors refer to changes in the financial markets, which in turn influence the economy. In 1994 China abolished its long-running dual exchange rate system and reformed the exchange rate system, with the consequence that China's international tourist receipts reached another high.

Natural factors include natural disasters (such as earthquakes, tsunamis and flood disasters), and infectious diseases. It is universally known that China suffered from catastrophic floods in 1998 and the pandemic of severe acute respiratory syndrome (SARS) in 2003, which negatively affected China's international tourism and caused a decrease in international tourism income in those two particular years (and even negative growth).

Domestic Tourism

After the 1979 reforms China's domestic tourism developed rapidly from almost nothing. Before 1996 the growth rate of China's domestic tourist numbers was as high as 20% per annum. However, from 1996 to 2003 the growth in China's domestic tourist numbers almost ceased, for which there were many reasons. The first was the imbalanced development of China's economy due to the previous rapid development, which resulted in more sluggish development of domestic tourism for a few years. However, under the centralised economic policies commencing in 2004 that encouraged domestic consumption, China's domestic tourism began to accelerate and maintained at least a double-digit growth rate. In 2007 China's domestic tourism still maintained a rapid development. According to the China National Tourism Administration (CNTA), China received 92.2 million tourists during the *Golden Week of Spring Festival* in 2007, which represented a 17.7% increase over the same period in the previous year; tourist arrivals also reached 179 million in the *Golden Week of Labor Day* in 2007 – 22.7% over the same period in the previous year. Tourism consumption has become a major and dynamic sector of the new emphasis on domestic consumer spending as a source of GDP growth. The vitality of China's tourism development can be mainly attributed to the following three aspects.

(1)   Chinese residents' consumer spending is being encouraged under current economic policies, as growth based on export earnings becomes more

limited due to the recession in export markets in 2008–2012. In 2006, the Engle coefficient of urban households in China was 35.8%, and represents a threshold level for further improvements in consumer spending and household developments.

(2) The continuous improvement of the infrastructure in China makes tourism activities more convenient and accessible. With the development of the national economy, China's infrastructure, especially public facilities such as transportation, has been remarkably improved; destination accessibility has also been greatly improved, and the rapid growth of private car ownership and consumption has accelerated domestic tourism growth.

(3) The tourism industry has obtained significant governmental support. Tourism is believed to play a role in enhancing domestic demand, increasing employment and promoting harmonious regional economic development and social coordination (Zeng & Ryan, 2012). Tourism development has been valued by both the government and the whole of Chinese society. Different levels of government bodies have given priority to tourism to ensure its stable and rapid development through favourable tourism development policies. A few years back, China issued RMB 650 billion in total of long-term construction treasury bonds, including RMB 150 billion in 2002, and RMB 140 billion in 2003. In the context of a national policy of withdrawing active fiscal intervention through issuing government bonds, the national tourism bonds in 2003 reached RMB 2 billion, more than twice the amount of RMB 800 million tourism bonds made available in 2002. Thus, it can be seen that the government has more than sustained its efforts in developing the tourism industry. Encouraged by central government policies, local governments also show an increasing enthusiasm for tourism development. In recent years, the Chinese government has made adjustments to its public holidays and the Golden Week holiday system, reinforcing leisure holidays as citizens' right of consumption and guaranteeing time availability for citizens' holiday leave. The government's positive attitude towards tourism is thus evident.

Nonetheless, China's domestic tourism has also experienced adverse fluctuations caused by major events such as the June 4 Tiananmen Square incident in 1989, the Asian financial crisis in 1997, the outbreak of SARS in 2003, the South China snow disaster in early 2008 and the Wenchuan earthquake in Sichuan. According to CNTA, China's disasters of freezing low temperatures, rainstorms and blizzards from middle January to early February in 2008 caused direct economic losses of about RMB 6.97 billion, and the Wenchuan earthquake brought a loss of RMB 53.369 billion to the tourism systems in earthquake-stricken provinces, among which Sichuan suffered a loss of RMB 52.831 billion (CNTA, 2008).

Further Discussions on TDCS Evolution

A further review of relevant theoretical models and academic debates regarding the tourism destination life cycle documented in Butler's theoretical model (see Figure 11.7) may help clarify the essence of the TDCS evolution mechanism.

Butler's tourism area life cycle model is actually based on the process of changes between tourism supply and demand. With the demand of a small number of tourists (venturers) at the initial phase, the tourism destination steps into the early development stage of its life cycle, with little tourism supply. As a few local residents start providing simple lodgings to visitors and knowledge of the tourism destination expands gradually, tourism demand also increases. At this stage, the destination needs to deal with the situation in which demand exceeds supply: the tourism industry grows quickly and employment in the industry is on a rise; a number of local and foreign investments accelerate the growth of tourism supply; both tourism demand and supply develop synchronically. Due to the rapid development of the destination, the destination development moves to the next stage in which tourism supply and tourism demand achieve a dynamic equilibrium where tourist arrivals and economic income at the destination attain the highest level, matching the destination's then current environmental carrying capacity, although it may be noted that natural and physical environments now differ from the initial starting position.

However, the 'boom phase' of a destination cannot last long. Because increasing tourist numbers will eventually exceed the overall environmental capacity, a series of negative impacts on the destination will happen. Problems of crowding, pollution and product quality decline will arise,

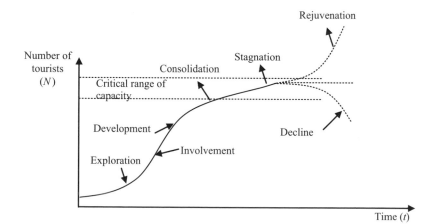

Figure 11.7 Model of resort life cycle (adapted from Butler, 1980)

leading to a decline in tourist demand and the destination's recession. At the early stage of declining profits and eventually demand, some local and foreign investors will begin to reduce or withdraw their investment in tourism. Consequently, the destination's economy begins to decline due to gradually diminishing tourism supply and either unemployment or less remunerative employment. Furthermore, reduced travel demand, surplus supply and product price cuts reduce further the profits of tourism enterprises, inhibiting them from further investment in the industry. Accordingly, tourism revenues will continue to fall and eventually the economy of the destination will decline to become tired, lacking investment and uncompetitive with new destinations. The situation is characterised by unemployment, underemployed tourist facilities, financial losses on the part of tourism enterprises and even bankruptcy. At this stage, the destination is confronted with the options of either decline or recovery.

There is no need for further discussion if a tourism destination goes into greater decline and impoverishment, existing like British seaside resorts on nostalgia and little else. On the other hand, if the tourism destination adopts revivalist policies at its evolutionary bifurcation point, it will attract visitors once again by exploring the potentials of existing tourism resources or developing new attractive tourism resources, which often falls within the terrain of the public sector (Ryan, 2003). With a rejuvenated business environment, tourism enterprises would consider increasing investment, increasing jobs and gradually expanding tourism supply, thus forming the recovery phase of the destination evolution process. The recovery stage is characterised by the elevation of tourism supply and demand, an increase in employment and the increased investment in the destination. With demand, supply and employment continuing to expand, and prices rising, the whole destination gradually moves toward a new prosperity phase and steps further into the next cycle process.

Conclusion

Based on the foregoing analyses and discussions, the following can be concluded regarding TDCS evolution:

- First, the evolution of TDCS is inevitable, deterministic, and independent of human subjective intentions. The S-shaped development process of a destination's birth, peak, decline and death follows the common laws of evolution and is determined by both its system structure and function. Once visitors appear in a place with tourism development potential, the relationship between tourism demand and supply is formed. The cause-and-effect relationship between demand and supply and its feedback loops are coupled together to form a system with new structure and function. The system is called the tourism destination complex system, which has been the focus of discussion in this chapter and the previous one. Moreover, through the S-shaped evolutionary curve, the development and evolution of the TDCS move in a circular track.

- Second, a TDCS is always directed at a relatively definite *target* throughout the process of its evolution cycle, no matter how complicated and treacherous the path of evolution. This target often corresponds to one or more natural limit values (i.e. travel environmental carrying capacity threshold values). These threshold values are not determined unilaterally by the TDCS or the environment, not even regulated in advance by other unrelated things, but commonly decided by the composition, structure and function of the TDCS itself, together with the interactions between the TDCS and the environment. Only after the TDCS evolves into its target state (the final state) can it remain stable or be transformed into a different system (i.e. a critical state of the TDCS evolution), thus representing a completion of one evolution cycle.

As a result, it is understood that any TDCS is bound to experience a cycle from birth to death and correspondingly follows an S-shaped evolution curve. The number of tourists to a destination will reach a level at the destination's peak stage of evolution and the destination's actual carrying capacity will attain its maximum threshold value. Afterwards, the TDCS will face an evolutionary bifurcation set to select, either actively or passively, the evolution track of either decline or recovery.

Future Research Direction

To further explore the evolutionary mechanism and regularities of TDCS, future research can build upon the basis of this qualitative inquiry to: (a) introduce related space-time dimension parameters that can reflect the essential characteristics of the TDCS evolution and control the development and evolution of the whole tourism destination; and (b) develop the dynamic evolution model of tourism destinations with functions of mathematical analysis. By so doing, the inherent evolution mechanism and regularities of TDCS can be illustrated and quantified, and the issue of a lack of a comprehensive, systemic, dynamic and predicting study in this particular field can also be addressed. We suggest future research probe into the following three aspects:

(a) *Constructing a dynamic evolution model of TDCS*: A dynamic evolution model of TDCS can be constructed based on the coupling relationships between two subsystems, i.e. the tourism destination life cycle (tourism supply and demand as the main components and the tensions between supply and demand as research subjects) and tourism environment carrying capacity. Both subsystems' evolution curves bearing temporal and spatial characteristics can represent the future track of a tourism destination. On the one hand, mathematical models can be developed to quantify maximum tourist arrivals as a core issue, based on the combination of the tourism destination life cycle and tourism environment carrying capacity, and with the introduction of the time dimension indicators, the pace and direction of TDCS changes; on the other hand, the call for more systematic, dynamic, predictive studies is more likely to be echoed through the establishment of tourism-related indicators to determine the stage of TDCS evolution and duration of each stage. Thus, the outcomes will be conducive to establishing a sound tourism destination planning and management system.

(b) *Establishing reasonable thresholds of tourism environment carrying capacity and monitoring the system of TDCS evolution*: Based on the efforts of building a dynamic evolutionary model of tourism destination development, by extending the *Logistic* curve model and introducing spatial and temporal parameters, the evolutionary curve and associated formula of the tourism environment carrying capacity can be explored. Such an attempt can realise the measurement of both reasonable and limited threshold values of tourism environmental carrying capacity. At the same time, such measurement can be adopted to (i) understand both the cumulative effect of the tourism environment carrying capacity and the system-enduring operating mechanisms among the reasonable threshold values (this mechanism is formed by the up-and-down oscillation around the equilibrium point of TDCS, under the TDCS's role of being a self-regulating mechanism), (ii) build the monitoring system of TDCS evolution, and (iii) enable early warning and subsequent management control of the TDCS evolution and development.

(c) *Conducting research on strategic management and decision-making*: The game relationships among all the stakeholders at tourism destinations, as one of key factors determining the development sustainability of tourism destinations, play a vital role in the evolution process of TDCS. Guided by the theory of TDCS evolution, future research can examine these relationships from the perspective of time and space for both the evolution process and its regularities, regarding the relationships among different stakeholders in a destination. The emphasis of such research can range from analysing the nature of the complex relationships among stakeholders from the perspective of economics to examining people's behaviours, attitudes, relationships and various social phenomena, taking a management perspective. On the basis of this, an adaptive management model matching the evolutionary process of the relationships between different stakeholders at a tourism destination can be built in the hope of achieving the destination's sustainable development.

References

Butler, R. (1980) The concept of the tourist area lifecycle of evolution: Implications for the management of resources. *Canadian Geographer* 24, 5–12.

CNTA (China National Tourism Administration) (2008) *China Tourism Statistics Public Report 2006*, accessed 27 September 2011. http://zhuanti.cnta.gov.cn/news_detail/newsshow.asp?id=A200861124436458767.

Dong, G. and Liu, F. (2005) The characteristics of variation in time to stay at scenic area – taking Shenzhen Happy Valley as an example. *Social Scientists* 1, 132–135.

Feller, W. (2006) *Probability Theory and its Applications* (3rd edn) (D. Hu, trans.). Beijing: People's Post Press.

Gu, H., Ryan, C. and Yu, L. (2012) The changing structure of the Chinese hotel industry: 1980–2012. *Tourism Management Perspectives* 4, 56–63.

Hamilton, J.M., Maddison, D.J. and Tol, R.S.J. (2003) Climate change and international tourism: A simulation study. Research Unit Sustainability and Global Change Working Paper No. FNU-31. Centre for Marine and Climate Research, Hamburg University.

Hu, Y. and Ritchie, J.R.B. (1993) Measuring destination attractiveness: A contextual approach. *Journal of Travel Research* 32 (2), 25–34.

Kuang, L. (2000) An analysis of the economic cycle in China's tourism industry. *Tourism Tribune* 20, 9–17.

Li, B. (2004) *Great Strategies and the Changes of New Military*. Beijing: PLA Publishing.

Li, J. (2006) Tour elusion in Golden Weeks and countermeasures – revelation from dynamic analysis on tourism market in Golden Weeks of year 2005. *Journal of Beijing Technology and Business University (Social Science)* 21, 73–78.

Li, Y. and Sun, G. (1998) Foundation and significance of background trend line of Xi'an city's abroad tourism. *Journal of Northwest University (Natural Science)* 28, 339–343.

Lise, W. and Tol, R.S.J. (2002) Impact of climate on tourism demand. *Climatic Change* 4, 429–449.

Liu, Z. (2006) The empirical research on the impact of Golden Week holiday system on travel demand – the case of Dr Sun Yat-sen's mausoleum scenic area. *Inquiry Into Economic Problems* 8, 84–87.

Luo, F. (2007) The impact of exchange rates on Chinese inbound tourism demand – evidence from Japan's tourism in China. *Industrial Technology and Economy* 26, 86–88.

Ryan, C. (2003) *Recreational Tourism: Demand and Impacts*. Clevedon: Channel View Publications.

Sun, G. (2000) The establishment of tourism bottom trend line for the six international tourist source markets. *Systems Engineering Theory and Practice* 1, 140–143.

Sun, G. (2001) The dynamic tendency and fluctuation cycle of inbound tourism in Xi'an city. *Journal of Northwest University (Natural Science)* 31, 514–517.

Sun, G. (2007) An analysis of tourist climate comfortable degree and yearly variation of tourist traffic in Xi'an. *Tourism Tribune* 22, 34–39.

Wang, C., Sun, G. and Ma, Y. (2004) Analysis and the reason of the fluctuation cycle of Chinese inbound tourism. *Journal of Ningxia University (Natural Science Edition)* 25, 174–179.

Wei, X. and Yu, L. (2005) Measurement methods of quantifying the short-term economic fluctuations of tourism destinations. *Statistics and Decision* 9, 13–15.

Yan, F. (2004) A study on the temporal-spatial changes of tourist flows in Zhangjiajie City, its impact and solutions. *Ecological Economy* S1, 208–212.

Zeng, B. and Ryan, C. (2012) Assisting the poor in China through tourism development: A review of research. *Tourism Management* 33 (2), 239–248.

Zhang, H. and Lu, L. (2004) An analysis of the cycles of tourist number to China. *Journal of Anhui Normal University (Natural Science)* 27, 457–460.

Zhang, Q.H. (1999) On the importance of national income, currency exchange rate and crime rate to the visitor to Hong Kong. *Tourism Tribune* 15 (2), 71–74.

12 Local Governments' Roles in Developing Tourism

Songshan (Sam) Huang, Chris Ryan and Chunyu Yang

Introduction

This chapter reviews and compares the roles of local and central government in developing tourism in China by examining policies and media appraisals of those policies. It was found that while central government appeared to be more conservative and cautious, utilising a 'trial-and-error' approach, local governments were bolder and more adventurous in developing tourism policies.

As stated in other chapters, China's tourism industry has developed rapidly since the early 1980s. Such a rapid development required institutional change in China's governmental system in general and more specifically in tourism administration. Those changes illustrate the dichotomies inherent in the processes described by Chunyu Yang in other chapters in this book. As described by Ryan and Gu (2009) in their analysis of the decay of Statism in China, the administrative reform has not followed the same path of deconstructed Statism as evidenced in other former Communist regimes. On the other hand, it has encouraged a private sector where previously none existed, but equally in the devolution of former central powers it has delegated more decision making to the provincial and municipal governments, who have formed partnerships with the private sector to create a new 'transformation path' (Ryan & Gu, 2009: 144). Centralised Statism has been replaced by a fusion of private and public sector local initiatives that paradoxically reinvent the power of the state as the state dismantles past regimes, although as Yang points out, the duration of interim stages may well be uncertain. Given this, within the academic literature it is suggested that degrees of confusion remain. For example, the model of government as a unified entity in China's tourism development has often been cited (e.g. Hao, 1999; Jia & Wu, 2002; Kuang, 2001; Zhang, 1998) even as recently as 2009 (Zhang & Yan, 2009). These studies relate to an undefined 'government' role within policy making, leaving the roles of local governments undifferentiated from those of the central government. Furthermore, these studies overlooked the dynamics within China's government system itself, which is represented by longitudinal interactions between the central government and local governments.

The aim of this chapter is to critically review and analyse the roles of local governments in developing China's tourism industry. We take two perspectives in our analysis. A historic perspective was adopted to provide contextual understanding of China's institutional change, while a comparative perspective permits an examination of the relationships and interactions between central and local governments over those years.

Literature Review

Matthews and Richter (1991), Hall (1994, 2003) and Lane (2004) are among those who analyse the role of politics in the formation of tourism policies and argue that the political framework established the broad context and overall direction of tourism development. For their part, Jenkins and Henry (1982) claimed that government involvement in tourism in most developing countries is required not only to attain long-term objectives but to compensate for the absence of a strong and tourism-experienced private sector. In the Western political system, local government is certainly deemed important in tourism development and promotion. For example Wilson *et al.* (2001) found that, in rural tourism in the USA, the importance of local government in tourism is embodied in areas of funding, the creation and maintenance of necessary infrastructure, zoning and community policies, and in education and occupational support. Applying network theory, Dredge (2006) examined the formal and informal relationships between local government and the tourism industry in Australia and concluded that maintaining a good public–private partnership between local government and the industry requires careful management because the interests and power allocations in a network are asymmetrical. However, these research findings from the Western political context may not be able to fully explain what has happened and is happening in China, due to differences in the political systems (Ryan & Gu, 2009).

China's emergence as a tourism power has attracted research attention from both Chinese and international researchers. Richter's (1983) early commentary on the political implications of Chinese tourism policies suggested that the earlier opening-up of China's tourism frontier by the Chinese authorities had actually enabled China to avoid many of the social and economic costs associated with tourism development elsewhere. Indeed, endowed with a political system different from most Western countries and a political culture inherited from its long history of intellectual bureaucracy, she suggested China should be treated as a unique laboratory for tourism policy research. As noted in earlier chapters of this book by Yang, early tourism development focused more on attracting much needed foreign exchange to help initiate modernisation (Huang, 2010; Tisdell & Wen, 1991; Zhang *et al.*, 2000), with subsequent policies addressing issues in developing domestic tourism and outbound tourism (Tse & Hobson, 2008; Wu *et al.*, 2000).

These changing policies have attracted research construed in different paradigms and dimensions. For example, Zhang *et al.* (2002) studied China's tourism policy implementation from an enterprise perspective. They found that Chinese tourism policies had established a legal framework for the administration, management and operation of tourism enterprise while at the same time following a 'top-down' and 'trial and error-correcting' model. Zhang *et al.* (1999) also analysed tourism policy development in China and identified six roles of the government, namely: operator, regulator, investment simulator, promoter, coordinator and educator. Implicitly, these roles were attributed to the central government of China. Sofield and Li (1998) took a broader perspective to examine China's tourism policies in its social context of modernisation, socialism, traditional conservatism and economic development. Like Richter's (1983) early conclusions, Sofield and Li (1998) claimed that tourism in China had exerted a centripetal influence on its social tensions and helped ameliorate the country's economic and social transitions.

More recently, York and Zhang (2010) analysed official documentation to identify the determinants of China's Golden Holiday system. Xu *et al.* (2010) examined China's policies on foreign-invested travel agencies based on its World Trade Organisation (WTO) membership commitment. 'Red tourism', as a highly politicised term or tourism form in China, was also studied by some scholars (e.g. Li & Hu, 2008). Yang *et al.* (2006) were among those who examined Chinese governmental perspectives in ethnic tourism development, taking a case study of Xishuangbanna Dai Autonomous Prefecture in Yunnan Province. Their study discloses that different levels of government (national vs. local) play key but different roles in development through regulation of production, consumption and investment in tourism, and nuanced government policies could mitigate many of the potential tensions between demand, supply and possible adverse impacts. Yan and Bramwell (2008) studied the changing attitudes of the Chinese national government over tourism development at a World Heritage Site, namely Qufu in Shangdong province. They found that even in highly centralised regimes, the central government sometimes has to respond to social pressures and local government initiatives in order to maintain its political hegemony. In this study, a gradual acceptance by the central government of tourism and traditional cultural activities in Qufu's cultural tourism development is related to growing tensions and instabilities in Chinese society and to a slow decentralisation of government policy making. Studying the same location, Ma *et al.* (2009) found examples of a lack of cooperation between the different ministries responsible for tourism development with a consequent lack of coordinated policy even while commercialisation of a 'Confucius' brand was occurring.

Airey and Chong (2010) studied the key players and institutional processes involved in policy making for China's tourism sector since 1978. They identified key policy makers in China's political and administrative system to include paramount Chinese Communist Party (CCP) and central government leaders, the China National Tourism Administration (CNTA), the National Development and Reform Commission (NDRC), the Ministry of Finance, the State General Administration of Quality Supervision, Inspection and Quarantine, local governments and the Chinese Academy of Social Sciences (CASS). A multi-faceted and multi-level involvement of government organisations in tourism development policy making is evident in China. Huang (2010) provided a comprehensive review on the evolution of China's tourism policies. He noted that while the changes in China's tourism policies witnessed a transition from seeing tourism as a subset of political affairs to becoming an important tertiary industry due to Deng Xiaoping's reform and opening-up policies in the last century, after the turn of the century the Chinese government has still tended to integrate tourism into policy agendas to achieve various economic, social, political and environmental development goals.

There seems to be a growing interest in studying government influences and interventions in different aspects of tourism development in China. Wang and Xu (2011) examined the influences of government intervention on tourism investment in China using a sample of Chinese listed companies that have diversified into the tourism sector. Government intervention was measured on the basis of a company CEO's political connections, the relations between the government and the market, and the degree of financial market development. They suggest greater local government awareness of policy implementation should be in place to avoid unfair competition between state owned enterprises (SOEs) and non-SOEs and to target the long-term positive development of the tourism industry in China. Wang and Bramwell (2011) used a political economic approach to examine the government's role in determining priorities between heritage protection and tourism development at heritages sites in China. They studied two heritage schemes at West Lake in the city of Hangzhou, Zhejiang Province and concluded that, while tourism development remains a prominent driver to form a powerful policy community, it was only recently that a wider stakeholder perspective began to emerge in policy formation and implementation.

While policy research in China tourism has covered different areas of policy practices and government roles in developing tourism, the term 'government' as used by many of these authors remains blurred. Although the institutional transition and decentralisation of government economic management functions have prompted a need to look into the relationships between the central government and local governments in China's tourism policy framework, little research has actually attempted to address such an issue. Indeed Gu *et al.* (2013) have suggested that, in a transitional economy with uncertainty of administrative procedures, traditional values of *guanxi*, *li* and other aspects of Chinese culture serve to hold the whole together as new forms of administration, policy formation and implementation continue to evolve.

Transition of China's General Administration System

Since 1979 the restructuring of the fiscal system has been one key factor in determining the shape of transition of China's general administrative structure. Four major structural adjustments were attempted in 1980, 1985, 1988 and 1994, respectively (Hu, 2002), to which might be added the more recent one of 2009–2011 as the Chinese government sought to ensure flows of credit without overheating the domestic economy in the aftermath of the global financial crisis and the debacle of the Eurozone. The fiscal system reforms have redefined the relationship between the central and local governments. Each adjustment was quite effective in generating more active local government involvement in economic development, while at the same time maintaining and strengthening the fiscal capacity of the central government. Over the years, local governments have gradually been allocated more power in different areas of their jurisdictions, albeit recently with a growing stress on provincial and municipal governmental budgets due to over-investment in infrastructure and prestige projects. One example is the RMB 210 billion debt inherited by Guangzhou after hosting the 2010 Asian Games which went well over budget, while the 2011 Shenzhen World Student Games also went well over budget, with both cities now possessing stadia that, like the Beijing's 'Bird's Nest' have had little usage after their respective Games (Wang, 2012). Equally the same source, *Caixin Magazine*, reported in September 2011 that the Yunnan Highway could no longer pay interest or principal on its 100 billion RMB debt (Zhang & Zhao, 2011).

Such changes and potential debt risks cannot but help impact on China's tourism development. Two different evolutionary paths in tourism administration can be identified, namely 'decentralisation' of the central government and 'concentration' of power to local governments. In theory, the central government coordinates all stakeholders in the industry, promotes the nation's destination image and improves the business environment by promulgating necessary industry regulations and policies; on the other hand, local governments implement the 'government-led' tourism development strategy, and consequently play more active roles in all aspects of tourism development. In practice, many issues of corruption and false padding of contracts have emerged.

Evolution of the Central Government's Roles in Tourism Development

During the process of China's tourism development, the central government has played three different roles at separate periods of time (Jiang, 2006). In the early stage, the central government acted as a pioneer to initiate China's tourism development. By assembling all the economic resources it could mobilise, the central government accelerated the nation's tourism development at an unprecedented speed and quickly formed a substantial industry and supply capacity. The central government was actively and directly involved in introducing foreign direct investment (FDI) for the first batch of joint-venture hotels such as Jianguo Hotel in Beijing and the White Swan Hotel in Guangzhou. After the tourism industry gained its growth momentum, the central government changed its role to being a regulator. A series of regulations and policies were promulgated to ensure healthy operations in the industry. These included the Provisional Regulations on Travel Agencies Administration announced in 1985, the Chinese Star Rating Standards in 1987 and the Provisional Regulations on Tourist Guides first promulgated in 1987. In addition, the central government has also played an enabling role by coordinating different forces in society, encouraging tourism business development, protecting consumers' rights, and promoting the nation's image among international markets. In 1999, in consideration of both economic and social demand, the central government started to implement the Golden Week holiday system, which greatly facilitated the country's domestic tourism development. After the turn of the century, Chinese outbound tourism emerged as a significant force in the world travel market. The central government revised its Administrative Measures on Chinese Citizens' Outbound Travels in 2002, which by 2011 also included free independent travel to Taiwan, while hotels were required to adhere to more environmentally aware standards in 2011 following the Green Hotel policies announced in January of that year.

For their part, Zhang et al. (1999) identified six roles played by the state in tourism policy and it is pertinent to review how these roles have evolved over China's relatively short but impressive tourism development history. Using the year 2000 as an arbitrary point of comparison, as shown in Table 12.1, the role of central government as an operator in tourism had almost ceased after the turn of the century. Until 1998 the central government, represented by CNTA, had been operating government-owned tourism

Table 12.1 Evolution of roles of the central government in tourism development

Role	Description[a]	Before 2000	After 2000
Operator	Involving ownership and provision of the infrastructure for tourism development and operation of tourism business activities	Operating government-owned tourism business until 1998	Former tourism businesses completely separated from government functions
Regulator	Formulating and implementing regulations to guide industry development and tourism business operations	Increasingly seeking a strong status in the central government structure by the CNTA	More regulating activities in emerging tourism sectors, (e.g. Chinese outbound tourism)
Investment stimulator	Stimulating tourism investment through the provision of financial incentives	Actively and directly involved in distributing national tourism development bonds and other funds	More regulatory exercises than direct involvement
Promoter	Spending money on the promotion of tourism in the international market	Core function of CNTA	Still the core function
Coordinator	Coordinating activities of different government departments with respect to tourism	Coordinating at both prime ministerial level and minister level with CNTA in a less powerful position	Coordinating at both prime ministerial level and minister level with CNTA in a more powerful position
Educator	Establishing a system of tourism education institutions and providing tourism education and training programmes	Micro-management: formulating education and training policies and implementing industry human resource programmes directly (e.g. national tour guide certification examination, national travel managers training and examination, hotel managers training)	Macro-management: more focus on developing industry-wide education and training policies

Note: [a]The description was adapted from Zhang et al. (1999).

businesses but, after the restructuring of government that occurred in the People's Republic at that time, that role was changed significantly. One prominent feature of the restructuring was the split of central government agencies from their directly owned and managed 'central government enterprises'. Until 1998, CNTA owned and appointed senior executives from among its personnel for several of its directly run tourism businesses, including Beijing International Hotel, Zhaolong Hotel, China International Travel Service (CITS) and China Tax-free Merchandising (Group) Co. Ltd. Also, in 1998, other central government agencies surrendered their affiliated tourism businesses. For instance, China Travel Service (CTS) was separated from its ministerial parental government agency – the Overseas Chinese Affairs Office of the State Council. After 2000, especially after China's entry into the WTO in 2001, all central government organisations virtually ceased their direct business operations.

On the other hand, central government has strengthened its regulatory role in tourism. As in other cases of industry reform, the central government has been taking an incremental approach (触摸石头过河, *touching the stones to cross the river*) in developing tourism. Earlier administrative legislative efforts were mostly labelled 'provisional', which meant that the policies were temporary and perceived to be changing in the context of China's rapid social and economic transition. During these earlier processes CNTA may have found itself less powerful in coordinating issues pertinent to tourism when compared to other central government authorities. As a sub-ministerial central government agency not on a par with other more powerful ministries, CNTA had worked hard to enhance its status in the central government organisational structure with the growing importance of the tourism industry to the national economy. Among many departmental regulatory efforts initiated by CNTA to advance its status was the promulgation of a national tourism attraction standard (from A to AAAAA) resembling the national hotel star-rating system and its associated certification method. The standards and their implementation are believed to have permitted CNTA to gain more prestige in the central government hierarchy and the responsibilities held by the Ministry of Construction with reference to scenic tourist attractions were transferred to CNTA. After 2000, as the state's regulatory role (as against an operational role) was further authenticated by legislation at both State Council and ministerial levels, CNTA saw its status improve while still remaining a sub-ministerial central government agency.

The involvement of central government as an initiator and supplier of investment has been greatly reduced since 2000. This is not hard to understand as the market takes more control of the nation's economy with China's transition into a market economy, albeit with Chinese characteristics that still retain a role for government as a regulator and occasional partner in ostensibly private sector investments in tourism such as Xi'an's Cultural Heritage initiatives based on the theme of the Tang dynasty. Similarly, as evident in other countries, the central government's role as a national promoter has been strengthened. This is corroborated by the recent establishment of offices in new significant tourist source markets such as India and Russia. While official overseas tourism promotions have been almost exclusively conducted by CNTA, other central government agencies, such as the Ministry of Culture and the Overseas Chinese Affairs Office of the State Council have also been indirectly involved in tourism-related overseas promotions in their respective portfolio-related overseas activities. For instance, the latter has been sending itinerant cultural performance delegations overseas to cities with significant migrant Chinese residents during the Chinese Spring Festival in recent years, and performances under such slogans as 'Cultures of China – Festival of Spring' have created positive destination branding effects. Such activities may be in line with China's recent national image strategy to demonstrate its 'soft power', which has so far included two short video advertisements featuring a number of influential contemporary Chinese figures broadcast on Times Square in New York. The national image project was initiated and supported by the State Council Information Office.

As mentioned above, even within the central government portfolio, different departmental agencies would have their responsibilities and functions covering tourism or tourism-related industries to a greater or lesser degree. As tourism is such a multifaceted industry or cluster of industries, the administration of tourism is divided between various government agencies, particularly at regional level. Therefore, the coordinating role of the central government has been and remains prominent in China's tourism development. Initially when tourism was still regarded as part of foreign affairs and had not earned recognition as an independent administrative body, tourism-related work under the State Council was chaired by one of the then vice premiers (He, 1999). Such a general coordinating mechanism is still evident today with some inter-ministerial meetings institutionalised by the State Council. For instance, the National Holiday Tourism Inter-Ministerial Coordination Meetings consist of senior officials from 18 ministerial organisations including CNTA and the NDRC and the meetings are normally chaired by one of the secretary generals of the State Council. Another level of coordination occurs in the performance of general functions by CNTA. On different occasions, CNTA has to coordinate with relevant central government agencies and local governments at different levels (e.g. provincial, municipal and city). Since 2000 CNTA has been engaging itself more with local governments for different aspects of its responsibilities. A couple of reasons explain this. First, as tourism legislation and policy systems become more formally established, there is less need to conduct inter-departmental horizontal coordination; on the other hand, ensuring that existing policies are implemented requires top-down coordination between CNTA and local governments. Second, the current CNTA chairman held a provincial governor's position in Yunnan Province before being appointed to head CNTA, which possibly predisposes him to liaise with local governments in the development of various tourism agendas.

CNTA, as the responsible central government tourism administrative body, has undertaken a significant role in tourism training and education. Before 2000 CNTA itself was directly involved in various forms of education and training activities to provide industry-needed human resources. In the early stages of tourism development (the 1980s), CNTA had close contact with universities and provided initial funding to establish tourism programmes in eight universities (e.g. Nankai University, Xi'an International Studies University, Sun Yatsen University and Beijing International Studies University) (Huang, 2001). Later, Beijing International Studies University became a university directly affiliated to CNTA. CNTA also provided scholarships to send teaching staff from these universities overseas to gain up-to-date tourism disciplinary knowledge. In 1989 CNTA initiated the first nationwide tour guides qualification certificate examination, accompanied by systematic tour guide training (Huang & Weiler, 2010). In the other industry sectors, CNTA also managed the travel managers' certificate examination and hotel managers' certification training. However, after 2000 there is an apparent transition with regard to CNTA's role as an education and training provider. In line with the fourth central government restructuring requirements, CNTA had to reconsider its involvement in providing industry training and education. It started to retreat from micro-management to macro-management; instead of providing training activities and administering industry-wide qualification examinations directly, it empowers provincial tourism administrations to take over these responsibilities and positions itself only as a policy maker and overseer for industry training and examinations.

In general, and particularly during the last decade, the Chinese central government has gradually transferred its power in tourism to local governments. This gradualist approach bears an innate nature of 'trial and error-correction', in part because of caution in introducing and yet still wishing to control a market economy. At each key stage of the economic reforms since 1979, the central government has sought to consolidate the achievement of its previous efforts and determine the next objective and path choice – a process that at times has been far from certain, as demonstrated by the events of 1989. Hence the process of encouraging local governments to be more active and creative requires the delegation of decision-making powers to a provincial, municipal and eventually village level, while maintaining a certain degree of tolerance towards local governments' behaviours when local governments go beyond what is considered necessary (He, 2007). Additionally, central government needs to be aware of policies contrary to 'social harmony' in cases of poor administration, as evidenced in riots at Wukan, Guangdong in the last months of 2011. It thus walks the tightrope of social tension of encouraging 'proper' local initiatives yet retaining corrective powers to penalise improper initiatives that are often related to land grabs, corrupt practices and simply poor administration.

Evolution of Local Governments' Roles in Tourism

As a new growth point in the national economy, tourism quickly demonstrated a significant capacity to lead the development of regional economies. From the mid-1990s, a majority of provincial-level governments started to recognise tourism as one of their key pillar industries and promulgated a series of regulations and policies facilitating tourism development. In 1995 Hainan province pioneered the first provincial-level regulation on tourism administration. From 1995 to 2000, 18 out of 31 provincial governments legislated for new tourism administrative regulations under their respective jurisdictions (Wang, 2005). By December 2005, except for the government of Tianjin, all provincial governments in China had initiated administrative regulations for tourism development. The pace of provincial legislation in tourism has been impressive. There are two reasons for this. First, the legislative acts were driven by the rapid development of the tourism industry itself as it sought to obtain recognition and legislative status. Second, through their own legislation efforts, local governments hoped to strengthen their power base to better administer and control tourism resources within the emergent mixed economy.

Just as central government has assumed the six roles listed above, so too does local government. However, while local government may currently have less of a coordinating role given its freedom to operate within its territorial zone, this will become more important as the private sector expands, particularly given a current model of private–public sector partnerships in major projects. Additionally, this process requires a more proactive approach to the roles of regulator, educator and promoter. In recent years, some provincial governments have started to send tourism promotion delegations to their major source markets. The investment stimulator role performed by local governments has seen variations between the eastern developed and western less-developed provinces. A scarcity of capital in western China may have prompted local governments in the western regions to play a more active role as a source of investment stimulation. As disclosed by Bao and Zuo in Chapter 4, western local governments have sought to overcome local investment funding deficiencies through adopting policies favourable to outside investors, even at the cost of incurring losses through leakage effects.

Nevertheless, among the six roles, the operational role is becoming more prominent with local governments in China. Generally speaking, local governments are becoming a major force in tourism development in the new institutional arrangement. Their capacity to directly run enterprises that were inherited from the former planned economy system has enabled them to initiate local projects as a part of local economic policy and urban regeneration as evidenced by cities like Xi'an or Dalian. Two aspects may be highlighted in this process – those of operating tourism enterprises and those of managing tourism resource rights.

Local government operating tourism enterprises

In July 1984 the State Council approved the CNTA report on guidelines for tourism development, including 'speeding up the construction of tourism infrastructure by gathering resources at national, local, departmental, collective and individual levels, combining self-reliance with foreign capital investment'. This report marked the beginning of China's reform in its tourism administration. With the release of the report, local governments were encouraged to take an initiating role in tourism development and began accumulating power through direct investment in tourism. In 1998 half of the star-rated hotels were owned by governments and their departments at different levels, with a considerable number of them being local-level government bodies. In addition, local governments also ran travel agencies and almost every provincial government had its affiliated travel agencies.

The favourable political and economic environment of the period 1989 to about 2000 stimulated rapid development in the hotel and travel agency sectors. However, the rates of returns often disappointed for a number of reasons, one being over-stimulation, with the increase in hotel capacity exceeding the growth of market demand at various times including the mid-1990s and again in 2010 (Gu et al., 2012). Due to a shortfall in available equity, many hotels had to operate with heavy debts and the burden of bank interest payments, and from 1996 occupancy rates, operation revenues and profitability decreased gradually. In 1998, an industry-wide deficit occurred for the first time with operating profits dropping to –5.84% (China Tourist Hotels Association, 2006). Although measures were taken to alleviate the deficit, losses in the whole industry were still as high as RMB 2.6 billion at the end of 2000. Since that time, however, profits have recovered along with confidence and, as described by Gu et al. (2012), the Chinese hotel industry is now embarking on overseas mergers and acquisitions. Travel agencies faced a similar situation. In 2002 the total number of travel agencies reached 11,552, nine times more than in 1987. However, from 1991 to 2002, average profits were gradually declining. During 1996–2002, average profit rates in the travel agencies industry dropped below 3%, in some years even less than 2%.

Local government managing tourism resource properties

Since the mid-1990s, there has also been an apparent transition in local governments' roles in tourism development, with a movement away from managing enterprises to one of managing land and other types of tourism resources. This change has been accompanied by some contextual government initiatives such as the transfer of natural resources property rights to local public and private companies, reform in the hotel and travel agencies sectors, and the transition of a national tourism product development strategy to a holiday focus rather than being sightseeing oriented. The relationship between the central government and local governments falls into two stages. The first (from the mid-1990s to 2001) was marked by the transfer of management rights to large-scale tourist scenic zones to local governments who in turn invited private sector partners. The second stage (after 2002) saw renewed central government intervention to correct problems that arose from the first period.

Managing natural resources in tourism scenic zones

In 1997, the Hunan provincial government transferred the management right of Zhangjiajie Huanglong Cave and Baofeng Lake scenic zones to China Datong Co. Ltd. (Beijing) through entrusted contract and lease. Since then, other local governments have also started to explore new ways of managing tourism scenic zones. For example, in 1998 Sichuan Wan'guan Group signed an agreement with the Ya'an municipal government to exclusively develop the Bifengxia scenic zone. In 2000 Shandong Confucius International Tourism Co. Ltd. purchased the management rights to nine large tourist attractions, including the world heritage sites of the Temple of Confucius, the Family Mansion of Confucius and the Cemetery of Confucius. Half the shares of the Company were held by the Shenzhen Overseas Chinese Town Group. Other shareholders included Qufu Confucius Tourism Co. Ltd., Shandong Cable Shareholding Co. Ltd. and Shandong China International Travel Service Co. Ltd. In 2001 the Sichuan Government announced the transfer of management rights of 10 large tourism attractions including the Sanxingdui Heritage Site and the Jiuzhaigou Valley. In the same year, the German company Abbe Erle took over the management rights to the Xingwen Stone Forest scenic zone for 50 years through acquiring 49% of the shares of Yibin Cast Tourism Development Co. Ltd. Abbe Erle thus became the first foreign company investing in China's tourist attraction development.

Despite the public and often official opposition to transferring management rights in tourism scenic zones to the private sector that was expressed by a variety of central government ministerial authorities, more provincial governments joined the queue to transfer the management rights of large tourist attractions under their jurisdictions to private or semi-private companies for many reasons, including, it was thought, for personal gain. It is estimated that by the end of 2004 more than 300 tourism scenic zones and spots in over 20 provinces, municipalities and autonomous regions had their management rights transferred in different forms.

Management leases normally ranged from 25 to 30 years. Some might be as long as 50–70 years (Lai, 2005).

To counter suspicions about these arrangements, a number of regulations at local level came into force. For instance, in 2001 the Anji municipal government in Jiangxi Province indicated that they would transfer management rights of the Jinggangshan scenic zone, and the Yingtan government in Jiangxi province also declared that the management rights to its tourism attractions, including the famous Longhu Mountain, could be transferred. Equally, the Shandong provincial government also undertook similar policies, but in these cases attempts were made to separate ownership from management rights and efforts were made to attract different types of investors to develop and manage tourism attractions through leasing, contracts and an auction of management rights. Tang (2007) notes that these policies placed the central government in an ambiguous position with reference to its own policies, for while it sought to encourage the private sector and local initiatives, it was also keenly aware of growing concerns about conservation and protection (e.g. Zhang et al., 2009).

Managing tourism real estate

Another way in which local government managed tourism resources is the 'Tourism + Real Estate' development model, which was stimulated by the valuation of land resources in China's tourism scenic zones.

Because a higher profit could be generated from the transactions of properties based on tourist accommodation, real estate developers could see a mutual reinforcement between tourism development and real estate development. This was exemplified through the business growth path of the Shenzhen-based Overseas Chinese Town Group. This group accumulated its initial profits through developing and managing large tourist attraction projects like *Windows of the World* and *Splendid China* (Zhang & Zhang, 2009). It then started to develop tourism-based real estate projects. After 2002, the group's operation revenues were mainly from its real estate projects and real estate came to be the focus of its business. In the first nine months of 2002, 2003 and 2004, the contribution from its real estate projects to the group's pre-tax gross profits were 71%, 99% and 70%, respectively (Xu, 2005). Such a shift in business focus is also witnessed in other large tourism group companies in China such as the Hangzhou Songcheng Group and the Zhejiang Nandu Group. These cases signalled a tourism business development pattern unique to China's political and socio-economic situation.

The aforementioned two patterns of local governments' involvement in managing tourism attractions should be understood by the 'alliance of interest' formed between local governments and tourism enterprises. Such an alliance enables tourism enterprises to obtain potential benefits from local government officials who in turn are able to circumvent regulations regarding state ownership of tourism resources through their relationship with the private sector. In return, local governments share these benefits through gaining non-taxable government revenue generated from the management rights transfers.

The second stage of local government involvement in tourism resources development commenced in about 2002. With an increasing numbers of cases being exposed (particularly through social media) of tourism attraction property rights and management rights transfers, central government agencies such as the Ministry of Construction, the State Administration of Cultural Heritage, and the Ministry of Forest explicitly expressed opposition to such local government actions. In March 2002 the Ministry of Construction, in its letter of response regarding the issue of transferring management rights of tourism scenic zones in Sichuan Province, was careful to state that no government body or department has the right to transfer the management rights of tourism scenic zones, either in their entirety or partially, to private sector business enterprises. In August 2002 the Ministry of Construction, in its National Urban and Rural Planning and Scenic Zones Protection Video Conference, stressed that any form of transferring tourism scenic resources and land is strictly forbidden. In the same year, the State Administration of Cultural Heritage stated that 'some regions and organisations have transferred the management rights of cultural protection units without permission under the flag of separating ownership from management right; some even opened bids of contract to domestic and foreign companies for cultural heritage management. We firmly oppose such actions.' Later, in September 2005, the Ministry of Construction, in one of its working conferences, noted that 'no substantial transfer of tourism scenic zone tickets management rights should be allowed'. In 2006 the Ministry publicised those organisations which had committed illegitimate transfer of tourism scenic zone management rights and requested them to rectify the situations within a designated period (Tang, 2006).

The evidence implies that central and local governments act as two different parties of interest in China's tourism development. The central government and its ministerial authorities adopt a conservative approach towards the transfer of management rights of tourism zones to the private sector, yet this has been a practice that is common and indeed welcomed by many local governments as a means of attracting investment and new infrastructure into their cities. China's past economic reform and institutional change were based on an incremental policy of 'crossing the river by feeling the stones', but the future is more uncertain as current tensions in policy making continue to work towards new directions. It should be acknowledged that some central government agencies, like the Ministry of Construction, are exploring new means of managing tourism property rights through granting interim rights in tourism resources management in joint partnerships between provincial authorities and the private sector.

Conclusion

It has been noted that the relationship between politics and tourism has been an under-researched subject (Hall, 1994). Yet there is little doubt, especially in China, that the government's role in tourism is important, and this role has attracted more attention in the literature as evidenced by the work of Zhang (1998), Hao (1999), Kuang (2001), Jia and Wu (2002) and Zhang and Yan (2009). However, much of this work has been founded on trying to discern consistent principles in what has been an evolving and often particularistic set of case studies, as the tensions noted above have played out through mixtures of self- and communal interests and escalating property prices. A dyadic relationship may exist between central and local governments in China, and until recently central government has held a conservative but tolerant attitude towards local government initiatives in developing tourism. In contrast, local governments in China have been far more proactive, driven by a motivation to gain more direct benefits from tourism development. That dyadic relationship has in part been motivated by central governmental concern over vested self-interests inherent in some property deals and developments, while in recent years it has also turned towards sustainable tourism as a means of a more holistic stance while also inhibiting developments solely motivated by short-term profit motives. Based on their different interests, central and local governments may have different attitudes in promoting tourism sustainability. The key to unravelling the tensions and tackling issues of low income and employment generation through tourism may be through a form of sustainable tourism development that recognises financial sustainability as much as those other environmental and social issues more normally considered – at least in Western literature. To achieve this will require provincial and municipal governments to take a longer term perspective of development rather than simply buying into property developments that offer the 'instant modernisation' that meets needs for prestige on the part of local officials. It is perhaps these developments that can be the subject of future studies, and which in turn can inform future policies.

References

Airey, D. and Chong, K. (2010) National policy-makers for tourism in China. *Annals of Tourism Research* 37 (2), 295–314.

Bramwell, B. and Lane, B. (eds) (2004) *Tourism Collaboration and Partnership: Politics, Practice and Sustainability.* Clevedon: Channel View Publications.

China Tourist Hotels Association (2006) *20 Years of China Tourist Hotels.* Beijing: China Tourism Press.

Dredge, D. (2006) Policy networks and the local organisation of tourism. *Tourism Management* 27 (2), 269–280.

Gu, H., Ryan, C. and Yu, L. (2012) The changing structure of the Chinese hotel industry: 1980–2012. *Tourism Management Perspectives* 4, 56–63.

Gu, H., Ryan, C., Li, B. and Gao, W. (2013) Political connections, *guanxi* and adoption of CSR policies in the Chinese hotel industry: Is there a link? *Tourism Management* 34, 231–235. doi:10.1016/j.tourman.2012.01.017.

Hall, C.M. (1994) *Tourism and Politics: Policy, Power and Place*. Chichester: Wiley.

Hall, C.M. (2003) Politics and place: An analysis of power in tourism communities. In S. Singh, D.J. Timothy and R.K. Dowling (eds) *Tourism in Destination Communities* (pp. 99–112). Wallingford: CABI Publishing.

Hao, S. (1999) Thoughts on the tourism administration system in Shannxi. *Tourism Tribune* 14 (5), 40–42.

He, G. (ed.) (1999) *50 Years of China's Tourism*. Beijing: China Tourism Press.

He, X. (2007) Local governments' roles and their behavioural logics in the process of marketisation – a local government perspective. *Journal of Zhejiang University (Humanity and Social Sciences Edition)* 37 (6), 25–35.

Hu, S. (2002) *Relationship Between Central and Local Governments in the Economic Development – A Study on China's Fiscal System*. Shanghai: Shanghai People Press.

Huang, S. (2001) Problems and solutions on tourism higher education development in China. *Journal of Guilin Institute of Tourism* 12 (2), 66–69.

Huang, S. (2010) Evolution of China's tourism policies. *International Journal of Tourism Policy* 3 (1), 78–84.

Huang, S. and Weiler, B. (2010) A review and evaluation of China's quality assurance system for tour guiding. *Journal of Sustainable Tourism* 18 (7), 845–860.

Jenkins, C.L. and Henry, B.M. (1982) Government involvement in tourism in developing countries. *Annals of Tourism Research* 9 (4), 499–521.

Jia, S. and Wu, A. (2002) Institutional transition and China's tourism development stages and solutions. *Tourism Tribune* 17 (4), 19–23.

Jiang, S. (2006) An analysis of government functions and positions in China's tourism development. *Yunnan Geography and Environment Studies* 18 (5), 108–112.

Kuang, L. (2001) Centralize or decentralize: Government dilemma in developing tourism. *Tourism Tribune* 16 (2), 23–26.

Lai, D. (2005) In-depth comment: How many tourism scenic zones to sell? *Beijing Modern Commercial News*, 10 October, 2.

Li, Y. and Hu, Z. (2008) Red tourism in China. *Journal of China Tourism Research* 4 (2), 156–171.

Ma, A., Si, L. and Zhang, H. (2009) The evolution of cultural tourism: The example of Qufu, the birthplace of Confucius. In C. Ryan and H. Gu (eds) *Tourism in China: Destinations, Cultures and Communities* (pp. 182–196). New York: Routledge.

Matthews, H.G. and Richter, L.K. (1991) Political science and tourism. *Annals of Tourism Research* 18 (1), 120–135.

Richter, L.K. (1983) Political implications of Chinese tourism policy. *Annals of Tourism Research* 10 (3), 395–413.

Ryan, C. and Gu, H. (2009) Destinations and cultural representations: The importance of political context and the decay of Statism. In C. Ryan and H. Gu (eds) *Tourism in China: Destinations, Cultures and Communities* (pp. 139–156). New York: Routledge.

Sofield, T.H.B. and Li, F.M.S. (1998) Tourism development and cultural policies in China. *Annals of Tourism Research* 25 (2), 362–392.

Tang, L.X. (2006) Structural change of China's tourism industry and tourism industry policy selection. *Finance and Economics* 12, 101–103.

Tang, L. (2007) A study on the institutional transition of scenic zones property rights. Unpublished doctoral dissertation, Sichuan University, China.

Tisdell, C. and Wen, J. (1991) Foreign tourism as an element in PR China's economic development strategy. *Tourism Management* 12 (1), 55–67.

Tse, T.S.M. and Hobson, J.S.P. (2008) The forces shaping China's outbound tourism. *Journal of China Tourism Research* 4 (2), 136–155.

Wang, Z. (2005) An empirical study of local governments' policy support to tourism development in China. *Dongyue Forum* 26 (5), 69–76.

Wang, Y. and Bramwell, B. (2011) Heritage protection and tourism development priorities in Hangzhou, China: A political economy and government perspective. *Tourism Management* 33 (4), 988–998.

Wang, C. and Xu, H. (2011) Government intervention in investment by Chinese listed companies that have diversified into tourism. *Tourism Management* 32 (6), 1371–1380.

Wang, Y. (2012) *Empty Nest Syndrome for Post-Olympics Beijing*, Caixin China Weekly Finance and Economics, 25 July 2012.

Wilson, S., Fesenmaier, D.R., Fesenmaier, J. and Van Es, J.C. (2001) Factors for success in rural tourism development. *Journal of Travel Research* 40 (2), 132–138.

Wu, B., Zhu, H. and Xu, X. (2000) Trends in China's domestic tourism development at the turn of the century. *International Journal of Contemporary Hospitality Management* 12 (5), 296–299.

Xu, G. (2005) Overseas Chinese town real estate president Chen Jian: The going-out tourism real estate, accessed 25 January 2011, http://www.f024.com/html/news/200611/200511415303.htm

Xu, J., Zhang, H. and Wu, J. (2010) China's policies on foreign invested travel agencies upon its entry to the WTO: What can foreign investors do? *International Journal of Contemporary Hospitality Management* 22 (3), 360–381.

Yan, H. and Bramwell, B. (2008) Cultural tourism, ceremony and the state in China. *Annals of Tourism Research* 35 (1), 969–989.

Yang, L., Wall, G. and Smith, S.L.J. (2006) Ethnic tourism development: Chinese government perspectives. *Annals of Tourism Research* 35 (3), 751–771.

York, Q.Y. and Zhang, H.Q. (2010) The determinants of the 1999 and 2007 Chinese Golden holiday system: A content analysis of official documentation. *Tourism Management* 31 (6), 881–890.

Zhang, S. (1998) Reflection on the 'government-led' tourism development strategy. *Tourism Tribune* 13 (6), 21–22.

Zhang, H.Q. and Yan, Q. (2009) The effects of power, ideology, interest groups, and the government on tourism policy making – a conceptual model. *Journal of China Tourism Research* 5 (2), 158–173.

Zhang, N. and Zhang, W. (2009) Overseas Chinese town: A case study of the interactive development of real estate and tourism. In C. Ryan and H. Gu (eds) *Tourism in China: Destinations, Cultures and Communities* (pp. 88–98). New York: Routledge.

Zhang, H.Q., Chong, K. and Ap, J. (1999) An analysis of tourism policy development in modern China. *Tourism Management* 20 (4), 471–485.

Zhang, H.Q., Chong, K. and Jenkins, C.L. (2002) Tourism policy implementation in mainland China: An enterprise perspective. *International Journal of Contemporary Hospitality Management* 14 (1), 38–42.

Zhang, G., Pine, R. and Zhang, H.Q. (2000) China's international tourism development: Present and future. *International Journal of Contemporary Hospitality Management* 12 (5), 282–290.

Zhang, C.Z., Xu, H.G., Si, B.T. and Ryan, C. (2009) Visitors' perceptions of the use of cable cars and lifts in Wulingyuan World Heritage Site. *Journal of Sustainable Tourism* 17 (5), 551–567.

Zhang, Y. and Zhao, J. (2011) *Highway Builders Discover Dead End for Debt.*, Caixin China Weekly Finance and Economics, 15 September 2011.

13 The Meetings, Incentives, Conferences and Events (MICE) Industry in Hang Zhou: What Do Residents Think of Such Policies?

Chao (Nicole) Zhou and Chris Ryan

Introduction

It has become a cliché that tourism is a means by which economic regeneration or advantage can be obtained by countries, regions and cities, although that has been questioned in terms of the consequences whereby tourism may crowd out alternatively more profitable enterprises (Bresson & Logosah, 2011; Dwyer *et al.*, 2000). Certainly, as a mature phenomenon, tourism is displaying an increased range of product based on specialisations located within the specificities of a destination's assets. One of these is that of meetings, incentives, conferences and events (MICE), and in the last few decades competing cities and regions have developed new conference centres and exhibition halls. Having built such assets, three subsequent developments occur. First, city and regional tourism authorities seek to attract business to fill those centres to the point that the International Congress & Convention Association (ICCA) was able to claim in its 2004 report 'that each year the ICCA figures are anxiously awaited by destinations around the world, all of which compete fiercely for a larger share of this lucrative market' (ICCA, 2004). Second, tourism destination marketing organisations become proficient at creating new product that can be sold to domestic, out of region and international visitors – whether such events be business or recreation based. Third, not every new venue succeeds, as oversupply has occurred in many different market places – although this may be a combination of structural factors (an inherent over-supply of overly ambitious products), new modes of meetings via the use of new communication technologies, and temporary downturns in business cycles that dampen demand.

A further issue in considering the MICE market is that the public sector is often heavily engaged in the development of centres and the promotion of events. In Western societies expenditure on such centres can be questioned, as residents pay for such developments through property taxes and may then hold elected officials to account. In China, while the political processes differ, promoters of such investments can still be held to account on the premise that each such investment has an opportunity cost, part of which cost may be the very opaqueness of decision making that can give rise to accusations of corrupt practices. Consequently, while residents and other stakeholders may have a less direct means of holding promoters of MICE investments to account, in the final resort no ruling party can afford to ignore the views of those who eventually 'pay the bills'. As a society in transition, with an active blogging community that continually scrutinises the actions of publicly elected officials, surveys of residents' views increasingly have significance within the Chinese setting.

The purpose of this chapter is therefore to examine the responses of residents in Hang Zhou to the development of a MICE policy as part of its tourism promotions. The first part of the chapter will briefly review the literature. The second part of the chapter will briefly describe Hang Zhou as a tourism destination and the nature of past Expos and their role within the tourism assets of that city. Thirdly, a concept pertaining to attitudinal development towards such events is suggested, and it will then describe research undertaken to examine residents' views on the use of MICE by the Hang Zhou city government. The method used was one of qualitative research based on premises of social construction in a post-positivist paradigm – that is, it is thought possible to identify attitudes that exist independent of the researcher, and thus these can be 'discovered' even while the researcher interprets the comments made by respondents (Fontana & Frey, 2000; Guba, 1990).

Literature Review

There exists an extensive Western literature relating to the impacts that tourism has on local communities, their economies, culture, society and built and natural environments, while the same is now emerging in China as evidenced by other chapters in this book. Among the earliest conceptualisations is that of Doxey (1975) and the Irritation Index (Irridex). This argued that residents passed through varying stages of welcome, indifference, annoyance and hostility in their attitudes towards tourism as it developed over time. Akin to this were the implications of the Tourist Area Life Cycle envisaged by Butler (1980, 2006a, 2006b) and the destination spatial models of land use as illustrated by Young's (1983) model of a Maltese fishing village. This was envisaged to develop from being a small village comprising the cottages of local farmers and fishermen to become a modern resort complex complete with marina, hotels, apartments and retail malls. These become subject to extensive planning legislation to control further development.

A second stage in the literature then followed when the impacts began to be better described and measured, especially in the 1980s with the evolution of community- and environment-oriented planning mechanisms. These required social and environment impact assessments as a necessary part of regional planning and development as demonstrated by legislation in many countries. Early Western studies included those of Belisle and Hoy (1980), Liu et al. (1987), Davis et al. (1988) and Long et al. (1990), and from this it was but a short stage to better delineate the determinants of resident perceptions of tourism impacts. These determinants included psychographics, duration of residency, nature of employment, age and nature and frequency of contact with tourists (e.g. Fredline & Faulkner, 2000). Separate from the tourism literature, a broadening range of measures were being identified and adopted by those involved in town and country planning, and social assessment measures that included traffic counts and congestion, litter collection, crime statistics, retail patterns, patterns of land usage, air and water quality, house prices and building starts were being collected and analysed – all of which were applicable to the impacts caused by tourism (for early studies, see Gunn, 1988; Smith, 1992).

Associated with these changing understandings was an attempt to better conceptualise the patterns of resident attitudes towards tourism. Ap (1995) proposed the use of social exchange theory, whereby attitudes could be explained on the premise of mutual advantage. Lindberg et al. (1999) argued that residents engage in a series of trade-offs in which they require the positive impacts of tourism to be greater than the negative. For their part, Ryan et al. (1998) argued that changes were based upon value systems that increasingly tested altruistic motives as tourism developed and increasingly impinged upon daily life patterns. Consequently, altruism (e.g. tourism creates jobs for others) might be overwhelmed by the personal (e.g. tourists get in my way).

Inherent in these changing perspectives was an appreciation that tourism might be just one economic activity that co-exists among many that, in a post-modern world, are increasingly dependent on image and experience (Pine & Gilmore, 1998). Thus the tourism industries (Leiper, 2008) would often be ensconced in a site of multi-layered economic activities possessing a strong recreational, heritage and cultural ambience independent of tourism, even as tourism utilised and complemented those facilities. In short, tourism's developments and impacts could occur within the small, newly discovered location envisaged by Young (1983), the totally new and previously non-existent such as Cancun (Haywood, 1986) or the well-established commercial and post-industrial centre such as Birmingham (Lutz & Ryan, 1997).

This last cited paper has specific reference to the subject matter of this paper. As previously noted, MICE tourism has emerged as an inherent part of urban planning, restoration and renovation. It has thus become a commonplace that events are important success factors for the marketing of tourism and its development (Getz, 1997; Peters & Weiermair, 2000). It is therefore not uncommon for the public sector to be responsible for a large proportion of the special events provided for the community, and the majority of local governments now have a substantial and varied events programme (Thomas & Wood, 2004). Indeed, in many countries local authorities have personnel who have the specific role of devising a portfolio of events and conferences and the encouragement of the private sector to initiate conferences, conventions and meetings. Another factor that binds public and private sectors into partnership arrangements is the incorporation of MICE centres into wider portfolios of property, recreation and tourism developments. For example, Kasarda (2008) notes the emergence of airports as conference, retail and leisure hubs. Yet, despite the growth in the importance of events and the increasing public sector role in providing special events, the public service provision for entertainment, culture and the arts remains a non-mandatory requirement (Borrett, 1991; Shone & Parry, 2001). Furthermore, because of the interest in economic regeneration, research has been dominated by economic impact assessments and resident reactions have been much less studied. Consequently, this study can be justified on the grounds that it extends the research on resident perceptions of tourism impacts to the specifics of event tourism, while secondly it is looking at a country where tourism is both relatively new in itself and new as a subject of research.

Consequently, when Chinese scholars began to consider planning issues and tourism impacts, they had access to a mature literature that identified determinants of change and the possible outcomes of those changes. For their part, Yu et al. (2010) noted the existence of 30 national convention and exhibition research institutes with 10 specialist journals, in addition to the more general journals reporting research into the MICE and related industry.

It is nonetheless possible to identify a trend in some of this Chinese literature. There was still, for example, a literature that sought to define and discuss exactly what the MICE sector was, and this can be further classified as that part which simply sought to describe and explain Western approaches to a Chinese audience and then tried to identify specific Chinese characteristics that differentiated the Chinese situation from those in other countries. Feng (2008) and Wang (2004) are examples of the former. Wang (2004), for example, noted that while at the time of writing China had over a decade of MICE promotion and exploitation, research was for the most part atheoretical and had achieved little. Nonetheless, in 2002 the same author had advanced ideas relating to the optimising of MICE tourism in China, drawing on that country's situation (Wang, 2002), while Zhao and Li (2005) had analysed inter-sectoral relationships within the Chinese industry. Case study analysis was also popular, one such example being that of Luo and Ding (2004), who argued that the MICE industry had the potential to achieve a 'breakthrough' in the development of Yiwu's tourism. Equally, with the news that Shanghai would host the World Expo in 2010, a number of studies were written to speculate about the likely outcomes (e.g. Guo, 2003; Liu et al., 2000).

By the latter half of the last decade much more sophisticated analyses had also appeared alongside a continuing series of case studies, as authors argued that context remained important. Thus Jin et al. (2012) examined the emergence of clusters of China's exhibition centres and their impacts on destinations from the perspectives of exhibitors. They noted the importance of pre-existing industrial strengths in determining the degree to which second- and third-tier cities would be able to secure success. Wu (2005), like the Western counterparts noted above, also placed MICE development within the broader framework of urban development and recreation with his spatial analysis of sightseeing patterns. Another example, Dai and Bao (2005), generated a measure of mega-events using statistics derived from consumer sociology and social geography to argue that spaces moved from what they termed the sacred to the secular. They also argued that longer term sustainability was only possible if the exhibition industry immersed itself into regional tourism development.

Part of that integration, it can be argued, also includes the role and perceptions of residents, and this was the topic of Luo's (2006) study of the impact of the MICE industry on Houjie Town, Dongguan City. Using a statistical analysis including clustering, four groups were identified, namely: 'lovers', 'in-betweeners', 'rationalists' and the 'indifferent'. This is one of a comparatively small number of Chinese studies that take into account residents' views, and this chapter builds upon that research. However, it is also notable that much of the research reported builds either upon observation, case studies or statistical studies, and few attempt to build upon textual analysis derived from interviews and conversations. This chapter tries to do this to introduce a further element into Chinese research.

The Context of the Research

This study was initially commenced as a reaction to the 2006 Hang Zhou World Leisure Expo. Hang Zhou is the capital city of Zhejiang Province, which lies fourth in Chinese provincial GDP ranking. Hang Zhou City has long been well regarded as a tourism destination in China because it possesses notable historical and cultural features. A traditional saying is 'In the sky there is heaven ... on earth there is Hang Zhou'. One of its main features is West Lake, which is largely artificial and is surrounded by mountains. The city's history is a long one, and dates back to the Neolithic Hemudu culture of 7000 years ago. The West Lake itself still possesses as a feature a dyke built in 1089 by Su Shi, and when Marco Polo visited it he hailed it as one of the finest cities in the world (Barmé, 2011). It has thus marketed itself for both domestic and international tourism as a city of leisure based on cultural and heritage assets (Zheng & Liu, 2005). It has a population of 6 million people and in 2010 attracted 2.2 million overseas visitors and 45.5 million domestic visitors (Hangzhou.gov.cn, 2011).

Based on the city's leisure facilities, the first world leisure exposition was held in Hang Zhou from 22 April to 22 October 2006, and lasted for 6 months. This exposition was mainly organized by the World Leisure Organization, based on the theme 'Leisure – changing human life', with the purpose of building an 'oriental leisure charm'. This world exposition was not a single themed event as it also included the annual Hang Zhou West Lake exhibition and thus became a multiple event that focused on various themes which included culture, heritage and tourism and incorporated the Zhejiang Provincial Museum of Cultural Relics and Fine Art Special Exhibition Series and The Third Hang Zhou West Lake Chorus Festival. Other themed events were also linked with the Exposition and were drawn from sport, business and social activities. Examples included the Miss International Tourism Finals and the 2006 Hang Zhou International City 'Business Cup' Go Competition.

Some of these subsidiary and complementary events had a long history in their own right. For example, the West Lake World Exposition has been held since 1929, when it was the fourth international exposition after the 1893 Chicago Exposition, the 1900 Paris Exposition and the 1927 Philadelphia Exposition. The West Lake Exposition has been re-held annually since 2000. For the 2006 Expo a 'three Lake Park' was also built – which proved controversial due to perceived negative impacts on the environment.

Taking into account the location of the research and the above cited literature it was expected that residents would be supportive of the events on the general grounds that economic improvements would result for the city. However, a reconsideration on further probing could occur, and past evidence suggests that residents are more cautious about claiming social and environmental benefits, and can reconsider economic gains on the grounds as to whether the costs, both financial and other, are too high. Additionally, respondents can be prompted to assess to what degree they gain from the impacts created by MICE tourism, and eventually an overall assessment is gained based upon an evaluation of these factors filtered through personal value systems. Figure 13.1 indicates these anticipated response sets.

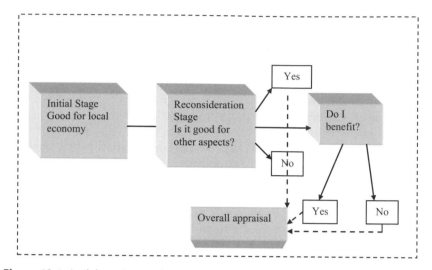

Figure 13.1 Anticipated sets of responses

Research Methodology

Given that much of the literature on the impacts of tourism as cited above is derived from the English-speaking world, a qualitative study was adopted in order to elicit responses from residents while using a semi-structured questionnaire to prompt conversational data, whereby the questionnaire provided a framework to ensure some commonality of subject matter across the various respondents. The questions are indicated in more detail below, but related to residents' perceptions of Hang Zhou, the benefits it derived generally from tourism, and then more specifically as to reactions to the Hang Zhou World Leisure Exposition. The research methodology is premised on social constructionism; that is, the researcher constructs perceptions from answers by an immersion in the text of the conversation. Conversation as a research tool implies many nuances. The researcher and respondent are potential equals in the research process; the respondent can control the research agenda as much as the researcher, yet it is the researcher who will offer the interpretive act. Feminist writers have redefined interviews as a dialogue that engages in openness and the sharing of emotion, and as a narrative that can challenge the concepts of scientific positivism (e.g. Fontana & Frey, 2000). However, in this instance the research methodology sought an 'unbalanced conversation' in the sense that the researcher sought responses and adopted a phenomenographic perspective whereby the role was to prompt increasing details of response and recall from the respondents (Bowden, 1994; Dall'Alba, 1994). However, conversational structures were adhered to, and the data were sequentially organised, contextually oriented and interactive (Gubrium & Holstein, 2000). Interviews were recorded and, additionally, after each interview, the first author immediately took notes on a laptop of key impressions, phraseology and other notes as part of the dataset. The first author is a native of Hang Zhou and thus conversant with the local dialect.

Respondents were selected through a filter question that asked whether they had attended any of the events associated with the 2006 Expo and, secondly, whether they were residents of Hang Zhou so as to ensure their familiarity with the events. The sample was divided almost evenly between local residents who had and had not attended an event associated with the World Leisure Expo. Interviews took place in cafés where people were resting and expected to spend some time so that they could engage in conversations that could be quite long (up to an hour). A cross-section of the general public was selected and the total of 40 respondents represented an equitable mix of gender and age above 18 years. Data were analysed in two ways. The first author immersed herself in the text, identifying themes and also creating a translation into English for the second author. He then independently analysed the text using the software programs *CatPac* and *Thought View*, and subsequently the two authors compared notes and understandings of the text to arrive at a consensual interpretation. This discourse is complex, and the process implies a post-positivistic perspective of a 'truth' independent of the research. It becomes, however, a decontextualised 'truth', for it has been separated from the initial series of conversational interplays, but the credibility of the interpretation becomes understood within another context, that of the wider tourism literature, and of shared recognitions of the categories that are formulated and discussed below.

Data Analysis

Question 1 asked respondents if they had attended events, and if so, what type. Just over half of the sample (56%) indicated that they had, while the most common reason for not going was not a lack of interest but a lack of time or a perceived lack of an interesting event to attend. Thus two respondents replied simply, 'No, no time' while another stated, 'No, no time and no interesting shows'. Of those that had gone to an event or show, three categories emerged from the text, these being: (a) a high attendee of shows, perhaps because of occupation or business; (b) a more selective attendee who went to shows solely because they possessed a specific interest, but who nonetheless had seemingly been to a number of events, conferences or shows; and (c) the occasional attendee. The range of shows and events mentioned ranged from academic conferences to car shows, agricultural shows, home and housing shows, beauty shows and exhibitions of museums and arts and crafts. Car shows were the most commonly mentioned, as were trade-related shows.

Within the academic literature there exists at least one conundrum. On the one hand, a common motivation for the development of an events portfolio is the further development of tourism whereby delegates attracted to a conference, festival, trade show or similar event not only engage in expenditure associated with that event, but also may prolong stays in order to visit other attractions and so swell the numbers of tourists visiting attractions otherwise not related to the trade show, conference, etc. However, some research into festivals and sporting events (e.g. Ryan & Lockyer, 2001; Ryan & Saleh, 1993) has indicated that in the majority of cases those going to an event are primarily motivated by a wish to attend that specific event, and there is little visitation to other attractions. Consequently, one might expect to find that the present sample would exhibit the same intended behaviours. This was generally found not to be the case. Of the 40 respondents, only five said that they would not find time to travel to other attractions in the region of the event. Of the remaining 35, the majority indicated that they would definitely make such visits, or normally did so, while just five indicated that they would usually do so dependent upon available time and money. Thus, one respondent stated:

> Yes, I will spend a little time on it, but it depends on the schedule, if the event is in the city where I live I will not spend time to make such visits. If the event is in other cities, I will travel around because I have already paid the transportation fees.

Indicative of the majority opinion were the two respondents who stated:

> Definitely I will do that because otherwise the opportunity (to travel) is hard to come by.

> Yes, I will also take some travel because I do not always have time to go travelling. During the event time one can both do the work and travel, which is good.

That this is the case is commonly noted within the Chinese situation. Thus Wang (2007) noted that a significant proportion of both internal and domestic travel was related to official business travel, and that it was common for people within such trips to have organised visits for recreational purposes.

The third question specifically sought to know whether respondents were aware of the Hang Zhou World Leisure Exposition and, if so, what was the source of their information. All respondents knew of the Expo, and nearly all stated that they received their information through TV and newspapers.

The questioning then turned toward residents' perceptions of Hang Zhou as a destination in itself, its capabilities of hosting such major Expos and its competitive positioning. First, all the respondents agreed that Hang Zhou had the capacity to host such an event given its rate of economic development, infrastructure and convention buildings. Thus one respondent noted:

> Hang Zhou definitely has the capability. In the last ten years Hang Zhou's economy has dramatically developed, so the economy is one of the strong foundations. Secondly, Hang Zhou city government has the daring and resolution (to do this); finally the leisure and tourism environment is good.

In terms of competitive positioning, almost all of the respondents commented that the competition was very strong, but that Hang Zhou possessed significant advantages that permitted it to compete. One of the most important of these were the natural features of Hang Zhou and its reputation, at least within China, for being a beautiful city with lakes and gardens. Other advantages lay in the city possessing an appropriate infrastructure, experience in hosting such events and access to substantial population – including that of Shanghai.

Respondents were then asked to consider potential visitors to MICE type events and to assess what would attract them to Hang Zhou. The answers fell into two main categories, and Figure 13.2 represents a simplified perceptual diagram derived from the textual analysis software *CatPac* and *Thought View*. The two classifications were (a) content and interest of the event itself to a potential visitor and (b) the nature of Hang Zhou as a host city. Figure 13.2 indicates that the two main dimensions had little direct interaction; they stood as two separate perceptual dimensions with little interaction between them. However, the second dimension, the beauty of Hang Zhou, had two sub-themes – the number of tourism attractions that were often based on natural features, and fame and culture, the last drawing in part on

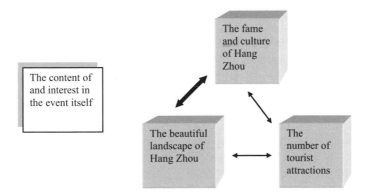

Figure 13.2 Perceptual map of Hang Zhou as a host city

events like the Hang Zhou Silk Cultural Festival and the Ghost Festival (Zhongyuan) which is specifically a feature of local life even though celebrated in many parts of China.

The questioning then began to assess how events can impact upon people, and at first the questioning was at a general rather than a personal level. Thus people were asked how hosting an event like the Leisure Expo impacted on Hang Zhou. Nearly all respondents recognised economic benefits that could accrue to the city, and the dimensions of these responses were three-fold and interlinking. The classifications were as follows, and indicative quotes are provided as being illustrative of the content of the dimensions:

(a) Of general economic benefit to the city;
     'The event is good for the city's tourism development and it also can bring many economic opportunities.'
(b) Of benefit to the tourism industry, which in turn benefits the city;
     'The main purpose of holding the event is to attract more tourists, so this benefit should be completed. The event is not a single event; it includes many different kinds of small shows; many of them relate to business. Many foreign companies were attracted to attend this event so the economic opportunities are obvious.'
(c) Of benefit to specific attributes of the city.
     'The major benefit from the event is to attract more tourists to view the new garden that was built for the 2006 Leisure Expo. The event can attract many foreign businesses, so it is good for city's economy and its development.'

When asked what were the actual benefits to the city, a relatively long list of advantages was produced, including not only economic benefits, but infrastructure development, better branding and knowledge of the city, including knowledge by foreigners, development of overseas links, both business and personal, environmental improvement through tree and flower planting and garden enhancement, cultural development through care of heritage buildings and the development of recreational facilities. Additionally, half of the sample felt able to point to specific examples of such improvements, while some referred to the more fashionable appearance of the city and its inhabitants and a feeling that the city was more lively as evidenced by the growth of neon lights and signs. However, five of the 40 respondents were unsure in terms of either not being able to identify specific improvements, or being unsure of how much of the improvement could be attributed to tourism and the MICE industry.

Respondents were then asked to what extent they had been influenced directly by these changes. Of the 40 respondents, 26 answered that there had been impact. Of the remaining 14, the changes noted tended to be psychological rather than physical, being in terms of feeling pride in the city and its achievements, having some enhancement in their leisure lifestyles through use of some of the facilities that had been developed for various events such as new gardens, or through being introduced to new foods. None of the respondents had been involved in any direct way through community action with these events, and indeed there was some doubt expressed as to what degree these events had involved local communities. Events like the Leisure Expo were seen as being organised by 'government' and a professional cadre of event organisers that had little impact on or involvement with the grassroots of local citizenry. This was not to argue that there were no benefits, and as already noted respondents were able to point to economic and other benefits at a city level, but little direct involvement or impact on personal lives seem to have been perceived as resulting from the Expo or similar events.

The final questions then were related to cost and to whether the expenditures involved in such Expos were indeed worth it. Indeed, might not the same results for the city in terms of infrastructure development have occurred in any case at possibly a lower cost if there had been no Expo? How can one really allocate or estimate returns from such events when, as noted, some of the returns are psychological rather than material? In terms of negative impacts, half of the respondents immediately made mention of the growth in traffic. Second, almost as many mentioned a gradual degradation in the environment, and most of those who also identified worsening traffic were at pains to mention this additional degradation was an additional and not solely traffic-related observation. A fifth of the respondents made reference to rising costs of living, of which property was the most immediately identified. A related issue was that local residents were bearing the cost of the event in many ways – one of which was that ticket prices to the events themselves were often too high. For example, one resident said:

> The total service is not good enough and some prices like the Leisure Expo garden ticket price is really high, which cannot be accepted by local normal residents. The Leisure Expo cannot be compared with the Olympics and World Expo [in attractiveness].

There was some mention of events like the Olympics. A small number felt that Hang Zhou had been used as a trial with the Leisure Expo to learn lessons for the Olympics, while a few others felt Hang Zhou should learn lessons from other event cities as to how to handle the negative impacts that occur from such events.

Figure 13.3 attempts to summarise the perceptual map derived from the software. The size of the boxes illustrate the frequency of response, while the arrows indicate linkages between the dimensions that comprise attitude toward perceived negative impacts of this form of tourism. The first observation is the degree of disconnectedness that exists – the components lie

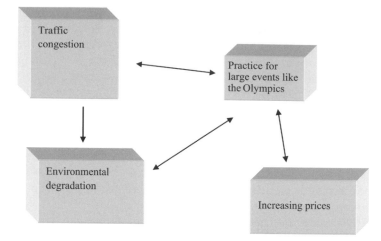

Figure 13.3 Dimensions of perceived negative impacts

united in that they create a negative impact on Hang Zhou – but the articulation of their inter-relatedness is not well formed in the responses given. Traffic congestion adds to environmental degradation, but there are other issues of environmental degradation linked to crowding due to the presence of visitors from outside the city, and an overuse of leisure and recreational facilities, both of which are perceived separate from simple road traffic congestion. The perception that Hang Zhou is an experiment for other larger events to be hosted by China is only thinly linked to the other aspects (as shown by thin dotted lines), while increasing prices both generally and specifically related to housing stands separate from the other concerns.

Given that respondents could identify negative impacts, the responses to the question, 'Is it worth the government spending money on these events?' overwhelmingly produced a positive response where just under two-thirds of the respondents stated that it was worthwhile, with two specifically using the phrase 'Of course it is worthwhile'. The reasons given for this positive response were the economic benefits, the development of future tourism development and the strengthening of the city brand. Of the remaining one-third of the respondents, most approved of the expenditure, but with varying caveats, while only about one-sixth of the respondents expressed criticism of such expenditure, arguing that the costs involved exceeded the benefits gained. Typical of these last classifications of comments were:

> I heard that the expenditure was too much and caused an imbalance between the input and return. Currently, the situation is in deficit. The problem is that the government should learn from this experience. [It should] try to attract more social communities to be involved in this and use more smaller investors, which can bring the most economic benefits.

It is not worth [the expenditure], the government has put lots of money into promotion and marketing but it did not attract enough foreign tourists and attendees.

On the other hand, there was a wide recognition that Hang Zhou is a 'tourism city' and thus needs to develop its tourism further to sustain its image and advantages.

Discussion

The results indicated that residents tend towards response sets whereupon economic benefits are immediately identified as being associated with an event like the World Leisure Expo. The data also indicate, at least in part, the basis of these perceptions. First, there is a very high awareness based upon media usage and media reports that not only referred to content of the Expo, but also to estimates of an anticipated economic gain based on estimates of the 2000 West Lake Exposition generating RMB 16 billion of foreign investment (West Lake Exposition Hang Zhou, 2006). Second, evidence of economic benefits was observed and included the development of the lakes, improvements in roads, and the development of Mei Jia Wu village on the fringe of Hang Zhou. Separate from but related to tourism is the fact that the city is due to increase its population with a new urban district, Hang Zhou Gulf Town, being built, which will house 800,000 people. Thus the signs of economic development are obvious. As was predicted though, while economic growth occupies a salient awareness, one can question the degree to which it becomes a determinant of attitudes when the nature of the questioning changes. Degradation of the environment is equally obvious in many parts of Zhejiang Province, and air and water quality has been negatively impacted by industrialisation (Swanson et al., 2004). A significant reason for this has been the failure to implement legislative safeguards and the under-resourcing of environmental agencies (Swanson et al., 2004). A tension thus arises in answers between perceived economic growth that can, at least in part, be attributable to developing tourism and specifically to events like the World Expo on the one hand, and a perception that these impacts bring about congestion, environmental degradation and little immediate direct benefit. For the moment, though, the evaluations are being filtered through perceptions of pride in the development of the city and the increased international attention that such Expos bring. Much of this can be explained by reference to the policies enacted prior to the opening of the Chinese economy to the outside world, policies that meant a city the size of Hang Zhou would have been generally unrecognised in the wider world. Thus to some extent attitudes are explicable by reference to an evolutionary process of establishing a self-belief and city identity for Hang Zhou as not only a major Chinese city, but also as a major international city capable of managing, establishing and exploiting events like the World Leisure Expo.

Such conclusions need, however, to be assessed within the framework of the study. It is a qualitative study, and thus has the advantages and disadvantages of such methodologies. It is well known that it is difficult to generalise from such studies, but equally such studies provide rich descriptions of processes as perceived by the actors in the study, and can be an excellent means of establishing attitudinal dimensions that can be subsequently assessed by quantitative means. In the discussions with respondents, informants tended to give willingly of their time and were articulate over their concerns, and that too is both a strength and a weakness. It is a strength in the collection of data; it is a weakness in that it provides a voice to the articulate and perhaps silences the less articulate, the more reluctant or the less able to voice a view. In short, this study needs to be contextualised with many dimensions – that of the tourism research on MICE and residents' attitudes, and that of the continuing understandings of qualitative research. One conclusion, however, is that the nature of the debate initiated within a Western context is also applicable to contemporary Chinese society, and thus one finding is that lessons from Western experiences are applicable also to the new China that is now emerging.

Acknowledgements

This chapter is based on a paper initially published in *The Journal of Hospitality Applied Research* by the authors and reworked for this book.

References

Ap, J. (1995) Residents' perceptions on tourism impacts. *Annals of Tourism Research* 19 (4), 665–590.

Barmé, G.R. (2011) A Chronology of West Lake and Hangzhou. *China Heritage Quarterly*, 28 December, 1–9.

Belisle, J. and Hoy, D. (1980) The perceived impact of tourism by residents: A case study in Sante Maria, Columbia. *Annals of Tourism Research* 7 (1), 83–99.

Borrett, N. (1991) *Leisure Services UK*. London: Macmillan.

Bowden, J.A. (1994) The nature of phenomenographic research. In J.A. Bowden and E. Walsh (eds) *Phenomenographic Research: Variations in Method – The Warburton Symposium* (pp. 1–17). Melbourne: RMIT.

Bresson, G. and Logosah, K. (2011) Crowding out effects of cruise tourism on stay-over tourism in the Caribbean: Non-parametric panel data evidence. *Tourism Economics* 17 (1), 127–158.

Butler, R. (1980) The concept of tourist area cycle of evolution: Implications for the management of resources. *Canadian Geographer* 24, 5–12.

Butler, R.W. (2006a) *The Tourism Area Life Cycle: Applications and Modification*. Clevedon: Channel View Publications.

Butler, R.W. (2006b) *The Tourism Area Life Cycle: Conceptual and Theoretical Issues*. Clevedon: Channel View Publications.

Dai, G.-Q. and Bao, J. (2005) Characteristics of mega-exposition and the change of the property of its venue – a case study of Expo '99, Kunming and Floriexpo 2001, Shunde. *Tropical Geography* 25 (3), 258–262.

Dall'Alba, G. (1994) Reflections on some faces of phenomenography. In J.A. Bowden and E. Walsh (eds) *Phenomenographic Research: Variations in Method – The Warburton Symposium* (pp. 73–88). Melbourne: RMIT.

Davis, D., Allen, J. and Cosenza, R.M. (1988) Segmenting local residents by their attitudes, interests, and opinions toward tourism. *Journal of Travel Research* 27 (2), 2–8.

Doxey, G.V. (1975) A causation theory of visitor-resident irritants: Methodology and research inferences. *Proceedings of the Sixth Annual Conference of the Travel Research Association, San Diego, CA* (pp. 195–198). San Diego, CA: Travel Research Association.

Dwyer, L., Forsyth, P., Madden, J. and Spurr, R. (2000) Economic impacts of inbound tourism under different assumptions regarding the macroeconomy. *Current Issues in Tourism* 3 (4), 325–363.

Feng, X-H. (2008) Who benefits? tourism development in Fenghuang Country, China. *Human Organization* 67 (2), 207–220.

Fontana, A. and Frey, J.H. (2000) From structured questions to negotiated text. In N.K. Denzin and Y.S. Lincoln (eds) *Handbook of Qualitative Research* (2nd edn) (pp. 645–672). Thousand Islands, CA: Sage.

Fredline, E. and Faulkner, B. (2000) Host community reactions: A cluster analysis. *Annals of Tourism Research* 27 (3), 764–785.

Getz, D. (1997) *Event Management and Event Tourism*. New York: Cognizant Communication Corporation.

Guba, E. (1990) *The Paradigm Dialogue*. Newbury Park, CA: Sage.

Gubrium, J.F. and Holstein, J.A. (2000) Analyzing interpretive practice. In N.K. Denzin and Y.S. Lincoln (eds) *Handbook of Qualitative Research* (2nd edn) (pp. 487–508). Thousand Islands, CA: Sage.

Gunn, C. (1988) *Tourism Planning*. New York: Taylor and Francis.

Guo, Y. (2003) An analysis of effects on the tourism development potential of 2010 Shanghai World Expo. *Tourism Tribune* 18 (5), 52–56.

Hangzhou.gov.cn (2011) About Hang Zhou, accessed 6 March 2011. http://eng.hangzhou.gov.cn.

Haywood, M. (1986) Can the tourist-life cycle be made operational? *Tourism Management* 7 (3), 154–167.

ICCA (International Congress and Convention Association) (2004) *ICCA Statistics 2003*, accessed 18 July 2006. http://www.iccaworld.com.

Jin, X., Weber, K. and Bauer, T. (2012) Impact of clusters on exhibition destination attractiveness: Evidence from Mainland China. *Tourism Management* 33 (6), 1429–1439.

Kasarda, J.D. (2008) Shopping in the Retail City and Aerotropolis. *Research Review* 15 (2), 50–55.

Leiper, N. (2008) Why 'the tourism industry' is misleading as a generic term and the case for the plural variation, 'tourism industries'. *Tourism Management* 29 (2), 237–251.

Lindberg, K., Dellaert, B.G.C. and Rassing, C.R. (1999) Resident tradeoffs: A choice modeling approach. *Annals of Tourism Research* 26 (3), 554–569.

Liu, J.C., Sheldon, P.J. and Var, T. (1987) Residents' perception of the environmental impacts of tourism. *Annals of Tourism Research* 14 (1), 1–37.

Liu, Z., Jin, H. and Liang, B. (2000) Some thoughts on bidding for the World Expo Shanghai 2010. *Tourism Science* 4 (1), 1–4.

Long, P.T., Perdue, R.R. and Allen, L. (1990) Rural resident tourist perceptions and attitudes by community level of tourism. *Journal of Travel Research* 28 (3), 3–9.

Luo, G-Y. and Ding, W-Y. (2004) MICE tourism – the turning point to develop tourism industry in Yiwu. *Economic Geography* 24 (6), 857–860.

Luo, Q.-J. (2006) A study on community perceptions that affect MICE industry in Houjie town, Dongguan City. *Tourism Tribune* 21 (3), 77–82.

Lutz, J. and Ryan, C. (1997) Impacts of inner city projects: the case of the international convention centre, Birmingham. In P. Murphy (ed.) *Quality Management in Urban Tourism* (pp. 41–53). Chichester: John Wiley.

Peters, M. and Weiermier, K. (2000) State-management and marketing. *Tourism Jahrbuch 2000,* 105–124.

Pine, B.J. and Gilmore, J.H. (1998) Welcome to the experience economy. *Harvard Business Review* 76 (4), 97–105.

Ryan, C. and Lockyer, T. (2001) An economic impact case study: The South Pacific Masters' Games. *Tourism Economics* 7 (3), 267–276.

Ryan, C. and Saleh, F. (1993) Jazz and knitwear – factors that attract tourists to festivals. *Tourism Management* 14 (4), 289–297.

Ryan, C., Scotland, A. and Montgomery, D. (1998) Resident attitudes to tourism development – a comparative study between the Rangitikei, New Zealand and Bakewell, United Kingdom. *Progress in Tourism and Hospitality Research* 4 (2), 115–130.

Shone, A. and Parry, B. (2001) *Successful Event Management: A Practical Handbook.* London: Continuum.

Smith, R.A. (1992) Beach resort evolution: Implications for planning. *Annals of Tourism Research* 19 (2), 304–332.

Swanson, K.E., Kuhn, R.G. and Xu, W. (2004) Environmental policy implementation in rural China: A case study of Yuhang, Zhejiang. *Environmental Management* 27 (4), 481–491.

Thomas, R. and Wood, E.H. (2004) Event-based tourism: A survey of local authority strategies in the UK. *Local Governance* 29 (2), 127–136.

Wang, C.-L. (2002) A research on building the optimized developing model of China's MICE tourism. *Tourism Tribune* 17 (2), 44–48.

Wang, C.-L. (2004) A commentary of domestic research on MICE tourism. *Journal of Guilin Institute of Tourism* 15 (6), 77–81.

Wang, D. (2007) *China's Outbound Travel Market.* Beijing: Ivy Consulting and China Outbound Tourism.

West Lake Exposition Hang Zhou (2006) *West Lake Exposition Hang Zhou,* accessed 10 May 2007. http://www.hzdjy.com/.

Wu, C. (2005) Research for spatial units and spatial structure of recreation and tourism in cities. *Urban Planning Forum* 157 (3), 82–87.

Young, B. (1983) Touristisation of traditional Maltese fishing-farming villages. *Tourism Management* 12 (1), 35–41.

Yu, H., Fu, Q. and Zhou, J. (2010) An overview of China convention and exhibition research and higher education. *Journal of Quality Assurance in Hospitality and Tourism* 11 (4), 283–291.

Zhao, Y. and Li, X. (2005) Several relationships in MICE tourism requiring orders. *Journal of Southwest China Normal University (Philosophy and Social Sciences Edition)* 31 (2), 92–97.

Zheng, S. and Liu, J. (2005) A city of leisure in the world: Hangzhou's CI position in the 21st century. *Tourism Tribune – Chinese Tourism Research Annual* (English version) 2005, 127–137.

Part 3

Planning

14 Planning for Tourism Places

Chris Ryan and Songshan (Sam) Huang

Introduction

There is little doubt that tourism planning has attracted significant attention from tourism academics, as planning most often has been seen as the means by which long-term environmental, social and economic sustainability can be achieved (Hall, 2007; Inskeep, 1991). The use of planning controls such as zoning whereby permitted and prohibited usage of land or marine areas is carefully delineated by area and/or time is probably one of the most common planning tools used, although a number of alternative techniques exist at both macro and micro levels. Ryan (2003) provides a list and description of such means, including the use of 'honey pot' destinations designed to be a focal point of tourism development thereby leaving other areas undisturbed, the careful design and construction of footpaths that both lead visitors to points of interest and away from more fragile areas, the use of soft tourism development whereby tourism is permitted only to fit into existing patterns of economic development and not dominate it (e.g. as in some forms of agri-tourism), and more altruistic measures such as appeals to adhere to given codes of conduct.

The Need for Planning

The nature of such appeals is exemplified by Corak (2006). Writing about the Opatija Riviera in Croatia she notes a period of decline in the 1930s, a rebuilding of mass tourism after World War II, further infrastructure decline and a need for investment after the break-up of Yugoslavia, and the turmoil that accompanied that period. Thus she notes:

> Assuming that the Opatija Riviera opts for a successful expanded tourism future, development should not be left to uncontrolled, sporadic activities, as has been the case in the past. A planned approach to tourism, which identifies and evaluates the optimal development options, should be applied. (Corak, 2006: 284)

The call for planning is thus understandable, especially when considering what is required to seek solutions to correct and avoid past mistakes. Agarwal (2002: 36–37) points out that: 'Specific product reorganisation strategies include investment and technical change, centralization and product special-ization. Product transformation strategies include service quality enhance-ment ... , environmental quality enhancement ... , repositioning, diversification, collaboration, and adaptation.' Given that within a single organisation such a task would require careful preparation and planning, how much more would this be true of tourism destinations that are often composed of multiple products?

The belief in planning approaches to tourism is also reinforced by its adoption in the national park administrative systems in the English-speaking Western world. In those countries with significant unspoilt land areas such as the USA, Canada, Australia and New Zealand, national and regional parks as protected areas prohibit a wide range of activities, and even access by humans in some instances. Even in the UK where over 80% of the land area may be in private ownership and used for commercial activities, zoning regulations require compliance with a range of regula-tions that may, for example, control the type of materials to be used in construction, the type of recreational activity to be followed or the locating of buildings. Indeed, in New Zealand, almost 37% of that country's land area is 'Conservation Estate' where human intrusion is carefully controlled if permitted at all. Much of the literature on natural area planning and the techniques to be used thus emanate from such areas, as is typified by Newsome *et al.* (2002).

However, outside the special areas of national parks, tourism planning tends to be piecemeal, more noted by its absence than its presence and, when present, is little more than a series of coordinated promotional attempts aimed at securing more visitors almost regardless of any attempt to adhere to an assessment of carrying capacity. The issue of the gap between the academic discourse on the need for tourism planning and the limited application of practical planning other than in the promotion of tourism has been examined by Hall in a series of books (e.g. Hall, 2007) and papers (e.g. Hall, 1999) and others (e.g. Ryan & Zahra, 2004; Zahra & Ryan, 2005, 2007). Hall (2007) examines the changing pattern of govern-ment involvement in wider social and environmental issues in Western societies. At the time of his writing, the political spectrum had swung toward market-oriented solutions and in many instances even National Parks were under pressure to find means of revenue generation (Eagles, 2002). Consequently, the emphasis tended to be on tourism promotion and economic benefits, but at the end of the 1990s and as the first decade of the 21st century commenced the political pendulum tended to swing back to new means of governmental intervention under various concepts of 'public good' in some countries such as the UK and New Zealand.

One of the issues that Hall considers in destination planning is the role of politics and the types of influence stakeholders possess, and the implications of consensus building that can occur as those in a network such as envisaged by Dredge (2006). Hall agrees with Evans' (1997: 8) statement that:

> ... if environmental planning for sustainability ... is to be anywhere near effective, the political processes of public debate and controversy, both formal and informal, will need to play a much more significant role than has hitherto been the case.

Indeed, the swings of the political pendulum can be relatively rapid. In the second decade of the current century, and partly as a reaction to the 2008 global financial crisis, governmental policies have again changed to reduce an emphasis on environmental issues, to be replaced by concerns about economic stability, reductions in government budgetary expenditures, and paradoxically quantitative easing (extending the money supply), all to sustain employment.

Elsewhere, Hall (1999) specifies why the informal as much as the formal is required in a planning and associated political process. The problem that he sees with many of the networks that become involved in planning is that they favour those stakeholders able to organise within the network, and in tourism this is generally members of the local or regional tourism industry. Networks thereby create biases in the planning processes that exist within political imperatives, requiring plans to be developed within given periods of time and within required budgetary implications. Hall (1999: 285) notes that 'The relationship between the tourism industry and government tourism agencies clearly raises questions about the extent to which established policy processes lead to outcomes which are in the "public interest" and which contribute to sustainability rather than meeting just narrow sectoral interests'. In fact he goes further and argues that the omission of key stakeholders from within the community actually, over time, lessens the ability of government to undertake effective planning in the tourist destination.

One countervailing view is that such an argument implies that a consensual view can be achieved. Ryan (2003), drawing on the experiences of the Province of Alberta in Canada in the late 1980s and early 1990s when significant effort went into community consultation in tourism planning (Jamal & Getz, 1995), argues that the assumption that communities are homogeneous and can arrive at a common solution is an ideal that does not always exist in practice. In fact local planning has often been characterised in Western societies by the twin phenomena of 'not in my backyard' (NIMBY) and 'locally unwanted land use' (LULU) responses by local communities, who are often resistant to change to a desired status quo. For her part, Schively (2007) also identifies other local groups that can emerge during proposals for planned change, and these include NIABY (not in anyone's backyard), NIMTOO (not in my term of office), BANANA (build absolutely nothing anywhere near anyone), NOPE (not on planet Earth), and CAVEs (citizens against virtually everything). Schively (2007) argues that planning processes under these circumstances are subject to an array of factors that include perceptions of risk to health and other concerns associated with change, perceptions of the authority responsible for the process, the dangers of conflicting scientific evidence created by the adversarial nature of proceedings, and issues of the fairness of the process. She is also not alone in recognising that often local groups are placed in a position of reaction to a proposal that may be initiated by commercial interests from outside the locality rather than them being empowered to initiate proposals from within the wider community.

For their part, Ryan and Zahra (2004) and Zahra and Ryan (2005, 2007) have argued that this failure emanates, in part, from the patterns of local politics. In an ideal environment it might be argued that proactive tourist destination planning would develop means by which local communities would be able to discuss what it is that they wish to achieve for their local communities and make proposals to the planning authorities. Indeed Zahra and Ryan (2007) trace the rise and fall of individual regional tourism organisations in New Zealand as the pendulum swings within local politics, inferring that such processes are not always consistent with any form of scientific rationalism, but are more attuned to the personal interests of local councillors that may be more or less altruistic in terms of their perceptions of community 'good' (Ryan & Zahra, 2004).

Tourism Planning Research and Practice in China

Tourism planning is one of the inclusive core research issues among tourism researchers in China. As revealed by various review studies (e.g. Hsu et al., 2010; Wu et al., 2001), tourism resources/attractions/product development and planning is the most prevailing recurrent research theme among tourism journal publications in China. The influence of politics in tourism planning and various political issues as have concerned Western authors like Hall (1999) and Dredge and Jenkins (2007) may more or less find their counterparts in the context of China, albeit in a more contextualised way and bearing more Chinese characteristics (Ying & Zhou, 2007). As early as the late 1970s when China decided to open up, a few researchers in China, mostly geographers in training, pioneered new directions in tourism research in the disciplines of geography and tourism planning (Wang, 1996). Deng Xiaoping's speech in Huangshan in July 1979 directing that 'the province (Anhui) should have a plan' (for Huangshan) was believed to have politically sanctioned all planning efforts ever since from both government agents and academia (Xu, 2003a). In 1984 the planning project completed by Professor Guo Laixi from the Institute of Geography of Chinese Academy of Science was deemed by Chinese tourism academics to be the first completed by the wider academic body in China (Xu, 2003a).

As determined by China's general stage of tourism development and government discourses, tourism planning has been favoured by various stakeholders in the process of tourism development, apparently including the government, academia and industry. It went even further in that tourism planning is somehow perceived as a profession in which some tourism students aspire to work. Unlike their Western counterparts, tourism academics in China are more motivated to undertake tourism planning projects because of the financial and prestige rewards that can be gained. On the one hand, working in planning projects brings in additional income for academics, who are mostly insufficiently remunerated in the current Chinese university system; on the other hand, planning project results, mostly as written master plan reports, are recognised as research outputs for academic planners. Practising in tourism planning also seems to advance an academic career in that tourism academics can publish journal articles and books on the basis of their planning projects. At the same time they develop *guanxi* with governmental bodies that is also generally advantageous for both their academic careers and future income opportunities.

Despite that, in the government agenda tourism planning has been mostly product driven and oriented, and planning practices undertaken by academics have demonstrated awareness of the tourist market from the very beginning (Chen & Bao, 1988; Xu, 2003b). Xu (2003a, 2003b) reviewed the different stages of market research development in China's tourism planning and noted that, after the turn of the century, market research in tourism planning has been more mature and systemic. Nevertheless, tourism planning practices, driven more by pragmatic regional development needs and government concerns than by theoretical innovations and research requirements, seem to have overwhelmed planning research in China. Consequently it is believed that tourism planning research, in the research sense per se, remains largely in the 'pre-paradigm' stage without clear and systemic theoretic guidance (Fan & Hu, 2003; Xu, 2003a).

The fact of government intervention and influence in the tourism planning process is obvious, and the government is prominent in the role of *State Planner*. Huang, Ryan and Yang in Chapter 12 of this book note, however, that in the current evolutionary process of the Chinese administrative reforms, regional and local governments are increasingly more actively involved in tourism planning than central government. Equally, land development and the associated tourism and real estate added values are becoming more of a tourism planning issue as recounted in several chapters in this book.

Although both the central government and different levels of local governments enthusiastically participate in tourism planning and practices in China, the way in which they influence those processes and ultimately shape outcomes as the major stakeholder in the multi-party/stakeholder networks has attracted far less attention in Chinese publications than in English. There is relatively little to compare with the work of Western commentators such as Dredge (2006). It is suggested that this is primarily due to the Chinese institutional environment that forges tourism research and publication behaviours as discussed the concluding chapter.

The patchwork of planning authorities and the seizing of 'solutions' that permit the maintenance of given interests, particularly those of the commercial sector, are seemingly common in China. For example, Ma et al. (2009) identify the many governmental agencies involved in the planning of Qufu, the birthplace of Confucius, and how product enhancement through the introduction of festivals, events and extended trails has created a whole series of new tourist experiences that has led to a branding of Qufu that possibly is inconsistent with the original nature of the town (Ma et al., 2009). Similarly there have been many disputes over the role of the commercial sector in opening up National Parks and reserves to higher numbers of visitors, such as that relating to the introduction of lifts and cable cars at Wulingyuan World Heritage Site (Zhang et al. 2009).

Nonetheless, both the community-based planning approach on the basis of stakeholder theory and sustainable tourism development ideologies have been adopted and appreciated in the tourism planning practices in China. For example, Zou et al. (in press), building on a critical review of different planning approaches including the community-based tourism planning approach, the Community Benefit Tourism Initiative (CBTI) and the pro-poor tourism (PPT) approach as advocated by UNWTO, have developed a community-driven model on the basis of planning practices in three rural tourism development cases in suburban Beijing. The community-driven development (CDD) model of rural tourism, as proposed by the authors, includes three interrelated planning principles: localisation of supply chain, community–external investor symbiosis, and democratization of decision making. The research represents an inductive, bottom-up approach which derives data from grass-roots village tourism planning and development exercises, and is differentiated from the official top-down tourism planning. As also promoted by different government discourses, both environmental and social sustainability need to be addressed in tourism planning (Bao & Zuo, 2012; Zhou, 2004). Hence some scholars (e.g. Chi et al., 2010) see China as entering a new stage of economic transition and social change where GDP growth will be less emphasised by government, and instead social equity/harmony issues and sustainable development will be increasingly emphasised by government policy. Such an institutional change will also bring more future attention to environmental and social issues in tourism.

The Following Chapters

It is hard to capture the whole picture of China's tourism planning realities in a few book chapters; the task may prove to be daunting even for a whole volume of books. Nevertheless, the following chapters in this part provide some additional views to those currently found in the general literature of Chinese tourism planning.

In the next chapter, Hu offers a viewpoint to integrate peripheral environments into the core tourist attraction in tourism planning. The concept of Peripheral Environments of Tourism Attraction (PETA) is thus developed with reference to the importance of coordination mechanisms. These are seen as critical, as coordination itself involves multiple players in the process, and when put into practice in the Chinese situation with its multilayer complexities, generally proves never to be an easy task. In most cases, PETA is subject to the management of authorities other than those of tourism. The complexities of interdepartmental coordination in tourism policy implementation are discussed in other chapters, such as those by Wang and Ap and Huang, Ryan and Yang. The complexity of coordination between PETA and the core attraction may go beyond simple interdepartmental coordination as other stakeholders, such as local communities residing in the PETA, may express concerns in any mooted coordination process. Yet the conceptualisation of PETA in Hu's chapter has its practical relevance and significance. As in many examples in China, imbalanced or incompatible landscapes are seen in the core tourist attraction and its associated PETA. Destruction of past heritage may be even more rampant in PETA than the artful configurations of the core attraction area. Yang's chapters on the evolution of the complex tourism destination system in the previous part may offer complementary theoretical underpinnings in explaining the complexities of PETA coordination.

Religious tourism is covered in Chapter 16. Wong and Ryan offer an alternative emic perspective in a study which depicts the co-existence of the mundane and spiritual perceptions of tourism development among Buddhist monks and nuns on Putuoshan who, as a key stakeholder group in religious tourism and being themselves mostly indispensable in forming a religious tourism experience in the tourism market, have not let their voice be heard in the tourism literature in China. The planning implications here lie in that both secular and spiritual concerns need to be accommodated in planning religious tourism sites. While the secular enables the viability of daily operations at the religious site (and its tourism operations), the spiritual perspective seems able to conserve the core, intangible part of the attraction, and perpetuate cultural authenticity and sustainability. Such a need for balance may prove to be even more prevalent in other cases of religious tourism development such as that at the Buddhist Shaolin Temple in Henan Province

(Shi, 2012). Concurrently, Ryan and Gu (2010), in their field trip to the Wutaishan Buddhist Festival, suggested that multiple perspectives existed (e.g. official versus Buddhist) in interpreting the cultural festival as a religious tourism attraction.

In Chapter 17 Wen provides a systemic view supported by a holistic conceptual framework on the formation and development of iconic tourist attractions. The chapter is based on Wen's PhD work with the World Heritage Site of Danxiashan. As noted by the author, the iconic tourist attraction as a concept has been studied by different authors in the literature, albeit under different names or nomenclature. Taking Danxiashan as a typical case of iconic attraction, Wen presents a conceptual model identifying 10 developmental factors that influence the formation of an iconic attraction and its development and allocating them to three dimensions, namely, value, association and subject. In a practical sense, identifying these influential factors along different dimensions provides tourism planners with a good reference for justifying resource allocation in the planning process of such attractions.

Chapter 18, contributed by Ai, Song, Ryan and Gu, reports later stage results of a longitudinal study from which earlier findings can be found in Ryan and Gu (2007) and Gu and Ryan (2008, 2012). This chapter examines residents' perceptions and attitudes towards tourism development in Beijing's Shi Cha Hai hutong. Both quantitative survey and qualitative interview findings are summarised. The Hutong residents' expressed concerns are contextualised in the general development of metropolitan Beijing after the Olympics. Rich information as disclosed by the interview data captures the issues and problems reflected in the current social and economic milieu. For instance, the pedicab business, mostly taken by migrant residents outside the city, proves to a certain degree to be a disturbance to long-term hutong residents who may have a higher level place attachment to where they live. As the city develops, traffic jam and parking problems emerge as being more prominent and seeming to be a greater influence on hutong tourism. The mixed method investigation helped identify the tourism planning problems as perceived by the grass-roots hutong residents. As hutongs also represent the old Beijing lifestyle and its traditions and architectural culture, the chapter offers implications for different tourism planning concerns, seemingly covering the issues of intangible heritage preservation in tourism development and community participation, and incorporating social development concerns in tourism planning.

The four chapters included in this part can by no means reveal the whole picture of tourism planning in China. However, many issues pertinent to tourism and destination planning in China are explicitly or implicitly covered in these chapters as in others in this book. Those planning issues that still see further need for research include more integrated and coordinative planning (Chapters 15 and 17), sustainable development and planning (Chapters 15, 16 and 18), social equity and heritage preservation in planning (Chapters 16 and 18), and religious and cultural tourism planning (Chapter 16).

References

Agarwal, S. (2002) Restructuring seaside tourism. *Annals of Tourism Research* 29 (1), 25–55.

Bao, J. and Zuo, B. (2012) Legislating for tourism attraction rights. *Tourism Tribune* 27 (7), 11–18.

Chen, J. and Bao, J. (1988) Tourist behaviour studies and their practical significance. *Geography Studies* 7 (1), 44–51.

Chi, F., Fang, S. and Kuang, X. (2010) *Change of China's Development Models at the Crossroads.* Beijing: China Intercontinental Press.

Corak, S. (2006) The modification of the tourism area life cycle model for (re)inventing a destination: The case of the Opatija Riviera, Croatia. In R.W. Butler (ed.) *The Tourism Area Life Cycle Vol. 1: Applications and Modification* (pp. 271–287). Clevedon: Channel View Publications.

Dredge, D. (2006) Policy networks and local organisation of tourism. *Tourism Management* 27 (2), 269–280.

Dredge, D. and Jenkins, J. (2007) *Tourism Planning and Policy.* Milton: John Wiley and Sons Australia.

Eagles, P. (2002) Trends in park tourism: Economics, finance and management. *Journal of Sustainable Tourism* 10 (2), 132–153.

Evans, B. (1997) From town planning to environmental planning. In A. Blowers and B. Evans (eds) *Town Planning Into the 21st Century* (pp. 1–14). London and New York: Routledge.

Fan, Y. and Hu, Q. (2003) On the developing course and research progress of China's tourism planning. *Tourism Tribune* 18 (6), 25–30.

Gu, H. and Ryan, C. (2008) Place attachment, identity and community impacts of tourism – the case of a Beijing hutong. *Tourism Management* 29 (4), 637–647.

Gu, H. and Ryan, C. (2012) Tourism destination evolution: A comparative study of Shi Cha Hai Beijing hutong businesses' and residents' attitudes. *Journal of Sustainable Tourism* 20 (1), 23–40.

Hall, C.M. (1999) Rethinking collaboration and partnership: A public policy perspective. *Journal of Sustainable Tourism* 7 (3/4), 274–289.

Hall, C.M. (2007) *Tourism Planning: Policies, Processes and Relationships* (2nd edn). Harlow: Prentice Hall.

Hsu, C.H.C., Huang, J. and Huang, S. (2010) Tourism and hospitality research in mainland China: Trends from 2000 to 2008. In D. Pearce and R. Butler (eds) *Tourism Research: A 20:20 Vision* (pp. 147–160). Oxford: Goodfellow Publishers.

Inskeep, E. (1991) *Tourism Planning: An Integrated and Sustainable Development Approach* New York: John Wiley and Sons.

Jamal, T.B. and Getz, D. (1995) Collaboration theory and community tourism planning. *Annals of Tourism Research* 22 (1), 186–204.

Ma, A., Si, L. and Zhang, H. (2009) The evolution of cultural tourism: The example of Qufu, the birthplace of Confucius. In C. Ryan and H. Gu (eds) *Tourism in China: Destinations, Cultures and Communities* (pp. 182–196). New York: Routledge.

Newsome, D., Moore, S.A. and Dowling, R.K. (2002) *Natural Area Tourism: Ecology, Impacts and Management.* Clevedon: Channel View Publications.

Ryan, C. (2003) *Recreational Tourism – Impacts and Demand.* Clevedon: Channel View Publications.

Ryan, C. and Gu, H. (2007) The social impacts of tourism in a Beijing hutong – a case of environmental change. *China Tourism Research* 3 (2), 235–271.

Ryan, C. and Gu, H. (2010) Constructionism and culture in research: Understandings of the Fourth Buddhist Festival, Wutaishan, China. *Tourism Management* 31 (2), 167–178.

Ryan, C. and Zahra, A. (2004) The politics of branding cities and regions: The case of New Zealand. In N. Morgan, A. Pritchard and R. Pride (eds) *Destination Branding: Creating the Unique Destination Proposition* (2nd edn) (pp. 79–110). Oxford: Butterworth Heinemann.

Schively, C. (2007) Understanding the NIMBY and LULU phenomena: Reassessing our knowledge base and informing future research. *Journal of Planning Literature* 21 (3), 255–266.

Shi, Y. (2012) Shaolin Temple Abbot Shi Yongxin: Shaolin Temple will preserve its traditions. *QQ News*, 8 March, accessed 15 September 2012. http://news.qq.com/a/20120308/000409.htm

Wang, X. (1996) Development and prospects of the contemporary tourism geography in China. *Human Geography* 11 (S1), 72–78.

Wu, B., Song, Z. and Deng, L. (2001) A summary of China's tourism research work in the past fourteen years – academic trends as reflected in 'Tourism Tribune'. *Tourism Tribune* 16 (1), 17–21.

Xu, C. (2003a) On the course of market research of China's planning. *Tourism Tribune* 18 (3), 5–9.

Xu, C. (2003b) On the course of market research of China's planning (second part). *Tourism Tribune* 18 (4), 52–57.

Ying, T. and Zhou, Y. (2007) Community, governments, and external capitals in China's rural cultural tourism: A comparative study of two adjacent villages. *Tourism Management* 28 (1), 96–107.

Zahra, A. and Ryan, C. (2005) National tourism organisations – politics, functions and form: A New Zealand case study. *Anatolia: An International Journal of Tourism and Hospitality Research* 16 (1), 5–26.

Zahra, A. and Ryan, C. (2007) From chaos to cohesion – complexity in tourism structures: An analysis of New Zealand's regional tourism organizations. *Tourism Management* 28 (3), 854–862.

Zhang, C.Z., Xu, H., Su, B.T. and Ryan, C. (2009) Visitors' perceptions of the use of cable cars and lifts in Wulingyuan World Heritage Site, China. *Journal of Sustainable Tourism* 17 (5), 551–566.

Zhou, L. (2004) Progress on the research of stakeholder theory in tourism planning and management. *Tourism Tribune* 19 (6), 53–59.

Zou, T., Huang, S. and Ding, P. (in press) Towards a community-driven development model of rural tourism: The Chinese experience. *International Journal of Tourism Research*, OnlineFirst, DOI: 10.1002/jtr.1925.

15 Peripheral Environments of Tourist Attractions: Definition, Assessment and Coordination

Weixia Hu

Introduction

The increasing expectations of tourists regarding the quality of the environmental settings within which tourism attractions are found have created an urgent need for tourism planners and developers to better address the relationship between the tourism attraction and its surroundings. In addition, growing competition between destinations will lead to a consideration of not only the core spatial area of those attractions, but also the peripheries that surround them. Hence, in turn, these peripheral environments will also come to rely on effective planning and integrative management to create a wider tourist zone that will appeal to both domestic and international tourists. In order to effectively plan and manage these peripheral zones their specific geographic spatial coverage needs to be clearly defined. Furthermore, evaluations are required so that the periphery and the core attraction form a coordinated system. This chapter aims to discuss the characteristics of a harmonious peripheral and core attraction zone. It argues that the value of peripheral environments must be recognised in order to ensure the future sustainable development of tourist attractions, and that proactive conservation measures should be taken to plan and manage the tourist attraction peripheral environments in ways consistent with the core.

Since the 1990s, the speed of China's urbanisation has accelerated, and an increasing number of Chinese cities and towns have been 'modernised', causing an unprecedented change in urban landscapes in China. In this process, problems have arisen because of disharmony between peripheral environments and the generally urban-based core tourist attractions. Numerous cases of 'developmental damage' or 'creative destruction' (Huang *et al.*, 2007) have occurred in the urban tourist attractions while, to make matters worse, the suburban rural tourist attractions that surround the urban cores have themselves become replicas of the urban. Any previous authentic cultural atmosphere found in these peripheral rural attractions has largely given way to an overwhelming pervasiveness of commercialism, pursued by both local residents and tourism businesses; an idyllic and relaxing rural lifestyle has been turned upside down by competing neon light advertising boards. Five phenomena can be identified. These are commercialisation, urbanisation, artificiality, modernisation, and the repetitious planning and design of peripheral environments. This 'patterned planning' of tourist attraction environments means repeated use of large green areas, public squares and garden zones in the surroundings of tourist attractions, but they come to replicate each other. Abrahamson (2007: 68) notes that historically 'Uniformity, regularity, hierarchy, cellularity, and the ritual symbolism of urban space have been celebrated as an expression of state power and administrative effectiveness in China since early times …' and it can be argued that, with local government still playing an important development partnership with an emergent private sector, the same characteristics currently persist.

On the other hand, with the current social and economic development in China, tourists in China are increasingly demanding a high-quality environment that also reflects local characteristics rather than state imperatives. These peripheral environments of tourist attractions (PETA) are increasingly being integrated into objects appreciated by the tourists of the 21st century. Yet there is a significant tension between the local and the desire to be modern by imitating what are deemed to be symbols of modernity. This is exemplified by residential gated communities such as The Orange County on the banks of the Wenyu River, Beijing, which replicates those found in the USA. The author's prior research work with World Heritage Sites in China indicates that tourists' evaluations of the quality of attraction has gone beyond the attraction itself and includes evaluation of the peripheral environments (Hu, 2009, 2010). Therefore, competition among tourist attractions in the future will not only depend on the resources within the attraction, but also on those of its periphery.

Currently many tourism attractions in China are ordered within their walls or other boundaries, but the outside environments remain chaotic and messy. Such a situation endangers the tourism attraction's authenticity, completeness and diversity, as well as its value and meaning. It also negatively impacts on any satisfaction that tourists may gain, and ultimately adversely impacts on the tourism attraction's sustainable development. It is recommended that planning for the coordinated development of core and periphery be placed at the centre of tourist attraction planning and management.

The Concept of PETA and its Functions

The concept of PETA was initiated in the *Xi'an Manifesto* written by the International Council on Monuments and Sites (ICOMOS) in 2005. While initially referring only to historical heritages, and emphasising historical and cultural environments, the concept and its underlying rationale also apply to nature-based tourist attractions. In this chapter, PETA refers to the districts that have close relations with the core attraction in terms of social and economic activities, and which are strongly identified by residents for their physical proximity to that attraction and which cover a certain geographic space surrounding the attraction. They are combinations of geographical regions and environments (Li, 2005). PETA differ from a 'controlled development zone' in heritage protection and the 'buffer zone' in nature reserves in the following aspects:

- *Different scope*. A tourist attraction that is included in the buffer zone of a nature reserve is generally smaller than the buffer zone; peripheral environments can be in the transition area, the buffer zone or in both. They usually extend beyond the 'controlled development zone' in heritage protection zones.
- *Different perspective*. Both the 'buffer zone' and the 'controlled development zone' serve to protect the target area, but the peripheral environments surrounding tourist attractions arise as a result of tourism and focus on development, utilisation and, where appropriate, protection and/or complementarity.

Desirable PETA should be compatible with the core resource of a tourist attraction and perform the following functions:

- acting as a 'buffer zone' between the attraction and outside bustling world;
- complementing the nature of the attraction;
- increasing the attractiveness of the core and the ability to generate higher levels of tourist satisfaction;
- advertising and marketing the attraction;
- allocating and utilising attraction resources more effectively to promote both protection and development; and
- promoting local social progress and economic development.

Defining the Coverage of PETA

Clarifying the coverage of PETA would help allocate management responsibilities. Many PETA lack planning, development and management, and thus are prevented from reaching their full potential of positively enhancing the attraction. Under current regulations, the scope of both the controlled development and the buffer zones is ambivalent and thus administrative responsibilities cannot be clearly allocated. For example, in many cases of cultural relics' protection, the separation of the peripheral heritage environments from a local economy and its communities often results in weak protection because of a separation of holistic site management (Ma et al., 2009). Therefore, a clear definition of the physical coverage of PETA is the first step for evaluating the quality of PETA and conducting further planning and development.

PETA lie in an area where the tourist attraction overlaps with the outside region. Its size depends on measurements of horizontal distances and non-continuous spatial coverage, which take the attraction as the centre point and measure the extension widths in different directions along the peripheral environments where subsidiary attractions can be found. Accordingly, PETA can be circular, rectangular or irregularly shaped. Although they have different radii of influence, PETA usually generate 'corridors' that emerge from the centre which is the tourism attraction.

Generally, tourist attractions with large vertical distance have large width bands for their PETA, large attractions have long rim lines of PETA, and attractions possessing dynamic patterns of change and high levels of interaction with tourist-generating zones will also tend to have large PETA. Shapes of PETA are also related to the tourist flow directions: thus along the tourist flows the PETA are more dense. The shape and scope of the PETA is also influenced by the core attraction itself (including nature of the attraction, rim effect, and attraction direction and level), spatial structure (including basic structure, vertical structure, natural geographical location and distance from central cities), and regional policies and seasonality. However, the existence of a large PETA does not necessarily benefit all the stakeholders in the attraction. Equally, the spatial characteristics of a PETA need not coincide with the region's being administered by any specific governmental departments. Generally speaking, attractions based on different resources, no matter whether natural, village-based, urban or town-based or rural-urban (suburban) connection attractions, can all be marked with their PETA boundary lines on the basis of the style of the attraction and the business service activities derived from tourism development.

Assessment of PETA Coordination

Before describing modes of coordination between PETA and core attractions, the problems and contradictions inherent within PETA need to be identified.

Establishing the coordination model

From a spatial perspective, existing research has mostly focused on the coordination of subsystems, aspects of general development and land usage within a region (Huo *et al.*, 2006; Xiong *et al.*, 2006; Yang *et al.*, 2005; Zhou & Li, 2006), or on comparisons between different regions on the basis of evaluating different subsystems and elements (Du & Yu, 2007; Song *et al.*, 2007; Yang *et al.*, 2005; Zhan, 2006; Zhang *et al.*, 2004). Only seldom has the coordination between different regional systems been researched. Furthermore, while economic subsystems form the basis of coordination studies, most research has actually focused on the characteristics of wider ecological-economic-social subsystems (e.g. Du & Yu, 2007; Song *et al.*, 2007; Yang *et al.*, 2005) rather than on issues of coordination per se. From a temporal perspective, while some studies focus on the coordination of subsystems at a given time (e.g. Du & Yu, 2007; Zhang *et al.*, 2004; Zhou & Li, 2006), others have examined different development stages and sought to forecast the trends in subsystem coordination by comparing different times and stages (e.g. Jin, 2007; Li & Di, 2006; Liu *et al.*, 2006; Song *et al.*, 2007).

Coordination models can be classified into two categories based on the dimension of time. A dynamic model judges the level of coordination by calculating degrees of the synchronisation of dynamic changes experienced by systems (Zhan, 2006). This is done on the basis of the *time of occurrence of a given stage* for each of the systems. This type of model can be used for long-term time-series trend analysis with relative indicators (Zhan, 2006). A static model establishes comparisons without time parameters. It can be used to (a) run comparative analysis on the coordination between different development stages or different regions, and (b) calculate the trend line of coordination levels, albeit using the time series of the coordination indicators (Zhan, 2006). The static model applies to the coordination between PETA and the attraction.

Coordination models can also be divided into gap and comprehensive models. Gap coordination looks into system coordination using system similarity indicators (Dai & Huang, 2006; Zhan, 2006). It can be used to compare the levels of coordination in different stages or different regions, and to identify the trend and strategies of coordination development. There are two subforms. The relative approach analyses the relative change of one subsystem to another (Dai & Huang, 2006; Zhan, 2006). The absolute gap approach aims to measure the ratio of mean score of a subsystem over that of the current whole system. In this chapter, the model is based on the relative form.

Based on the above discussions, considering the study context, we construct the PETA–Attraction coordination model as follows:

$$I_E = \sum_{i=1}^{n_E} F_{Eli} \times W_{Eli} \quad I_S = \sum_{j=1}^{n_S} F_{Slj} \times W_{Slj}$$

And with $\sum_{i=1}^{nE} W_{Elj} = 1$ and $\sum_{j=1}^{nS} W_{Slj} = 1$

$$\text{Coordination level:} \quad C = \sum_{i=1}^{nE} F_{Eli} \times W_{Eli} \Bigg/ \sum_{j=1}^{nS} F_{Slj} \times W_{Slj}$$

In the above formula, C represents the coordination level between the two systems, IE and IS are the overall indices of each system, respectively; $FEli$ and $FsIj$ represent assessment value of the ith system indicator and the jth respectively; $WEli$ and $WsIj$ denote the corresponding weights, nE and nS represent numbers of equation indicators. When comparing the same level indicators between PETA and the attraction, $\sum_{i=1}^{nE} W_{Elj} \neq 1$ and $\sum_{j=1}^{nS} W_{Slj} \neq 1$.

Establishing the coordination assessment indicators

In selecting system indicators, reference should be made to both the literature and raw data (often accessed from regional development statistical yearbooks). The values of indicators should be standardised in order to enable comparability among complex indicators from different systems and different quantities. In the study of PETA, some indicators are hard to obtain from existing statistical data. Even such hard data as indices of air pollution, ratios of rural to urban land, and water quality in the attraction and its PETA may be difficult to obtain and at best are only indirect measures of variables that determine the tourist experience. Furthermore, because PETA are neither independent areas nor standard units of statistical data collection, independent statistical data in relation to PETA are rarely available, and so undertaking quantitative analysis always proves to be difficult. However, as PETA share certain characteristics of the tourist attraction in terms of physical landscape, structure, functions and atmosphere, it becomes possible to attribute data to the PETA to permit comparison between the subsystems of the basic core attraction and wider environments. Thus data can be acquired mainly through measuring visitors' personal feelings and perceptions about their tourism activities.

As the purpose of coordination is to improve the role of the PETA in complementing the centre, measurement should be based on the PETA and its relationship to the core attraction. For example, when assessing Pingyao Ancient Town in Shanxi Province to its hinterland, general indicators can include coherence of architectural styles, tourist atmosphere, local custom and orderly layout; thus variables that are used to evaluate the attraction may include sightseeing values, uniqueness, history and culture, artistic value and scenic variation.

Weighting

Weightings to be applied to the indices will normally be determined from values obtained from survey respondents. They vary in terms of different contextual situations and reflect the authenticity and consistency of the tourist experience. The weighting model is generally determined by the ratio of the importance of a certain indicator over all indicators, thus:

$$S_i = \frac{\sum\limits_{i=1}^{m} xij}{i - \sum\limits_{i=1}^{n}\sum\limits_{j=1}^{m} xij} \times 100\%$$

with S_i being the ratio of the importance of the ith indicator to PETA and the attraction, and xij being the importance score of the ith indicator in the jth sample; n and m are the numbers of indicators and samples, respectively.

Cross-sectional surveys in examining the coordination level between PETA and the attraction are not sufficient. It is necessary to compare results at different time periods. After initial measures to improve the PETA are taken, subsequent monitoring should be conducted and pre- and post-measure coordination levels compared to identify the results of policies and to identify future management directions.

Coordination Mechanisms

Factors that enable periphery and core to become better coordinated may emanate from the core attraction, the PETA or both. Attraction-induced forces tend to regulate and adjust PETA in order to better meet the needs of tourists, but to reinforce the role of the centre against the periphery, although economic development is promoted in the region and improves the image of the tourist attraction through enhancing its PETA (as in Figure 15.1). Conversely, if the tourism-enhancing policies originate from the region, demand from the region will require more direct adjustment and management of the PETA. This, in turn, leads to the prosperity of the attraction itself, which again reinforces regional social and economic development as shown in Figure 15.2.

The effectiveness of either approach is determined to a large part by the spatial allocation of land use patterns in the peripheral environments (Wu & Zhou, 2007). Thus three key components of the coordination should include:

- ideology, a recognition of the value of PETA and the attraction as a *whole*;
- regulation, emphasing the coordination of policies and relationships of interest groups; and
- planning guidance, providing both technical and ideological guidelines.

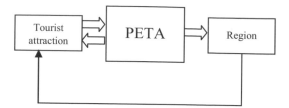

Figure 15.1 Attraction–induced coordination

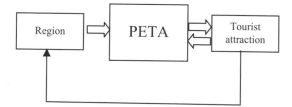

Figure 15.2 Region-induced coordination

Ideological Innovations

Conscious construction of PETA

A tourist attraction comprises a spatial location of natural or cultural sightseeing assets in either an urban, human-influenced rural or natural setting. Generally speaking, the larger the combined planned tourist attraction/PETA area, the more numerous are the tourism elements that can be supported. In some ways, the construction of a PETA extends the scope of tourism and recreation resources in a harmonious association with the core tourist attraction. It brings aesthetic enjoyment to tourists, provides a good basis for future tourist attraction development, and preserves the tourist attraction. With reference to carrying capacities, while these may be limited at the core, the use of peripheries that can fulfil some of the same functions may permit the wider region to develop while retaining capacity capability.

Acknowledging the value of PETA

While not meeting the main motivational needs of tourists, corridors in peripheral regions may direct tourists to the core while providing a range of commercial services of value to the tourists as they travel along the corridor. Such a potential will further foster the market demand for various resources in PETA, and help promote competition which leads to the formation of a variety of visual and service attractions. Indeed, it is possible that the activities in a PETA may overtake those in the original core attraction, creating a series of other problems and opportunities for the total region.

Such a potential requires destination management to be proactive with a clear vision as to the respective roles and potentials of the core attraction and its PETA. Another Chinese issue is that, in reality, those who benefit from the PETA are not always held accountable for their illegal behaviours, if any. In the Chinese situation a key to development is ownership of property rights, and normally the government may possess property rights in the PETA, which may be under a different jurisdiction from that of the core attraction. Many of the unresolved problems relating to relationships between the PETA and the core attraction and their respective development are often due to complex jurisdictions and an overemphasis on tourism as an economic activity with little regard to community, social and environmental issues, and the need for complementarity between the core and its peripheral zones. Consequently, government departments and local communities should recognise that PETA can be largely influenced and constrained by the attraction, and should not be subject to random development.

Planning PETA needs to be in the attraction's master plan

Planning is needed for maintaining the coordination between PETA and the attraction. Planning with reference to a PETA should not only be one that compensates for any prior damage but should be preventative. In the past, the planning of PETA is usually included in a regional plan, with little reference to the needs of tourism development. Such planning is, for tourism, a reactive remedy. This is certainly the case if tourism carrying capacities are exceeded in the PETA. To rectify this, first, the PETA should be included in the planning of tourist attractions. Second, considering PETA, attraction planning should be in line with regional planning. The construction of the PETA should be considered in the big picture of the whole region's social and economic development. Regional planning should have specifications referring to the PETA as a tourist attraction, thereby making the PETA more valued as a zone in the regional plan.

Defining PETA scope and assessing the level of coordination

There should be an audit of physical geographical features to assess scenic value, social and natural resources with the PETA to better assess its relationship with the core attraction.

Coordination of Policies and Regulations

Improving policies and regulations

As noted above, there may be differences of administrative jurisdictions between the PETA and the core attraction, but problems may also arise due to a lack of expertise and resources within the PETA, and possibly also due to the absence of relevant laws and regulations. Alternatively, although regulations may exist as to the development of PETA, they may lack detail and are difficult to effectively implement. The *Xi'an Manifesto* of 2007 contains regulations on the peripheral environments of cultural heritages and adheres to international conventions such as those of ICOMOS and UNWTO. It is here recommended that China should refer to successful cases from other countries and enact laws that monitor environment and resources in PETA.

More policy and regulation support

Currently there are neither rigid standards nor regulated monitoring of PETA zones and effective measures are lacking to prevent tourism resources in PETA from being damaged (Li, 2005). After identifying the PETA's spatial zone, there is a need to adopt the relevant policies and regulations to approve development projects. Due to the close relationship between tourist attractions and PETA, the ideal approach is to include PETA in the planning and management of the core tourist attraction.

Management coordination

Apart from local governments, many PETA are also subject to supervision by different government departments, such as the forestry and water conservation authorities. There are differences in regulation, management, planning and conservation between these authorities and the attraction management. On one hand, the attraction and PETA are under the administration of more important government agencies. On the other hand, the local government will supervise the branch offices of these senior administrative agencies. At the same time, the local government needs to coordinate organisations in the attraction and PETA. In such an administrative system, departmental management of the tourist attraction appears to be weaker in its powers when compared to the local government. Therefore, a local government-led system in the management and coordination of tourism attractions and PETA is necessary and is realistic. Local governments should have a specialised agency in charge of all resources development and tourism services in PETA. The agency should be under the direct supervision of the local government.

Integrative coordination and benefit sharing

The establishment of a specialised management agency and its operation need to be reinforced by benefit sharing. The government should turn itself from being a direct stakeholder to that of an indirect coordinating agency, attempting to establish a reasonable benefit coordination and allocation system. After PETA and the attraction are combined as a 'grand attraction', stakeholders including the resident community and relevant bodies will form a 'commonwealth' in combined attractions. It is necessary to compensate and subsidise various stakeholders for their efforts and sacrifices to preserve the resources in the PETA and the attraction. Such subsidies and compensation can highlight the importance and value of PETA, and encourage different sorts of development activities in accordance with the theme of the attraction. Local governments can allocate special funds or financial means to support the planning of PETA. Funding in such purposes can be allocated through various fiscal arrangements, tourist tickets revenue or part of the general income generated from the attraction.

Coordinating the relationship with local residents

Because tourists are generally less able to protect their consumer rights, the destination management will need to ensure that these are met. Major stakeholders in PETA development should be local residents and the attraction management. It is usually through benefit sharing that local residents can be connected to the attraction management. According to the author's survey in May–June 2007 (Hu, 2008, 2009), with further development of PETA local communities may still fail to voluntarily respect tourists' consumer rights or preserve tourism resources in the attraction and PETA. When local communities come to consolidate their status and acquire a greater share in revenues and other benefits, the local economic and social structure begins to change, and with these changes new sources of tension will also emerge. Within these new dynamics tourists may simply come to be seen as a resource to be exploited, and thus means and organisations will be required to avert this for the longer term interests of residents and local communities.

Guidelines for PETA planning and management

- *Local features.* Local landscapes form one of the basic geographical features of tourist attractions (Gunn & Var, 2005). There should be thematic extensions and innovations in the PETA to reinforce or enhance the unique features of the attraction, and emphasise aesthetic values in local history and culture.
- *Integrity and continuity.* PETA should contribute to the integrity and continuity of the core attraction by consistently displaying the theme and style in its architecture and design. Yet, while keeping the consistent theme and style, a reasonable zone of disjunction should be established for tourists to differentiate the attraction from its PETA.
- *Focusing on both economy and culture.* Although PETA planning originally serves the purpose of local economic improvement, with subsequent social and economic development, specific local culture components in the PETA will be increasingly emphasised to increase tourist satisfaction, preserve resources and improve the integration of

local communities to the region, thereby increasing a need for careful management and marketing.

- *Multiple utilisation.* PETA should not only serve the attraction and local tourism industries, but also form close relations with other local business sectors such as leisure and recreation and real estate development. As such, PETA can play multiple functions and roles with more value-added results.

Conclusion

A tourist attraction is not an isolated system. It is closely associated with its peripheral environments. Good peripheral environments for tourist attractions are those where desirable tourist activities can be conducted. This chapter focuses on PETA as a future research topic. The following points have been addressed: first, PETA should be compatible with the core attraction to aid the market competitiveness of the tourist attraction; second, PETA should be responsible for protecting the tourist attraction; third, management for tourist attractions and PETA should not be completely separate and coordination between the attraction and PETA should be the core task; and lastly, PETA must be protected and partially managed by the tourist attraction in order to sustain its tourist appeal and integrity.

References

Abrahamson, D.R. (2007) The dialectics of urban planning in China. In F. Wu (ed.) *China's Emerging Cities: The Making of New Urbanism* (pp. 66–86). London: Routledge.

Dai, S. and Huang, J. (2006) Analysis on the evaluation methods of sustainable development coordination. *Sci-Tech and Management* 6, 22–23.

Du, X. and Yu, X. (2006) Evaluation of the urban environment – economy coordination in Hebei Province. *Economic Issues* 217 (7), 109–110.

Gunn, C.A. and Var, T. (2005) *Tourism Planning: Basics, Concepts, Cases* (4th edn; Chinese translation). Dalian: Dongbei University of Finance and Economics Press.

Hu, W. (2008) A study on tourist attraction settings: Definition, evaluation, and coordination. Unpublished doctoral dissertation, Shaanxi Normal University, Xi'an, China.

Hu, W. (2009) On the coordinative evaluation between surrounding environment and tourist attractions: An empirical analysis of Pingyao ancient city, Shanxi Province. *Tourism Tribune* 14 (10), 57–62.

Hu, W. (2010) Exploring the coordinated mechanism between tourist attractions and their settings – case studies of some key scenic spots in Shanxi and Shaaxi Provinces. *Economic Geography* 30 (4), 682–687.

Huang, H.Y.B., Wall, G. and Mitchell, C.J.A. (2007) Creative destruction: Zhu Jia Jiao, China. *Annals of Tourism Research* 34 (4), 1033–1055.

Huo, X., Pan, Y. and Zhang, L. (2006) Evaluating the coordination level in eco-city development using weighting analysis methods. *Drought Zone Resources and Environment* 20 (1), 140–145.

ICOMOS (International Council on Monuments and Sites) (2005) *Xi'an Manifesto.* ICOMOS 15th Conference, Xi'an, October 2005.

Jin, Y. (2007) Evaluation on water use and national strategic development coordination. *Statistics and Decision Making (Theory)* 1, 36–38.

Li, S. and Di, Y. (2006) An exploration of the use of Gray correlation in the evaluation of sustainable development coordination. *Journal of Liaoning Industrial Institute* 8 (2), 77–80.

Li, Y. (2005) Thoughts on the rim characteristics of China's World Heritage Sites. *Tourism Tribune* 20 (3), 23–32.

Liu, F., Pan, X. and Shi, D. (2006) Evaluation and analysis on Liaoning Province's economy – technology coordination development. *Research and Development Management* 18 (5), 94–98.

Ma, A., Si, L. and Zhang, H. (2009) The evolution of cultural tourism: The example of Qufu, the birthplace of Confucius. In C. Ryan and H. Gu (eds) *Tourism in China: Destination, Culture and Communities* (pp. 182–196). New York: Routledge.

Song, Y., Tang, H. and Ni, C. (2007) Analysis and evaluation on the coordination between ecological environment and economic development of Nanchang. *Environment and Sustainable Development* 1, 39–41.

Wu, J. and Zhou, N. (2007) Construction of wetland parks and preservation of wetland tourism resources. *Human Geography* 97 (5), 124–127.

Xiong, J., Yu, R. and Liu, C. (2006) Suburban land development structural evaluation and coordination under the background of rapid urbanization – the case of Hannan District of Wuhan City. *World Geography Studies* 15 (4), 80–85.

Yang, S., Gao, W. and Sui, P. (2005) An evaluation study of the coordination of ecological, economic, and social systems in Ziyan, Hunan Province. *China Populations: Resources and Environment* 15 (5), 67–70.

Zhan, Y. (2006) Evaluation on the measurement methods of coordination between military and economics. *Military Economics Studies* 10, 22–24.

Zhang, X., Wang, C. and Wang, Y. (2004) A study on the coordination measurement of population, economic development and ecological environment system. *Ecological Economics* 6, 123–126.

Zhou, X. and Li, W. (2006) Trial assessment for regional economic and social development coordination: Models and cases. *Exploration* 2, 90–97.

16 Tourism at Buddhist Shrines on Putuoshan: A Co-existence of the Secular and Profane

Cora Un In Wong and Chris Ryan

Introduction

This chapter examines reasons for the patronage of religious tourism by the Chinese Communist Party, and then considers the impacts of tourism upon monastic orders in Putuoshan and the classifications of tourists who attend such a site. The data on which this chapter is based were generated through different means, including observation, participation in various Buddhist rituals, interviews and conversations with Buddhist monks which included the recording of the more formal interviews, and structured self-completion questionnaires by visitors. The textual data were analysed with the help of *Atlas.ti* and SPSS was used to analyse the statistical data. However, it is not the purpose of this chapter to engage in detailed analysis of the results, which are published elsewhere (Wong *et al.*, 2013, in press), but rather to provide an overview of the development of religious tourism in China and, using the case study of Putuoshan, indicate the impacts and managerial issues such development poses for members of the monastic orders.

Putuoshan is a major Buddhist site with several centuries of history, and is famed for special devotion to Guan Yin, also known as Bodhisattva Avalokitesvara. Chinese history records a number of visions of the Bodhisattva who, though initially male, became transformed into a female form, and in this form reputedly appeared in ad 668, and again in ad 939, and at varying stages until the present period (Naquin & Yu, 1992; Wang, 1999). The island of Putuoshan is easily accessible from the cities of Ningbo and Shanghai and in 2012 was attracting approximately 6 million visitors a year. However, while being one of the most significant sites of religious tourism in China along with others like Wutaishan, the issues that have emerged there are quite typical for both large and small centres of the Buddhist and Taoist religions, and hence the observations made in the following text are quite generic, as can be seen from the readings developed by Oakes and Sutton (2010) in their book, *Faiths on Display: Religion, Tourism, and the Chinese State.*

Religious Tourism in China

In the second decade of the 21st century the one-party Chinese state has sought to legitimise its continuing rule by reference to traditions that predate 1949 and the Maoist period. From 1949 the state's Maoist ideologies were based initially on the egalitarianism of Karl Marx but variants of Marxian philosophy became increasingly inappropriate after Deng Xiaoping famously declared that it was no bad thing to be rich, although it should also be noted that he commented that not all would become rich at the same time, but those who did become rich would in turn help others to subsequently enrich themselves (Vogel, 2011). Deng was certainly not the first Chinese politician who sought to ensure that China would emerge as a rich nation, but as indicated in his saying, 'I do not care if the cat is black or white, what matters is it catches mice', he was perhaps the most pragmatic, and arguably, especially after 1989, pragmatism was the ideology most wanted by many Chinese.

Yet pragmatism alone may be insufficient for sustaining government, for there remains a need for both performance and legitimacy, although the former may serve to enhance the latter. Certainly, China has emerged as an economic power in the last three decades as described in other chapters of this book, but there remains a deep-seated aversion to the goal of simply seeking to be rich as a governing ideology. Arguably, such a process inherently undermines a society by the very disparities it creates. As a country with cultural, historic and religious traditions extending back thousands of years, and additionally a country used to strong central government based on a respect for authority historically exercised through mutual sets of responsibilities between governed and governors, China possessed a rich stream of thought that could be, and is, used as providing legitimacy to the status quo of a one-party state and rule by the Chinese Communist Party. The traditions of Confucianism, with its respect for authority with the teachings of Buddhism and Taoism that seek natural harmonies between men and between man and nature, have increasingly been used by the Chinese state to provide an ideology that justifies its rule – for the Chinese Communist Party is the state as surely as was any past Chinese emperor. Yet emperors were overthrown, and thus the current state continues to create its national stories and engender economic progress to ensure stability – both political and social.

Consequently, the proceedings of Party Congresses are of importance for the language used by the leadership, and for several years the Party has now sought to achieve a 'harmonious society based on scientific advancement with Chinese characteristics'. One issue that thus arises is how to make real such statements, and how to inculcate them into the normality of daily life. One way has been through the use of tourism and the development of tourism that reinforces traditional patterns of thought that equate progress within societal belief systems congruent with the interests of the state. Three aspects of Chinese domestic tourism achieve this. The first is the conjuring of past traditions of Chinese culture – that sense of being Chinese, and the sense of societal obligation. Consequently, tourism based upon the great traditions of Buddhism, Confucianism and Taoism has been carefully nurtured. Great centres of Buddhism have been restored and have become centres of visitation, partly for pilgrimage, but also for reinforcing aesthetics, cultural tradition and sightseeing. Locations like Wutaishan have attracted new infrastructure, restoration of the monasteries and patronage by the state of festivals and arts development (Ryan & Gu, 2010). Yet even here the state has trodden a selective path. While Islam has been an intrinsic part of some areas of China such as in the northwest in provinces such as Xinjiang, and renovation of mosques have taken place – the state remains cautious in light of radical Islamic movements that are perceived as seeking goals inimical to Chinese interests. Equally, Chinese authorities have spent millions of RMB on the restoration of Buddhist sites in Tibet (Qin & Xu, 2011; Wang, 2012) with a view to developing religious tourism. Essentially, this normalises an experience for many – but that normalisation has been criticised as a Hanisation of various areas such as Tibet. In consequence, the state has generally trodden a careful path between promoting its secular activities, seeking the support of various religious hierarchies, maintaining core belief systems and trying not to alienate those who resist what is perceived as state interference in personal belief systems. On the other hand, it is been stated that many Chinese would not perceive such intervention as curious, for such has been the key role of the Chinese state in many arenas of social life.

A second approach has been to evoke the heroic traditions of the early revolution and this has led to the development of 'red tourism' that recalls the sites and events of the Long March and revolutionary times (Li & Hu, 2008; Li et al., 2010). Two factors create a congruency with current state interests. The first contextualises the March within a historical context and a wider tourism appeal such as 'red-green' tourism that combines the historical with nature-based tourism (Liu et al., 2011). Examples of this include Jinggangshan, which combines tourism product based on the Long March with trips such as drifting down the river on large rafts (Gu et al., 2007). Secondly there has been the adoption of a Maoist cult, who has been 'mystified into a deity, and worshiped as a secular god' (Yu, 2010: 95). This in itself is consistent with Taoist belief systems where humans could become gods through good works or works of significance.

The third approach has been the very pattern of the development of Chinese domestic tourism as part of the social and economic development of China. As the Chinese middle classes grow in number and affluence, they seek to replicate the lifestyles of their Western counterparts by the purchase of more luxurious homes, cars and travel – both domestically and overseas. From the initial institution of Golden Weeks to the subsequent abandonment of the Labour Day week and the establishment of more, shorter long weekends (thereby giving people a greater degree of freedom over the selection of dates for travel and the ability to add paid holiday times to long weekends), the process of tourism has become for many a normal part of life and no longer an aspiration. In hand with other policies such as the designation of sites as, for example, AAAA Historic Areas (Ryan *et al.*, 2009) or the accreditation of sites as World Heritage Sites, Chinese tourists are encouraged to consume places of heritage and history as well as patronise hotels, bars and resorts.

The Impact of Tourism on the Religious Sites of Putuoshan

Putuoshan received in 2012 about 6 million visitors, while the island itself has an area of only about 12.5 km². During Golden Weeks and special festivities, crowding at the more popular sites is thus an issue. Equally, not all of the 28 monasteries have equal accessibility to the main port area, and that too poses an issue of overcrowding for the more popular sites. Finally, it should be stated that the island is very popular as a tourist destination, and is classified as an 'AAAAA National Tourism Destination' by the China National Tourism Administration (the highest classification). The current resident population comprises approximately 5000 lay people and 3000 belonging to the monastic orders. The visitor-to-resident ratio is thus very high.

The topic of how Buddhist monks and nuns perceive tourism at their religious and sacred sites has not been the focus of previous research. This chapter reports such views based on the ethnographic research of the first author, herself a devoted Buddhist who spent several months in both 2010 and 2011 establishing links with the nuns and monks, attending *pujas* and other religious ceremonies, observing tourist behaviours, and in addition undertaking a more formal structured quantitative-based study of departing tourists at the main ferry embarkation point.

That quantitative survey had a sample of 640 respondents, of whom the overwhelming majority were domestic visitors. Of the total sample, only 10% were primarily on a pilgrimage tour. A total of 444 visitors had made their own travel arrangements and it should be noted that regular ferry services depart from locations such as Shanghai and Ningbo. The profile of the visitors was found to be very close to those found at many other domestic tourism sites; that is, the sample is dominated by a well-educated, above-average income grouping primarily aged between 25 and 55 years of age.

Visitors were asked to assess the importance of various motives for visiting the island on a seven-point scale, and it is evident that the main reasons were for sightseeing (6.56), seeing something of Chinese culture (6.03) and relaxation (5.99) on this scale. Religious motivation was unimportant in that the score for attending *pujas* was only 2.93.

A cluster analysis of the sample showed that tourists could be divided into five classifications, these being designated as: 'general traditionalists' (17.2% of the sample); 'casual sightseers' (26.3%); 'good fortune seekers' (20.8%); 'enlightenment seekers' (18%); and finally 'cultural sightseers' (17.8%). Essentially the 'general traditionalists' generally score highly on the scales but seem to be drawn by a combination of culture, history and traditional religious ritual. 'Casual sightseers' simply view the island and its attractions as a pleasant place to visit, 'good fortune' seekers maintain a folkloric perspective and come to pray for specific factors such as success in exams, or to become pregnant, or for more generic reasons such as to be wealthy, successful and healthy. 'Cultural sightseers' are more purposeful in that they possess an interest in antiquity and the role of classical Chinese religious belief systems in Chinese culture, albeit not necessarily possessing a strong Buddhist belief system of their own. 'Enlightenment seekers' do possess a curiosity about Buddhism and want to find out something about the belief system, or have come more specifically to further their understanding.

It is therefore evident that Putuoshan acts primarily as a general tourist attraction, but in terms of the nature of its attractions it is consistent with a promotion of a sense of being Chinese based upon tradition, classic references, Chinese culture and a belief system of respect. Additionally, it may be argued that concepts of self-fulfilment and self-awareness are primarily inward directed. Many of these attributes would be congruent with a politically approved message of social harmonisation where to threaten that sense of harmony would be to deny what it means to be Chinese.

Perspectives of the Nuns and Monks

However, while these issues of wider political significance may indeed help to reinforce the structures of the Chinese state, an alternative perspective also exists, and that is the Buddhist view of the tourists that come to the island. This is not the place in which to explain the tenets of the Buddhist faith, but those tenets emerged strongly in the interviews undertaken by the first author with varying members of the monastic orders. From a specific Buddhist perspective, all visitors, regardless of their knowledge or belief, were viewed as commencing at the very least, a journey of better understanding of Buddhism. Indeed Wong (2011) discerns two sets of attitudes, what she describes as 'mundane-me' (or a secular perspective) and the 'Buddhist-me' viewpoint. It was possible to trace a continuum from the secular to the Buddhist, with a mid-point where both views were held as of equal importance. Thus, at one end of the continuum, some monks would tend to the secular perspective dominating, while at the other end the 'Buddhist-me' would be primary.

Citing three examples from the notes and interviews provides possibly a better flavour of these distinctions.

Examples of the 'Mundane-me' perspective

In this case two quotations are given because they provide a classification of the tourists based on degrees of belief and behaviour observed by the monks.

Monk Pu-Huan: Generally speaking, you can divide them into two groups: the Jushis[1] and Shinshis.[2] Jushis are Buddhists who practise Buddhism at home. To be a Jushi, you have to make the vow that you will follow the path of Buddhism ... Shinshis are, on the other hand, individuals who to a certain extent believe in Buddhism, but they are not Buddhists.

Monk Zhang Jie: ... tourists are those who come here with sightseeing as their main purpose; some may believe in Buddhism to a certain degree, so they purchase incense sticks from here ... you can call them Shinshis, meaning those who believe in Buddhism. Xiankes are those who are devoted in their belief in Buddhism, so they bring their own incense sticks to Pu-Tuo, together with other gifts to offer as tribute to the Bodhisattva. You can also call them Shinshis; it is one kind also, but the difference is that the Xiankes bring along their tributes and offerings when they come to Pu-Tuo and usually they come repeatedly. Another type is called Jushis; they do not simply believe, they also learn. In any case, many people come to Pu-Tuo to pray, not to learn; about one visitor out of one hundred comes to you and wants to learn Buddhism from you. Jushis usually come here to attend pujas[3] ... they are here to redeem themselves from their bad karmas,[4] to clear their minds, to attend Buddhist lectures and to participate in pujas. They are quite different from the others.

Example of the duality of mundane and Buddhist

Monk Yuan Guang's reply exhibits a duality of worldviews.

... on the basis of their behaviour at the monastery, then you have tourists and *Xiankes*[5] ... yet from the Buddhist understanding, they are all the same, no matter if they are *Xiankes* or tourists. They all have good seeds, so they can come to Pu-Tuo. It is because they all believe in Buddhism and believe in the Bodhisattva that they come to Pu-Tuo. Or else there are many cultural places in China, also in many cities where you can find even older Buddhist monasteries. If it is not because of the fact that you believe in Buddhism, why do you need to come to Pu-Tuo? You can very well go and visit other places. That is why I say that they are all the same, no matter what their main reason to come might be and whether they are here to pray for fortune, for health or for other purposes. The nature of the origin of all the sentient beings is all the same.

Example of the 'Buddhist-me' perspective

The following again is an extract from field notes.

Cora: Who do you think are the people who come to Pu-Tuo?
Nun: They all have good fates and destinies and so they have a chance to come to the place of the Bodhisattva.
Cora: In your eyes, do they appear different from each other? For example some believe in Buddhism and some do not.
Nun: There is no difference and there is no need to differentiate. It is just the matter of who learns Buddhism first; some believe in Buddhism earlier and some will do it later. As long as they come, they have made a good tie and planted a good seed in their life; soon they will become Buddhists too. Everyone is good; we are all the same.

The respondent in this case was an 80-year-old nun, and she was the only one of all the respondents who did not make any distinction when assessing the tourists, but saw all as Buddhists joined by following a *dao* to *dharma*, and all are 'good'.

Implications for the Management of Monastic Sites

The above text illustrates not simply a classification of tourists, but one that has an implication for the modes of behaviour that are expressed. There are those who wish to photograph everything, and indeed may have little respect for those engaged in religious ritual. In order to manage these potential intrusions, the monasteries respond with a series of strategies. One is to hold *pujas* in the early hours of the morning and not open the monastery gates until after the service is completed. This therefore requires attendees to stay in the monastery overnight, but it has been found that some visitors have taken advantage of this to obtain a cheap night's accommodation. A second is to simply to close the monastery at times. This is made possible because, as previously noted, there are 28 monasteries, and thus the closure of one would still provide an opportunity for visitors to visit others. This does raise issues of coordination between the various abbots, and the need for communication to the visitors, not all of whom visit the tourist information office near the ferry landing stage.

A second requirement is for the monks to be present at all the shrines to ensure that no actions are taken that may harm the premises. At times a monk may be required to make a request of visitors, and there is possible recourse to secular security guards in very rare cases if any extreme adverse behaviours are exhibited. Being present at these shrines is also an opportunity for monks and nuns to answer questions, but again this seems relatively uncommon in that most visitors do not approach the monks.

A third strategy is the use of notices that bear requests. A growing problem is related to the burning of incense sticks. As numbers of visitors grow, the number of incense sticks being burnt is rapidly increasing. A second factor associated with this is that more of the sticks contain chemicals and substances other than simply incense due to the cost of incense. A third feature that has been observed is that incense sticks are becoming larger in size. Two responses have been initiated. In the first case those wishing to pray before the statue of Buddha are asked to use no more than three sticks in their ritual. For those wishing to use more sticks, they are asked to place the sticks in holders outside the actual temple of shrine buildings. Two reasons dictate this. The first is the risk of fire as the majority of the buildings are not only several centuries old, but are also constructed of wood. The second is that the smoke from the sticks is beginning to have a significant impact on the patina of the statues and ceilings, while the chemicals may cause damage to the paintings.

Generally, however, in spite of the very large numbers of visitors to the shrines, these controls are still low key, and for the most part appear to rest on assumptions that most tourists will comply with the norms of good behaviour, and indeed the presence of so many tourists will in itself inhibit any overt negative behaviour.

Nonetheless, some concessions are being made. Many visitors have taken to throwing coins into fountains, attempting to lodge coins in the higher tiers of multiple-layered fountains. This appears to be on the basis of it being an entertainment in itself, but also in the belief that the higher the coin 'sticks', the more good fortune the successful player will have. This is accompanied by laughter, shouting and good banter, but it does add to the total noise generated by the stream of tourists.

The end result is that monasteries are often not an oasis of peace and quiet conducive to quiet reflection during the main hours of the day, but come to resemble a busy thoroughfare of people seeking to take photographs and buy souvenirs from the various vendors at the site. The reactions of the monks are, however, determined by their own belief systems and the maturity they have reached as deep believers in Buddhism.

At this point, it is perhaps necessary to illustrate some aspects of the Buddhist approach to life. Rather than attempting to provide a structured explanation, the belief system may be quickly captured by providing illustrative text from Buddhist works. First, two passages are cited from the *Jing Si Aphorisms* of Master Cheng Yen, a Buddhist nun:

> How bitter life is when we have desires!
> Our demands on others bring endless misery. (Yen, n.d.: 58)

> The first step on the path of Buddhism is to lessen our desires and be satisfied with what we have. Then our minds will relax and we will begin to gain wisdom. (Yen, n.d.: 64)

And again, Venerable Master Hsing Yun, in his commentary on the Platform Sutra, writes:

> Good Dharma friends, the Way must flow freely, how can it be obstructed? If the mind does not abide in phenomena, then the Way flows freely. If the mind abides in phenomena, this is called binding ourselves. (Yun, 2010: 108)

He goes on to observe that those who form attachments become deluded. In essence we have key Buddhist teachings. Buddhist seek their *dharma*, follow their *dao* (Way) to achieve nirvana, the highest state of holiness, and the world is a place of facades. Master Hsing Yun implies in his work that non-thought, non-form, non-abiding does not represent emptiness, and emptiness is not nothing, but is a means to achieve higher states of being.

Given this, the monastic responses to the noise and behaviour of many tourists is that such intrusions may be disregarded. Indeed the logic of the above extracts would imply that even if a mislaid incense stick did cause a fire that burnt a shrine, that too, in the wider scheme of things, would be of little importance. However, it is recognised that shrines and temples have their role to play in the commencement of *dao* and that meaning comes through adherence to the *dao*. As Master Hsing Yun notes, the world is an illusion, and meditation is not an end, but a means to freeing oneself of illusions.

Discussion and Conclusion

Given these Buddhist perspectives of the world, and the desire of the Chinese Communist Party to further develop tourism, it can be noted that while very different in their philosophical premises, co-existence is possible because of the tolerance of the former. This tolerance extends beyond the state adhering to those things that belong to the state when such responsibilities are perceived from a Western perspective of 'rendering to Caesar those things that belong to Caesar' (Matthew 22: 21, *The Holy Bible*) with an implication of a separation of the religious and secular in the administration of the state. However, in China that contemporary perspective[6] based initially in Christianity is subsumed into a wider Confucian sense of reciprocal patterns of obligation.

Legally there is freedom of religion under Article 36 of the Chinese Constitution, which article also provides freedom from persecution on the basis of religious belief. However, ever since 1994 the State Council has deemed it necessary for all places of worship to be registered with government religious affairs bureaux. In September 1999 President Jiang Zemin noted that it was the role of government to '... energetically give guidance to religion so that it will keep in line with the Socialist society and serve ethnic unity, social stability, and modernization'. This is consistent with the Constitution in that the same Article 36 that provides for religious freedom also states that 'No one may make use of religion to engage in activities that disrupt public order, impair the health of citizens or interfere with the educational system of the State'.

There is a congruence of interests between (a) the devout who believe that the increased numbers of tourists visiting Buddhist shrines permits the embryonic Buddhist seed within each visitor to begin to flourish, and continue a search for *dharma*; (b) the interests of a state that seeks to implant a consciousness of what it means to be Chinese – proud of the past, imbued by patterns of thought where respect for order is an inherent component of Chinese tradition; and (c) the third interest of economic development through the promotion of tourism.

There is little doubt that religious tourism is a growing niche within China. Not only does Putuoshan attract 6 million visitors, but other sites attract people in their tens of thousands. For example, in late June/early

July 2011, 10,000 people a day visited Beijing's Yunju Temple to attend the display of Buddha sarira found in the cremation ashes of Shakyamuni. These sarira will become the centrepiece of a RMB 300 million development of Sutra-inscribed stone tablets being constructed at the same temple. In Tibet RMB 300 million was spent on repairs to the Potala Palace, and Ryan (2011) notes the resurgence in religious festivals throughout China over the last three decades. In short, the growth of tourism has created an opportunity for the development of not only secular concerns of income and employment, but is also fashioning an awareness of the spiritual beliefs of China. However, since the research was undertaken in 2011 other issues have emerged. In July 2012 Zhang Shaolei of the Putuo Mountain Scenic Management Committee announced that the committee was seeking to raise approximately RMB 750 million (US$117 million) through a stock market floatation of shares 'to bolster the site's development' (Branigan, 2012: 17). This would not be the first time such an action has taken place, for on 1997 the Emei Shan Tourism Company did likewise to help fund the construction of a cable car to the shrine on that particular mountain. Equally, as described by Li, Wang and Ryan in Chapter 5 of this book, a cable car was built at Qiyunshan, while similar plans are being mooted for Wutaishan and Jiuhuashan in Shanxi and Anhui Provinces, respectively. The corporations and governments argue that such initiatives have little to do with religion, but are oriented solely towards the tourism industry, and thus seek to distinguish between the two. Yet it is undeniable that the core of the attraction is the heritage, culture and the religious practices from which that heritage emerges. For some, these initiatives represent a triumph of commercialism and even a moral decline in China, and even the state-sanctioned *Global Times* of 2 July 2012 was initially moved to comment that pilgrims to holy places now kneel before listed corporations, in a comment that now seems to have been removed from the associated web page.

Notes

(1) Jushi [居士] is a Buddhist term used to describe a student of Buddhism. Literally, it means someone who practices Buddhism at home. The Jushis are also called Buddhist practitioners (as opposed to 'believers' or 'worshippers'). They are people who have taken Buddhism seriously and have formally 'gone for refuge to the Buddha' in a Buddhist ritual ceremony conducted by High Lamas or Senior enlightened monks. In this ritual ceremony, a Jushi has to make the vow that from the current life onwards until the day of enlightenment, he or she will never kill, lie, steal, commit adultery or consume alcohol (Too, 2003: 259).

(2) Shinshi [信士] literally means Buddhist believer. It is a term used by monastic members to describe those who believe to a certain extent in Buddhism, but who have not yet gone for refuge to the Buddha.

(3) Puja is a Buddhist term to describe the Buddhist ritual in which monks recite Buddhist scriptures and chant holy mantras (Too, 2003). It is equivalent to a Catholic mass.

(4) Karma (skt.) literally means action or deed. In Buddhism, it is interpreted as the driving force for cause and consequence. A bad karma is equivalent to an accumulation of sins in Catholicism (Too, 2003).

(5) Xianke [香客] literally means a guest who burns incense sticks.
(6) In Western history that distinction was not always clear. For example, the English Civil War was in part due to the insistence by Charles I on his rights under the Divine Right to Rule.

References

Branigan, T. (2012) Chinese shrine seeks stock market path to financial bliss. *Guardian Weekly*, 13 July.

Gu, H., Ryan, C. and Zhang, W. (2007) Jinggangshan Mountain: A paradigm of China's red tourism. In C. Ryan (ed.) *Battlefield Tourism: History, Place and Interpretation* (pp. 59–58). Oxford: Pergamon.

Li, Y. and Hu, Z. (2008) Red tourism in China. *Journal of China Tourism Research* 4 (2), 156–171.

Li, Y., Hu, Z.Y. and Zhang, C.Z. (2010) Red tourism: sustaining communist identity in a rapidly changing China. *Journal of Tourism and Cultural Change* 8 (1/2), 101–119.

Liu, Z., Yang, Z. and Wang, S. (2011) Research on leisure agricultural development based on red tourist area in Ningxiang County of Huban Province, China. *Journal of Landscape Research* 3 (4), 37–41.

Naquin, S. and Yu, C.F. (1992) Pilgrimage in China. In S. Naquin and C.F. Yu (eds) *Pilgrims and Sacred Sites in China* (pp. 1–38). Berkeley, CA: University of California Press.

Oakes, T. and Sutton, D.S. (2010) *Faiths on Display: Religion, Tourism, and the Chinese State.* Lanham, MD: Rowman and Littlefield Publishers.

Qin, J. and Xu, F. (2011) Based on deep ecological theory of Buddhism cultural tourism development – Guiping Xishan. *Journal of Zhejiang Tourism Vocational College* 3 (1).

Ryan, C. (2011) Religious Tourism in China. In F. Xu (ed.) *Religious Tourism in Asia and the Pacific* (pp. 110–124). Madrid: United Nations World Tourism Organization.

Ryan, C. and Gu, H. (2010) Constructionism and culture in research: Understandings of the Fourth Buddhist Festival, Wutaishan, China. *Tourism Management* 31 (2), 167–178.

Ryan, C., Gu, H. and Meng, F. (2009) Destination planning in China. In C. Ryan and H. Gu (eds) *Tourism in China: Destinations, Cultures and Communities* (pp. 11–37). New York: Routledge.

Vogel, E.F. (2011) Deng Xiaoping and the transformation of China. Cambridge, MA: Harvard University Press.

Wang, L.X. (1999) *The Monograph of Potalaka.* Shanghai: Shanghai Ancient Script Press.

Wang, Y. (2012) Potential demand market segments of the Tibetan Buddhist cultural tourism experiences. *Nationalities Research in Qinghai* 1 (1).

Wong, U.-I. (2011) Buddhism and tourism at Pu-Tuo-Shan, China. Unpublished PhD thesis, Department of Tourism and Hospitality Management, University of Waikato Management School.

Wong, U.-I., McIntosh, A. and Ryan, C. (2013) Buddhism and tourism: Perceptions of the monastic community. *Annals of Tourism Research* 40, 213–234.

Wong, U.-I., Ryan, C. and McIntosh, A. (in press) The monasteries of Putuoshan, China: Sites of secular or religious tourism. *Journal of Travel and Tourism Marketing*.

Yen, C. (n.d.) *Jing Si Aphorisms.* Hualien: Tzu Chi Merits Society.

Yu, L.R. (2010) Pilgrim or tourist? The transformation of China's revolutionary holy land. In T. Oakes and D.S. Sutton (eds) *Faiths on Display: Religion, Tourism and the Chinese State* (pp. 79–102). Rowman and Lanham, MD: Littlefield Publishers.

Yun, H. (2010) *The Rabbit's Horn: A Commentary on the Platform Sutra.* Los Angeles, CA: Buddha's Light Publishing.

17 Development of Iconic Tourism Attractions: The Case of World Heritage Danxiashan

Tong Wen

Introduction

An iconic attraction is a tourist attraction within a destination that has a high tourism value. It is usually in a central location within the destination, represents the image and theme of the destination, and undergoes stable and ongoing development. Iconic attractions in a destination represent those 'must-sees' for tourists. The study presented in this chapter uses the World Heritage Site, Danxiashan, as a case study. The analysis shows that the formation and development of an iconic attraction is influenced by three dimensions simultaneously. The three dimensions are *value, association* and *subject*, respectively. Basic resources, brand, spatial formations, infrastructural fallibilities, peripheral attractions, government, residents, tourists, businesses and third-party forces are 10 factors that affect an iconic attraction. These factors all work from different angles; the direction and strength of change induced by the individual factors in the same dimension form a collective impact of that dimension, which demonstrates an accumulative cause–effect interaction among different forces, ultimately determining the development of iconic attractions.

Research Background

Within the system of tourism attractions that comprise a destination, one or more of the attractions will usually become 'must-see' spots for tourists because of characteristics such as resources, culture and quality. At the end of the 1960s a few Western scholars started to see these attractions as symbols representing the tourism destinations from sociological, anthropological and semiotic perspectives. In 1976 MacCannell argued in *The Tourist: A New Theory of the Leisure Class* that the nature of tourism activity lays in the 'decoding' of the semiotic symbolism in the modern tourism system (MacCannell, 1976). He pointed out that tourism attractions form a series of related 'sign systems' during the sacralisation process of tourism, and further become centres of tourist 'gatherings'. He labelled the semiotic meaning of tourism attractions on the basis of prior research as a 'semiotic attraction' (MacCannell, 1976). Both Chinese and international tourism scholars commonly believe that iconic attractions influence tourism growth at a destination. For example, Pearce (1995) identified the key effects of iconic attractions on the tourism supply of a destination; Guo and Cao (2004) suggested that iconic attractions represent the most important factor in building the competitive power of tourism destinations; Yang *et al.* (2004) pointed that iconic attractions determine the scale of the tourism industry at a destination; Tooman (1997), Batle and Robledo (2000), Deng (2000) and Tao and Dai (2002), among others, provided case studies showing that iconic attractions boost the competitive power of destinations.

The development of tourism in China since the 1970s has relied on a group of high-quality iconic attractions, such as the Great Wall in Beijing, Lijiang River in Guilin, West Lake in Hangzhou, and the Suzhou Gardens. Because of their special attributes, these attractions are seen as key targets for restoration and renovation and they influence the direction and progress of destination tourism development in their role as the main subject of a destination's brand and image creation. The past development of tourism destinations in China has shown a high regard for the potential role of iconic attractions, and this has supported the creation of classification schemes of landscapes, historic monuments and cities (Ryan *et al.*, 2009). Certainly tourism per se has promoted itself as being important. At the 2007 National Tourism Work Conference, Shao Qiwei, Chairman of the China National Tourism Administration (CNTA), stated that CNTA 'promotes quality tourism development and improves the development of tourism destinations' (Shao, 2007); local tourism authorities have also stressed the construction and development of tourism attractions in hope of promoting the local tourism economy as a whole. The State Council has identified the tourism industry as a 'strategic pillar industry', as stated in other chapters in this book, and it is anticipated that in the future the Chinese tourism industry will continue to seek the development of iconic attractions as a means of supporting local economic development. However, studies of planned local tourism development in China based upon iconic attractions reveal a mixed pattern of success for several reasons which include opportunism uninformed by good theory or practice. This has led to high costs and unrealised hopes in several instances and, worse, has left local communities with high levels of debt as evidenced elsewhere in this book (e.g. Chapter 12 by Huang, Ryan and Yang).

To address such an issue, this research provides a case study on a typical iconic attraction – the World Heritage Danxiashan Mountain. The research framework is based on inductive reasoning following Wallace's model of scientific research reasoning (Li, 2004). On the basis of statistical data, surveys, interviews and field observations, the research illustrates the mechanisms underlying the attraction's development path and the factors that (mis)guided it.

As a famous tourist attraction in Guangdong, Danxiashan was known as the 'Captain of Guangdong's Four Great Mountains' and 'Tourism Resort of Lingnan'. It is designated as a National Scenic Zone, a Natural Reserve and a National Geological Park. It became a World Geological Park in 2004 and was listed as a World Heritage Site in 2010. All these classifications illustrate Danxiashan Mountain as being a typical iconic attraction in the Chinese context and so suitable for this study.

Literature Review

MacCannell's research has influenced a range of scholars who gradually took an interest in studying iconic attractions, and many of them have used different names for iconic attractions depending on their areas of focus. Examples include 'leading tourist destination' (Formica & Uysal, 1996), 'major destination' (Sofield & Li, 1998), 'key elements' (Pearce, 1999), 'festival site' (Cybriwsky, 1999), 'popular destination' (Nepal, 2000) and 'central attractions' (Uysal et al., 2000). These examples (shown in Table 17.1) represent the diversity of scholars' understandings of iconic attractions, and reflect the current state of iconic attractions as a new research focus.

Based on the understanding that an iconic attraction is the core of a tourism destination's 'sign system', MacCannell (1976) proposed the semiotic attraction theory that systematically construes the formation and development of tourism attractions. He argued that the formation of a tourism attraction is the process of sacralisation, and divided this process into five phases: 'naming', 'framing and elevation', 'enshrinement', 'mechanical reproduction', and 'social reproduction'. Jacobsen (1997) and Seaton (1999) respectively applied this theory to analyse the case of North Cape, Norway and that of Waterloo, Canada, and found that even though the theory was consistent generally with the cases, there were some limitations. Jacobsen found that in the tourism development of North Cape, 'mechanical reproduction' occurred during the second phase, and characteristics proposed as different phases sometimes occurred in the same stage. Seaton also pointed out that the effects that take places in the phases of 'framing and elevation' and

Table 17.1 Alternative names for iconic attractions

Name	Author	Time	Perspective of understanding
Semiotic attraction	Dean MacCannell	1976	Subjective meaning to tourists
Leading tourist destination	Sandro Formica	1996	Tourism attraction power
Major destination	Trevor H.B. Sofield	1998	Importance to the destination
Key elements	Douglas G. Pearce	1999	Concentration of tourists
Festival site	Roman Cybriwsky	1999	Development potential
Popular destination	Sanjay K. Nepal	2000	Number of tourists
Central attractions	Muzaffer Uysal	2000	Marketing

'enshrinement' are significantly weaker than those of other phases, and thus drew his conclusion that the formation process can be simplified to two phases, 'naming' and 'mechanical reproduction'.

One of the common foci of international research in this area is analysing the factors that affect the formation and development of iconic attractions. Bhattacharyya (1997) analysed the travel guides introducing Indian tourism in the *Lonely Planet* books, and found that the iconic attractions that represent the tourism destination are often at the centre of advertising, as well as the focus of tourists' attention. Sirgy and Su (2000) argued that choice of destination made by tourists is directly influenced by advertising and travel guides, and the iconic attractions described in detail in these publications often become a 'must-see' for tourists. Hanlan and Kelly (2005) also believed that official and independent advertising play a large part in expanding the market pulling power for iconic attractions.

Research also shows other factors such as the local economy, planning techniques, accessibility and government can influence the formation and development of iconic attractions. Formica and Uysal (1996) found that, due to the level of economic development, even though Southern Italy has many famous tourism attractions, only 10% of international tourists and 17.9% of overnight tourists chose southern Italy as their travel destination. In a study of public space in the cities of New York and Tokyo, Cybriwsky (1999) noted that recreational use in urban public spaces, including those of iconic attractions, is becoming increasingly important. However, after comparing the actual uses of newly planned urban public spaces, he argued that imitating Disney theme parks might damage historic and cultural connections in cities, resulting in low rates of utilisation, 'planned wastelands' and 'new urban deserts'. Pearce (1999) studied major religious and commercial tourism attractions in Paris from a micro-perspective and found that tourists are concerned about traffic conditions in the destination. Henderson (2000) noted that, due to the importance of Chinatown in the history of Singapore, the Government of Singapore had recognised its enormous value and turned it into a unique tourism attraction with appropriate policies of protection and development. She concluded that government leadership decisions had played a central role in maintaining the area and making it a viable tourist space. Jacobsen (1997) argued that, in the North Cape case study, new tourism activities were important in the formation of the North Cape as an iconic attraction, and the importance of creativity in tourism product creation was emphasised.

Some scholars have analysed tourists' perceptions of iconic attractions and the implications of these. Moore (1985) conducted surveys of Japanese tourists in Los Angeles and found that the sites they visited most were not considered to be iconic attractions by local residents. The analysis showed that variables such as educational level, occupation and social class determined tourists' perceptions of what constituted an iconic attraction. Urry (1990) and Leiper (1990) both stressed that tourists' perception of iconic attractions affected the ways in which iconic attractions developed.

Researchers in China have started to pay increasing attention to iconic attractions since 2000 and most research focuses on exploring the factors that have affected the development of iconic attractions.

Internal and external transportation systems have been found to play a crucial role in the developmental process. Cui et al. (1997) analysed the effects of internal traffic systems on the balanced development of iconic attractions, and suggested that, to solve the problem of excessive tourist concentration, more paths should be built to split the flow of tourists. Fei (2000), Zhu and Guo (2002) and Wang (2005) used different cases to demonstrate the importance of traffic management. Fei (2000) analysed Wudang Mountain's tourism development and believed that the lack of traffic facilities has compromised the mountain as a tourism brand and hindered its development. Zhu and Guo found that traffic inconvenience between Tunxi and Huangshan (the Yellow Mountain) limited the number of tourists going from Tunxi to Huangshan, and suggested building circular roads to solve this problem. Wang (2005) studied the Stone Forest in Yunnan Province and found that even though improved traffic management brought more tourists to the attraction, the result was a reduction in both travel time and duration of stay in the vicinity. In general, scholars concluded that the major use of traffic systems is to divide flows of tourists to and through an attraction to increase carrying capacities and visitor satisfaction. Good internal traffic systems help speed the flow of tourists on site, and this is negatively correlated with the tourist flow volume at certain hub points. Better external or access traffic systems help increase the number of tourists and provide links by which the iconic attraction is connected to the external local, regional and global environment.

Researchers in China have also analysed other factors through conceptual explorations and case studies. Zhan (1993) listed qualification standards for key tourism attractions, and stated that the quality of the resource and its distinguishing features were the most important criteria. Jiang *et al.* (2004) analysed the tourism development of south China's historic water towns and found that the popularity of a tourism attraction and tourists' travel purposes are the main factors that shape an iconic attraction. Li and Niu (2001) and Li and Zheng (2006) found that tourism resource branding is central in the tourism industry. They highlighted the importance of tourism brand management, and pointed out that cultural significance and hospitality management may be crucial to building a tourism brand. Chen (2003) studied the locations of National 4A tourism attractions, and found the majority were distributed in eastern China. It was concluded that economic development is an important factor in the distribution of 4A tourism attractions. Yang (2006) further researched the development of national high-ranking tourism attractions, suggesting that tourism development in western China could be promoted by a more market-oriented approach to its attractions.

It is worth mentioning that longitudinal studies have been undertaken to better observe the development of major Chinese attractions. Lu and colleagues conducted a long-term research project on Huangshan and the Jiuhuashan Mountain (Lu, 1994, 1995, 1997). They found that an even and stable flow of tourists, a low concentration of tourists, and strong tourism appeal have helped sustain these high-ranking mountain attractions as viable, attractive tourist locations for several years. On the other hand, Zhong *et al.* (2008) noted with reference to Zhangjiajie National Park that its evolution appeared to consist of various turning points, something that is consistent with the work on Yang's theory of complex destination evolution in this book. On the other hand, within the context of a Beijing hutong over a three-year time period, Gu and Ryan (2012) highlight a growing integration of wider urban and tourism planning that is beginning to create a new fusion of recreation and leisure foci, which observation fits into this thesis of the wider social trend creating new reiterative actions between place and resident and visitor behaviours.

Both Chinese and international researchers seem to agree that, compared to other attractions, iconic sites have a more stable life cycle and are much more important to the development of spatially wider tourist destinations. Relatively less research has been completed by Chinese scholars on the effects of such factors as marketing, planning, government and the economy. However, Chinese scholars seem to have extensively researched traffic as a factor and drawn conclusions similar to those of international research. This in itself is reflective of wider patterns of globalisation.

On the whole, iconic attractions have been researched by both Chinese and other scholars within a similar research framework. Much of the research has focused on analysing the impacts of single factors on iconic attractions, and there has been little systematic theoretical construction. In part this reflects concerns about marketing, control of visitors and site management, reflecting immediate pragmatic concerns where each site has been considered individually with little reference to wider, comparative issues. In light of this, while the current paper uses Danxiashan as the study case, it does analyse its development using a framework derived from the above-mentioned studies to assess the degree to which general principles might be established.

Case Study

Overview of tourism development in Danxiashan

Danxiashan is situated in the Shaoguan Prefecture of Guangdong Province. It is one of the six significant Danxia landform sites in China. Its main characteristic resources are its natural red cliffs and dramatically shaped rock platforms. This landform was discovered and classified by Chinese geologists in the 1930s as Danxia, after which Danxiashan was named. The area is also known as the 'Redstone Park of China'.

Danxiashan has abundant natural and cultural resources upon which its tourism development has been built. It was already a tourism site early in the Sui and Tang Dynasties (589–906 ce) and was known as one of the 'Four Great Mountains of Guangdong'. In the 1960s the Guangdong Provincial Government, acknowledging the site's importance and historical significance, developed Danxiashan into a tourist attraction by providing and improving its infrastructure including roads, hotels and shops. In 1980 Danxiashan was officially opened to the public and attracted large numbers of tourists. In 1985 it was listed as one of the first scenic zones in Guangdong, becoming the 'flagship' in Shaoguan's tourism product portfolio. It also became the only National Key Scenic Zone in Shaoguan in 1988, and it is in this period that its local iconic status emerged.

Subsequently, Danxiashan became a National Natural Reserve, a National Geological Park and a National 4A Tourism Attraction due to its unique landform, scenic qualities and heritage, thereby enabling Shaoguan to be a key tourism destination zone in Guangdong Province. In 2004 Danxiashan was classified as a World Geological Park. Hence, by 2010 it was the only site in Guangdong with all three titles: World Natural Heritage, World Cultural Heritage and World Geological Park. Table 17.2 indicates the evolution of Danxiashan's tourism status.

Currently, the World Heritage Site Danxiashan covers an area of 290 km². The Danxia landforms are concentrated in an area of 180 km². Developed attractions include the Zhanglao Peak, Yangyuanshi, the Jinjiang Scenic Corridor, the Xianglong Lake and the Shaoshishan Ecotourism Zone, which have welcomed large numbers of tourists over the years as shown in Figure 17.1.

Table 17.2 Timeline of Danxiashan tourism development

Timeline	Characteristics	Developer
Before 1960	Religious site; spread by word of mouth	The public
1969–1979	Production-oriented functions; government becomes main manager; values presented as geological site	Government
1980–1985	First time formally established as a tourism site; development and advertising from government as main manager; main tourist body formed; golden developmental phase	Government
1986–1988	Prominent recreational commercial zone; strong links between local economy and tourism; expert intervention	Government, professionals
1989–1994	Decline of tourist numbers; strong need for developing new attractions; steady business investment	Government, professionals, industry
1995–2003	Restart of new attraction market; strengthened tourism brand development; closer links between local economy and tourism industry; second golden developmental phase	Government, professionals
After 2004	World Geological Park and World Heritage Site; rapid increase in number of tourists; rapid increase in inflowing tourism investment	Government, professionals, industry

Source: Wen (2007)

Factors affecting Danxiashan as an iconic attraction

Danxiashan demonstrates the typical process of development from an embryonic tourist destination to an iconic tourist attraction. The formation of its iconic status is inevitably affected by both internal and external factors. The following 10 factors were identified as salient in the formation of Danxiashan as an iconic attraction.

Resources

Danxiashan possesses plentiful resources for tourism development. Its natural scenery has high scenic value; its ancient temples and villages reflect its rich humanity and history; Yangyuanshi (the Male-Power-Origin Stone) represents a Chinese erotic culture. These form the major part of Danxiashan's tourism appeal. In a survey conducted by the author in 2003, 76.8%

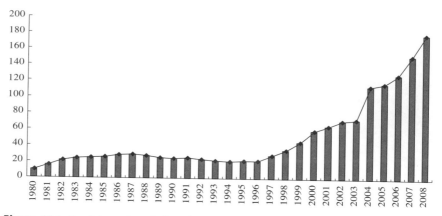

Figure 17.1 Tourist numbers in Danxiashan, 1980–2008
Source: Shaoguan Tourist Bureau; Shaoguan Danxiashan Scenic Zone Management Commission, 2009

($N = 587$) of respondents stated 'sightseeing' as their main purpose in visiting Danxiashan.

Brand

In the developmental process, Danxiashan underwent a series of branding exercises that reflect its resource base and increased governmental recognition of the site. Table 17.3 identifies the cores of the different brands and associated images. The consequence of this growing recognition is that Danxiashan is comparable to other famous iconic tourist attractions such as Huangshan, Taishan and Wuyishan.

Table 17.3 The development of the Danxiashan brand

Title	Time of recognition	Brand level
Captain of Guangdong's Four Great Mountains	Pre-1900	Public
Tourism Resort of Lingnan	Pre-1900	Public
Discovery Site of Danxia Landform	1930s	Academic
Guangdong Provincial Tourist Scenic Zone	1985	Provincial
National Key Tourist Scenic Zone	1988	National
Guangdong Provincial Natural Reserve	1994	Provincial
National Natural Reserve	1995	National
Guangdong Provincial Civil Tourist Zone example	1998	Provincial
National Geological Park	2001	National
National 4A Tourist Attraction	2001	National
World Geological Park	2004	International
World Natural Heritage	2010	International

Spatial features

Danxiashan covers an area of 290 km². This scale allows for plenty of space for development. With reference to spatial patterns, the whole Danxiashan region demonstrates a characteristic of a series of 'large openings and small enclaves'. The Zhanglao Peak and Yangyuanshi form enclaves where tourists can only access and exit through given entrances. However, the majority of the Danxiashan region is open to surrounding roads. Such a high level of openness enables the whole region, especially the Baizhai and Yanyan Zones, to be used as areas for hiking and self-drive tourists. Nonetheless, the inbound routes for existing scenic zones in the Danxiashan region limited tourist activities and have arguably negatively impacted on Danxiashan's status as an iconic attraction.

Infrastructural facilities

Danxiashan is situated in a suburban area 50 km away from urban Shaoguan. Its mountainous nature has permitted the retention of rural landscapes and low levels of urbanisation. Accordingly, most of the service facilities are concentrated within the attraction itself; most of the hotels and restaurants in the area are currently located in the tourist scenic zone. Commercial tourism services complexes have thus formed in major scenic areas such as Zhanglao Peak and the Jinjiang Scenic Zone.

Peripheral attractions

Due to the size of Danxiashan, there are relatively few other tourist attractions in its vicinity. These attractions tend to have weaker market influence and are dependent on tourism flows to Danxiashan. While smaller and less important, they form a complementary product that further reinforces Danxiashan as the major attraction.

Government

The government took a leading role in the formation of Danxiashan as an iconic attraction. It undertook investment and marketing initiatives, and the local government was the developer and manager at every stage of Danxiashan's tourism development. It also formed a management committee to coordinate the management work on Danxiashan. As shown in Table 17.4, there have now been four decades of government involvement with the development of Danxiashan's tourism.

Residents

Danxiashan residents include villagers inside the tourism zone as well as those living in Shaoguan city. Shaoguan city is a source of frequent and repeat visitation to Danxiashan, and in a survey conducted by the author in 2003, 9.06% of tourists visiting Danxiashan lived in Shaoguan and had the highest revisit rate amongst all respondents. However, it is the villagers living in the Danxiashan region who form a highly relevant stakeholder group in Danxiashan's development. In a resident survey conducted by the

Table 17.4 Danxiashan's management organisations

Management organisation	Year of establishment	Notes
Renhua County Danxiashan Forestry Range	1963	
Renhua County Danxiashan Management Office	1976	
Renhua County Danxiashan China Travel Service (CTS)	1980	
Renhua County Tourism Bureau	1986	Office shared with Renhua CTS
Renhua County Danxiashan Scenic Zone Administration	1989	Personnel shared with Renhua CTS and Renhua Tourism Bureau
Renhua County Danxiashan Tourism Economy Development Experiment Zone Management Commission	1992	
Renhua County Danxiashan Scenic Zone Management Commission	1993	Joint office with the Experiment Zone
Renhua County Danxia Township Government	1995	Joint office with the Experiment Zone and the Scenic Zone
Shaoguan Danxiashan Scenic Zone Management Commission	2004	Directly under the supervision of Shaoguan Government

author in 2004, 95.6% ($N = 113$) of the respondents strongly support Danxiashan's tourism development, 87.6% hoped to work in the tourism industry, and 92.9% supported an expansion of the tourism zone to the extent that they would consider relocation.

Tourists

The ever-increasing numbers of tourists reflect the market appeal of Danxiashan as well as an acceptance of its iconic status by tourists. It was well illustrated in the results of visitor surveys conducted by the author in 2003. Of the respondents: 41.6% ($N = 587$) had visited Danxiashan before; 80.1% ($N = 587$) stated they would visit the place again; and 91.8% ($N = 587$) would recommend Danxiashan to a friend.

Tourism business operators

The initial government stance limited opportunities for private sector involvement in Danxiashan. However, as the government could not supply enough funds for tourism development, the scale of current tourism zones has been limited. Over time a private sector has emerged, aided also by the post-1994 changes in economic policy that provided a bigger role for the private sector in the economy. Nonetheless, in this instance, although tourism business operators have played an active role in providing tourism services and some infrastructure in accommodation and retail provision, their impact on the overall development of Danxiashan has been comparatively weak. However, since Danxiashan became a World Geological Park and World Heritage Site, there has been more private sector interest in investment in the region, given the current opportunity for higher rates of return on venture capital.

Third-party forces

Third-party forces mainly refer to professional groups that have had an effect on Danxiashan's tourism development. Professionals, experts and academics have been creating more awareness of Danxiashan's geological value through a variety of research activities, which have contributed to achieving the status of being a World Geological Park and World Heritage Site. Professional groups have also been involved in tourism planning, consultations and heritage title applications on many occasions.

Analysis of Iconic Attraction Formation Mechanism

Categorisation of factors

From the above analysis, it could be suggested that the formation, recognition and reinforcement of iconic attractions are affected by resources, branding exercises, spatial features, infrastructure, peripheral attractions, government, residents, tourists, business operators and third party forces. Regardless of the varying strengths of the different factors, each has an impact. In terms of the nature and mechanisms of the factors, resources, branding, and spatial features can be categorised as factors internal to the destination, and the remaining seven factors as external environmental factors. In terms of the mechanisms or processes of generating impacts, resources, branding and spatial features represent the touristic value of the attraction itself (and are endogenous forces); infrastructure and peripheral attractions represent the factors external to the attraction, are complementary to the iconic attraction and are operated in direct positive correlation with the degree to which the main destination is indeed iconic. Although government, residents, tourists, business operators and third party forces are also exogenous factors, their main role is that of initiating agencies and developers of an iconic attraction. This classification is shown in Table 17.5.

The affecting factors can be further divided into three dimensions, the *value, association* and *subject*, as shown in Figure 17.2. As internal value factors, resources, branding and spatial features mainly reflect the inherent tourism value of the iconic attraction itself, and therefore belong to the *value* dimension, which may or may not be fully realised dependent upon exiting degrees of destination development. In other words, a continuum exists from

Table 17.5 Categorisation of factors affecting iconic attractions

Dimension	Factors	Nature of effect	Mechanism	Functional effect
Value	Resource; brand; spatial features	Endogenous	Internal value	Basic
Association	Infrastructural facilities; peripheral attractions	Exogenous	Radiation objects	Supporting
Subject	Government; residents; tourists; business operators; third-party forces	Exogenous	Development subject	Initiating

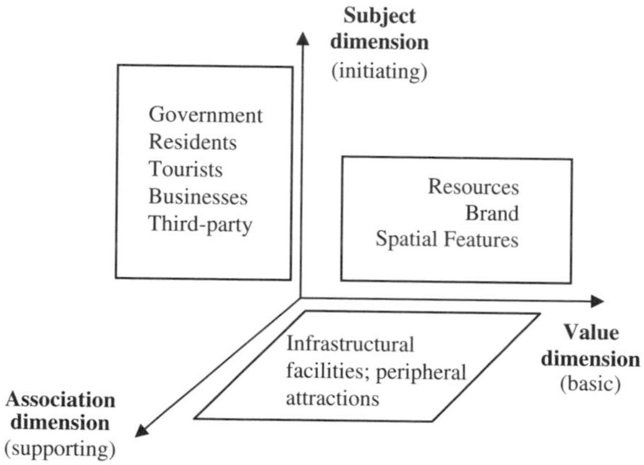

Figure 17.2 Formation of an iconic attraction

potential to fully exploited value. Exogenous factors (infrastructure and peripheral attractions) interactively affect iconic attractions and belong to the *association* dimension, reflecting the degree to which *value* is exploited. Government, residents, tourists, business operators and third-party forces lead the development and reinforcement of iconic attractions externally, have a central function in the formation of an iconic attraction, and are therefore placed on the *subject* dimension. The formation of an iconic attraction is thus determined by the three dimensions and 10 factors, as demonstrated in Figure 17.2. These individual factors work from different angles, but form a combined force while interacting with other factors of the same dimension and thus have a significant collective influence on the development of an iconic attraction.

Mechanism and processes of iconic attraction formation

The three dimensions have differing impacts on the formation of an iconic attraction. The three factors on the *value* dimension form the 'appeal' of the iconic attraction and its promotional opportunities, i.e. what there is to be advertised and marketed. The greater the appeal, the more likely the site is to become an iconic tourism attraction. The resources factor represents the iconic attraction's base value; branding reflects its market value; and spatial features strengthen distribution channels to expand its values. The association dimension shows and affects the impacts on surroundings from the iconic attraction as well as the positive reiterative relationship with those surroundings. Infrastructure provides 'hardware support' for the attraction and either limits or encourages the association dimension.

The effect of the tourist factor is especially worth noting. Due to the characteristics of tourism, production and consumption occur simultaneously. In this sense, tourists play the roles of co-producers as well as consumers in the formation of an iconic attraction. The flow of tourists causes interaction between factors of the value and association dimensions. As represented in Figure 17.3, the value dimension factors have a reiterative effect on the association dimension factors; the latter have a reverted influence on the former, which process strengthens the status of an iconic attraction. Tourist consumption and production also occur with the movement of the tourist flow. At the same time, government, business operators and residents led the simultaneous improvement of iconic attraction development together with infrastructure and peripheral attractions development; third-party

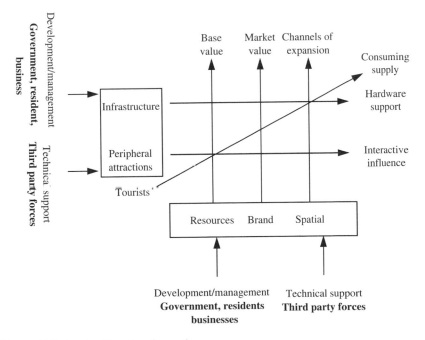

Figure 17.3 Iconic attraction formation

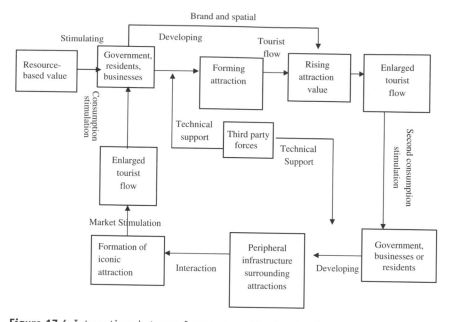

Figure 17.4 Interactions between forces generating iconic attractions

forces provided professional and technical guidance and support to the development and management of the attraction.

The mechanism causing interacting forces between factors is shown in Figure 17.4. Resource-based values stimulate and cause government, businesses and residents to initiate development and management, which is supported by third party forces, leading to the formation of an iconic attraction. Subsequently, tourists arrive. Continuing development raises the tourism value of the site in terms of branding and spatial formations and further enhances tourist flows. Increased tourist flows further sanction the need for more infrastructure facilities and reinforce the existence of peripheral attractions, which are developed to improve profit, provide hardware support and positively influence the iconic attraction itself in a reiterative fashion. The positive cycle of interacting forces constantly forms and reinforces the iconic status of the attraction.

Discussion and Conclusion

The status of Danxiashan as an iconic tourist destination has been gradually recognised, emerging as it has from a local tourism attraction to being recognised as a World Heritage Site and World Geological Park. Its development was based on its inherent geological and scenic qualities, its heritage values, professional expertise and marketing initiatives.

The formation of an iconic attraction is the product of forces derived from the three dimensions of value, association and subject. Each dimension also contains a system of influential factors that determine the nature, speed and direction of change induced by itself. The value dimension forms the basis from which an iconic attraction begins to develop. The association dimension comprises environmental factors which provide external support to the attraction. The subject dimension includes stakeholders that are the centre of the model and initiate the development of the iconic attraction.

The resource base, government, businesses and residents can initiate tourism development, yet technical support is required from third-party forces. Over time the tourist attraction appears and tourists arrive in growing numbers. In turn, further developments and operations improve the branding and values based on spatial formations, and reinforce and enhance the volume of tourist flows. The economic demand generated by those tourist flows will subsequently stimulate supplies of peripheral infrastructure and attractions, which lead to new rounds of tourism developments and operations driven by profits. Both infrastructure and peripheral attractions will interact with the iconic attraction in a reiterative manner, and an interactive mechanism among the factors becomes established, creating a self-reinforcing circle that explains the generation, development and reinforcement of an iconic attraction.

Even though some factors have similar functions, there remain differences in emphasis, mechanisms and degrees of effectiveness from a micro perspective. The effects of individual factors on iconic attractions thereby remain a key problem for future research, requiring monitoring and management, but this chapter has sought to provide a classification that will help those responsible for such actions.

Acknowledgements

The writing of this chapter has been supported and helped by many colleagues; among them special thanks go to Professor Liu Renhuai of Jinnan University, Professor Peng Hua of Sun Yat-sen University, Mr Hou Rongfeng, Director of Shaoguan Danxiashan Scenic Zone Management Commission, and Dr Songshan (Sam) Huang of the University of South Australia.

References

Batle, J. and Robledo, M.A. (2000) Rethinking tourism in the Balearic Islands. *Annals of Tourism Research* 27 (2), 524–526.
Bhattacharyya, D.P. (1997) Mediating India: An analysis of a guidebook. *Annals of Tourism Research* 24 (2), 371–389.
Chen, L. (2003) An analysis on the corresponding relationships between China's 4A tourist attractions and tour routes – the case of Eastern China. *Journal of Guilin Tourism Higher Learning Institute* 14 (6), 65–69.

Cui, F., Zhang, J. and Yang, Y. (1997) A preliminary research on the tempo-spatial distri-
    bution of tourism demand and tourist behavioural characteristics in Taishan.
    Economic Geography 17 (3), 62–67.
Cybriwsky, R. (1999) Changing patterns of urban public space: Observations and
    assessments from the Tokyo and New York metropolitan areas. *Cities* 16 (4),
    223–231.
Deng, M. (2000) An analysis of the characteristics of international tourism market flows
    in Chengdu. *Economic Geography* 20 (6), 115–117.
Fei, Z. (2000) A study on Wudang tourism transportation. *Journal of Shiyan Vocational
    College* 13 (1), 32–35.
Formica, S. and Uysal, U. (1996) The revitalization of Italy as a tourist destination.
    Tourism Management 17 (5), 323–331.
Gu, H. and Ryan, C. (2012) Tourism destination evolution: A comparative study of Shi
    Cha Hai Beijing Hutong businesses' and residents' attitudes. *Journal of Sustainable
    Tourism* 20 (1), 23–40.
Guo, S. and Cao, N. (2004) An explanation of tourism destination competitiveness.
    Nankai Management Review 7 (2), 95–99.
Hanlan, J. and Kelly, S. (2005) Image formation, information sources and an iconic
    Australian tourist destination. *Journal of Vacation Marketing* 11 (2), 163–177.
Henderson, J. (2000) Attracting tourists to Singapore's Chinatown: A case study in con-
    servation and promotion. *Tourism Management* 21 (5), 525–534.
Jacobsen, J.K.S. (1997) The making of an attraction: The case of North Cape. *Annals of
    Tourism Research* 24 (2), 341–356.
Jiang, Z., Wu, G. and Bai, G. (2004) A spatial analysis of the image of tourist destinations:
    A case study on historical water towns in southern China. *Tourism Tribune* 19 (2),
    32–36.
Leiper, N. (1990) Tourist attraction systems. *Annals of Tourism Research* 17 (3), 367–384.
Li, H. (2004) *Management Research Methodology* (2nd edn). Xian: Xian Jiaotong University
    Press.
Li, J. and Zheng, S. (2006) Study on the spatial distribution of brand tourism resources in
    China. *Resources Science* 28 (1), 174–179.
Li, Y. and Niu, Z. (2001) Study on building brand image for tourist attractions. *Journal of
    Beijing International Studies University* 5, 59–66.
Lu, L. (1994) A study on visitor flows of mountain tourist attractions – the case of
    Huangshan, Anhui. *Geography Science* 49 (3), 236–246.
Lu, L. (1995) A study on the distribution of tourism zones in South Anhui. *Geography
    Science* 15 (1), 88–95.
Lu, L. (1997) Research on the life-cycle of mountain tourist destinations – an empirical
    analysis on Huangshan and Jiuhuashan in Anhui Province. *Geography Science* 17 (1),
    63–69.
MacCannell, D. (1976) *The Tourist: A New Theory of the Leisure Class*. New York: Schocken.
Moore, A. (1985) Rosanzerusu is Los Angeles: An anthropological inquiry of Japanese
    tourists. *Annals of Tourism Research* 12 (4), 619–643.
Nepal, S.K. (2000) Tourism in protected areas: The Nepalese Himalaya. *Annals of Tourism
    Research* 27 (3), 661–681.
Pearce, D. (1995) *Tourism Today: A Geographical Analysis*. Harlow: Longmans.
Pearce, D.G. (1999) Tourism in Paris: Studies at the microscale. *Annals of Tourism Research*
    26 (1), 77–97.
Ryan, C., Gu., H. and Fang, M. (2009) Destination planning in China. In C. Ryan and
    H. Gu (eds) *Tourism in China: Destination, Cultures and Communities* (pp. 11–37).
    New York: Routledge.
Seaton, A.V. (1999) War and thanatourism: Waterloo 1815–1914. *Annals of Tourism Research*
    26 (1), 130–158.

Shao, Q. (2007) Key work points of this year, accessed 18 January. http://www.cnta. gov.cn.

Sirgy, M.J. and Su, C. (2000) Destination image, self-congruity and travel behaviour: Toward an integrative model. *Journal of Travel Research* 38 (4), 340–352.

Sofield, T.H.B. and Li, F.M.S. (1998) Tourism development and cultural policies in China. *Annals of Tourism Research* 25 (2), 362–392.

Tao, W. and Dai, G. (2002) The cooperation–competition model of regional tourism development: A case study on three ancient towns in southern Jiangsu Province. *Human Geography* 17 (4), 29–33.

Tooman, L.A. (1997) Applications of the life-cycle model in tourism. *Annals of Tourism Research* 24 (1), 214–234

Urry, J. (1990) *The Tourist Gaze*. London: Sage.

Uysal, M., Chen, J.S., and Williams, D.R. (2000) Increasing state market share through a regional positioning. *Tourism Management* 21 (1), 09–96.

Wang, X. (2005) The interaction between tourism development and transportation in the Stone Forest Scenic Zone. *Yunnan Architecture* 2, 16–10.

Wen, T. (2007) An analysis of the life-cycle of Danxiashan World Geological Park. *Economic Geography* 27 (3), 496–501.

Yang, W. (2006) Exploring the sustainable development of national level tourist attraction. *Journal of Changchun Normal University (Natural Sciences)* 25 (1), 96–99.

Yang, X., Ma, X. and Huo, Y. (2004) Research on Tourism Destination District (TDD) and its spatial structure – the case of Xian. *Geography Science* 24 (5), 620–626.

Zhan, B. (1993) Explorations of several principles of screening large tourism projects. *Special Zone Economics* 10, 28–29.

Zhong, L., Deng, J. and Xiang, B. (2008) Tourism development and the tourism area life cycle model: A case study of Zhangjiajie National Forest Park, China. *Tourism Management* 29 (5), 841–856.

Zhu, L. and Guo, C. (2002) Study on the regional space of Huangshan tourism. *City Planning* 26 (12), 49–54.

18 Developments in a Beijing Hutong

Le Ai, Xu (Melody) Song, Chris Ryan and Huimin Gu

Introduction

In recent decades the growth of tourism has created places of entertainment for both visitors and local residents, thereby generating nodes of entertainment and recreation within many cities. From an economic perspective tourism has become one of the strongest sources of development in many countries and fulfils an important role in the global economy, generating higher levels of consumer spending and creating new jobs and incomes, especially in previously marginal zones (OCN, 2012). Because of these changes and the generally rapid development of China's industries and services, China's natural environment, cultural and historical resources and social communities have more or less been influenced by the changes caused by both economic development and the growth of tourism businesses. While increasing numbers of tourism-related workers benefit from the growth of tourism businesses, so too do residents who live in or around the tourism destinations increasingly experience the inconvenience caused by tourists and the businesses that service them. This chapter assesses the impact of tourists on place attachment to Beijing Shi Cha Hai Hutong as a place of residence, and examines the relationship between place attachment and place change due to tourism. It does this by reference to a mixed methods mode of study.

Background

Tourism within China

The World Tourism Organization (WTO, 2001) had predicted that China would become the world's largest tourist market by 2020. Additionally,

China has also developed into one of the most popular tourist destinations in the world (Kong & Baum, 2006). China has mapped out its 20-year tourism development plan, which estimates that by 2020 the country's tourism revenue will exceed US$398.7 billion, equal to 8% of the country's total GDP (Jiang & Tribe, 2009). According to the China National Tourism Office (CNTO, 2006), the yearly average growth rate of tourism revenues is 12%, which is much higher than the overall GDP growth rate of 7%. At present there are around 6 million people employed in the tourism industry and over the next 10 years nearly 1 million additional job vacancies will be generated (CNTO, 2006). All of these reasons indicate that, in China, tourism could significantly add further to economic development, increase the employment rate and promote the development of traditional culture (OCN, 2012).

Beijing and Shi Cha Hai Hutong

Beijing is the capital city of China, and is located on the Hua Bei flat plain. The long-term registered residents (i.e. residents with Beijing Hukou) in this city exceed over 10 million, while there are also a significant number of unregistered residents. It is estimated that, based on available statistics, that there are additionally 4–5 million people living or working in Beijing for the most of the year. Indicative of the success of the tourism industries in Beijing, the numbers of hotels continue to increase, as do their profits (Gu et al., 2012). Since China entered the World Tourism Organization (WTO), won and then hosted its first Olympic Games, the image of China has increasingly become more of an economic and commercial power, and indeed by 2010 when measured by gross GDP it became the second largest economy in the world, although by GDP per capita it still remains far down the ranking of countries, in 93rd place. This growth has also been associated with a reduction in many prohibitive regulations and policies that placed restrictions on hotel ownership, especially since 2002, after which more foreign investors could hold a majority stake in hotels. Fully foreign-owned hotels were also permitted by the government four years later. All these factors have significantly influenced the speed of development of the tourism industries, and provided an impetus for an extensive expansion in foreign-owned hotels (Sands, 2008).

The word 'hutong' in Beijing's local dialect means 'a narrow lane', and it was originally named and defined by the Mongolians during the Yuan dynasty. A hutong lane is not only a place in which people live and grow up; it also provides shelter from the strong winds and consists of many old buildings such as Si-He-Yuan (quadrangle homes) and courtyards. Local guidebooks refer to features of the hutong thus: 'In the Si-He-Yuan house, the main building (Zheng Fang) is perfectly located on the northern side of the courtyard facing south, with two sub rooms to either side (Er Fang). On the Western and Eastern sides are Xiang Fang. The south side comprises a building facing the street (Dao Zuo Fang) and a shadow wall (Yin Bi)' and 'Si-He-Yuan buildings are timber framed, with brick walls and tiled roofs. The reddish colour of the painted timber beams and pillars contrast with the grey bricks and tiles'. Today many buildings in Shi Cha Hai still retain these architectural styles.

At present, this architecture has made Shi Cha Hai's historical and cultural area a tourism attraction and a recreational zone for Beijing's residents, and is arguably one of the most attractive tourist attractions in Beijing (Shichahai, 2009). Shi Cha Hai is located in the west side of old Beijing city, just north of the Forbidden Palace. It used to be part of the old Grand Canal of the Yuan Dynasty 600 years ago (Travel China Guide, 2013), and now it is circled by the former palaces of ministers, temples and well-kept Si-He-Yuans, as well as residences of past celebrities (Travel China Guide, 2013). 'Shi Cha Hai' literally means 'ten temple lakes'. Shi Cha Hai area or Shi Cha Hai Lake is also the name of three connected lakes – Qian Hai Lake, Houhai Lake and Xihai Lake (Travel China Guide, 2013). The area used to have 10 temples scattered around the lakes, hence Shichahai Lake (Travel China Guide, 2013).

Literature Review

Recent tourism development in Shi Cha Hai

In Shi Cha Hai, in order to give foreign tourists and those attending the Olympic Games an impressive experience of Beijing's historic past and cultural traditions, the local government of Xi Cheng District started to regulate the hutong area, and take direct action to protect its environment. For example, in 2006 the government demolished most of the illegal buildings surrounding Shi Cha Hai, which included 88 illegal bars and restaurants, two old rebuilt buildings at Ya Er Hutong, and all the illegal buildings at No. 50 Bei Yan (CRI, 2006). Government spokespeople stated at the time that the government would focus on all the illegal buildings in Shi Cha Hai, the general state of the hutong lanes, its traffic jams and parking issues arising from the narrow lanes, and the total regulation of the hutong tourism market (CRI, 2006). During this period significant photographic evidence of the hutong was created. Based on this evidence, a government team was appointed to enforce the law to remove illegal buildings, manage the narrow parking areas and to clean and tidy the streets as necessary.

In 2008, to encourage tourism businesses to develop in a smooth and positive way, the government started to formulate a small tourism business market policy. Key activities included the provision of special permissions and licences to the hutong tourism workers and a reduction in the total number of pedicabs from over 1000 to 300 (BTA, 2007). Furthermore, the government also regulated the work of the pedicab workers, such as controlling their working places, requiring uniforms and the provision of regular training (BTA, 2007). Additionally, if any new companies wished to enter the pedicab business, then the relevant department conducted checks on the company including on its history and finances. Companies could only commence their pedicab business once they met governmental standards. If companies or individuals failed to obtain these licenses and illegally ran pedicab businesses, then the government would take action by closing the business and enacting penalties against the company and its management (BTA, 2007).

Social benefits of tourism

Tourism provides a number of benefits to destination communities, such as the generation of revenue and employment, regional development and an overall increase in living standards (Archer & Cooper, 1994). Tip (2009: 22) argued that: 'A company built on the principles of responsible tourism is not only setting itself up for long-term success, but also responding directly to current consumer demand, which has never before been so focused on sustainability, and at the local community level, there's an unprecedented opportunity for micro-enterprises to become a part of the organized tourism supply chain.' In addition, travel and tourism employment, investment and added value exceed those of such major industries as steel, automobiles, textiles and electronics in virtually every country (Harry & Foden, 1992).

Negative social, economic and environmental impacts

On the other hand, the quality of the natural and man-made environment is very important to tourism, but many tourism activities could potentially cause adverse impacts on the environment. These adverse influences are caused by the construction of the basic infrastructure of tourism attractions, such as the construction of roads, bus termini, railway stations and airports, and the supporting infrastructure including resorts, hotels, restaurants, shops, information centres, parking, public toilets and recycling systems. Furthermore, these buildings may also cause waste water and water shortages by over-using water resources, and a subsequent deficient water supply could put huge pressure on places around tourism attractions with a potential reduction in the plants and animals associated with a region. This is a sensitive issue in Beijing due to the existing deficiencies in Beijing's water supply. Additional issues are associated with inflation, including that of real estate. Moreover, serious noise pollution from aircraft, cars, buses (and in the hutong, pedicabs) can lead to annoyance, stress and hearing loss, and alter animals' natural activity patterns (Weaver, 2010).

Again, air pollution from the transportation of tourism activities has increased at a global level, and the growing demand for energy usage in transportation has led to a greater volume of carbon dioxide emissions. As a classic example of air pollution, in Beijing city residents are increasingly aware of the city's poor air quality. Because of the increasing number of cars and many manufacturing plants being sited within the inner city, and the increasing number of tourism activities and transport movements associated with tourism, sometimes it may be safely said that the air quality can be less than optimal (Sands, 2008). Although the Beijing City Government have identified this as a serious issue and have taken steps to stop more air pollution, such as requiring 200 heavily polluting manufacturing factories to move out of the city, the air quality still remains a worry for city residents (Sands, 2008) and imposes inconveniences such as controls on the use and purchase of private vehicles in an attempt to cope with Beijing's notorious traffic jams. Therefore, a US$12.2 billion sustainable development plan was designed and accepted by Beijing City Government. This involved launching 20 projects to change the serious situation of Beijing's environment, including new wastewater treatment plants, solid waste processing facilities, air source heat pump systems, the replacement of 47,000 old taxis and 7000 diesel buses, the adoption of EU emission standards to check vehicles, the use of natural gas, geothermal and wind-powered electricity generating plants, increasing the area of trees and lawns, and the establishment of additional natural reserves to protect forests, wild animals, wetlands and geological formations (Sands, 2008). By the 2008 Beijing Olympic Games, the city's environment gradually changed in a positive way and attempts to further improve the city's environment have continued since that date.

In addition, there are many other negative impacts of tourism development such as increased prices in restaurants and rents, unsustainable employment; large corporations may invade local small business areas and tourism may accelerate a polarized economy (Tsundoda & Mendlinger, 2009). When the cost of living is rising, wages often may not keep pace (Stefano, 2004). The seasonal nature of the tourist industry has also left people unemployed (Stefano, 2004). Moreover, social and cultural impacts are getting clearer. Tourism may increase social interactions (Tsundoda & Mendlinger, 2009). Conflicts between tourists and locals and the diversification of tastes and lifestyles have become a major social phenomenon (Tsundoda & Mendlinger, 2009). Ryan (1991) also suggested that tourism has contributed to the bastardisation of culture and the creation of social problems such as the commercial sex industry, drug abuse, unwanted demonstration effects and the displacement of some of the traditionally viable economic and industrial activities. The indifferent attitude of the tourism industry towards local communities and their sensitivities has led to accusations of tourism being a form of neo-colonialism (Kokkranikal & Morrison, 2002). Likewise, the destruction of natural areas has also stopped the sustainable development of tourism and other industries (Akpabio et al., 2008).

Research Methodology

This study sought to study the impacts of tourism on the Shi Cha Hai Hutong from the perspective of residents. It sought to answer the following research questions:

(a) What were the impacts identified as being significant by residents?
(b) What types of impacts were identified as being positive, and what were seen as negative, and how important were such impacts?
(c) Were there significant differences in the perceptions by socio-demographic features such as age, gender and duration of residency in the hutong?
(d) Were there differences in perceptions that could lead to the identification of psychographic groupings that were independent of socio-demographic factors?
(e) Was there any change in the desire to live in the hutong as a result of the impacts of tourism, i.e. could changes in the level of place attachment be identified?

Place attachment was thought important; Gu and Ryan (2008) argued that place attachment was an important variable when considering the perceptions that residents had of a place. Locating their work in Shi Cha Hai hutong, they argued that residents' self-esteem was in part shaped by the physical and social community within which they lived. If that community was significantly impacted on by tourism, then this too impacted on how residents perceived not only tourism, but also their own standing. Some might be excited by living in an area deemed to be 'lively' and 'attractive', while others would resist the changes, wishing to maintain the status quo. They also argued that 'self-efficacy' – the ability to influence and control the changes taking place – was a key determinant of place attachment, but that in the context of the Beijing hutong this variable was difficult for residents to both conceptualise and make operational. Since Gu and Ryan's (2008) work, residents of the hutong and the wider cultural community of Beijing have been shown to have such efficacy in their successful resistance to a planned retail and leisure development in that part of the hutong close to the Bell and Drum Towers. The traditional alleyways have now been retained and not replaced by the planned leisure development that in many ways would have simply replicated similar sites in other parts of the world.

The research used mixed methods of conversations, open-ended questionnaires and the use of a structured questionnaire.

Questionnaire design

The questionnaire comprised five parts. The first is about the resident's place of living, such as Shi Cha Hai Hutong, Xi Dan or Dong Dan. The second part asked respondents to note how they felt about the significant changes to Shi Cha Hai Hutong, such as the advantages and disadvantages of the changes. The third part asked respondents about the importance of tourism in the hutong. The respondents indicated the extent to which they agree or disagree by a scale of one to seven where seven represents the most positive response. A non-response option was also used. The last part sought general socio-demographic data.

The questionnaire was based on the literature identified in Table 18.1. This indicates the variables that could affect residents' views of tourism, and these can be summarised as:

(a)   the economic benefits of tourism;
(b)   the degree of place attachment to the hutong;
(c)   the perceived levels of intrusion on daily life;
(d)   the perceived enhancement of the living environment – both aesthetically and in terms of widening perceived recreational opportunities;
(e)   approval of governmental planning authorities' policies;
(f)   the nature of the tourists.

Survey Findings

The sample comprised 226 respondents of whom 53% were female. Of the sample 8% were aged 66 years or over, 8% were between the ages of 18 and 25 years, and the largest age cluster was that between the ages of 36 and 45 years (18.3%). With reference to years of residence in the hutong, 98% had lived for 10 or more years in Shi Cha Hai, and indeed 95% had lived for more than 20 years in the hutong. Only 10% felt that the changes induced by tourism had begun as early as 1990, but 50% identified the year 2000 as the one by which those impacts had started to become obvious. By the time of the Beijing Olympics in 2008 the overwhelming majority of the sample considered that tourism was already impacting on the hutong.

In terms of income, the sample was asked to self-assess their income levels; 59% indicated that they had an average income level, and 20% felt they had a below-average income. Only 2% felt they had a significantly above-average income.

The potential relationships examined in the research are identified in Figure 18.1. It is suggested that an evaluation of resident satisfaction with the impacts of tourism can be measured by their stated satisfaction with tourism and their willingness to continue living in the hutong. Single measures of satisfaction where respondents simply state degrees of satisfaction have been deemed to be valid measures (Ryan & Cessford, 2003; Scarpello & Campbell, 1983; Wanous et al., 1997). It is suggested that any evaluation of the impacts of tourism on residents' lives in the hutong is determined by: the perceived

Table 18.1 Summary of literature underlying research design

Potential determinant	Indicative items	Indicative literature
Economic benefits	Tourism has created job opportunities in the hutong. The tourism industry is good for the hutong's economy. My income has increased with the introduction of tourism. The money spent locally to attract more tourists is a good investment.	Cui & Ryan, 2011; Franquesa, 2011; Kytzia et al., 2011; Liu & Var, 1983; Nunkoo & Ramkisson, 2011; Perdue et al., 1990; Pratt, 2011; Schofield, 2011
Place attachment	With the changes I see I would like to move out of the hutong. The hutong are special places in Beijing history and should be protected. I really enjoy living in the hutong. Personally, I would like to see the hutong demolished and more modern houses for local people built.	Amsden et al., 2011; Andereck & Nyaupane, 2011; Cristoforetti et al., 2011; Gu & Ryan, 2008; Kyle et al., 2004a, 2004b
Intrusions on daily life	Tourists create traffic and parking problems in the hutong. I think visitors are far too intrusive in our everyday lives. There are already some things I do not do in the hutong at certain times because of the tourists. The tourists are far too noisy for my liking. Tourism means that the area is losing a number of shops that served the interests of local people.	Andereck & Nyaupane, 2011; Aref, 2011; Ji & Wall, 2011; Nunkoo & Ramkisson, 2011; Percue et al., 1990; Schofield, 2011; Sheldon & Var, 1984

Perceived enhancement	The hutong is now a lot smarter and cleaner because of tourism.	Nunkoo & Ramkisson, 2011; Ramkisson & Nunkoo, 2011; Schofield, 2011; Ward & Berno, 2011
	I believe the tourism industry can improve the quality of life in the hutong.	
	I am able to go to the new restaurants that meet the needs of tourists.	
	The hutong would be a dull place if it were not for the attempts to attract tourists.	
Governmental planning	The tourism /planning authorities do an excellent job in balancing the needs of local residents with the desire to increase tourism.	Kask et al., 2011
	I feel the hutong's tourism planning authorities do an excellent job in making the right decisions about the area I live in.	
	The tourism planning authorities pay little attention to the views of local residents when making decisions about the future of the hutong.	
Nature of the tourists	The tourists I have seen in the hutong generally have little consideration for the local population.	Schofield, 2011; Ward & Berno, 2011
	The tourists that come to the hutong are usually very friendly.	
	When I see tourists coming here I am envious of their way of life.	
General work on hutong and Chinese heritage tourism		Gu & Ryan, 2008; Heath & Tang, 2010

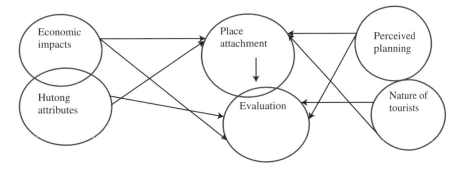

Figure 18.1 Potential determinants of hutong resident-perceived impacts

economic impacts (often benefits); the perceived impact upon social and environmental aspects of life in the hutong (e.g. congestion, intrusion effects – these are categorized as 'hutong attributes' in the above diagram); the perceived nature of the tourists (e.g. are they desired and/or seen as being friendly?); the degree of attachment to being part of the hutong; and the efficacy of local administration planning for the future of the hutong. Equally it is possible that economic and other impacts, local authority planning and the nature of the tourists also affect place attachment, and it is possible that an interactive effect may exist between a sense of place attachment and an evaluation of the impacts of tourism on daily life.

Prior to undertaking the analysis the data were examined for sample adequacy and reliability. As a measure of the former, the Kaiser–Meyer–Olkin score was 0.83, while the Cronbach alpha coefficient for the scaled items was 0.73, while the deletion of individual items meant that the alpha coefficient remained consistently above 0.70 other than the removal of the item that related to the desire for a job in tourism, when the alpha coefficient fell to 0.69.

The basic descriptive statistics are displayed in Table 18.2. From this it can be seen that a common concern is the build-up of traffic and congestion, and this reinforces past findings. However, in the interim period since the initial work of Gu and Ryan (2008) it seems that this issue has become even more pronounced.

There may well be good reasons for this as in the intervening years the Beijing Tourism Administration and the Beijing Municipal Authority have continually sought to develop the hutong as not only a tourist attraction but as a recreational and leisure site for local people. One example is the development of the hutong festival started in 2001, and which has since increased in duration and in the area in which it is located.

The advantages of tourism are recognized along with the disadvantages. Tourism is perceived as good for the local economy (5.53), the hutong is now smarter and cleaner than before (5.18), and there is job creation (5.10). On the

Table 18.2 Descriptive statistics

	Number	Mean	Standard deviation
The hutong are special places in Beijing history and should be protected.	223	6.46	0.99
Tourists create traffic and parking problems in the hutong.	224	6.44	0.96
There will be problems of traffic congestion and accidents if more tourists come.	223	6.18	1.25
The problem is that the hutong does not have enough facilities to cope with tourists.	223	5.80	1.38
The tourism industry is good for the hutong's economy.	222	5.53	1.48
Local residents are the people who suffer most from living in a tourist area.	220	5.48	1.55
The development of tourism facilities and attractions is a threat to the local environment.	219	5.35	1.61
Tourism in the hutong might lead to more petty crime.	217	5.32	1.53
The hutong is now a lot smarter and cleaner because of tourism.	222	5.18	1.64
Tourism has created job opportunities in the hutong.	220	5.10	1.81
The tourists are far too noisy for my liking.	219	5.08	1.72
I feel that tourism is growing too fast for the hutong to cope with.	218	4.98	1.63
The tourism authorities pay little attention to the views of local people.	211	4.95	1.66
The tourists that come to the hutong are usually very friendly.	212	4.94	1.34
Local tourism planer should invest more money in the construction of tourism destinations.	218	4.92	1.67
The money spent locally to attract more tourists is a good investment.	215	4.73	1.67
I think visitors are far too intrusive in our everyday lives.	216	4.72	1.72
I often talk to the visitors who come to the hutong.	223	4.67	1.65
The hutong has a wide selection of tourist attractions.	214	4.65	1.51

Statement	N	Mean	SD
I think that attracting more tourists to the hutong is a good idea.	217	4.64	1.74
I feel the hutong's tourism planning authorities should encourage further tourism developments in the area.	210	4.60	1.48
Tourism is one way of protecting the houses and courtyards of the hutong.	223	4.54	1.65
The hutong has a number of good quality restaurants because of tourism.	217	4.51	1.72
Tourism means the area is losing shops that once served local people.	215	4.49	1.78
The hutong is becoming too expensive for me to live in because of tourism.	219	4.43	1.92
I am quite happy with tourism and its impacts on the hutong.	222	4.40	1.70
Tourism encourages a wide variety of cultural and other activities.	219	4.38	1.77
The tourists I have seen in the hutong generally have little consideration for the local population.	222	4.33	1.70
I feel that the hutong planning authorities should consider plans to restrict the growth of tourism.	216	4.25	1.90
I believe the tourism industry can improve the quality of life in the hutong.	218	4.15	1.75
I feel the hutong's tourism planning authorities do an excellent job in making the right decisions about the area I live in.	203	3.98	1.67
I would prefer it if visitors stayed overnight in the hutong.	217	3.97	1.63
The area would be better off if tourists did not come.	214	3.88	1.67
I no longer go to some shops in the hutong because of the tourists.	211	3.87	1.92
There are already some things I do not do in the hutong because of tourists.	215	3.74	1.87
The benefits of tourism get distributed widely through the hutong.	191	3.72	1.74
Shopping hours in the hutong should be extended to cater better for tourists.	218	3.68	1.79
I am able to go to the new restaurants that meet the needs of tourists.	212	3.64	1.61
The tourism/planning authorities do an excellent job in balancing the needs of local residents with the desire to increase tourism.	208	3.53	1.65

Table 18.2 (*Continued*)

	Number	Mean	Standard deviation
The hutong would be a dull place if it were not for the attempts to attract tourists.	222	3.52	1.84
I would like to have a job in tourism.	216	3.40	2.11
When I see tourists coming here I am envious of their way of life.	221	3.27	1.62
Tourism is the only way the hutong can survive in the future.	208	3.05	1.68
My income has increased with the introduction of tourism.	208	2.50	1.89
Personally, I would like to see the hutong demolished and more modern houses for local people built.	212	2.43	1.71
With the changes I see I would like to move out of the hutong.	199	2.31	1.68

other hand, the hutong residents feel that the hutong is more congested with traffic (6.44), adversely affecting local residents (5.48), and further development is seen as potentially threatening the hutong environment (5.35). There is a high degree of agreement with the notion that the hutong is a special place and should be protected (6.46). By the same token, in spite of the growing intrusion being caused by tourism, these mainly older residents have no desire to move out of the hutong (2.31) and neither do they wish to see the hutong demolished and replaced by something more modern (2.43). This last viewpoint was made quite evident when proposals to demolish part of the hutong around the Bell and Drum Towers was significantly resisted to such a degree that in February 2011 the Beijing authorities announced the abandonment of the idea to develop a modern shopping mall and entertainment centre in that area.

The opposition to these proposals is also reflected in the generally low scores relating to the degree of approval of the planning authorities. For example, the items 'I feel the hutong's tourism planning authorities do an excellent job in making the right decisions about the area I live in' and 'The tourism/planning authorities do an excellent job in balancing the needs of local residents with the desire to increase tourism' attract scores of 3.98 and 3.53, respectively (below the mid-point of the scale). By the same token, the item 'I think that attracting more tourists to the hutong is a good idea' attracts at best a moderate degree of support, with a score of 4.64.

Reverting to Figure 18.1, the relationships within the diagram were assessed. Using as a dependent variable the item 'I am quite happy with tourism and its impacts on the hutong' and a stepwise linear regression routine from Predictive Analytics Software (PASW), it was found that 10 items generated an adjusted coefficient of determination of 0.65. The Durbin–Watson test statistic was 1.92, indicating that auto-correlation was not an issue. Categorising respondents as 'low', 'indifferent' and 'high' in their satisfaction with the impacts of tourism and incorporating income as a possible determinant in light of the findings discussed below, an ordinal logistic multinomial regression was calculated. This is possible because the determined variable is ordered from low to high. The reduction in the number of cells can be justified owing to the high data demands, and on this basis the income groups were also simply grouped as below average, average and above average on the grounds that, as noted above, those with incomes significantly above average accounted for only 2% of the sample. Nonetheless, while the result may be designated as 'encouraging', given that the Cox and Snell Pseudo Coefficient of Determination was 0.85, the initial result was problematic because it generated too many empty cells in the calculations for 'above average income' and thwarted an attempt to calculate likelihood ratios.

An alternative approach is to adopt discriminate analysis to predict membership of those groups categorized as being happy with the impact of tourism upon the hutong. Using this approach indicated an overall success rate of 73.4%, with 91.9% of those categorized as 'more than happy' and 81.4% of those less than happy being correctly predicted. This meant that it was the mid-group for which the predicting variables were least efficient. Examining the Squared Mahalanobis Distance Matrix simply confirmed the 'leakage' of the mid-points to the two extremities, as was also clearly indicated by the canonical distribution chart generated by PASW.

Data Derived from the Qualitative Study

The following highlights issues that emerged from conversations with the residents of the hutong during the first stage of the project. Over 40 such conversations were held and a thematic analysis was used.

Dog issues

Many hutong respondents commented that, as the living standards of the hutong residents improved, many are taking to feeding and keeping dogs rather than the traditionally kept fish or birds. While dogs are proving to be excellent pets, dog droppings are also seriously influencing the hutong environment. The animals generate yet more noise in the morning or at night with their barking. Some car drivers commented that they worry about hurting dogs when the lane is narrow and the light is not good at dusk or at night. If the dogs are out of the control of their owners and jump out from the darkness, they may pose problems to drivers, even to the degree of causing damage or harm when drivers try to avoid these small animals. It does appear that these issues are becoming harder to control by the local government, as well causing local residents to worry about their dogs possibly being hurt in accidents.

Pedicab issues

The pedicab has been a major tourist business in the Beijing Shi Cha Hai area for over a decade. As a successful small business type, it reputedly makes millions of yuan income every year. It has, for over much of its history (Gu & Ryan, 2008), attracted Chinese migrants originally resided outside Beijing to Shi Cha Hai to make money by starting up or working in a pedicab business. While too many people and too many companies are doing this, the impact it has is also huge. Consequently, more than half of the long-term hutong residents interviewed, especially those living around Prince Gong's Palace, identified pedicab workers as creating intrusive noise throughout the day and so significantly adversely affecting their daily rest patterns.

For the most part, the pedicab workers generally have no background in higher education and most are from families in a state of poverty; they therefore concentrate on making money without considering the feelings of others. Respondents had noted that these workers often smoke and throw their cigarette butts onto the streets or into the lake. The smell of the cigarettes also lingers in the hutong air and permeates the lanes. Respondents also claimed that the lake water is being polluted by them and by other tourists. Furthermore, it was claimed that some pedicab workers swear a lot and make dirty jokes and residents are offended by both this and by the fact that they do it in front of the residents' children. Residents are also afraid of their children getting hurt when pedicab workers ride in the hutong lanes. One respondent described a conflict between two pedicab companies, causing fights on the street and a lot of people being badly hurt or wounded. The reason for this conflict was that the two companies were focusing on the same customer and, in negotiating the price together, one side felt the other broke the informal rules of this business, and called on others to become involved in the argument which then escalated into violence. This feedback reconfirms original work by Gu and Ryan (2008), who also commented on the need for better controls on the pedicab business; however, these comments also indicate that the improvements noted after the Olympics have been short lived (Gu & Ryan, 2012).

Traffic jams and parking problems

Every resident interviewed had witnessed a significant traffic jam in or around the hutong. Year by year, month by month, week by week, day by day, such jams are repeated again and again. This issue is caused by increasing numbers of domestic and international tour groups and local small business operators. It is very hard to cater for the thousands of tourists in the high tourist season in the narrow lanes. Additionally, the number of private cars in Beijing is increasing rapidly. All these reasons mean the hutong residents have come to think of a traffic jam as being as normal as sunrise and sunset. The related traffic issue is that of parking. Some inhabitants stated that parking is right now the most annoying problem for them, because there are always unknown cars or buses parked outside their houses blocking them in when they wish to come and go. Cars also bring noise and air pollution. It is no use denying that cars have already occupied most of the spare space in the hutong lanes, but building more parking lots is not really a feasible solution for the government. The government has committed to hutong protection, and cannot destroy more old buildings to make way for new parking areas. Therefore, traffic jams and parking issues can be seen as one of the more challenging tasks facing the local government.

Protection of the hutong

Most respondents support protection of the hutong because it is seen as a special place very different from the remainder of Beijing. It means not only a place to which people are strongly attached to live, but it also represents hundreds of years of Chinese history.

The hutong involves Chinese culture, tradition, custom and personality. Even when the government planned to remove the old buildings and build more modern houses and apartments for the older residents, which meant larger room sizes and a better living environment for them, the Shi Cha Hai inhabitants expressed the view that they would not accept these alternatives because Shi Cha Hai is their home. Furthermore, other inhabitants think Shi Cha Hai has been and should be protected by the Chinese government and tourism organizations. From a practical perspective, with the current prices of houses in Beijing, many residents do not have too many choices as to where they could live. If they had to move out from this area, they would have to live in somewhere beyond the 6th ring road, which is far from the centre of Beijing, but would represent the only parts of Beijing where they could afford to purchase a property. The hutong remains close to the centre of Beijing and its main governmental and business sector. Indeed, such has been the strength of local opinion that the local administration has abandoned plans for the 'upgrading' of the area around the Bell and Drum Towers.

Public security and crime

The majority of Shi Cha Hai Hutong residents are registered as possessing residency rights in Beijing. However, there is still a *floating population* (liudong renkou), including illegal migrants. Following a rapid increase in the number of migrants and the high turnover rate of tourism workers, more and more small businesses managers started to rent out rooms in the hutong for their out-of-town employees. As the numbers of such employees have increased, so too is crime becoming a social issue at the local level. Some respondents described a situation where these employees normally have no regular timetable for work, but on the other hand would always work overtime when it is available. Consequently, the rooms in which they live would be empty during much of the day. Break-ins and theft happen very frequently in these areas, especially where foreigners live. The most commonly stolen items include cash, bicycles, small cars and expensive electronic items. Cars are also subject to broken windows. Hence the signs as shown in Figure 18.2.

Noise

Any one of local residents, foreign and domestic tourists, animals, pedicab operators, private cars and tour buses can be a reason for intrusive noise. Some inhabitants mentioned that at night in Shi Cha Hai, some foreign tourists tend to drink in the bars until the early hours. While people try to sleep at home, tourists sing 'the strange songs', turn up their loudspeakers, speak loudly and shout at each other; drunks vomit in the lake or on the street and, at worst, fights break out.

Figure 18.2 Warning notices in a hutong alley

In the daytime there are sounds of car horns, tourists talking loudly and merchants advertising their wares; all these inhibit the ability of nearby residents to have a good rest. Additionally, there are old buildings that need to be refurbished and the construction of new buildings permitted by government plans or by the private sector. Therefore, heaps of building materials are piled on the ground in hutong lanes. Sand and concrete dirty the hutong environment. Noise and chaos consequently accompany such construction. However, things are slowly improving and there are now even electric pedicabs as illustrated in Figure 18.3.

Figure 18.3 Electric pedicab

Cleanliness

Although noise and chaos are becoming one of the most serious issues in hutong lanes, most respondents still accept that the current hutong streets and lanes are much cleaner and tidier than was previously the case.

Many years ago, the hutong lanes did not have many street lights and rubbish bins. At night, people had to walk or work in the dark, and if they had some cooking waste to drop, they would tend to just dump it at convenient spots; therefore rubbish would be everywhere next morning. These reasons directly caused hutong lanes to be dirty and smelly for a very long time. Nowadays, environmental and hygiene management have been incorporated into the hutong management system, and it is recognised that local government has been doing a very good job in keeping the hutong lanes cleaner and lighter. Only a very small part of the hutong area still looks a mess because of either unlicensed building or being too close to pubs and restaurants.

Water pollution

Because of the construction of the restaurants and bars with little concern about the environment, Shi Cha Hai inhabitants have been watching a growing serious problem of water pollution in Shi Cha lake for a long time. Some respondents commented that, although the government has done a good job on water resource protection through, for example, the collection of weed during the summer months, they are not employing enough people to manage garbage and rubbish such as cans, bottles, bags, papers and rocks which are being dumped in the lake. Actually, there are hundreds of buildings around the lake, and most are profit-oriented business premises. While customers sit and consume goods, rubbish will be generated. Lack of good maintenance will lead to higher levels of water pollution in a very small part of Shi Cha Lake. The good news is that water pollution is very limited in Shi Cha Hai, and many respondents realize this, but equally many are intolerant of the situation. Some respondents said that water is not perfect and as clean as in the past, but it is still possible to swim and fish in the lake away from the rubbish which gathers in the southwest part.

Conclusion

Shi Cha Hai Hutong is an old, cultural and unique part of Beijing city, and it attracts both tourists coming to Beijing and local people for recreational purposes, making the hutong and the lake a major tourism and recreational centre. Its culture represents one of the more valuable heritage sites of Chinese social history, both recent and from the classical periods. While increasing numbers of people experience this location, it is changing step by step. No one knows for how much longer the present pattern of hutong culture can be sustained, for the modernization of the buildings is transforming their traditional use and the culture associated with them. Quadrangle homes are being converted into hotels, restaurants and retail outlets, or are being gentrified by the newly affluent middle classes seeking a home near their place of work. Property prices are increasing. Some local residents have already recognized the importance of protecting the hutong environment, and are taking further action to protect the area on their own initiative. Fortunately, the local government has also initiated laws relating to hutong protection in terms of the physical assets while seeking to preserve patterns of culture, albeit sometimes through commercialised means such as the annual festival. At the same time, whether consciously or not, a degree of 'demarketing' exists in that the Visitor Information Centre at Shi Cha Lake displays comparatively little literature in any language for visitors, although maps are available.

Thus far at least, efforts by inhabitants and the government have maintained much of the character of the area, although the greater threat may be from gradual gentrification and changing patterns of resident population rather than, perhaps, tourism. Indeed, sustainable tourism would require the conservation of these historic areas of Beijing.

Recommendations

According to the research findings and feedback from respondents, there are many issues that need to be addressed in order to maintain the hutong as a sustainable tourism attraction.

First, illegal extensions to buildings should be managed, regulated or removed in the last resort if required. Penalties may be introduced to curb unlicensed alterations or changes of use, and would need to be properly implemented. Certainly one can recognise the desire of occupants to acquire modern facilities, especially given the high numbers of properties without modern toilet facilities, but major architectural features should be retained and as a minimum the traditional facades retained. A number of initiatives are already being carried out, including the removal of overhead wires and the relocation of them underground, thereby creating hutong lanes that look tidier and cleaner. Of course, in itself this represents a change, for just over a decade ago many of these lanes were not paved and comprised little more than muddy alleyways in the winter months.

Second, with reference to the traffic jams and parking problems, there is a need for local government to arrange enough places for the locals to park their cars. However, there is little open space within the hutong on which public parking can be developed and it is too expensive to build new parking lots. Therefore, developing underground parking for the tour groups and individual tourists might be considered in the local government plan. For those who still park in inconvenient places such as in front of local residents' front doors, oral warnings and reasonable penalties should be applied to stop such behaviour. One possibility is to consider parking sites at the periphery of the hutong with pedicab (or electric pedicab) services being available to take residents to their homes. Such 'park and ride' schemes may also create employment, but would need consideration as to how such a service might be paid for. Once the hutong lanes have been regulated, the streets would be wider through the removal of cars that obstruct the traffic flow and all the noise caused by car horns would disappear.

Third, concerning dog issues, every dog must have a legal ID, be registered and wear a dog tag on its neck, so people can know the dog is 'legal'. Furthermore, microchips into the dog's body can be used to check the dog's ID. When someone finds a missing dog, then by scanning the chip he or she could know who the owner of the dog is and find the owner's address. Secondly, the dog's owners should be responsible for their dog's safety and the removal of the dog's droppings. Leashes must be used to control dogs to stop potentially hazardous behaviour on the part of the dogs. Dog catchers and a dog pound are required for strays, and the local government could follow the overseas practice of permitting the adoption of such dogs instead of having them put down. Certainly, there must be great care to ensure that a problem of feral dogs does not ensue.

Fourth, as some respondents have commented, the green lanes should be preserved and more public facilities should be provided. At locations where there are famous tourism attractions such as Prince Gong's Palace, normally there would be a very high tourist flow rate and tourism-related workers are employed to assist in the management of tourist flows while also continually cleaning and sweeping the site. There is a need for more public facilities like rubbish bins and public toilets. Such simple measures would both reduce complaints from the residents, and also help protect the hutong environment.

Fifth, the government provides, and should continue to provide strong support for the maintenance and improvement of Shi-He-Yuan buildings. The traditional hutong buildings have a very long history and heritage. Without outside maintenance, the structure of the buildings may become unsafe, and not every householder has the resources to undertake repairs themselves; indeed, government action may be required because of patterns of partial or joint ownership or even unclear ownership.

Additionally, to retain the traditional beauty and aesthetics of the hutong buildings and provide visitors with reasons to take pictures and appreciate them, skilled painters are needed to maintain these buildings on a regular basis, especially those in the areas of main tourist flow, and this too may fall within the remit of the local authorities. Furthermore, if someone illegally causes critical damage or even destroys the buildings, then punishment must be based on the law and additionally there should be a requirement to rebuild the building in the style of the original.

Sixth, residents suggest a limit should be imposed on the development of pedicab businesses and better regulation of existing pedicab businesses. According to the anecdotal evidence as well as the more formal feedback of many Shi Cha Hai inhabitants and visitors, most possess a strong antipathy towards this business. Today the Shi Cha Hai area cannot afford yet more pedicab companies, for many who run such businesses are not achieving desirable returns and individual drivers are not earning as much as they would wish. The noise and damage caused by pedicabs on the environment are becoming increasingly less tolerated by residents. The conflicts between pedicab workers also bring instability to tourism pricing structures through discounts, with a mounting threat of petty crime. But any regulation of this business will require patience and perseverance. The local government should define and implement a more effective policy to control the increasing number of pedicabs and limit their times of operation; for example, the pedicabs could be limited to periods only between 10 am and 5 pm To reduce the number of unlicensed pedicab workers, the companies should not only require workers to wear uniforms but also more prominently display their ID. During the Olympic Games of 2008 the business was carefully regulated and monitored, but those policies have not apparently been sustained and evidence derived from walking through the area several times indicates that there is again a growing number of unlicensed drivers.

It can be argued that tourism in the hutong is moving into a later stage of the Butler tourist area life cycle, and further development must be more carefully considered within a wider framework of urban development. A greater integration of tourism policy and development is called for within the wider perspective of zonal planning that identifies areas of leisure and recreation – in this case including Beihai Park which is immediately adjacent to the hutong and the lakes. Each must be seen as part of an integrated whole, not as separate components with little relationship to one another. This call is supported by the evidence generated in this study, but it also has future implications for research. Thus far, most research has concentrated upon specific aspects of the hutong and little integrative or longitudinal research has been reported. There is also a significant silence in the English literature; few if any interviews have been held with those actually responsible for planning the hutong. Such dialogues are also necessary for future sustainable tourism in the area.

References

Akpabio, I.A., Eniang, E.A. and Egwali, E.C. (2008) Socio-economic potentials and environmental implications of coastal tourism at Adiabo, Cross River State, Nigeria. *Environment, Development and Sustainability* 10 (3), 249–265.

Amsden, B.L., Stedman, R.C. and Kruger, L.E. (2011) The creation and maintenance of sense of place in a tourism-dependent community. *Leisure Sciences* 33 (1), 32–51.

Andereck, K.L. and Nyaupane, G.P. (2011) Exploring the nature of tourism and quality of life perceptions among residents. *Journal of Travel Research* 50 (3), 248–260.

Archer, B. and Cooper, C. (1994) *The Positive and Negative Impacts of Tourism*. Oxford: Global Tourism Butterworth Heinemann.

Aref, F. (2011) The effects of tourism on quality of life: A case study of Shiraz, Iran. *Life Sciences Journal* 8 (2), 26–30.

BTA (Beijing Tourism Administration) (2007) 什刹海胡同游2008年实施特许经营. http://ly.beijing.cn/lykx/n214056599.shtml.

CNTO (China National Tourism Office) (2006) *China Tourism Statistics*, accessed 26 August 2006. http://www.cnto.org/chinastats.asp.

CRI (2006) 什刹海开拆88处违建酒吧. http://gb.cri.cn/9523/2006/04/06/421@982962.htm.

Cristoforetti, A., Gennai, F. and Rodeschini, G. (2011) Home sweet home: The emotional construction of places. *Journal of Aging Studies* 25 (3), 225–232.

Cui, X. and Ryan, C. (2011) Perceptions of place, modernity and the impacts of tourism – differences among rural and urban residents of Ankang, China: A likelihood ratio analysis. *Tourism Management* 32 (3), 604–615.

Franquesa, J. (2011) 'We've lost our bearings': Place, tourism, and the limits of the 'mobility turn'. *Antipode* 43 (4), 1012–1033.

Gu, H. and Ryan, C. (2008) Place attachment, identity and community impacts of tourism – the case of a Beijing hutong. *Tourism Management* 29 (4), 637–647.

Gu, H. and Ryan, C. (2012) Tourism destination evolution: a comparative study of Shi Cha Hai Beijing Hutong businesses' and residents' attitudes. *Journal of Sustainable Tourism* 20 (1), 23–40.

Gu, H., Ryan, C. and Yu, L. (2012) The changing structure of the Chinese hotel industry: 1980–2012. *Tourism Management Perspectives* 4, 56–63.

Harry, G. and Foden, C.E.D. (1992) Destination attractions as an economic development generator. *Economic Development Review* 10 (4), 69–72.

Heath, T. and Tang, Y. (2010) Beijing's hutong and siheyuan: Conservation of an urban identity. *Proceedings of the Institution of Civil Engineers: Municipal Engineer* 163 (3), 155–161.

Ji, S. and Wall, G. (2011) Visitor and resident images of Qingdao, China, as a tourist destination. *Journal of China Tourism Research* 7 (2), 207–228.

Jiang, B.L. and Tribe, J. (2009) 'Tourism jobs – short lived professions': Student attitudes towards tourism career in China. *Sport & Tourism Education* 8 (1), 4–19.

Kask, S., Kline, C. and Lamoureux, K. (2011) Modeling tourist and community decision making. *Annals of Tourism Research* 38 (4), 1387–1409.

Kokkranikal, J. and Morrison, A. (2002) Entrepreneurship and sustainable tourism: The houseboats of Kerala. *Tourism and Hospitality Research* 4 (1), 7–20.

Kong, H.Y. and Baum, T. (2006) Skills and work in the hospitality sector: The case of hotel front office employees in China. *International Journal of Contemporary Hospitality Management* 18 (6), 509–518.

Kyle, G., Graefe, A., Manning, R. and Bacon, J. (2004a) Effects of place attachment on users' perceptions of social and environmental conditions in a natural setting. *Journal of Environmental Psychology* 24 (2), 213–225.

Kyle, G., Mowen, A.J. and Tarrant, M. (2004b) Linking place preferences with place meaning: An examination of the relationship between place motivation and place attachment. *Journal of Environmental Psychology* 24 (4), 439–454.

Kytzia, S., Waltz, A. and Wegmann, M. (2011) How can tourism use land more efficiently? A model-based approach to land use efficiency for tourist destinations. *Tourism Management* 32 (3), 629–640.

Liu, J. and Var, T. (1983) The economic impacts of tourism in metropolitan Victoria, B.C. *Journal of Travel Research* 22 (2), 8–15.

Nunkoo, R. and Ramkisson, H. (2011) Residents' satisfaction with community attributes and support for tourism. *Journal of Hospitality and Tourism Research* 35 (2), 171–190.

OCN (2012) *Report on China Tourism Industry, 2012–2016*. Beijing: CI Consulting.

Perdue, R.R., Long, P.T. and Allen, L. (1990) Resident support for tourism development. *Annals of Tourism Research* 17 (4), 586–599.

Pratt, S. (2011) Economic linkages across the TALC. *Annals of Tourism Research* 38 (2), 630–650.

Ramkisson, H. and Nunkoo, R. (2011) City image and perceived tourism impact: Evidence from Port Louis, Mauritius. *International Journal of Hospitality and Tourism Administration* 12 (2), 123–143.

Ryan, C. (1991) *Recreational Tourism: A Social Science Perspective*. London: Routledge.

Ryan, C. and Cessford, G. (2003) Developing a visitor satisfaction monitoring methodology: Quality gaps, crowding and some results. *Current Issues in Tourism* 6 (6), 457–507.

Sands, L.M. (2008) The 2008 Olympics' impact on China. *China Business Review*. https://www.chinabusinessreview.com/public/0807/sands.html.

Scarpello, V. and Campbell, J.P. (1983) Job satisfaction: Are all the parts there? *Personnel Psychology* 36, 577–600.

Schofield, P. (2011) City resident attitudes to proposed tourism development and its impacts on the community. *International Journal of Tourism Research* 13 (3), 218–233.

Sheldon, P.J. and Var, T. (1984) Resident attitudes to tourism in North Wales. *Tourism Management* 5 (1), 40–47.

Shichahai (2009) 什刹海简介, accessed 8 November. http://www.shichahai.com/travel/1.asp.

Stefano, D.D. (2004) Tourism, industry, and community development: Whitefish, Montana, 1903–2003. *Environmental Practice* 6 (1), 63–70.

Tip, B.P. (2009) Sustainable tourism. *International Trade Forum* 1, 21–23.

Tsundoda, T. and Mendlinger, S. (2009) Economic and social impact of Tourism on a small town: Peterborough, New Hampshire. *Service Science & Management* 2, 61–70.

Wanous, J.P., Reichers, A.E. and Hudy, M.J. (1997) Overall job satisfaction: How good are single-item measures? *Journal of Applied Psychology* 82 (2), 247–252.

Ward, C. and Berno, T. (2011) Beyond social exchange theory: Attitudes towards tourists. *Annals of Tourism Research* 38 (4), 1556–1569.

Weaver, D. (2010) *Tourism Management* (4th edn). Milton: John Wiley and Sons.

WTO (World Tourism Organization) (2001) *Tourism 2020 Vision: Vol. 3, East Asia and Pacific*. Madrid: WTO.

Travel China Guide (2013) Shichahai. Beijing: China Travel Guide, accessed 21 February 2013. www.travelchinaguide.com/attraction/beijing/shichahai.htm

19 Chinese Tourism Research: An International Perspective

Chris Ryan and Songshan (Sam) Huang

Defining Chinese Tourism Research

At the end of this volume, we feel there is a need to fit this collective work into the broad *landscape* of 'Chinese tourism research'. The term Chinese tourism research is preferred, although in the literature or on various research platforms and outlets (e.g. journals and conferences), 'China tourism' and 'Chinese tourism' have been used interchangeably and without clear differentiation. For the sake of academic clarity and rigour, we argue for a conceptual distinction between the two terms and are inclined to adopt the latter for our discussion in this chapter. As a matter of definition, we see 'Chinese tourism' as being more inclusive in its scope than what is literally meant by 'China tourism'. 'Chinese tourism', as a refined academic term, thus refers to any tourism phenomenon which has happened, is happening or is about to happen in relation to China as a nation/country and the Chinese as a people. The term involves therefore two fundamental elements in the tourism system: people and place. The two are not necessarily congruent, because many Chinese live outside China as noted below. But it can also be interpreted in a second way, and that is that Chinese tourism research is that research undertaken by Chinese people about tourism, which may or may not be occurring in China. Indeed, a third definition simultaneously occurs, and that is that Chinese tourism research is research about China, the Chinese and tourism that is conducted, whether or not the researchers are Chinese. The definitions therefore have their own separate foci, but two essentials remain. Firstly there is the place, and secondly there are the people. These differing ways of defining the term 'Chinese tourism research' are listed in Table 19.1. It is evident that this is not a totally exhaustive examination of the term, but it is sufficient to indicate that what appears to be a self-evident term is in fact one with several nuances. Equally, however, it implies the importance of culture and language.

Table 19.1 Defining Chinese tourism research

Research about tourism in China (domestic tourism and inbound tourism)	This may be conducted by either Chinese or non-Chinese researchers.
Research about tourism undertaken by Chinese citizens (domestic and outbound tourism)	This may be conducted by either Chinese or non-Chinese researchers.
Research about tourism undertaken by Chinese citizens and the wider Chinese diaspora (tourism within and outside China)	This may be conducted by either Chinese or non-Chinese researchers.
Research about tourism undertaken by Chinese researchers concerning tourism carried out by Mainland Chinese citizens (domestic and outbound tourism)	This is conducted by Chinese researchers who may be: (a) Chinese citizens working within China; (b) Chinese citizens working outside China; (c) those of Chinese ethnicity working outside China, e.g. Hong Kong.
Research about tourism undertaken by Chinese researchers concerning tourism carried out by those of Chinese ethnicity and culture (domestic and outbound tourism)	This is conducted by Chinese researchers who may be: (a) Chinese citizens working within China; (b) Chinese citizens working outside China; (c) those of Chinese ethnicity working outside China, e.g. Hong Kong.

Table 19.1 is also interesting in that it seeks to make clear a distinction that is not generally sought. For example, do researchers write about 'British tourism research', although in recent years there have been comments that have sought to demarcate a US–UK nexus of research that has been and continues to be important? This importance is due to the role of English assuming an international importance through economic, business and colonial histories. It also reflects the emergence of tourism as an important economic activity within those economies and the emergence of tourism and leisure as subjects for study within their universities (the position of hospitality being, arguably, a little more complex due to the Swiss and wider mainland European traditions). The emergence of China, and the Chinese and their researchers reflects a new reality and dynamic that challenges the hegemony of the Western academic tradition in tourism scholarship. Indeed, when one looks simply at the number of universities where tourism and hospitality is studied, taught and researched, it is clear that in the last decade the critical mass of scholarship has shifted to China. Chinese names are increasingly prevalent in English language journals and, in tourism thus far, only belatedly and still only too rarely are English names to be found in journals like *Tourism Tribune* and *Human Geographies* that are published in Mandarin.

Returning to the first understanding of what constitutes 'Chinese tourism research', China as a place can be seen as a destination potentially attracting the yet-to-be largest inbound tourist flow as forecast by UNWTO (2001) and possessing a very significant domestic tourist market considering the country's population base of well over 1 billion people and its growing wealth. Additionally, the Chinese mainland is undoubtedly emerging as an influential place of outbound tourism growth to justify the title of the world's leading outbound travel market, as proudly claimed by the China Tourism Academy (CTA, 2012). The sheer size of the Chinese population both within and outside China prompts broader thinking with regard to Chinese tourism research as indicated in Table 19.1. In this sense, Chinese tourism can be said to extend across the administrative borders of the Chinese mainland and should include tourism in relation to those Chinese people resident in Hong Kong, Macao and Taiwan, and further to overseas Chinese now dwelling virtually in every corner of the world. Chinese people in different localities within or outside China could be related to tourism as either tourists or residents, or as other types of stakeholder in tourism, thus adding various layers to Chinese tourism research as discussed below.

Such a broader Chinese tourism research scope requires an international perspective in surveying the overall terrain. Several issues warrant scrutiny in the making and understanding of Chinese tourism research. The first is pertinent to researchers. It is evident that researchers working on Chinese tourism research come from both within and outside China or the greater China region (including Hong Kong, Macao and Taiwan). These researchers can be divided into different communities by applying various criteria. The community comprising tourism researchers working in research institutions in mainland China is seemingly more distinct from the others, even though to some extent mainland China tourism researchers may share common ground with their counterparts in Taiwan. Two sets of commonality may be defined. The first is the cultural aspect of being Chinese. While Taiwanese scholars can argue for an unbroken tradition of classical Chinese thought as evidenced by their retention of an older form of written Chinese in everyday life, nonetheless China is still perceived as the origin country. The great traditions of Taoism, Buddhism and Confucianism still retain a hold on thought. But across these traditions is now imposed the scientism of Western thought, often empirical and generally but not wholly due to American positivistic and post-positivistic patterns of thought, as evidenced in articles littered with statistical tables. China has its history of scientific thought, but the technological and to some extent the mathematical advances made by China were halted by the Qing dynasty as it isolated itself from the rest of the world. Hence Wen (2010) discerns a gap from about 1652 when he describes Wang Fuzhi's writings as representing the highest point of Chinese philosophical thought and that of 1919 when Hu Shi made his attempt to incorporate Western thought into Chinese epistemological systems. That process of integration, broken by the Maoist period (other than considerations of Marxist thought) has, arguably, only recently been restored, at least in the field of tourism research, as Chinese thinkers seek to establish their own voice. In doing so they make recourse to other traditions, such as the European philosophical traditions of the constructionists and interpretivists who acknowledge social constructions of truth, and the holistic understandings of varying native peoples who adhere to human–nature relationships as being important. Chinese researchers thus occupy various worlds, the world of being immersed in a Chinese culture, a world of respect for scientific traditions and the authority of the scientific tradition, and the hybrid world where both are entwined.

Performing Chinese Tourism Research: Researchers and Research Camps

If, therefore, we adopt the above argument that the tourism research community in China demonstrates distinctive characteristics in making and contributing to Chinese tourism research when compared to their counterparts outside China, wherein lie the practical determinants of that difference? Possibly their research activities and behavioural patterns can best be explained by the institutional environment within which they work. We should note that while language remains a factor in making the distinction, an increasing number of researchers in China seem to be adept in both reading and writing English. However, there is an informational asymmetry between tourism researchers in China and their international counterparts who mainly work in the English academic language environment. While tourism researchers in China are increasingly able to access and process English academic literature, a large number of overseas scholars (particularly from the English language environment) undertaking research in and about China seemingly lack the capacity to access and integrate into their works the Chinese language literature produced by their counterparts in China. Having said that, we must acknowledge this situation is also changing and being reduced by: (a) collaborations between the two; (b) Chinese tourism scholars working overseas, increasingly bridging such a gap; and (c) the increasing availability of access to sources such as CKNI by overseas scholars. Admittedly, globalisation is also bringing researchers closer to each other.

Nevertheless, tourism academics in China remain in a largely enclosed community of their fellow researchers despite a small number actively publishing their works, mostly in collaboration with outside researchers, in international tourism journals. While the increasing numbers of international journal publications and cross-country collaborations represent a transition, or the beginnings of a transition, a sense of a more integrated tourism research agenda with overseas colleagues as hoped for by Chinese tourism researchers has thus far not fully materialised (Chen & Huang, 2008; Song et al., 2006). Currently, the majority of research outputs emanating from Chinese scholars remain within the academic body that forms the Chinese tourism research community. Liu (2008) reviewed tourism grants projects under both the National Natural Science Foundation and the National Social Science Foundation schemes from 1987 to 2007. To the knowledge of these writers, among the 78 grant projects reviewed by Liu, none seemed to have had its results communicated in journals outside China. Two examples were found of grants and publications in English outlets (Kim et al., 2005; Wu & Cai, 2006) with similar titles, but further examination showed that the publication attempts were before the grant award years and apparently the publications served as a basis for the researchers to win the grants, rather than as results derived from grant-aided research. It is worth mentioning, however, that the two chapters authored by Yang in this volume (Chapters 10 and 11) appear to come from the author's project in the National Social Science Foundation scheme awarded in 2006.

Caution should be exercised in differentiating the camps of researchers within and outside China, as the boundary lines between the two camps are becoming increasingly blurring and intermingled. This is especially true when considering researchers based in Hong Kong, a Special Administrative Region (SAR) of China. Undeniably, due to different institutional requirements, tourism researchers in Hong Kong mainly publish in international English journals, thereby distinguishing themselves from their mainland colleagues. Hence, there appears to be a division in the Chinese language world, between those who mainly publish their research in the Chinese language and those, primarily outside China, who mainly publish their research work in English language academic journals. With the exception possibly of Hong Kong, something of a similar distinction can also be seen, at least partly, for Chinese scholars working in Taiwan and Macao. There are those within China who do regularly publish in both Chinese and English journals, but they are relatively few in number, and some of them are represented in this book.

This classification logically leads to the recognition and allocation of researchers into one or other category of researcher. Those researchers of Chinese ethnicity primarily based outside China publishing in English about Chinese matters have been increasingly prolific. Review studies (e.g. Cai et al., 2008; Gross et al., 2013; Tsang & Hsu, 2011) demonstrate that Chinese tourism research publications in English academic journals have been increasing in number over the past two or three decades; researchers publishing in this field come from institutions across the globe, but mainly from mainland China, Hong Kong, the USA, the UK, Australia, New Zealand and Canada.

The volume of such work has led to a second stage that reflects upon and reviews past work to develop a history of Chinese tourism research in general and in specific sub-fields (e.g. outbound Chinese tourism). Examples include reviews of work published in English (e.g. Cai *et al.*, 2008; Tsang & Hsu, 2011), in Chinese (e.g. Huang & Hsu, 2008) and writers using both English and Chinese publications (e.g. Hsu *et al.*, 2010). Equally there are reviews of such work in Chinese publications by authors mainly based in China on research published in English (e.g. Chen & Bao, 2011; Li & Zhao, 2007), on research published in Chinese (e.g. Cao & Hu, 2008; Wu *et al.*, 2001), and comparison studies of tourism research inside and outside China (e.g. Zhu & Liu, 2004). A comparison of such works between the two camps generally confirms that the mutual 'gaze' at each other's research work is unbalanced. While a significant number of Chinese articles are found on reviewing and evaluating research progress in the English literature, very little research has been found in the English literature critiquing and evaluating the progress of tourism research in China. What has happened inside China regarding tourism research activities in a community with an estimated number of at least 1500 researchers (Hsu *et al.*, 2010) has largely remained unseen outside China.

Among those working inside China, self-reflection and criticism about tourism research is not unusual. Critiques have been focused on the lack of standard research practice to ensure research quality and rigour, the lack of proper research question definition by researchers, a lack of a proper application of scientific research methods, and the possibly undue intervention of government-led agendas (Bao, 2010; Cao & Hu, 2008; Xie, 2003; Zhu & Liu, 2004). Some commentators have been concerned with the seemingly small contribution made to international mainstream tourism journals by researchers in China. It has been suggested that the reasons for this include (a) research perspective, (b) research methods/methodologies, and (c) the language barrier (Chen & Huang, 2008).

Generating Chinese Tourism Research: Institutional Issues

Interestingly, tourism researchers within China have seldom explicitly discussed the institutional factors that influence the development of tourism research in their country. This issue has been implicitly touched upon by some researchers in China, and flagged by those outside the country (e.g. Bao, 2009; Ryan, 2009). In this regard, Kuhn's (1970) theory of the paradigm, together with Foucauldian discourse theory, may shed some light on the matter. For Kuhn (1970), knowledge creation occurs at the level of the culture of disciplines; an analysis of how domains of knowledge emerge can be applied to other specific forms of knowledge organisation such as the culture of a certain research community. Similarly, in Foucault's (1969) lexicon, discourses, as practices that systematically form the objects of which a certain social or professional group members speak, consequently define the limits of truth claims, and legitimise and sanction some statements while silencing and denying others. Both theories postulate the argument that certain patterns of research practice should be considered as outcomes of the historical, social and cultural milieu within which researchers are living. Transferring this to the scenario of tourism research in China, we may argue that institutional environment factors, such as political ideologies, social and cultural norms, research evaluation criteria and so on, are forging the current status quo of tourism research undertaken by scholars in China.

Outside China, tourism researchers have also more or less continuously discussed institutional influences on tourism research, often in the English language publishing community subject to government-directed research assessment exercises or tenure systems that emphasise research outputs and influence (Hall, 2011; Huang, 2012; Page, 2003; Ryan, 2005; Tribe, 2003). Bibliometrics has developed as a research topic in its own right as journal rankings, ratings and impact factors have been developed and individual researchers and journals compare their h-indices.

China has not been immune to similar considerations, but has its own characteristics. First, the government's influence on the university system is generally more interventionist when compared to that of Western governments. In the latter, academic freedom and independence has long been defended along with the notion that standards are common across all universities, although, primarily based on their history, the research and resources of universities are far from equal. This inequality is formally recognised in China, where a tiered system of university status exists and the ability to offer research through doctoral degrees is a decision made by the Chinese Ministry of Education. Additionally, tourism itself has been generally directed (until very recently) by government economic policies. Consequently, via both educational and economic policies, government support has played a key role in fostering the higher tourism education system (Huang, 2001) and to a significant extent, the direction of research undertaken in tourism. Hence review studies have identified many articles published in the leading Chinese tourism academic journal *Tourism Tribune* that describe and analyse government actions and policy directions in developing tourism, particularly with reference to destination development (Huang & Hsu, 2008; Xie, 2003).

Second, China has a cultural tradition that selects government officials from its intelligentsia, as summarised by an old saying 'those who study well academically should be put into officialdom' ('学而优则仕'). In the Chinese research institutional system (which includes its various academies including the China Tourism Academy), academics who excel in research are commonly associated with university leadership and administrative positions. Additionally, being connected to or closer to the government at varying levels means access to more intangible research resources for academics in the Chinese *guanxi* society. Given these factors, and the generally low salaries associated with university teaching posts, researchers are naturally drawn to seek more research collaborations with government agencies. This process serves to reinforce the role of government influence on tourism research.

Third, in the current higher education system in China, tourism does not enjoy a high disciplinary status and consequently tourism researchers struggle to compete for more resources with researchers from other more established disciplines (Hu & Huang, 2011), although this situation is not unique to China (Tribe, 2003). One means of acquiring status is to develop systems of awards whereby members of an academic community acquire status and prestige, and thus Chinese academia has developed such a research reward system, which may be diversified and specific at institutional level and may remain opaque in its processes to outsiders. These systems, instead of simply being awards for past services or research, become over time motivations for research in given directions and are sought for career enhancement positions, and thus in themselves become directive and shape researchers' research activities and behaviours. Although this is hardly new, and similar situations have rapidly emerged in other counties (Huang, 2012) where now, for example, it is no longer sufficient to be a 'Professor' but Professors seek to be 'Distinguished Professors', we suspect the specificity of these arrangements plays a more distinct role in this regard within China. One outcome of this is the growing demand for Chinese scholars to acquire international recognition, and the research reward systems, as adopted by Chinese universities, are motivating more tourism researchers to seek publication in international Science Citation Index (SCI) and Social Science Citation Index (SSCI) journals. Indeed, that system has now permeated to the doctoral level where, for many universities, doctoral students can only gain their degree after acquiring three 'publication points' – and three points can be gained from publication in a SSCI journal. The reverse aspect of this is the worrying system of paying for publication in little-known journals published in Mandarin, as academics struggle to enhance their curricula vitae.

There are other, more nuanced institutional factors that exist and which are less easily observed. The Marxist world view and ideological system influenced the generations of researchers brought up immediately after the foundation of the People's Republic in 1949. Some evidence shows that tourism researchers tended to resort to dialectic thinking in writing research articles (Huang & Hsu, 2008), indicating an inheritance from Marxist dialectic materialism that still pervades, at least in a ghostly fashion, the writing of some Chinese tourism research. One consequence is that explicitly stated research paradigms, be they positivism, post-positivism, interpretivism or constructionism, are rarely consciously conceived and applied in their research publications by tourism researchers in China. As observed above, one paradoxical result has been an almost uncritical acceptance of empirical, quantitative research methods and thus an understatement of the cultural realities that inform Chinese tourism research (e.g. Yang et al., 2012).

The methods by which research achieves publication in China also represent another discourse. Double-blind peer review, as an internationally accepted research quality assurance mechanism in journal publications, is not commonly practised among Chinese tourism research journals. There also remains a suspicion that publishing houses, still mainly under state surveillance, may function to produce research books that reinforce mainstream interests and discourage research-led truth-seeking not compatible with prevailing social and cultural values. Just how much credence there is in such suspicions remains unclear, and the evidence is at best indirect, being based on counts of classifications of published research outcomes.

A Glimpse into the Future

In spite of such doubts, there are reasons for optimism about the future of Chinese tourism research. China is in a process of transition and transformation that is possibly unparalleled in past human history. Not only have China and Chinese society in China been transformed economically in the past three decades, but the country and its people have also seen great changes in social, cultural and even political circles. Such changes will continue. In the past 30 years the tourism industry in China has started from virtually nothing to become one of the country's pillar industries. Currently, Chinese tourism, in its broad sense as defined in this chapter, is growing to become the world's most significant domestic and outbound travel market and the world number one tourist destination.

Changes and transition will also occur in Chinese tourism research. Since the 1980s, the number of Chinese doctoral students studying tourism at overseas universities has been increasing. A number of Chinese scholars who gained their doctoral degrees (sometimes in tourism) early in the 1980s and 1990s and who are currently working in overseas universities are active members of the Chinese tourism research camp outside China, supplementing the work of their similarly qualified, contemporary colleagues within China. These efforts are additionally supplemented by a growing number of non-ethnic Chinese tourism scholars. Often they are connected to Chinese tourism research through supervising doctoral students of Chinese origin. Some actively collaborate with tourism researchers in China, and through visits to China slowly become more familiar with the on-the-ground realities of China, especially when undertaking visits independent of 'official' sponsoring bodies. While the 'outside-China' camp's research mainly results in English language publications, it is believed that they bring clearly defined research paradigms and methodologies that begin to influence tourism researchers in China. We foresee that, in this regard, the two camps will increase communication and collaboration between their members. Increasing collaborations between the camps will benefit both communities in advancing knowledge on a common ground, and on one of growing cross-cultural sensitivities. Inter-camp collaborations can also help to lessen the degree of information asymmetry between the two communities. The present book is one result of such a collaboration. Although co-authored journal publications have become common between authors within and outside China, this book provides a platform for some researchers in China to let their voice be heard by researchers outside China, which otherwise would not be easy. Some of the contributors to this book speak and write little English, and in this respect the role of the book editors in undertaking the translation and copyediting of original Mandarin texts represents a task not commonly undertaken by journal editors; hence books such as this represent a contribution to the collaborative process.

Holding an optimistic view of the future of Chinese tourism research, we offer the following as the concluding remarks of this book:

- Chinese tourism will continue to develop along with China's unprecedented transformation, and consequently Chinese tourism research will become increasingly significant at an international level.
- Tourism research in China will mature irrespective of various levels and aspects of institutional constraints. With a growing dialogue, communication and collaboration with international colleagues, paradigm and methodological research knowledge and skills transfer will be expedited and the research capacity of tourism researchers in China will be greatly enhanced.
- With the above-noted asymmetry of information gradually diminishing, international tourism research will be increasingly enriched by indigenous Chinese knowledge, theories and concepts such as the Chinese cosmology of Man and Nature in One Unity (天人合一的宇宙观), the *Yijing* Theory (the Chinese Theory of Change), and the Feng Shui concept. Increasing knowledge of past nuanced debates of Mencius or the Legalists will also come to the fore in Western consciousness and provide new hybrid forms of thinking that have yet to unfold.

References

Bao, J. (2009) From idealism to realism to rational idealism: Relection on 30 years of development in tourism geography in China. *Acta Geographica Sinica* 64 (10), 1184–1102.

Bao, J. (2010) On the lack of the research questions concerning China's tourism geography science and our rethinking. *Tourism Tribune* 25 (10), 13–17.

Cai, L.A., Li, M. and Knutson, B.J. (2008) Research on China outbound market: A meta-review. *Journal of Hospitality and Leisure Marketing* 16 (1–2), 5–20.

Cao, S. and Hu, S. (2008) Study on inspecting and reconsidering tourism research in China: Taking the journal of *Tourism Tribune* as an example. *Geography and Geo-Informaiton Science* 24 (4), 103–106.

Chen, G. and Bao, J. (2011) Progress on oversea studies on China's tourism: A review from the perspective of academic contributions. *Tourism Tribune* 26 (2), 28–35.

Chen, G. and Huang, Y. (2008) A study on the degree of international impact of China's tourism research: Comparative analysis and upgrading approach. *Tourism Tribune* 23 (5), 91–96.

CTA (China Tourism Academy) (2012) *Annual Report of China Outbound Tourism Development 2012.* Beijing: Tourism Education Press.

Foucault, M. (1969) *The Archaeology of Knowledge.* London: Routledge. Online at http://www.marxists.org/reference/subject/philosophy/works/fr/foucault.htm.

Gross, M.J., Gao, H. and Huang, S. (2013) China hotel research: A systematic review of the English language academic literature. *Tourism Management Perspectives* 6, 68–78.

Hall, C.M. (2011) Publish and perish? Bibliometric analysis, journal ranking and the assessment of research quality in tourism. *Tourism Management* 32 (1), 16–27.

Hsu, C.H.C., Huang, J. and Huang, S. (2010) Tourism and hospitality research in mainland China: Trends from 2000 to 2008. In D. Pearce and R. Butler (eds) *Tourism Research: A 20:20 Vision* (pp. 147–160). Oxford: Goodfellow Publishers.

Hu, R. and Huang, S. (2011) A review of doctoral thesis research in tourism management in China. *Journal of Hospitality, Leisure, Sport & Tourism Education* 10 (2), 121–125.

Huang, S. (2001) Problems and solutions on tourism higher education development in China. *Journal of Guilin Institute of Tourism* 12 (2), 66–69.

Huang, S. (2012) Similar exercises, different consequences: An examination of tourism research in national research assessment frameworks. *Tourism Management Perspectives* 2–3, 13–18.

Huang, S. and Hsu, C.H.C. (2008) Recent tourism and hospitality research in China. *International Journal of Hospitality and Tourism Administration* 9 (3), 267–287.

Kim, S.S., Guo, Y. and Agrusa, J. (2005) Preference and positioning analyses of overseas destinations by mainland Chinese outbound pleasure tourists. *Journal of Travel Research* 44 (2), 212–220.

Kuhn, T.S. (1970) *The Structure of Scientific Revolutions* (2nd edn). Chicago, IL: University of Chicago Press.

Li, X. and Zhao, W. (2007) Progress in international tourism research on China: Evidence from Annals of Tourism Research, Tourism Management, and Journal of Travel Research. *Tourism Tribune* 22 (3), 90–96.

Liu, Q. (2008) On the progress of China's tourism research in the past twenty years – academic trends as reflected in NSFC and NPOPSS Full Tourism Foundation Database. *Tourism Tribune* 23 (3), 78–84.

Page, S.J. (2003) Evaluating research performance in tourism: The UK experience. *Tourism Management* 24 (6), 607–622.

Ryan, C. (2005) The ranking and rating of academics and journals in tourism research. *Tourism Management* 26 (5), 657–662.

Ryan, C. (2009) Thirty years of tourism management. *Tourism Management* 30 (1), 1–2.

Song, Z., Wu, B. and Dang, N. (2006) A review of presentations at the International Conference on Tourism and the New Asia: Implications for research, policy and practice. *Tourism Tribune* 21 (9), 92–96.

Tribe, J. (2003) The RAE-ification of tourism research in the UK. *International Journal of Tourism Research* 5 (3), 225–234.

Tsang, N.K.F. and Hsu, C.H.C. (2011) Thirty years of research on tourism and hospitality management in China: A review and analysis of journal publications. *International Journal of Hospitality Management* 30 (4), 886–896.

UNWTO (UN World Tourism Organisation) (2001) *Tourism 2020 Vision, Vol. 7: Global Forecasts and Profiles of Market Segments.* Madrid: UNWTO.

Wen, H. (2010) *Chinese Philosophy: Chinese Political Philosophy, Metaphysics, Epistemology and Comparative Philosophy.* Beijing: Chinese International Press.

Wu B. and Cai, L.A. (2006) Spatial modelling: Suburban leisure in Shanghai. *Annals of Tourism Research* 33 (1), 179–198.

Wu, B., Song, Z. and Deng, L. (2001) A summary of China's tourism research work in the past fourteen years – academic trends as reflected in 'Tourism Tribune'. *Tourism Tribune* 16 (1), 17–21.

Xie, Y. (2003) Tourism and hospitality industry studies: A comparative research between China and overseas countries. *Tourism Tribune* 18 (5), 20–25.

Yang, J., Ryan, C. and Zhang, L. (2012) The use of questionnaires in Chinese tourism research. *Annals of Tourism Research* 39 (3), 1690–1693.

Zhu, H. and Liu, Y. (2004) Viewing the difference and trend of Chinese and foreign tourism researches by comparing the articles published on 'Tourism Tribune' and 'Annals of Tourism Research'. *Tourism Tribune* 19 (4), 92–95.

Index